FIVE STUART TRAGEDIES

FIVE
STUART TRAGEDIES

EDITED

WITH AN INTRODUCTION BY
A. K. McILWRAITH

OXFORD UNIVERSITY PRESS

LONDON OXFORD NEW YORK

1972

Oxford University Press

LONDON OXFORD NEW YORK

GLASGOW TORONTO MELBOURNE WELLINGTON

CAPE TOWN IBADAN NAIROBI LUSAKA ADDIS ABABA

DELHI BOMBAY CALCUTTA MADRAS KARACHI LAHORE DACCA

KUALA LUMPUR SINGAPORE HONG KONG TOKYO

ISBN 0 19 281129 0

First published in The World's Classics, 1953

First issued as an Oxford University Press paperback by
Oxford University Press, London, 1972

*Printed lithographically in Great Britain by
Hazell Watson & Viney Ltd,
Aylesbury, Bucks*

Contents

Introduction

It is convenient to call the literature of the reigns of James I and Charles I simply 'Stuart', leaving the qualification 'early' to be understood, since later Stuart literature has a label of its own. The present volume contains five tragedies written between the death of Queen Elizabeth in 1603 and the closing of the theatres in 1642. More plays survive from these forty years than from the previous generation, represented in a preceding volume, *Five Elizabethan Tragedies*, but the aim has again been to make a handy volume of plays to be read for pleasure.

When James I came to the throne the physical resources of the Elizabethan 'public' theatres had already been explored for a quarter of a century, and many conventions of the poetic drama had come to be recognized, if not always approved or observed. In the first ten or fifteen years of the new reign and the last few years of the previous one the poetic drama achieved a general level of excellence which it had not attained before and has never approached since. This was the age of Shakespeare's great tragedies and the romances which followed them, of Jonson's mature comedies, of Chapman's belated flowering in tragedy and comedy alike, of the début of Middleton, Beaumont, Fletcher, Webster, and others too many to name. Conditions favoured the dramatists. The adult companies of professional players now invaded the fashionable, sophisticated, and critical 'West End', and gained in substance and repute. A play for the Blackfriars or the Phoenix had to be well written, so well that it could afterwards stand perusal at leisure, without support from the communal magic of stage and audience; and the dramatists increasingly attended to the printing of their best plays. That is one reason why more plays survive from this period. It would be going too far, however, to say that in writing for the 'private houses' the dramatists cut themselves off from the old public life and from popular contacts and tradition. At the other end of the scale came coarse farce and topical scandalmongering for the vulgar stages of the Red Bull and its like, and the 'literary' dramatists were there too. Webster was not too intense, Chapman too profound, Fletcher too urbane, or Ford too idealistic to stage the latest murder, seduction, or swindle in exuberant pot-boilers, and Jonson had never been aloof from the life of London. These plays, not being meant to please the fastidious reader of their own or later days, were not usually printed, and so are often lost to us, but Sisson has collected lurid details of a few of them which brought the producers into the courts of law,[1] and a few which dealt with such notorious matters as witchcraft and politics have survived in print.

From earlier days the company of which Shakespeare was a member had been the principal one, and as its leading dramatist he had been at the head of his profession. On his withdrawal to Stratford Fletcher took his place at the Blackfriars theatre, to be succeeded on his death in 1625 by his collaborator Massinger, who lived and wrote until 1640. Their leading rivals were a succession of companies managed by Christopher Beeston, which played from about 1616 onwards at his

[1] C. J. Sisson, *The Lost Plays of Shakespeare's Age*, Cambridge, 1936.

theatre in Drury Lane called the Phoenix or the Cock-
pit. Other companies rose and fell in the polite world,
but of the plays here printed the first four were written
for or inherited by the Blackfriars company, and the
last was written for the Phoenix. This is probably no
accident. These flourishing theatres could command
the best work, and publishers prefer to print what they
can reasonably hope the public will buy. We may regret
the loss of Sisson's 'shockers', but, however incom-
pletely, our selection most likely represents a fair
cross-section of the Stuart plays that many people
would want to read then, now, or in between times.

. George Chapman was born about 1559, and was
older by twenty years or more than most of our other
authors, a longer-lived contemporary of Kyd and Marlowe and Shakespeare, but he turned to creative literature late, and when he wrote *Bussy D'Ambois*, probably
in 1604, his experience of the stage had been gained
from a few comedies written in the immediately preceding years. He makes good scenic use of the resources
of his stage, as in the entry of the Friar and Bussy from
the vault into Tamyra's chamber (II. ii), and the
theatrically effective scene (IV. ii) where Behemoth
rises in smoke from Hell with attendant spirits marked
by blue torches seen through the smoke, the errand
of Cartophylax being marked by a torch going out
when he leaves and shining again on his return. There
is powerful dramatic or melodramatic irony in the
appeal of Tamyra, tortured on the rack,

husband, oh, help me, husband,

to the man who is having her tortured concerning her
lover. Yet the magnificent opening lines of the play are
dramatically weak exposition, and the relation by a
classical Nuntius of the tripartite duel (II. i. 25 sq.) is

reminiscent of an earlier age; Parrott finds that when
the play was revised by the author before his death
(possibly with the advice of Nathan Field, who played
Bussy) all the 200 or so changes were designed to improve it as theatre. The discontented probing mind of
his friends and contemporaries Marlowe and Ralegh
lives in Chapman, and he seems in his most famous
play to be as much a philosophical or heroic poet as a
dramatic one.

Kyd, Heywood, the author of *Arden of Feversham*, and
other tragic dramatists of the old generation had im-
plicitly accepted the existence of a just moral law—
perhaps beyond man's power to follow, but not beyond
his power to know. In Chapman this has given place
to a defiant assertion of the supreme value of the indi-
vidual man, however powerless he may be. The denial
of order in the cosmos is explicit in the first line,

> Fortune, not Reason, rules the state of things,

and the futility of self-assertion in

> Man is a torch borne in the wind; a dream
> But of a shadow, summ'd with all his substance.

The image of smoke, fire, and darkness is taken up
again in the scene with Behemoth, and it pervades
Bussy's dying bravado,

> Nothing is made of nought, of all things made,
> Their abstract being a dream but of a shade.

> .   .   .   .   .

> Oh, frail condition of strength, valour, virtue,
> In me (like warning fire upon the top
> Of some steep beacon, on a steeper hill)
> Made to express it: like a falling star
> Silently glanc'd, that like a thunderbolt
> Look'd to have stuck and shook the firmament.

The high astounding terms are those of Tamburlaine,

but the proud rebellious spirit outgoes Faustus himself, and we catch echoes of it later in Ford's Giovanni.

   After Shakespeare and Jonson the part of our older
drama longest known and loved is that associated with
the corporate personality of Beaumont and Fletcher,
two younger men whose careers were beginning as
Shakespeare's drew toward its close. Modern scrutiny
of the fifty-odd plays has amplified the well-informed
protest of Sir Aston Cokaine (*d.* 1684) that

> Beaumont, of those many, writ in few
> And Massinger in other few,

without endorsing his further phrase,

> the main
> Being sole issues of sweet Fletcher's brain,

and without regarding this as an exhaustive list of the
possibilities. *Rollo, or The Bloody Brother*, the latest to
appear in a critical edition, is ascribed by its editor to
the collaboration of Fletcher, Chapman, Jonson, and
Massinger, the claims of other suggested collaborators
being rejected.[1] This is one of the extreme cases,
though it is not unique. Fortunately this and other
similar problems are not our concern. *The Maid's
Tragedy* is not one of the plays in which other hands
are suspected. It is generally recognized as the work of
Beaumont and Fletcher alone, and more Beaumont's
than Fletcher's.[2] It was their first joint success in

---

   [1] *Rollo, Duke of Normandy*, ed. J. D. Jump (Liverpool, 1948)
p. xxvi. 'Chapman, Daborne, Field, Jonson, Middleton, Rowley,
Wilkins and sundry Unknowns are the suggested claimants' to
those parts of the play not recognizably written by Fletcher or
Massinger.
   [2] Broadly speaking, Beaumont is held to have written the first
four acts except II. ii and IV. i, and Fletcher the fifth act except the
last scene.

tragedy, and its early and enduring popularity is easy to understand. Austere critics, who are clearly right, point out that Beaumont and Fletcher rely more on exciting turns of plot and on gripping situations than on depth of thought or imaginative revelation of human character. It would be idle to deny the further charge that in later years Fletcher often exploited similar situations and repeated similar broadly portrayed characters, or that his extraordinarily adaptable blank verse can take at will a note of quavering pathos as easily as one of hilarious gaiety. If we pause to analyse our spontaneous delight we may feel that we have been duped, and resent the trickery (or, more politely, the art); but that is not all, for here as elsewhere the whole is greater than the sum of the parts. Never, not even in Shakespeare, has the poetic drama a more magical power of creating illusion. The more remote it is from life the more wonderful is its enchantment. In the realm of fancy where it belongs,

> Where the daisies are rose-scented,
> And the rose herself has got
> Perfume which on earth is not,

The Maid's Tragedy belongs to the class of the very best. If the collaborators can be happily styled 'Fletcher, Beaumont & Co., Entertainers to the Jacobean Gentry'[1] it speaks well for the taste of the gentry who called forth their works.

Even the entertainers were aware that their audience had serious problems. Many of these gentry and their sons were less than forty years later to lose their lands or their lives in the cause of a king against subjects who defied him. It is worth our while to pause a moment over this, because it is not immediately recognizable as one of our own problems, and the form in

[1] The title of a recent study by L. B. Wallis, New York, 1947.

which it pervades *The Maid's Tragedy* is to us peculiarly
unreal. Amintor refuses to avenge himself on the adulterous king who has so grossly wronged him:

> Oh, thou hast named a word, that wipes away
> All thoughts revengeful! In that sacred word,
> 'The King,' there lies a terror: what frail man
> Dares lift his hand against it? Let the gods
> Speak to him when they please: till when, let us
> Suffer and wait.

We are trebly alienated: in our daily lives we no longer
punish adultery with death; we do not admit private
duels; we do not exempt royalty from human justice.
This alienation is unfortunate. As a dramatic convention we accept Othello's passionate killing of Des-
demona. As an historical fact Elizabeth, James I, and
their successors tried repeatedly and in vain to stamp
out duelling. And the king's rights were, as we have
seen, a practical matter of life and death. Beaumont and
Fletcher cannot answer the question how far a good
man should serve a bad king, any more than Massinger
could later, but Amintor's conflict of conscience be-
longed to the real world, not to fairyland. The question
is not unlike in principle to some raised by trials of
war criminals in our own day.

Conflict between a young widow who wishes to
marry again and her family who selfishly oppose her is
not peculiar to one epoch, and the central situation of
The Duchess of Malfi needs no paraphrasing in modern
terms. Only the episodes are extravagant, and they are
triumphantly carried off by the poetry. None the less,
and because of its poetry, it is a challenging play. We
cannot be quite satisfied with readings of it which have
to dismiss the dead man's hand and the madmen as
appeals to the groundlings, or to excuse the existence

of the fifth act after the death of the Duchess by a
reference to Webster's concern with extraneous moral
problems. They are part of the play, and we insist on
asking what part.

Webster is closer than his fellow-dramatists to the
mood of metaphysical poetry. The imagery of a play
lies not only in the mental pictures conjured up by the
words in the spectator's mind, but also in the actual
tableaux presented to his eyes on the stage by the
actors, all the more so if the acting is formally stylized.
The gay snatch of the conjugal felicity of Antonio, his
Duchess, and the familiar servant Cariola at the beginning of Act III, scene ii, indeed provides the occasion
for the fell appearance of Ferdinand with a poniard, but
the abrupt contrast of groupings enhances the effect
of the narrative. The exchange (IV. ii. 205 sq.) between the Duchess and Bosola is more shattering in its
abrupt transition than anything in earlier drama:

> I pray thee, look thou giv'st my little boy
> Some syrup for his cold, and let the girl
> Say her prayers ere she sleep.—Now what you please:
> What death?
> *Bosola.* Strangling.

The fusion of the utterly normal with the extremes
of violent cruelty is more than an appetizer for
jaded palates, it is the essence of the play, here and
throughout.

The contrast of good and evil is singularly strong in
The Duchess of Malfi, and localized with unusual clarity.
There is at least a hint in her direction for the prayers
of the little girl, but the firm religious faith of the
Duchess is often explicit. She is not afraid of death
(IV. ii. 214),

> Knowing to meet such excellent company
> In th'other world.

Antonio is equally clear (v. iv. 66–67) that this world
is evil and death an entrance into felicity:

> Pleasure of life, what is't? only the good hours
> Of an ague; merely a preparative to rest.

Nor should the central importance of Bosola escape us.
The play begins and ends with him. He is clearly im-
pressed on us from the first as a man driven to brutal
villainy by the ways of this world. He acts the hired
assassin in all the murders. Yet his pity for the children
and his remorse over the Duchess are no afterthoughts.
The spirit which has been distorted in him shows
through in his language.

> Look you, the stars shine still

is his mocking retort (IV. i. 95–98) to the outburst of
the Duchess,

> I could curse the stars.

But the stars haunt Bosola in Webster's mind:

> Princes' images on their tombs
> Do not lie, as they were wont, seeming to pray
> Up to heaven; but with their hands under their cheeks,
> As if they died of the tooth-ache: they are not carved
> With their eyes fix'd upon the stars.   (IV. ii. 158–62.)

Bosola is as unlike Chapman's Bussy as the Duchess is
unlike Tamyra, but he is essential to the play both as
theatre and as poetry, and it cannot end until we know
what becomes of him. There is nothing simple about
him.

When Massinger in 1629 called *The Roman Actor* 'the
most perfect birth of my Minerva' he had still over ten
years of writing before him, but there is no reason to
question his judgement or to suppose that he would
have changed his mind. It is not easy to define the

merit of the work. Some of its contributory assets are apparent enough: the dignified and lucid blank verse, highly praised by Coleridge;[1] the coherent and exciting plot; the use made in three different ways of the device of the 'play within the play', all naturally introduced.[2] These have been duly admired. Praise of the eloquent Defence of the Stage by Paris in Act I, Scene iii, has perhaps verged on the naïve. Paris was defending the acting profession against the charge of doing what he immediately proceeds to do, and it is hard to believe that Massinger's irony was wholly unintentional.

The craftsman is triumphant, but the spirit which inspires the whole is elusive. The characters who live in the memory are the Roman actor Paris himself, the 'great lord and god' Domitian, and Parthenius, Caesar's freedman. The other players, the senators, and Domitian's women-folk, including the important central figure of the Empress, are well done—better than Massinger's subsidiary figures usually are—but they do not attract much attention as individuals. Domitian is vain, superstitious, callous, affectionate, and a competent ruler of the world. There is no hint of insincerity in his magnificent address to the dying Paris (IV. ii. 284–308),

> . . . as thou didst live
> Rome's bravest actor, 'twas my plot that thou
> Shouldst die in action, and to crown it die
> With an applause enduring to all times,
> By our imperial hand.

Massinger presents us with a Caesar who thinks as highly of himself as that, and with servants like Paris

[1] *Lectures and Notes on Shakspere* (1883), p. 540.
[2] *The Cure of Avarice* (II. i) is a stage sermon, like *Gorboduc*. *Iphis and Anaxarete* (III. ii) betrays the feelings of a stage spectator as does the play in *Hamlet*. *The False Servant* (IV. ii) is used for a real killing, like the play in *The Spanish Tragedy*.

and Parthenius whose goodness is apparent, but who yet reverence the name and virtue of Caesar without being blind to his vice. Paris admits the justice of his execution (which is not really in dispute by the accepted standards of the stage), and the loyalty of Parthenius is not shaken by the abrupt (and here quite unwarranted) execution of the father whom he respected and sought to help. Massinger need not have conceived his characters in this way, for they are remote from history, and we wonder why he did.

It may be that here, as in others of his major plays, Massinger was puzzled himself, and was trying to work out an answer. The working out of the answer to a puzzle of character or conduct is at the heart of his serious work. He was less of an intuitive poet than most of his great contemporaries—his placid annexation of other men's images is a byword of criticism—and it does not seem that he was always very observant of manners and conversation. Yet he saw in London and Nottinghamshire and read in ancient and modern story that people do odd things, and he tried to explain why. He necessarily lacked the technique of the psychologist and the vehicle of the novel, but he seems in *The Roman Actor* to be aware of such questions as these: How can a man as debauched as Domitian rule an empire well? How could he find trustworthy men to obey him? What would induce good men to serve an evil master? When will their loyalty break? His answers to these questions are not those of modern historians, nor even those of the political thinkers of his own time; but they are those of an inquiring mind which will not be put off by cynical generalizations from the absorbing interest of real and understandable motives, and his search for them gives *The Roman Actor* a spiritual integrity underlying all its skilled stagecraft.

Despite its catchpenny title, *'Tis Pity She's a Whore* is a play to be reckoned with seriously, as poetry, as stagecraft, and as the expression of conflicting ways of thought. We can discern in Ford a mixture of scientific determinism (derived most immediately from Burton's *Anatomy of Melancholy*) and unbridled individualism.[1] The former element was apparently the more striking to his contemporaries, for Hemminge in the middle of the seventeenth century recorded that

> Deep in a dump Jack Ford alone was got,
> With folded arms and melancholy hat.

Yet the latter element is explicit in Giovanni's defiance of the laws of God and the ways of men, from the very beginning of the play. The story of Giovanni and Annabella is addressed to rebellious youth, not only in its blending of passion and eroticism to a degree without precedent, but also in the intransigence of its idealism. There is little show of moderation in Giovanni's arguments (though he does try to humour the poor old Friar), and there is none at all in Ford's plot. He does not try to persuade, as Chapman and Webster did, by asking or making terms with public opinion. He aggravates a scandalous defence of sensuality and adultery by wantonly linking it with the sexual love of brother and sister, with incest. It is an immature reaction to anticipated opposition to go to the farthest extreme and still present his theme as beautiful. The spectator or reader may be either enthralled or disgusted, but he will not be converted by this technique.

It was perhaps this ardent defiance of convention that made Ford seem specially modern to some critics earlier in the present century; it is not a quality which

[1] G. F. Sensabaugh, *The Tragic Muse of John Ford*, Stanford University (1944).

seems essentially modern to-day. Ford is no more modern than Donne or Webster, perhaps less so. Modernity necessarily changes with time, and it is not clear that it is ever a virtue.

The poet-philosopher asserts himself in Ford, but the stage playwright will not be neglected. He has been praised for the skill with which he portrays the important stages in the development of a character or a relationship, leaving the intermediate links so clearly implied that we do in fact understand them. To this is allied his clear discrimination between the movements of the spirit in man and woman as the history of Giovanni and Annabella proceeds. Both qualities derive from his sensitive intuition of human nature. In this he is akin to Webster, and equally far from the Stoic philosophical thought of Chapman and the careful study of Massinger. Annabella is not driven by her relentless fate like Tamyra, but she needs the exhortation and persuasion of Giovanni until her spirit is wholly won over to the tragic course, and then she is the equal of any man.

In more technical matters, too, Ford's mastery is evident. The simultaneous use of upper and lower stage (I. ii) is hardly more than the able use of a long-established conventional device, though editors who did not appreciate it have spoiled the effect by bisecting the scene. More striking is the pictorial grouping of the scene (v. vi) where Giovanni enters with Annabella's heart on his dagger. This has been condemned as mere striving after sensation, and on a realistically representational stage the verdict might be just. It is better conceived as a picture in three dimensions for which the dialogue supplies a commentary, like the text in the then fashionable books of emblems. In this light it appears as a symbol and epitome of the thought and feeling of the play. The killed heart is held high on the dagger's point before a group of incredulous and shocked people who will not understand or accept the worship due to the miracle of beauty.

In retrospect we see the Jacobean and Caroline dramatists as men of strong and diverse minds. It is true that they do not forget Shakespeare and his contemporaries. It would have been queer if they had. It may even be true that when they borrow scenes or characters or expressions they do not improve or recreate. But in their hands the English drama was revealing a new richness unlike anything that had gone before, and it was only in the last year or two that it became obscured by the nervous strain of the impending civil war.

In this anthology the spelling has generally been modernized for the reader's greater ease and comfort, but variant forms like 'vild' for 'vile' and 'murther' for 'murder' have been retained, as have spellings which might indicate the presence or absence of a syllable in pronunciation: thus the termination '-ed' has been printed in full when it so appears in the original spelling, but as '-'d' when the original has a shortened form, even though the variation may be due only to the caprice or convenience of a printer. The standard of accuracy in printed play-books was improving in these years with the increasing care taken by the authors over the printing of their works. The rules here followed should inconvenience no one, and may preserve the authors' intentions.

With two exceptions the texts are based on the first editions with necessary or desirable corrections proposed by modern editors. The problems in textual criticism raised by *Bussy D'Ambois* and *The Maid's Tragedy* are too complex for discussion in this modest volume, and these plays are reprinted by permission from the editions of T. M. Parrott and P. A. Daniel.

In all the plays a great deal is due to the critical editions cited for each author, to other scholars whose readings or explanations are quoted from time to time, and, of course, to the *Oxford English Dictionary*. The introductory notes on each author only suggest what collected editions are most likely to be accessible. Most of the footnotes are merely verbal glosses to save the reader trouble. No attempt has been made to produce a critical edition for the scholar or a textbook for the student.

Bussy D'Ambois

BY

GEORGE CHAPMAN

GEORGE CHAPMAN (*c.* 1559–1634)

Bussy D'Ambois

Acted probably in 1604; printed in 1607, second quarto, 'much corrected and amended by the Author before his death', printed in 1641, and the present text taken from the latter.

[*Comedies and Tragedies*, ed. R. H. Shepherd, 3 vols., 1873 (Pearson's Reprints), is in the original spelling; *Works*, ed. R. H. Shepherd, 3 vols., 1874, in modern spelling, includes the great translations; *Plays and Poems*, ed. T. M. Parrott (*Tragedies*, 1910; *Comedies*, 1914; complete works reprinted, 1961), in modern spelling, is the edition from which the text of this play is reprinted. There are recent new editions, with critical apparatus, of *Bussy D'Ambois*, ed. Robert J. Lordi, 1964 (Regents Renaissance Drama Series); ed. N. S. Brooke, 1964 (Revels Plays); ed. Maurice Evans, 1965 (New Mermaid).]

Buſſy D Ambois:

A TRAGEDIE:

As it hath been often Acted with great Applauſe.

Being much corrected and amended by the Author before his death.

LONDON:
Printed by *A. N.* for *Robert Lunne.*
1641.

DRAMATIS PERSONAE

HENRY III, *King of France.*

MONSIEUR, *his brother.*

The Duke of GUISE.

The Count of MONTSURRY.

BUSSY D'AMBOIS.

BARRISOR,
L'ANOU,
PYRHOT,
} *Courtiers; enemies of Bussy.*

BRISAC,
MELYNELL,
} *Courtiers; friends of Bussy.*

BEAUMOND, *an attendant on the King.*

COMOLET, *a Friar.*

MAFFÉ, *steward to Monsieur.*

Nuntius.

Murderers.

BEHEMOTH,
CARTOPHYLAX,
} *Spirits.*

Umbra *of the Friar.*

ELENOR, *Duchess of Guise.*

TAMYRA, *Countess of Montsurry.*

BEAUPRÉ, *niece to Elenor.*

ANNABLE, *maid to Elenor.*

PERO, *maid to Tamyra.*

CHARLOTTE, *maid to Beaupré.*

PYRA, *a court lady.*

Courtiers, Ladies, Pages, Servants, Spirits, &c.

PROLOGUE

Not out of confidence that none but we
Are able to present this tragedy,
Nor out of envy at the grace of late
It did receive, nor yet to derogate
From their deserts, who give out boldly that   5
They move with equal feet on the same flat;
Neither for all, nor any of such ends,
We offer it, gracious and noble friends,
To your review; we, far from emulation
(And, charitably judge, from imitation)   10
With this work entertain you, a piece known,
And still believed in Court to be our own.
To quit our claim, doubting our right or merit,
Would argue in us poverty of spirit
Which we must not subscribe to: Field is gone,   15
Whose action first did it name, and one
Who came the nearest to him, is denied
By his gray beard to show the height and pride
Of D'Ambois' youth and bravery; yet to hold
Our title still a-foot, and not grow cold   20
By giving it o'er, a third man with his best
Of care and pains defends our interest;
As Richard he was liked, nor do we fear
In personating D'Ambois he'll appear
To faint, or go less, so your free consent,   25
As heretofore, give him encouragement.

[Prologue] *From the edition of* 1641, *evidently written for a
revival by the King's Players after a previous revival by another
company.*

15 Field] Nathan Field, actor-dramatist, died in 1620.   21
a third man] *Eyllardt Swanston*   23 Richard] *In Shakespeare's
Richard III, revived a few months earlier*

ACTUS PRIMI, SCENA PRIMA

Enter Bussy D'Ambois, *poor.*

Bus. Fortune, not Reason, rules the state of things,
Reward goes backwards, Honour on his head;
Who is not poor, is monstrous; only Need
Gives form and worth to every human seed.
As cedars beaten with continual storms,   5
So great men flourish; and do imitate
Unskilful statuaries, who suppose,
In forming a Colossus, if they make him
Straddle enough, strut, and look big, and gape,
Their work is goodly: so men merely great   10
In their affected gravity of voice,
Sourness of countenance, manners' cruelty,
Authority, wealth, and all the spawn of Fortune,
Think they bear all the kingdom's worth before them;
Yet differ not from those colossic statues,   15
Which, with heroic forms without o'er-spread,
Within are nought but mortar, flint, and lead.
Man is a torch borne in the wind; a dream
But of a shadow, summ'd with all his substance;
And as great seamen, using all their wealth   20
And skills in Neptune's deep invisible paths,
In tall ships richly built and ribb'd with brass,
To put a girdle round about the world,
When they have done it, coming near their haven,
Are fain to give a warning-piece, and call   25
A poor, staid fisherman, that never pass'd
His country's sight, to waft and guide them in:
So when we wander furthest through the waves

27 waft] wave (*in signalling to the helm*)

Of glassy Glory, and the gulfs of State,
Topt with all titles, spreading all our reaches,   30
As if each private arm would sphere the earth,
We must to Virtue for her guide resort,
Or we shall shipwrack in our safest port.

[*Procumbit.*

Enter Monsieur *with two* Pages.

Mons. There is no second place in numerous state
That holds more than a cipher; in a king   35
All places are contain'd. His words and looks
Are like the flashes and the bolts of Jove;
His deeds inimitable, like the sea
That shuts still as it opes, and leaves no tracts
Nor prints of precedent for mean men's facts: 40
There's but a thread betwixt me and a crown,
I would not wish it cut, unless by nature;
Yet to prepare me for that possible fortune,
'Tis good to get resolved spirits about me.
I follow'd D'Ambois to this green retreat,   45
A man of spirit beyond the reach of fear,
Who (discontent with his neglected worth)
Neglects the light, and loves obscure abodes;
But he is young and haughty, apt to take
Fire at advancement, to bear state, and flourish;   50
In his rise therefore shall my bounties shine:
None loathes the world so much, nor loves to scoff it,
But gold and grace will make him surfeit of it.

[*Approaching* Bussy.

What, D'Ambois?
Bus.   He, sir.

30 Topt ... spreading ... reaches] under full sail   33 s.d.
Procumbit] falls on his face   39 tracts] traces   40
facts] deeds

8

Mons.   Turn'd to earth, alive?
Up, man; the sun shines on thee.
   Bus.   Let it shine: 55
I am no mote to play in't, as great men are.
   Mons. Callest thou men great in state, motes in the
     sun?
They say so that would have thee freeze in shades,
That (like the gross Sicilian gourmandist)
Empty their noses in the cates they love,   60
That none may eat but they. Do thou but bring
Light to the banquet Fortune sets before thee,
And thou wilt loathe lean darkness like thy death.
Who would believe thy mettle could let sloth
Rust and consume it? If Themistocles   65
Had liv'd obscur'd thus in th'Athenian state,
Xerxes had made both him and it his slaves.
If brave Camillus had lurk'd so in Rome,
He had not five times been Dictator there,
Nor four times triumph'd. If Epaminondas   70
(Who liv'd twice twenty years obscur'd in Thebes)
Had liv'd so still, he had been still unnam'd,
And paid his country nor himself their right;
But putting forth his strength, he rescu'd both
From imminent ruin; and like burnish'd steel,   75
After long use he shin'd; for as the light
Not only serves to show, but renders us
Mutually profitable, so our lives
In acts exemplary not only win
Ourselves good names, but do to others give   80
Matter for virtuous deeds, by which we live.
   Bus. What would you wish me?
   Mons.   Leave the troubled streams,
And live, where thrivers do, at the well-head.
   Bus. At the well-head? Alas, what should I do

   59 Sicilian gourmandist] Gnatho   72 still] always

With that enchanted glass? See devils there?   85
Or, like a strumpet, learn to set my looks
In an eternal brake, or practise juggling,
To keep my face still fast, my heart still loose;
Or bear (like dame schoolmistresses their riddles)
Two tongues, and be good only for a shift;   90
Flatter great lords, to put them still in mind
Why they were made lords; or please humorous ladies
With a good carriage, tell them idle tales
To make their physic work; spend a man's life
In sights and visitations that will make   95
His eyes as hollow as his mistress' heart;
To do none good, but those that have no need;
To gain being forward, though you break for haste
All the commandments ere you break your fast;
But believe backwards, make your period   100
And creed's last article, 'I believe in God':
And (hearing villanies preach'd) t'unfold their art
Learn to commit them? 'Tis a great man's part.
Shall I learn this there?
    Mons.   No, thou need'st not learn,
Thou hast the theory; now go there and practise.   105
    Bus. Ay, in a threadbare suit; when men come there,
They must have high naps, and go from thence bare:
A man may drown the parts of ten rich men
In one poor suit; brave barks and outward gloss
Attract Court loves, be in-parts ne'er so gross.   110
    Mons. Thou shalt have gloss enough, and all things
        fit
T'enchase in all show thy long-smother'd spirit:
Be rul'd by me then? The old Scythians
Painted blind Fortune's powerful hands with wings
To show her gifts come swift and suddenly,   115

    87 brake] carpenter's vice (*for holding things immovable*)
92 humorous] captious

Which if her favourite be not swift to take,
He loses them for ever. Then be wise:
Stay but awhile here, and I'll send to thee.
      [*Exit* Monsieur [*with the* Pages]. *Manet* Bussy.
   Bus. What will he send? Some crowns? It is to sow
      them
Upon my spirit, and make them spring a crown   120
Worth millions of the seed-crowns he will send.
Like to disparkling noble husbandmen,
He'll put his plow into me, plow me up;
But his unsweating thrift is policy,
And learning-hating policy is ignorant   125
To fit his seed-land soil; a smooth plain ground
Will never nourish any politic seed;
I am for honest actions, not for great:
If I may bring up a new fashion,
And rise in Court for virtue, speed his plow!   130
The King hath known me long as well as he,
Yet could my fortune never fit the length
Of both their understandings till this hour.
There is a deep nick in Time's restless wheel
For each man's good, when which nick comes, it
      strikes;   135
As rhetoric yet works not persuasion,
But only is a mean to make it work;
So no man riseth by his real merit,
But when it cries clink in his raiser's spirit.
Many will say, that cannot rise at all,   140
Man's first hour's rise is first step to his fall.
I'll venture that; men that fall low must die,
As well as men cast headlong from the sky.

Enter Maffé.

   Maf.--Humour of princes! Is this wretch indu'd
With any merit worth a thousand crowns?   145

Will my lord have me be so ill a steward
Of his revenue, to dispose a sum
So great with so small cause as shows in him?
I must examine this.—Is your name D'Ambois?
 Bus. Sir?
 Maf. Is your name D'Ambois?
 Bus.   Who have we here? 150
Serve you the Monsieur?
 Maf.   How?
 Bus.   Serve you the Monsieur?
 Maf. Sir, y'are very hot. I do serve the Monsieur,
But in such place as gives me the command
Of all his other servants. And because
His Grace's pleasure is to give your good   155
His pass through my command, methinks you might
Use me with more respect.
 Bus.   Cry you mercy!
Now you have open'd my dull eyes, I see you,
And would be glad to see the good you speak of;
What might I call your name?
 Maf.   Monsieur Maffé. 160
 Bus. Monsieur Maffé? Then, good Monsieur Maffé,
Pray let me know you better.
 Maf.   Pray do so,
That you may use me better. For yourself,
By your no better outside, I would judge you
To be some poet; have you given my lord 165
Some pamphlet?
 Bus. Pamphlet?
 Maf.   Pamphlet, sir, I say.
 Bus. Did your great master's goodness leave the
  good,
That is to pass your charge to my poor use,
To your discretion?

   147 revenue] *commonly pronounced* revénue

Maf.   Though he did not, sir,
I hope 'tis no rude office to ask reason   170
How that his Grace gives me in charge, goes from me?
   Bus. That's very perfect, sir.
   Maf.   Why, very good, sir;
I pray, then, give me leave; if for no pamphlet,
May I not know what other merit in you,
Makes his compunction willing to relieve you?   175
   Bus. No merit in the world, sir.
   Maf.   That is strange.
Y'are a poor soldier, are you?
   Bus.   That I am, sir.
   Maf. And have commanded?
   Bus.   Ay, and gone without, sir.
   Maf.—I see the man; a hundred crowns will make
   him
Swagger, and drink healths to his Grace's bounty,   180
And swear he could not be more bountiful;
So there's nine hundred crowns sav'd.—Here, tall
   soldier,
His Grace hath sent you a whole hundred crowns.
   Bus. A hundred, sir? Nay, do his Highness right;
I know his hand is larger, and perhaps   185
I may deserve more than my outside shows;
I am a poet, as I am a soldier,
And I can poetise, and (being well encourag'd)
May sing his fame for giving, yours for delivering
(Like a most faithful steward) what he gives.   190
   Maf. What shall your subject me?
   Bus.   I care not much.
If to his bounteous Grace I sing the praise
Of fair great noses, and to you of long ones.
What qualities have you, sir, beside your chain
And velvet jacket? Can your Worship dance?   195
   Maf.—A pleasant fellow, 'faith; it seems my lord

Will have him for his jester; and, by'rlady,
Such men are now no fools; 'tis a knight's place.
If I (to save his Grace some crowns) should urge him
T'abate his bounty, I should not be heard;   200
I would to heaven I were an arrant ass,
For then I should be sure to have the cars
Of these great men, where now their jesters have them.
'Tis good to please him, yet I'll take no notice
Of his preferment, but in policy   205
Will still be grave and serious, lest he think
I fear his wooden dagger.—Here, Sir Ambo!
   Bus. How, Ambo, sir?
   Maf.   Ay, is not your name Ambo?
   Bus. You call'd me lately D'Ambois; has your Wor-
     ship
So short a head?
   Maf.   I cry thee mercy, D'Ambois.   210
A thousand crowns I bring you from my lord:
Serve God, play the good husband; you may make
This a good standing living: 'tis a bounty
His Highness might perhaps have bestow'd better.
   Bus. Go, y'are a rascal; hence, away, you rogue!   215
   Maf. What mean you, sir?
   Bus.   Hence! Prate no more,
Or, by thy villain's blood, thou prat'st thy last!
A barbarous groom grudge at his master's bounty!
But since I know he would as much abhor
His hind should argue what he gives his friend,   220
Take that, sir, for your aptness to dispute.
                       [Strikes him. Exit.
   Maf. These crowns are set in blood; blood be their
     fruit!   *[Exit.*

205 preferment] promotion

ACTUS PRIMI, SCENA SECUNDA

Henry, Guise, Montsurry, Elenor, Tamyra, Beaupré,
Pero, Charlotte, Pyra, Annable.

Table, chess-board, and tapers.

Hen. Duchess of Guise, your Grace is much enrich'd
In the attendance of that English virgin,
That will initiate her prime of youth
(Dispos'd to Court conditions) under the hand
Of your preferr'd instructions and command,   5
Rather than any in the English Court,
Whose ladies are not match'd in Christendom
For graceful and confirm'd behaviours;
More than the Court, where they are bred, is equall'd.
   Guise. I like not their Court fashion; it is too crest-
     fall'n   10
In all observance, making demigods
Of their great nobles, and of their old queen
An ever-young and most immortal goddess.
   Mont. No question she's the rarest queen in Europe.
   Guise. But what's that to her immortality?   15
   Hen. Assure you, cousin Guise, so great a courtier,
So full of majesty and royal parts,
No queen in Christendom may vaunt herself.
Her Court approves it, that's a Court indeed,
Not mixt with clowneries us'd in common houses,   20
But, as Courts should be th' abstracts of their king-
     doms
In all the beauty, state, and worth they hold,
So is hers, amply, and by her inform'd.
The world is not contracted in a man

   12 old queen] *Elizabeth reigned at the time of Bussy's death (but
she must have been dead before these words could be spoken on the
London stage)*

With more proportion and expression,   25
Than in her Court, her kingdom. Our French Court
Is a mere mirror of confusion to it:
The king and subject, lord and every slave,
Dance a continual hay; our rooms of state
Kept like our stables; no place more observ'd   30
Than a rude market-place: and though our custom
Keep this assur'd confusion from our eyes
'Tis ne'er the less essentially unsightly,
Which they would soon see would they change their
    form
To this of ours, and then compare them both;   35
Which we must not affect, because in kingdoms
Where the king's change doth breed the subject's
    terror,
Pure innovation is more gross than error.
    Mont. No question we shall see them imitate
(Though afar off) the fashions of our Courts,   40
As they have ever ap'd us in attire;
Never were men so weary of their skins,
And apt to leap out of themselves as they,
Who, when they travel to bring forth rare men,
Come home deliver'd of a fine French suit;   45
Their brains lie with their tailors, and get babies
For their most complete issue; he's sole heir
To all the moral virtues that first greets
The light with a new fashion, which becomes them
Like apes, disfigur'd with the attires of men.   50
    Hen. No question they much wrong their real worth
In affectation of outlandish scum;
But they have faults, and we more; they foolish proud
To jet in others plumes so haughtily;
We proud that they are proud of foolery,   55
Holding our worths more complete for their vaunts.

29 hay] country dance   54 jet] strut

Enter Monsieur *and* D'Ambois.

Mons. Come, mine own sweetheart, I will enter thee.
—Sir, I have brought a gentleman to Court,
And pray you would vouchsafe to do him grace.
  Hen. D'Ambois, I think?
  Bus.   That's still my name, my lord, 60
Though I be something alter'd in attire.
  Hen. We like your alteration, and must tell you
We have expected th'offer of your service;
For we (in fear to make mild virtue proud)
Use not to seek her out in any man.   65
  Bus. Nor doth she use to seek out any man:
They that will win must woo her.
  Mons. I urg'd her modesty in him, my lord,
And gave her those rites that he says she merits.
  Hen. If you have woo'd and won, then, brother,
    wear him.   70
  Mons. Th'art mine, sweetheart. See, here's the
    Guise's Duchess,
The Countess of Montsurreau, Beaupré.
Come, I'll enseam thee. Ladies, y'are too many
To be in council; I have here a friend
That I would gladly enter in your graces.   75
  Bus. 'Save you, ladies.
  Duch. If you enter him in our graces, my lords, me-
thinks by his blunt behaviour he should come out of
himself.
  Tam. Has he never been courtier, my lord?   80
  Mons. Never, my lady.
  Beau. And why did the toy take him in th' head
now?
  Bus. 'Tis leap-year, lady, and therefore very good to
enter a courtier.   85

73 enseam] introduce

Hen. Mark, Duchess of Guise, there is one is not bashful.

Duch. No, my lord, he is much guilty of the bold extremity.

Tam. The man's a courtier at first sight.   90

Bus. I can sing prick-song, lady, at first sight; and why not be a courtier as suddenly?

Beau. Here's a courtier rotten before he be ripe.

Bus. Think me not impudent, lady; I am yet no courtier: I desire to be one, and would gladly take 95 entrance, madam, [*To the* Duchess] under your princely colours.

Enter Barrisor, L'Anou, *and* Pyrhot.

Duch. Soft, sir, you must rise by degrees, first being the servant of some common lady, or knight's wife, then a little higher to a lord's wife, next a little higher 100 to a countess, yet a little higher to a duchess, and then turn the ladder.

Bus. Do you allow a man, then, four mistresses, when the greatest mistress is allowed but three servants?   105

Duch. Where find you that statute, sir?

Bus. Why, be judged by the groom-porters.

Duch. The groom-porters?

Bus. Ay, madam; must not they pledge of all gamings i' th' Court?   110

Duch. You talk like a gamester.

Guise. Sir, know you me?

Bus. My lord?

Guise. I know not you; whom do you serve?

Bus. Serve, my lord!   115

Guise. Go to, companion, your courtship's too saucy.

116 companion] fellow (*contemptuous*)

18

Bus.—Saucy! Companion! 'Tis the Guise, but yet those terms might have been spared of the Guisard. Companion! He's jealous, by this light. Are you blind of that side, Duke? I'll to her again for that—Forth, 120 princely mistress, for the honour of courtship. Another riddle!

Guise. Cease your courtship, or by heaven I'll cut your throat.

Bus. Cut my throat? Cut a whetstone! Young 125 Accius Naevius, do as much with your tongue, as he did with a razor: cut my throat!

Bar. What new-come gallant have we here, that dares mate the Guise thus?

L'An. 'Sfoot, 'tis D'Ambois. The Duke mistakes 130 him, on my life, for some knight of the new edition.

Bus. Cut my throat! I would the King feared thy cutting of his throat no more than I fear thy cutting of mine.

Guise. I'll do 't, by this hand.   135

Bus.   That hand dares not do 't.
Y'ave cut too many throats already, Guise,
And robb'd the realm of many thousand souls,
More precious than thine own. Come, madam, talk on.
'Sfoot, can you not talk? Talk on, I say.   140
Another riddle!

Pyr.   Here's some strange distemper.

Bar. Here's a sudden transmigration with D'Ambois—out of the knights' ward into the duchess' bed.

L'An. See what a metamorphosis a brave suit can 145 work.

Pyr. 'Slight, step to the Guise and discover him.

Bar. By no means; let the new suit work; we'll see the issue.

131 of the new edition] courtier, not soldier (*contemptuous*)
147 discover] reveal (*sc. his identity*)

Guise. Leave your courting.   150
Bus. I will not.—I say, mistress, and I will stand
unto it, that if a woman may have three servants, a
man may have threescore mistresses.
Guise. Sirrah, I'll have you whipped out of the Court
for this insolence.   155
Bus. Whipped? Such another syllable out o' th'
presence, if thou dar'st for thy dukedom.
Guise. Remember, poltroon.
Mons.—Pray thee, forbear.
Bus. Passion of death! Were not the King here, he   160
should strow the chamber like a rush.
Mons. But leave courting his wife, then.
Bus. I will not. I'll court her in despite of him. Not
court her!—Come, madam, talk on, fear me nothing.—
[*To* Guise] Well may'st thou drive thy master from   165
the Court, but never D'Ambois.
Mons.—His great heart will not down, 'tis like the
      sea,
That partly by his own internal heat,
Partly the stars' daily and nightly motion,
Their heat and light, and partly of the place   170
The divers frames, but chiefly by the moon,
Bristled with surges, never will be won,
(No, not when th' hearts of all those powers are burst)
To make retreat into his settled home,
Till he be crown'd with his own quiet foam.   175
Hen. You have the mate. Another?
Guise. No more.   [*Flourish short.*
[*Exit* Guise; *after him the* King, Monsieur *whispering.*
Bar. Why, here's the lion, scared with the throat of
a dunghill cock; a fellow that has newly shaked off his
shackles; now does he crow for that victory.   180
L'An. 'Tis one of the best jigs that ever was acted.

176 mate] at chess

20

Pyr. Whom does the Guise suppose him to be, trow?

L'An. Out of doubt, some new denizened lord, and thinks that suit newly drawn out o' th' mercer's books.

Bar. I have heard of a fellow, that by a fixed imagina- 185 tion looking upon a bull-baiting, had a visible pair of horns grew out of his forehead, and I believe this gallant, overjoyed with the conceit of Monsieur's cast suit, imagines himself to be the Monsieur.

L'An. And why not? as well as the ass, stalking in 190 the lion's case, bare himself like a lion, braying all the huger beasts out of the forest?

Pyr. Peace, he looks this way.

Bar. Marry, let him look, sir, what will you say now if the Guise be gone to fetch a blanket for him? 195

L'An. Faith, I believe it for his honour sake.

Pyr. But, if D'Ambois carry it clean?

                                [Exeunt Ladies.

Bar. True, when he curvets in the blanket.

Pyr. Ay, marry, sir.

L'An. 'Sfoot, see how he stares on's. 200

Bar. Lord bless us, let's away.

Bus. Now, sir, take your full view, how does the object please ye?

Bar. If you ask my opinion, sir, I think your suit fits as well as if't had been made for you. 205

Bus. So, sir, and was that the subject of your ridiculous jollity?

L'An. What's that to you, sir?

Bus. Sir, I have observed all your fleerings; and resolve yourselves ye shall give a strict account for't. 210

        Enter Brisac *and* Melynell.

Bar. Oh, miraculous jealousy! Do you think yourself

195 blanket] *to toss him in*

21

such a singular subject for laughter that none can fall
into the matter of our merriment but you?

L'An. This jealousy of yours, sir, confesses some
close defect in yourself that we never dreamed of.   215

Pyr. We held discourse of a perfumed ass, that being
disguised in a lion's case, imagined himself a lion: I
hope that touched not you.

Bus. So, sir; your descants do marvellous well fit
this ground; we shall meet where your buffoonly 220
laughters will cost ye the best blood in your bodies.

Bar. For life's sake let's be gone; he'll kill's outright
else.

Bus. Go, at your pleasures, I'll be your ghost to
haunt you; and ye sleep on't, hang me.   225

L'An. Go, go, sir; court your mistress.

Pyr. And be advised; we shall have odds against you.

Bus. Tush, valour stands not in number! I'll maintain it, that one man may beat three boys.

Bris. Nay, you shall have no odds of him in number, 230
sir; he's a gentleman as good as the proudest of you,
and ye shall not wrong him.

Bar. Not, sir?

Mel. Not, sir: though he be not so rich, he's a better
man than the best of you; and I will not endure it.   235

L'An. Not you, sir?

Bris. No, sir, nor I.

Bus. I should thank you for this kindness, if I
thought these perfumed musk-cats (being out of this
privilege) durst but once mew at us.   240

Bar. Does your confident spirit doubt that, sir?
Follow us and try.

L'An. Come, sir, we'll lead you a dance.   [*Exeunt.*

FINIS ACTUS PRIMI.

215 close] secret   239–40 this privilege] *the Court, where*
they might not fight

ACTUS SECUNDI, SCENA PRIMA

Henry, Guise, Montsurry, [Beaumond], and Attendants.

Hen. This desperate quarrel sprung out of their
    envies
To D'Ambois' sudden bravery, and great spirit.
    Guise. Neither is worth their envy.
    Hen.   Less than either
Will make the gall of Envy overflow;
She feeds on outcast entrails like a kite;   5
In which foul heap, if any ill lies hid,
She sticks her beak into it, shakes it up,
And hurls it all abroad, that all may view it.
Corruption is her nutriment; but touch her
With any precious ointment, and you kill her: 10
Where she finds any filth in men, she feasts,
And with her black throat bruits it through the world
Being sound and healthful; but if she but taste
The slenderest pittance of commended virtue,
She surfeits of it, and is like a fly   15
That passes all the body's soundest parts,
And dwells upon the sores; or if her squint eye
Have power to find none there, she forges some:
She makes that crooked ever which is straight;
Calls valour giddiness, justice tyranny;   20
A wise man may shun her, she not herself:
Whithersoever she flies from her harms,
She bears her foe still clasp'd in her own arms;
And therefore, Cousin Guise, let us avoid her.

Enter Nuntius.

    Nun. What Atlas or Olympus lifts his head   25
So far past covert, that with air enough

13 Being sound and healthful] 'Envy keeps her own health after
consuming filth' (*Parrott*)

23

My words may be inform'd, and from their height
I may be seen and heard through all the world?
A tale so worthy, and so fraught with wonder
Sticks in my jaws, and labours with event.   30
   Hen. Com'st thou from D'Ambois?
   Nun.   From him, and the rest,
His friends and enemies; whose stern fight I saw,
And heard their words before and in the fray.
   Hen. Relate at large what thou hast seen and heard.
   Nun. I saw fierce D'Ambois and his two brave friends 35
Enter the field, and at their heels their foes;
Which were the famous soldiers, Barrisor,
L'Anou, and Pyrhot, great in deeds of arms:
All which arriv'd at the evenest piece of earth
The field afforded, the three challengers   40
Turn'd head, drew all their rapiers, and stood rank'd:
When face to face the three defendants met them,
Alike prepar'd, and resolute alike.
Like bonfires of contributory wood
Every man's look shew'd, fed with either's spirit;   45
As one had been a mirror to another,
Like forms of life and death, each took from other;
And so were life and death mix'd at their heights,
That you could see no fear of death, for life,
Nor love of life, for death; but in their brows   50
Pyrrho's opinion in great letters shone;
That life and death in all respects are one.
   Hen. Pass'd there no sort of words at their encounter?
   Nun. As Hector, 'twixt the hosts of Greece and Troy,
(When Paris and the Spartan king should end   55
The nine years' war) held up his brazen lance
For signal that doth hosts should cease from arms,
And hear him speak: so Barrisor (advis'd)
Advanc'd his naked rapier 'twixt both sides,

51 Pyrrho] *of Elis, the founder of scepticism*

24

Ripp'd up the quarrel, and compar'd six lives   60
Then laid in balance with six idle words;
Offer'd remission and contrition too;
Or else that he and D'Ambois might conclude
The others' dangers. D'Ambois lik'd the last;
But Barrisor's friends (being equally engag'd   65
In the main quarrel) never would expose
His life alone to that they all deserv'd.
And (for the other offer of remission)
D'Ambois (that like a laurel put in fire
Sparkled and spit) did much much more than scorn,   70
That his wrong should incense him so like chaff,
To go so soon out, and like lighted paper
Approve his spirit at once both fire and ashes;
So drew they lots, and in them Fates appointed
That Barrisor should fight with fiery D'Ambois,   75
Pyrhot with Melynell, with Brisac, L'Anou:
And then like flame and powder they commix'd
So spritely that I wish'd they had been spirits,
That the ne'er-shutting wounds they needs must open
Might as they open'd, shut and never kill: 80
But D'Ambois' sword (that lighten'd as it flew)
Shot like a pointed comet at the face
Of manly Barrisor; and there it stuck:
Thrice pluck'd he at it, and thrice drew on thrusts,
From him that of himself was free as fire;   85
Who thrust still as he pluck'd, yet (past belief)
He with his subtle eye, hand, body, scap'd;
At last, the deadly-bitten point tugg'd off,
On fell his yet undaunted foe so fiercely
That (only made more horrid with his wound)   90
Great D'Ambois shrunk, and gave a little ground;
But soon return'd, redoubled in his danger,

   60 Ripp'd up] set forth, explained   73 Approve] prove
78 spritely] spiritedly   81 lighten'd] flashed lightning

And at the heart of Barrisor seal'd his anger:
Then, as in Arden I have seen an oak
Long shook with tempests, and his lofty top   95
Bent to his root, which being at length made loose
(Even groaning with his weight) he gan to nod
This way and that, as loath his curled brows
(Which he had oft wrapt in the sky with storms)
Should stoop; and yet, his radical fibres burst,   100
Storm-like he fell, and hid the fear-cold earth:
So fell stout Barrisor, that had stood the shocks
Of ten set battles in your Highness' war,
Gainst the sole soldier of the world, Navarre.
   Guise. Oh, piteous and horrid murther!
   Beau.   Such a life. 105
Methinks had metal in it to survive
An age of men.
   Hen.   Such often soonest end.
—Thy felt report calls on; we long to know
On what events the other have arriv'd.
   Nun. Sorrow and fury, like two opposite fumes   110
Met in the upper region of a cloud,
At the report made by this worthy's fall
Brake from the earth, and with them rose Revenge,
Ent'ring with fresh powers his two noble friends;
And under that odds fell surcharg'd Brisac   115
The friend of D'Ambois, before fierce L'Anou;
Which D'Ambois seeing, as I once did see,
In my young travels through Armenia,
An angry unicorn in his full career
Charge with too swift a foot a jeweller,   120
That watch'd him for the treasure of his brow,
And ere he could get shelter of a tree,
Nail him with his rich antler to the earth:

   108 felt] stirring   121 treasure of his brow] *his horn, highly prized*

So D'Ambois ran upon reveng'd L'Anou,
Who eyeing th' eager point borne in his face,   125
And giving back, fell back, and in his fall
His foes uncurbed sword stopp'd in his heart:
By which time all the life-strings of the tw'other
Were cut, and both fell, as their spirits flew
Upwards, and still hunt honour at the view: 130
And now, of all the six, sole D'Ambois stood
Untouch'd, save only with the others' blood.
   Hen. All slain outright but he?
   Nun.   All slain outright but he,
Who kneeling in the warm life of his friends,
(All freckled with the blood his rapier rain'd)   135
He kiss'd their pale lips, and bade both farewell:
And see the bravest man the French earth bears.

         Enter Monsieur, *and* D'Ambois *bare.*

   Bus. Now is the time; y'are princely vow'd, my
         friend;
Perform it princely, and obtain my pardon.
   Mons. Else heaven forgive not me; come on, brave
         friend.   [*They kneel before* Henry.] 140
If ever Nature held herself her own,
When the great trial of a king and subject
Met in one blood, both from one belly springing,
Now prove her virtue and her greatness one,
Or make the t'one the greater with the t'other,   145
(As true kings should) and for your brother's love
(Which is a special species of true virtue)
Do that you could not do, not being a king.
   Hen. Brother, I know your suit; these wilful
         murthers

130 at the view] in close pursuit   137 s.d. bare] bare-
headed   149 sq.] *Public opinion was too strong for attempts to
suppress duelling, for which cf.* The Maid's Tragedy, V. iv. 64–66.

Are ever past our pardon.

   Mons.   Manly slaughter   150
Should never bear th'account of wilful murther;
It being a spice of justice, where with life
Offending past law equal life is laid
In equal balance, to scourge that offence
By law of reputation, which to men   155
Exceeds all positive law, and what that leaves
To true men's valours (not prefixing rights
Of satisfaction, suited to their wrongs)
A free man's eminence may supply and take.

   Hen. This would make every man that thinks him
      wrong'd   160
Or is offended, or in wrong or right,
Lay on this violence; and all vaunt themselves
Law-menders and suppliers, though mere butchers;
Should this fact (though of justice) be forgiven?

   Mons. Oh, no, my lord; it would make cowards fear 165
To touch the reputations of true men;
When only they are left to imp the law,
Justice will soon distinguish murtherous minds
From just revengers: had my friend been slain,
His enemy surviving, he should die,   170
Since he had added to a murther'd fame
(Which was in his intent) a murther'd man;
And this had worthily been wilful murther;
But my friend only sav'd his fame's dear life,
Which is above life, taking th'under value,   175
Which, in the wrong it did, was forfeit to him;
And in this fact only preserves a man
In his uprightness, worthy to survive
Millions of such as murther men alive.

   Hen. Well, brother, rise, and raise your friend withal 180

  157 prefixing] fixing in advance   164, 177 fact] deed
  167 imp] supply the defects of

From death to life; and, D'Ambois, let your life
(Refin'd by passing through this merited death)
Be purg'd from more such foul pollution;
Nor on your scape, nor valour, more presuming
To be again so daring.

 Bus.   My lord,   **185**
I loathe as much a deed of unjust death,
As law itself doth; and to tyrannize,
Because I have a little spirit to dare
And power to do, as to be tyranniz'd.
This is a grace that (on my knees redoubled), **190**
I crave, to double this my short life's gift,
And shall your royal bounty centuple,
That I may so make good what God and Nature
Have given me for my good; since I am free,
(Offending no just law), let no law make   **195**
By any wrong it does, my life her slave:
When I am wrong'd, and that law fails to right me,
Let me be king myself (as man was made),
And do a justice that exceeds the law;
If my wrong pass the power of single valour **200**
To right and expiate; then be thou my king,
And do a right, exceeding law and nature:
Who to himself is law, no law doth need,
Offends no law, and is a king indeed.

 Hen. Enjoy what thou entreat'st; we give but ours. **205**
 Bus. What you have given, my lord, is ever yours.
        [*Exit* Rex *cum* Beau, *etc.*
 Guise. Mort Dieu, who would have pardon'd such a
  murther?   [*Exit.*
 Mons. Now vanish horrors into Court attractions
For which let this balm make thee fresh and fair.
And now forth with thy service to the Duchess, **210**
As my long love will to Montsurry's Countess. [*Exit.*

 190 redoubled] bent, *perhaps (Parrott) for the second time*

Bus. To whom my love hath long been vow'd in
   heart,
Although in hand for shew I held the Duchess.
And now through blood and vengeance, deeds of
   height,
And hard to be achiev'd, 'tis fit I make   215
Attempt of her perfection; I need fear
No check in his rivalry, since her virtues
Are so renown'd, and he of all dames hated.   [*Exit.*

ACTUS SECUNDI, SCENA SECUNDA

Enter Monsieur, Tamyra, *and* Pero *with a book.*

Mons. Pray thee regard thine own good, if not mine,
And cheer my love for that: you do not know
What you may be by me, nor what without me;
I may have power t'advance and pull down any.

Tam. That's not my study; one way I am sure   5
You shall not pull down me; my husband's height
Is crown to all my hopes; and his retiring
To any mean state, shall be my aspiring:
Mine honour's in mine hands, spite of kings.

Mons. Honour, what's that? Your second maiden-
   head: 10
And what is that? A word: the word is gone,
The thing remains: the rose is pluck'd, the stalk
Abides; an easy loss where no lack's found:
Believe it, there's as small lack in the loss
As there is pain i'th' losing; archers ever   15
Have two strings to a bow; and shall great Cupid
(Archer of archers both in men and women)
Be worse provided than a common archer?
A husband and a friend all wise wives have.

213 in hand . . . held] played with

30

Tam. Wise wives they are that on such strings
    depend,   20
With a firm husband joining a loose friend.
Mons. Still you stand on your husband; so do all
The common sex of you, when y'are encounter'd
With one ye cannot fancy: all men know
You live in Court, here, by your own election,   25
Frequenting all our common sports and triumphs,
All the most youthful company of men:
And wherefore do you this? To please your husband?
'Tis gross and fulsome: if your husband's pleasure
Be all your object, and you aim at honour   30
In living close to him, get you from Court;
You may have him at home; these common put-offs
For common women serve: 'My honour! Husband!'
Dames maritorious ne'er were meritorious:
Speak plain, and say 'I do not like you, sir;   35
Y'are an ill-favour'd fellow in my eye';
And I am answer'd.
Tam.   Then, I pray, be answer'd:
For, in good faith, my lord, I do not like you
In that sort you like.
Mons.   Then have at you here!
Take (with a politic hand) this rope of pearl,   40
And though you be not amorous, yet be wise:
Take me for wisdom; he that you can love
Is ne'er the further from you.
Tam.   Now it comes
So ill prepar'd, that I may take a poison
Under a medicine as good cheap as it;   45
I will not have it were it worth the world.
Mons. Horror of death! Could I but please your eye,
You would give me the like, ere you would loose me:
'Honour and husband!'

    31 **close to**] privately with

Tam.   By this light, my lord,
Y'are a vile fellow, and I'll tell the King   50
Your occupation of dishonouring ladies,
And of his Court: a lady cannot live
As she was born, and with that sort of pleasure
That fits her state, but she must be defam'd
With an infamous lord's detraction: 55
Who would endure the Court if these attempts
Of open and profess'd lust must be borne?—
Who's there? [*To* Pero] Come on, dame, you are at
    your book
When men are at your mistress; have I taught you
Any such waiting-woman's quality?   60
    Mons. Farewell, 'good husband!'
                              [*Exit* Monsieur.
    Tam.   Farewell, wicked lord!

            Enter Montsurry.

    Mont. Was not the Monsieur here?
    Tam.   Yes, to good purpose;
And your cause is as good to seek him too,
And haunt his company.
    Mont.   Why, what's the matter?
    Tam. Matter of death, were I some husband's wife: 65
I cannot live at quiet in my chamber
For opportunities almost to rapes
Offer'd me by him.
    Mont.   Pray thee bear with him:
Thou know'st he is a bachelor and a courtier,
Ay, and a prince; and their prerogatives   70
Are to their laws, as to their pardons are
Their reservations, after Parliaments—
One quits another: form gives all their essence:
That prince doth high in virtue's reckoning stand
That will entreat a vice, and not command: 75

So far bear with him; should another man
Trust to his privilege, he should trust to death:
Take comfort, then, my comfort, nay, triumph
And crown thyself; thou part'st with victory:
My presence is so only dear to thee   80
That other men's appear worse then they be.
For this night yet, bear with my forced absence:
Thou know'st my business; and with how much weight
My vow hath charg'd it.
    Tam.   True, my lord, and never
My fruitless love shall let your serious honour;   85
Yet, sweet lord, do not stay; you know my soul
Is so long time without me, and I dead,
As you are absent.
    Mont.   By this kiss, receive
My soul for hostage, till I see my love.
    Tam. The morn shall let me see you?
    Mont.   With the sun   90
I'll visit thy more comfortable beauties.
    Tam. This is my comfort, that the sun hath left
The whole world's beauty ere my sun leaves me.
    Mont. 'Tis late night now, indeed; farewell, my light!   [*Exit.*
    Tam. Farewell, my light and life! But not in him,   95
In mine own dark love and light bent to another.
Alas, that in the wane of our affections
We should supply it with a full dissembling,
In which each youngest maid is grown a mother.
Frailty is fruitful, one sin gets another: 100
Our loves like sparkles are, that brightest shine
When they go out; most vice shows most divine.
—Go, maid, to bed; lend me your book, I pray:
Not, like yourself, for form; I'll this night trouble
None of your services: make sure the doors,   105

33

And call your other fellows to their rest.
   Pero. I will.—Yet I will watch to know why you
     watch.   [*Exit.*
   Tam. Now all ye peaceful regents of the night,
Silently-gliding exhalations,
Languishing winds, and murmuring falls of waters,   110
Sadness of heart and ominous secureness,
Enchantments, dead sleeps, all the friends of rest,
That ever wrought upon the life of man,
Extend your utmost strengths, and this charm'd hour
Fix like the Centre! Make the violent wheels   115
Of Time and Fortune stand, and great Existence
(The Maker's treasury) now not seem to be,
To all but my approaching friends and me!
They come, alas, they come! Fear, fear and hope,
Of one thing, at one instant, fight in me: 120
I love what most I loathe, and cannot live,
Unless I compass that which holds my death:
For life's mere death, loving one that loathes me,
And he I love, will loathe me, when he sees
I fly my sex, my virtue, my renown,   125
To run so madly on a man unknown. [*The vault opens.*
See, see, a vault is opening that was never
Known to my lord and husband, nor to any
But him that brings the man I love, and me.
How shall I look on him? How shall I live,   130
And not consume in blushes? I will in,
And cast myself off, as I ne'er had been.
                             [*Exit.*

       Ascendit Friar *and* D'Ambois.

  Friar. Come, worthiest son, I am past measure glad,

109 exhalations] comets, shooting stars   111 ominous
secureness] ill-omened sense of security   126 & 132 s.d.]
They ascend through the trap-door in the stage   132 cast . . .
off] dismiss

34

That you (whose worth I have approv'd so long)
Should be the object of her fearful love;   135
Since both your wit and spirit can adapt
Their full force to supply her utmost weakness:
You know her worths and virtues, for report
Of all that know is to a man a knowledge:
You know, besides, that our affections' storm,   140
Rais'd in our blood, no reason can reform.
Though she seek then their satisfaction
(Which she must needs, or rest unsatisfied)
Your judgment will esteem her peace thus wrought,
Nothing less dear than if yourself had sought: 145
And (with another colour, which my art
Shall teach you to lay on) yourself must seem
The only agent, and the first orb move
In this our set and cunning world of love.
    Bus. Give me the colour, my most honour'd father, 150
And trust my cunning then to lay it on.
    Friar. 'Tis this, good son; Lord Barrisor (whom you
      slew)
Did love her dearly, and with all fit means
Hath urg'd his acceptation, of all which
She keeps one letter written in his blood: 155
You must say thus, then, that you heard from me
How much herself was touch'd in conscience
With a report (which is, in truth, dispers'd)
That your main quarrel grew about her love,
Lord Barrisor imagining your courtship   160
Of the great Guise's Duchess, in the presence,
Was by you made to his elected mistress:
And so made me your mean now to resolve her,
Choosing (by my direction) this night's depth

135 fearful] timorous   148 first orb] *the* primum mobile
of the Ptolemaic system (Boas)   161 presence] *of the king*
163 resolve] inform

35

For the more clear avoiding of all note   165
Of your presumed presence; and with this
(To clear her hands of such a lover's blood)
She will so kindly thank and entertain you,
(Methinks I see how), ay, and ten to one,
Show you the confirmation in his blood,   170
Lest you should think report and she did feign,
That you shall so have circumstantial means
To come to the direct, which must be used;
For the direct is crooked; love comes flying;
The height of love is still won with denying.   175
    Bus. Thanks, honour'd father.
    Friar.   She must never know
That you know anything of any love
Sustain'd on her part: for, learn this of me,
In anything a woman does alone,
If she dissemble, she thinks 'tis not done;   180
If not dissemble, nor a little chide,
Give her her wish, she is not satisfied;
To have a man think that she never seeks
Does her more good than to have all she likes:
This frailty sticks in them beyond their sex,   185
Which to reform, reason is too perplex:
Urge reason to them, it will do no good;
Humour (that is the chariot of our food
In everybody) must in them be fed,
To carry their affections by it bred.   190
Stand close!

Enter Tamyra *with a book.*

    Tam. Alas, I fear my strangeness will retire him.
If he go back, I die; I must prevent it,
And cheer his onset with my sight at least,

186 perplex] complicated   191 close] hidden   192 strange-
ness] unfriendliness   retire] repel

And that's the most; though every step he takes   195
Goes to my heart, I'll rather die than seem
Not to be strange to that I most esteem.
     Friar. Madam!
     Tam.   Ah!
     Friar.   You will pardon me, I hope,
That so beyond your expectation,
And at a time for visitants so unfit,   200
I (with my noble friend here) visit you:
You know that my access at any time
Hath ever been admitted; and that friend
That my care will presume to bring with me
Shall have all circumstance of worth in him   205
To merit as free welcome as myself.
     Tam. Oh, father, but at this suspicious hour
You know how apt best men are to suspect us,
In any cause, that makes suspicious shadow
No greater than the shadow of a hair: 210
And y'are to blame. What though my lord and husband
Lie forth to-night, and since I cannot sleep
When he is absent I sit up to-night;
Though all the doors are sure, and all our servants
As sure bound with their sleeps; yet there is One   215
That wakes above, whose eye no sleep can bind;
He sees through doors, and darkness, and our thoughts;
And therefore as we should avoid with fear,
To think amiss ourselves before his search;
So should we be as curious to shun   220
All cause that other think not ill of us.
     Bus. Madam, 'tis far from that; I only heard
By this my honour'd father that your conscience
Made some deep scruple with a false report
That Barrisor's blood should something touch your
          honour;   225

          220, 232 &c. curious] careful

                         37

Since he imagin'd I was courting you,
When I was bold to change words with the Duchess,
And therefore made his quarrel, his long love
And service, as I hear, being deeply vow'd
To your perfections; which my ready presence,   230
Presum'd on with my father at this season
For the more care of your so curious honour,
Can well resolve your conscience is most false.
  Tam. And is it therefore that you come, good sir?
Then crave I now your pardon and my father's,   235
And swear your presence does me so much good,
That all I have it binds to your requital:
Indeed, sir, 'tis most true that a report
Is spread, alleging that his love to me
Was reason of your quarrel; and because   240
You shall not think I feign it for my glory
That he importun'd me for his court service,
I'll show you his own hand, set down in blood,
To that vain purpose: good sir, then come in.
Father, I thank you now a thousand fold.   245
                    [*Exit* Tamyra *and* D'Ambois.
  Friar. May it be worth it to you, honour'd daughter.
                            [*Descendit* Friar.

                FINIS ACTUS SECUNDI.

        ACTUS TERTII, SCENA PRIMA

    Enter D'Ambois, Tamyra, *with a Chain of Pearl.*

  Bus. Sweet mistress, cease, your conscience is too
    nice,
And bites too hotly of the Puritan spice.
  Tam. Oh my dear servant, in thy close embraces

242 court service] fashionable philandering   246 s.d.
Descendit] he *goes down through the trap-door*

                        38

I have set open all the doors of danger
To my encompass'd honour, and my life: 5
Before I was secure against death and hell;
But now am subject to the heartless fear
Of every shadow, and of every breath,
And would change firmness with an aspen leaf:
So confident a spotless conscience is,   10
So weak a guilty: oh, the dangerous siege
Sin lays about us, and the tyranny
He exercises when he hath expugn'd!
Like to the horror of a winter's thunder,
Mix'd with a gushing storm, that suffer nothing   15
To stir abroad on earth but their own rages,
Is Sin, when it hath gather'd head above us:
No roof, no shelter can secure us so,
But he will drown our cheeks in fear or woe.
    Bus. Sin is a coward, madam, and insults   20
But on our weakness, in his truest valour:
And so our ignorance tames us, that we let
His shadows fright us: and like empty clouds,
In which our faulty apprehensions forge
The forms of dragons, lions, elephants,   25
When they hold no proportion, the sly charms
Of the witch Policy makes him like a monster
Kept only to show men for servile money:
That false hag often paints him in her cloth
Ten times more monstrous than he is in troth: 30
In three of us the secret of our meeting
Is only guarded, and three friends as one
Have ever been esteem'd: as our three powers
That in one soul are as one united:
Why should we fear then? For myself, I swear,   35

13 expugn'd] taken by siege   29 cloth] picture adver-
tising a freak-show   33 three powers] *sc. vegetative, sensible,
reasoning* (Boas)

Sooner shall torture be the sire to pleasure,
And health be grievous to one long time sick,
Than the dear jewel of your fame in me
Be made an outcast to your infamy;
Nor shall my value (sacred to your virtues)   40
Only give free course to it, from myself:
But make it fly out of the mouth of kings
In golden vapours and with awful wings.
    Tam. It rests as all kings' seals were set in thee.
Now let us call my father, whom I swear   45
I could extremely chide, but that I fear
To make him so suspicious of my love
Of which, sweet servant, do not let him know
For all the world.
    Bus.   Alas, he will not think it!
    Tam. Come, then.—Ho! Father, ope, and take your
    friend.   [*Ascendit* Friar. 50
    Friar. Now, honour'd daughter, is your doubt re-
    solv'd?
    Tam. Ay, father, but you went away too soon.
    Friar. Too soon?
    Tam.   Indeed you did, you should have stay'd;
Had not your worthy friend been of your bringing,
And that contains all laws to temper me,   55
Not all the fearful danger that besieg'd us,
Had aw'd my throat from exclamation.
    Friar. I know your serious disposition well.
Come, son, the morn comes on.
    Bus.   Now, honour'd mistress,
Till farther service call, all bliss supply you!   60
    Tam. And you this chain of pearl, and my love only!
            [*Descendit* Friar *and* D'Ambois.
It is not I, but urgent destiny,
That (as great statesmen for their general end
In politic justice, make poor men offend)

Enforceth my offence to make it just.   65
What shall weak dames do, when th' whole work of
      nature
Hath a strong finger in each one of us?
Needs must that sweep away the silly cobweb
Of our still-undone labours, that lays still
Our powers to it: as to the line, the stone,   70
Not to the stone, the line should be oppos'd.
We cannot keep our constant course in virtue:
What is alike at all parts? Every day
Differs from other: every hour and minute;
Ay, every thought in our false clock of life,   75
Oft-times inverts the whole circumference:
We must be sometimes one, sometimes another:
Our bodies are but thick clouds to our souls,
Through which they cannot shine when they desire:
When all the stars, and even the sun himself,   80
Must stay the vapours' times that he exhales
Before he can make good his beams to us:
Oh, how can we, that are but motes to him,
Wandering at random in his order'd rays,
Disperse our passions' fumes, with our weak labours, 85
That are more thick and black than all earth's vapours?

Enter Montsurry.

  Mont. Good day, my love! What, up and ready too!
  Tam. Both, my dear lord; not all this night made I
Myself unready, or could sleep a wink.
  Mont. Alas, what troubled my true love, my peace, 90
From being at peace within her better self?
Or how could sleep forbear to seize thine eyes,
When he might challenge them as his just prize?
  Tam. I am in no power earthly, but in yours;

65 Enforceth] reinforces   71 oppos'd] adjusted
                87 ready] dressed

To what end should I go to bed, my lord,   95
That wholly miss'd the comfort of my bed?
Or how should sleep possess my faculties,
Wanting the proper closer of mine eyes?
   Mont. Then will I never more sleep night from thee:
All mine own business, all the King's affairs,   100
Shall take the day to serve them; every night
I'll ever dedicate to thy delight.
   Tam. Nay, good my lord, esteem not my desires
Such doters on their humours that my judgment
Cannot subdue them to your worthier pleasure: 105
A wife's pleas'd husband must her object be
In all her acts, not her soothed fantasy.
   Mont. Then come, my love, now pay those rites to
     sleep
Thy fair eyes owe him; shall we now to bed?
   Tam. Oh, no, my lord; your holy friar says   110
All couplings in the day that touch the bed
Adulterous are, even in the married;
Whose grave and worthy doctrine, well I know,
Your faith in him will liberally allow.
   Mont. He's a most learned and religious man;   115
Come to the presence then, and see great D'Ambois
(Fortune's proud mushroom shot up in a night)
Stand like an Atlas under our King's arm;
Which greatness with him Monsieur now envies
As bitterly and deadly as the Guise.   120
   Tam. What! He that was but yesterday his maker,
His raiser, and preserver?
   Mont.   Even the same.
Each natural agent works but to this end,
To render that it works on like itself;
Which since the Monsieur in his act on D'Ambois   125

   107 soothed fantasy] pleased fancy   119 envies]
pronounced envies

42

Cannot to his ambitious end effect,
But that, quite opposite, the King hath power,
In his love borne to D'Ambois, to convert
The point of Monsieur's aim on his own breast,
He turns his outward love to inward hate: 130
A prince's love is like the lightning's fume,
Which no man can embrace but must consume.

                                        [*Exeunt.*

ACTUS TERTII, SCENA SECUNDA

Henry, D'Ambois, Monsieur, Guise, Duchess,
Annable, Charlotte, Attendants.

Hen. Speak home, Bussy! Thy impartial words
Are like brave falcons that dare truss a fowl
Much greater than themselves; flatterers are kites
That check at sparrows; thou shalt be my eagle,
And bear my thunder underneath thy wings;   5
Truth's words, like jewels, hang in th' ears of kings.
  Bus. Would I might live to see no Jews hang there
Instead of jewels—sycophants, I mean,
Who use Truth like the Devil, his true foe,
Cast by the angel to the pit of fears,   10
And bound in chains; Truth seldom decks king's ears.
Slave Flattery (like a rippier's legs roll'd up
In boots of hay-ropes) with kings' soothed guts
Swaddled and strappled, now lives only free.
Oh, 'tis a subtle knave; how like the plague   15
Unfelt he strikes into the brain of man,
And rageth in his entrails when he can,
Worse than the poison of a red-hair'd man.
  Hen. Fly at him and his brood! I cast thee off,
And once more give thee surname of mine eagle.   20

        12 rippier] fishmonger   14 strappled] gaitered

43

Bus. I'll make you sport enough, then: let me have
My lucerns too, or dogs inur'd to hunt
Beasts of most rapine, but to put them up,
And if I truss not, let me not be trusted.
Show me a great man (by the people's voice,   25
Which is the voice of God) that by his greatness
Bombasts his private roofs with public riches;
That affects royalty, rising from a clapdish;
That rules so much more by his suffering king,
That he makes kings of his subordinate slaves: 30
Himself and them graduate (like woodmongers,
Piling a stack of billets) from the earth,
Raising each other into steeples' heights;
Let him convey this on the turning props
Of Protean law, and (his own counsel keeping)   35
Keep all upright—let me but hawk at him,
I'll play the vulture, and so thump his liver,
That, like a huge unlading Argosy,
He shall confess all, and you then may hang him.
Show me a clergyman, that is in voice   40
A lark in heaven, in heart a mole of earth;
That hath good living, and a wicked life;
A temperate look, and a luxurious gut,
Turning the rent of his superfluous cures
Into your pheasants and your partridges,   45
Venting their quintessence as men read Hebrew—
Let me but hawk at him, and, like the other,
He shall confess all, and you then may hang him.
Show me a lawyer that turns sacred law
(The equal rend'rer of each man his own,   50

22 lucerns] *wrongly used by Chapman for* hunting dogs; *they are*
cats (O.E.D.)   24 truss] clutch *(as a bird of prey)*   27
Bombasts] pads out   28 clapdish] beggar's bowl   44
cures] *sc. of souls, referring to pluralist clergy*   46 Hebrew]
is read backward (Parrott)

The scourge of rapine and extortion,
The sanctuary and impregnable defence
Of retir'd learning and besieged virtue)
Into a harpy, that eats all but 's own,
Into the damned sins it punisheth;   55
Into the synagogue of thieves and atheists,
Blood into gold, and justice into lust—
Let me but hawk at him, as at the rest,
He shall confess all, and you then may hang him.

Enter Montsurry, Tamyra, *and* Pero.

Guise. Where will you find such game as you would
    hawk at?   60
Bus. I'll hawk about your house for one of them.
Guise. Come, y'are a glorious ruffian, and run proud
Of the King's headlong graces; hold your breath,
Or, by that poison'd vapour, not the King
Shall back your murtherous valour against me.   65
Bus. I would the King would make his presence free
But for one bout betwixt us: by the reverence
Due to the sacred space 'twixt kings and subjects,
Here would I make thee cast that popular purple,
In which thy proud soul sits and braves thy sovereign. 70
Mons. Peace, peace, I pray thee peace.
Bus.   Let him peace first
That made the first war.
Mons.   He's the better man.
Bus. And, therefore, may do worst?
Mons.   He has more titles.
Bus. So Hydra had more heads.
Mons.   He's greater known.
Bus. His greatness is the people's; mine's mine own. 75

62, 116 &c. glorious] boastful   66 free] *sc. from the
prohibition of violence (cf.* I. ii. 239–40 *note)*

Mons. He's nobl[ier] born.

Bus.   He is not; I am noble.
And noblesse in his blood hath no gradation.
But in his merit.

Guise.   Th'art not nobly born,
But bastard to the Cardinal of Ambois.

    Bus. Thou liest, proud Guisard; let me fly, my lord. 80

    Hen. Not in my face, my eagle; violence flies
The sanctuaries of a prince's eyes.

    Bus. Still shall we chide and foam upon this bit?
Is the Guise only great in faction?
Stands he not by himself? Proves he th' opinion   85
That men's souls are without them? Be a duke,
And lead me to the field.

    Guise.   Come, follow me.

    Hen. Stay them! Stay, D'Ambois! Cousin Guise, I
      wonder
Your honour'd disposition brooks so ill
A man so good, that only would uphold   90
Man in his native noblesse, from whose fall
All our dissensions rise; that in himself
(Without the outward patches of our frailty,
Riches and honour) knows he comprehends
Worth with the greatest: kings had never borne   95
Such boundless empire over other men,
Had all maintain'd the spirit and state of D'Ambois;
Nor had the full impartial hand of Nature
That all things gave in her original,
Without these definite terms of Mine and Thine,   100
Been turn'd unjustly to the hand of Fortune,
Had all preserv'd her in her prime, like D'Ambois;
No envy, no disjunction had dissolv'd,
Or pluck'd one stick out of the golden faggot
In which the world of Saturn bound our lives,   105

    86 duke] = dux = leader

46

Had all been held together with the nerves,
The genius, and th' ingenuous soul of D'Ambois.
Let my hand therefore be the Hermean rod
To part and reconcile, and so conserve you,
As my combin'd embracers and supporters.   110
    Bus. 'Tis our King's motion, and we shall not seem
To worst eyes womanish, though we change thus soon
Never so great grudge for his greater pleasure.
    Guise. I seal to that, and so the manly freedom,
That you so much profess, hereafter prove not   115
A bold and glorious licence to deprave,
To me his hand shall hold the Hermean virtue
His grace affects, in which submissive sign
On this his sacred right hand, I lay mine.
    Bus. 'Tis well, my lord, and so your worthy great-
        ness   120
Decline not to the greater insolence,
Nor make you think it a prerogative,
To rack men's freedoms with the ruder wrongs,
My hand (stuck full of laurel, in true sign
'Tis wholly dedicate to righteous peace)   125
In all submission kisseth th' other side.
    Hen. Thanks to ye both; and kindly I invite ye
Both to a banquet, where we'll sacrifice
Full cups to confirmation of your loves;
At which, fair ladies, I entreat your presence;   130
And hope you, madam, will take one carouse
                        [*To the Duchess.*
For reconcilement of your lord and servant.
    Duch. If I should fail, my lord, some other lady
Would be found there to do that for my servant.
    Mons. Any of these here?
    Duch.   Nay, I know not that.   135

108 Hermean rod] caduceus, symbol of pacification
116 deprave] disparage

Bus.—Think your thoughts like my mistress,
  honour'd lady?

Tam. I think not on you, sir; y'are one I know not.

Bus. Cry you mercy, madam!

Mont.   Oh, sir, has she met you?

  [*Exeunt* Henry, D'Ambois, [*and*] Ladies.

Mons. What had my bounty drunk when it rais'd
  him?

Guise. Y'ave stuck us up a very worthy flag,   140
That takes more wind than we with all our sails.

Mons. Oh, so he spreads and flourishes.

Guise.   He must down,
Upstarts should never perch too near a crown.

Mons. 'Tis true, my lord; and as this doting hand,
Even out of earth, like Juno, struck this giant,   145
So Jove's great ordnance shall be here implied
To strike him under th' Etna of his pride:
To which work lend your hands, and let us cast
Where we may set snares for his ranging greatness:
I think it best, amongst our greatest women: 150
For there is no such trap to catch an upstart
As a loose downfall; for, you know, their falls
Are th' ends of all men's rising: if great men
And wise make scapes to please advantage[s]
'Tis with a woman: women, that worst may,   155
Still hold men's candles: they direct and know
All things amiss in all men, and their women
All things amiss in them; through whose charm'd
  mouths,
We may see all the close scapes of the Court.
When the most royal beast of chase, the hart,   160

145 Juno] *struck Typhon out of earth*   146 ordnance]
artillery (*sc. the thunderbolt*)   148 cast] calculate   155–6
women . . . candles] *Parrott explains this as meaning that the looker-
on sees most of the game*   159 close scapes] secret escapades

Being old, and cunning in his lairs and haunts,
Can never be discover'd to the bow,
The piece, or hound, yet where, behind some queach,
He breaks his gall, and rutteth with his hind,
The place is mark'd, and by his venery   165
He still is taken. Shall we then attempt
The chiefest mean to that discovery here,
And court our greatest ladies' chiefest women
With shows of love and liberal promises?
'Tis but our breath. If something given in hand   170
Sharpen their hopes of more, 'twill be well ventur'd.
    Guise. No doubt of that; and 'tis the cunning'st
        point
Of our devis'd investigation.
    Mons. I have broken
The ice to it already with the woman   175
Of your chaste lady, and conceive good hope
I shall wade thorough to some wished shore
At our next meeting.
    Mont.   Nay, there's small hope there.
    Guise. Take say of her, my lord, she comes most fitly.

        Enter Charlotte, Annable, Pero.

    Mons. Starting back?   180
    Guise. Y'are engaged, indeed.
    Anna. Nay, pray, my lord, forbear.
    Mont. What, skittish, servant?
    Anna. No, my lord, I am not so fit for your service.
    Char. Pray pardon me now, my lord; my lady
        expects me.   185
    Guise. I'll satisfy her expectation, as far as an uncle
        may.
    Mons. Well said, a spirit of courtship of all hands!

163 piece] gun   queach] thicket   179 Take say] make trial

49

Now, mine own Pero, hast thou remembered me for
the discovery I entreated thee to make of thy mistress?
Speak boldly, and be sure of all things I have sworn 190
to thee.

Pero. Building on that assurance, my lord, I may
speak and much the rather, because my lady hath not
trusted me with that I can tell you; for now I cannot
be said to betray her.   195

Mons. That's all one, so we reach our objects; forth,
I beseech thee.

Pero. To tell you truth, my lord, I have made a
strange discovery.

Mons. Excellent! Pero, thou reviv'st me; may I sink 200
quick to perdition if my tongue discover it.

Pero. 'Tis thus, then: this last night, my lord lay
forth, and I, watching my lady's sitting up, stole up at
midnight from my pallet, and (having before made a
hole both through the wall and arras to her inmost 205
chamber) I saw D'Ambois and herself reading a letter.

Mons. D'Ambois?

Pero. Even he, my lord.

Mons. Dost thou not dream, wench?

Pero. I swear he is the man.   210

Mons.—The devil he is, and thy lady his dam! Why,
this was the happiest shot that ever flew; the just
plague of hypocrisy levelled it. Oh, the infinite regions
betwixt a woman's tongue and her heart! Is this our
Goddess of chastity? I thought I could not be so 215
slighted, if she had not her fraught besides, and therefore plotted this with her woman, never dreaming of
D'Ambois.—Dear Pero, I will advance thee for ever;
but tell me now—God's precious, it transforms me
with admiration—sweet Pero, whom should she trust 220

202–3 lay forth] slept away from home

50

with this conveyance? Or, all the doors being made
sure, how should his conveyance be made?

Pero. Nay, my lord, that amazes me; I cannot by any
study so much as guess at it.

Mons. Well, let's favour our apprehensions with for- 225
bearing that a little; for, if my heart were not hooped
with adamant, the conceit of this would have burst it.
But hark thee.   [*Whispers [to* Pero.]

Mont. I pray thee, resolve me: the Duke will never
imagine that I am busy about's wife: hath D'Ambois 230
any privy access to her?

Anna. No, my lord; D'Ambois neglects her, as she
takes it, and is therefore suspicious that either your
lady, or the Lady Beaupré, hath closely entertained
him.   235

Mont. By'r lady, a likely suspicion, and very near the
life,—especially of my wife.

Mons. [*Aside to* Pero.] Come, we'll disguise all with
seeming only to have courted.—Away, dry palm!
Sh'as a liver as hard as a biscuit; a man may go a whole 240
voyage with her, and get nothing but tempests from
her wind-pipe.

Guise. Here's one, I think, has swallowed a porcu-
pine, she casts pricks from her tongue so.

Mont. And here's a peacock seems to have devoured 245
one of the Alps, she has so swelling a spirit, and is so
cold of her kindness.

Char. We are no windfalls, my lord; ye must gather
us with the ladder of matrimony, or we'll hang till we
be rotten.   250

Mons. Indeed, that's the way to make ye right open-
arses. But, alas, ye have no portions fit for such husbands as we wish you.

221 conveyance] trick   227 conceit] idea   234 closely
entertained] secretly accepted

Pero. Portions, my lord? yes, and such portions as
your principality cannot purchase.   255
Mons. What, woman! what are those portions?
Pero. Riddle my riddle, my lord.
Mons. Ay, marry wench, I think thy portion is a
right riddle; a man shall never find it out. But let's
hear it.   260
Pero. You shall, my lord.

> *What's that, that being most rare's most cheap?*
> *That when you sow, you never reap?*
> *That when it grows most, most you in it;*
> *And still you lose it when you win it?*   265
> *That when 'tis commonest, 'tis dearest,*
> *And when 'tis farthest off, 'tis nearest?*

Mons. Is this your great portion?
Pero. Even this, my lord.
Mons. Believe me, I cannot riddle it.   270
Pero. No, my lord: 'tis my chastity, which you shall
neither riddle nor fiddle.
Mons. Your chastity? Let me begin with the end of
it; how is a woman's chastity nearest a man when 'tis
farthest off?   275
Pero. Why, my lord, when you cannot get it, it goes
to th' heart on you; and that, I think, comes most near
you: and I am sure it shall be far enough off; and so we
leave you to our mercies.   [*Exeunt* Women.
Mons. Farewell, riddle!   280
Guise. Farewell, medlar!
Mont. Farewell, winter plum!
Mons. Now, my lords, what fruit of our inquisition?
Feel you nothing budding yet? Speak, good my lord
Montsurry.   285
Mont. Nothing but this: D'Ambois is thought negli-
gent in observing the Duchess, and therefore she is

suspicious that your niece or my wife closely enter-
tains him.

Mons. Your wife, my lord? Think you that possible? 290

Mont. Alas, I know she flies him like her last hour.

Mons. Her last hour? Why, that comes upon her the
more she flies it. Does D'Ambois so, think you?

Mont. That's not worth the answering. 'Tis miraculous to think with what monsters women's imagina- 295
tions engross them when they are once enamoured,
and what wonders they will work for their satisfaction.
They will make a sheep valiant, a lion fearful.

Mons. And an ass confident. Well, my lord, more will
come forth shortly; get you to the banquet.   300

Guise. Come, my lord; I have the blind side of one of
them.   [*Exit* Guise *cum* Montsurry.

Mons. Oh, the unsounded sea of women's bloods,
That when 'tis calmest, is most dangerous!
Not any wrinkle creaming in their faces,   305
When in their hearts are Scylla and Charybdis,
Which still are hid in dark and standing fogs,
Where never day shines, nothing ever grows,
But weeds and poisons that no statesman knows:
Not Cerberus ever saw the damned nooks   310
Hid with the veils of women's virtuous looks.
But what a cloud of sulphur have I drawn
Up to my bosom in this dangerous secret!
Which if my haste with any spark should light
Ere D'Ambois were engag'd in some sure plot,   315
I were blown up; he would be, sure, my death.
Would I had never known it, for before
I shall persuade th' importance to Montsurry,
And make him with some studied stratagem
Train D'Ambois to his wreak, his maid may tell it;   320
Or I (out of my fiery thirst to play

320 train ... wreak] lure ... vengeance

53

With the fell tiger, up in darkness tied,
And give it some light) make it quite break loose.
I fear it afore heaven, and will not see
D'Ambois again, till I have told Montsurry,   325
And set a snare with him to free my fears.
Who's there?

Enter Maffé.

Maf.   My lord?
Mons.   Go call the Count Montsurry,
And make the doors fast; I will speak with none
Till he come to me.
Maf.   Well, my lord.   [*Exiturus.*
Mons.   Or else
Send you some other, and see all the doors   330
Made safe yourself, I pray; haste, fly about it.
   Maf. You'll speak with none but with the Count
      Montsurry?
   Mons. With none but he, except it be the Guise.
   Maf. See, even by this there's one exception more;
Your Grace must be more firm in the command,   335
Or else shall I as weakly execute.
The Guise shall speak with you?
   Mons.   He shall, I say.
   Maf. And Count Montsurry?
   Mons.   Ay, and Count Montsurry.
   Maf. Your Grace must pardon me, that I am bold
To urge the clear and full sense of your pleasure;   340
Which whensoever I have known, I hope
Your Grace will say I hit it to a hair.
   Mons. You have.
   Maf.   I hope so, or I would be glad—
   Mons. I pray thee get thee gone; thou art so tedious
In the strict form of all thy services,   345

329 s.d. *Exiturus*] about to go out

54

That I had better have one negligent.
You hit my pleasure well, when D'Ambois hit you;
Did you not, think you?
   Maf.   D'Ambois? Why, my lord—
   Mons. I pray thee talk no more, but shut the doors:
Do what I charge thee.
   Maf.   I will, my lord, and yet   **350**
I would be glad the wrong I had of D'Ambois—
   Mons. Precious, then it is a fate that plagues me
In this man's foolery! I may be murther'd
While he stands on protection of his folly.
Avaunt about thy charge!
   Maf.   I go, my lord.   **355**
—I had my head broke in his faithful service;
I had no suit the more, nor any thanks,
And yet my teeth must still be hit with D'Ambois—
D'Ambois, my lord, shall know—
   Mons.   The devil and D'Ambois!
                         [*Exit* Maffé.

How am I tortur'd with this trusty fool!   **360**
Never was any curious in his place
To do things justly, but he was an ass;
We cannot find one trusty that is witty,
And therefore bear their disproportion.
Grant, thou great star and angel of my life,   **365**
A sure lease of it but for some few days,
That I may clear my bosom of the snake
I cherish'd there, and I will then defy
All check to it but Nature's, and her altars
Shall crack with vessels crown'd with every liquor   **370**
Drawn from her highest and most bloody humours.
I fear him strangely, his advanced valour
Is like a spirit rais'd without a circle,

358 teeth ... hit] 'hit in the teeth' = reproach   373 with-
out] outside   circle] *magically imprisoning raised evil spirits*

Endangering him that ignorantly rais'd him,
And for whose fury he hath learnt no limit.   375

Enter Maffé *hastily.*

Maf. I cannot help it: what should I do more?
As I was gathering a fit guard to make
My passage to the doors, and the doors sure,
The man of blood is enter'd.
 Mons.   Rage of death!
If I had told the secret, and he knew it,   380
Thus had I been endanger'd.

Enter D'Ambois.

         My sweet heart!
How now, what leap'st thou at?
 Bus.   O royal object!
Mons. Thou dream'st awake; object in th' empty air?
Bus. Worthy the brows of Titan, worth his chair.
Mons. Pray thee, what mean'st thou?
 Bus.   See you not a crown 385
Impale the forehead of the great King, Monsieur?
 Mons. Oh, fie upon thee!
 Bus.   Prince, that is the subject
Of all these your retir'd and sole discourses.
 Mons. Wilt thou not leave that wrongful supposi-
  tion?
 Bus. Why wrongful to suppose the doubtless right 390
To the succession worth the thinking?
 Mons. Well, leave these jests! How I am overjoy'd
With thy wish'd presence, and how fit thou com'st,
For, of mine honour, I was sending for thee.
 Bus. To what end?
 Mons.   Only for thy company,   395

388 sole] solitary

56

Which I have still in thought; but that's no payment
On thy part made with personal appearance.
Thy absence so long suffer'd oftentimes
Put me in some little doubt thou dost not love me.
Wilt thou do one thing therefore now sincerely?   400
   Bus. Ay, anything, but killing of the King.
   Mons. Still in that discord, and ill-taken note?
How most unseasonable thou playest the cuckoo,
In this thy fall of friendship!
   Bus.   Then do not doubt
That there is any act within my nerves,   405
But killing of the King, that is not yours.
   Mons. I will not, then; to prove which by my love
Shown to thy virtues, and by all fruits else
Already sprung from that still-flourishing tree,
With whatsoever may hereafter spring,   410
I charge thee utter (even with all the freedom
Both of thy noble nature and thy friendship)
The full and plain state of me in thy thoughts.
   Bus. What, utter plainly what I think of you?
   Mons. Plain as truth!
   Bus. Why, this swims quite against the stream of   415
     greatness;
Great men would rather hear their flatteries,
And if they be not made fools, are not wise.
   Mons. I am no such great fool, and therefore charge
     thee
Even from the root of thy free heart display me.   420
   Bus. Since you affect it in such serious terms,
If yourself first will tell me what you think
As freely and as heartily of me,
I'll be as open in my thoughts of you.
   Mons. A bargain, of mine honour! And make this,   425
That prove we in our full dissection
Never so foul, live still the sounder friends.

Bus. What else, sir? Come, pay me home; I'll bide
  it bravely.
Mons. I will, I swear. I think thee then a man
That dares as much as a wild horse or tiger,   430
As headstrong and as bloody; and to feed
The ravenous wolf of thy most cannibal valour,
(Rather than not employ it) thou wouldst turn
Hackster to any whore, slave to a Jew,
Or English usurer, to force possessions   435
(And cut men's throats) of mortgaged estates;
Or thou wouldst tire thee like a tinker's strumpet,
And murther market-folks; quarrel with sheep,
And run as mad as Ajax; serve a butcher;
Do anything but killing of the King: 440
That in thy valour th'art like other naturals
That have strange gifts in nature, but no soul
Diffus'd quite through, to make them of a piece,
But stop at humours, that are more absurd,
Childish, and villanous than that hackster, whore,   445
Slave, cut-throat, tinker's bitch, compar'd before;
And in those humours wouldst envy, betray,
Slander, blaspheme, change each hour a religion,
Do anything, but killing of the King:
That in thy valour (which is still the dunghill,   450
To which hath reference all filth in thy house)
Th'art more ridiculous and vain-glorious
Than any mountebank, and impudent
Than any painted bawd; which not to soothe,
And glorify thee like a Jupiter Hammon,   455
Thou eat'st thy heart in vinegar, and thy gall
Turns all thy blood to poison, which is cause
Of that toad-pool that stands in thy complexion,
And makes thee (with a cold and earthy moisture,

441 naturals] men without divine revelation   458 toad-
pool] tadpole

Which is the dam of putrefaction,   460
As plague to thy damn'd pride) rot as thou liv'st,
To study calumnies and treacheries,
To thy friends' slaughters like a screech-owl sing,
And to all mischiefs, but to kill the King.
   Bus. So! Have you said?
   Mons.   How think'st thou? Do I flatter? 465
Speak I not like a trusty friend to thee?
   Bus. That ever any man was blest withal;
So here's for me! I think you are (at worst)
No devil, since y'are like to be no king;
Of which, with any friend of yours, I'll lay   470
This poor stillado here, gainst all the stars,
Ay, and gainst all your treacheries, which are more;
That you did never good, but to do ill.
But ill of all sorts, free and for itself:
That (like a murthering piece, making lanes in armies, 475
The first man of a rank, the whole rank falling)
If you have wrong'd one man, you are so far
From making him amends, that all his race,
Friends, and associates fall into your chase:
That y'are for perjuries the very prince   480
Of all intelligencers; and your voice
Is like an eastern wind, that, where it flies,
Knits nets of caterpillars, with which you catch
The prime of all the fruits the kingdom yields:
That your political head is the curs'd fount   485
Of all the violence, rapine, cruelty,
Tyranny, and atheism flowing through the realm:
That y'ave a tongue so scandalous, 'twill cut
The purest crystal; and a breath that will
Kill to that wall a spider; you will jest   490

   471 stillado] stilleto (*erroneously. O.E.D.*)   475 murthering piece] small cannon   481 intelligencers] spies   489 crystal] diamond

With God, and your soul to the devil tender;
For lust kiss horror, and with death engender:
That your foul body is a Lernean fen
Of all the maladies breeding in all men;
That you are utterly without a soul;   495
And, for your life, the thread of that was spun
When Clotho slept, and let her breathing rock
Fall in the dirt; and Lachesis still draws it,
Dipping her twisting fingers in a bowl
Defil'd, and crown'd with virtue's forced soul: 500
And lastly (which I must for gratitude
Ever remember), that of all my height
And dearest life you are the only spring,
Only in royal hope to kill the King.
   Mons. Why, now I see thou lovest me; come to the
   banquet.   [*Exeunt.* 505

FINIS ACTUS TERTII.

ACTUS QUARTI, SCENA PRIMA

Henry, Monsieur *with a letter*, Guise, Montsurry,
   Bussy, Elenor, Tamyra, Beaupré, Pero, Charlotte,
   Annable, Pyra, *with four* Pages.

   Hen. Ladies, ye have not done our banquet right,
Nor look'd upon it with those cheerful rays
That lately turn'd your breaths to floods of gold;
Your looks, methinks, are not drawn out with thoughts
So clear and free as heretofore, but foul,   5
As if the thick complexions of men
Govern'd within them.
   Bus.   'Tis not like, my lord,
That men in women rule, but contrary;
For as the moon (of all things God created)
Not only is the most appropriate image   10

60

Or glass to show them how they wax and wane,
But in her height and motion likewise bears
Imperial influences that command
In all their powers, and make them wax and wane;
So women, that (of all things made of nothing)   15
Are the most perfect idols of the moon,
(Or still-unwean'd sweet moon-calves with white faces)
Not only are patterns of change to men,
But, as the tender moonshine of their beauties
Clears or is cloudy, make men glad or sad: 20
So then they rule in men, not men in them.
   Mons. But here the moons are chang'd, (as the King
     notes)
And either men rule in them, or some power
Beyond their voluntary faculty,
For nothing can recover their lost faces.   25
   Mont. None can be always one: our griefs and joys
Hold several sceptres in us, and have times
For their divided empires: which grief now in them
Doth prove as proper to his diadem.
   Bus. And grief's a natural sickness of the blood,   30
That time to part asks, as his coming had;
Only slight fools, griev'd, suddenly are glad;
A man may say t' a dead man, 'Be reviv'd,'
As well as to one sorrowful, 'Be not griev'd.'
And therefore, princely mistress, in all wars   35
                     [*To the* Duchess.
Against these base foes that insult on weakness,
And still fight hous'd behind the shield of Nature,
Of privilege, law, treachery, or beastly need,
Your servant cannot help; authority here
Goes with corruption, something like some States   40
That back worst men: valour to them must creep
That, to themselves left, would fear him asleep.

     17 moon-calves] born fools

Duch. Ye all take that for granted that doth rest
Yet to be prov'd; we all are as we were,
As merry and as free in thought as ever.   45
    Guise. And why then can ye not disclose your
       thoughts?
    Tam. Methinks the man hath answer'd for us well.
    Mons. The man? Why, madam, d'ye not know his
       name?
    Tam. Man is a name of honour for a king:
Additions take away from each chief thing.   50
The school of modesty not to learn learns dames:
They sit in high forms there, that know men's names.
    Mons.—Hark, sweetheart, here's a bar set to your
       valour!
It cannot enter here, no, not to notice
Of what your name is; your great eagle's beak   55
(Should you fly at her) had as good encounter
An Albion cliff, as her more craggy liver.
    Bus. I'll not attempt her, sir; her sight and name
(By which I only know her) doth deter me.
    Hen. So they do all men else.
    Mons.   You would say so   60
If you knew all.
    Tam.   Knew all, my lord? What mean you?
    Mons. All that I know, madam.
    Tam.   That you know! Speak it.
    Mons. No, 'tis enough, I feel it.
    Hen.   But, methinks
Her courtship is more pure than heretofore;
True courtiers should be modest, and not nice,   65
Bold, but not impudent, pleasure love, not vice.
    Mons.—Sweetheart, come hither! What if one should
       make
Horns at Montsurry? Would it not strike him jealous

52 high forms] dunces' stools (*Boas*)   65 nice] prudish

Through all the proofs of his chaste lady's virtues?
  Bus. If he be wise, not.   70
  Mons. What? Not if I should name the gardener
That I would have him think hath grafted him?
  Bus. So the large licence that your greatness uses
To jest at all men, may be taught indeed
To make a difference of the grounds you play on,   75
Both in the men you scandal, and the matter.
  Mons. As how? As how?
  Bus.   Perhaps led with a train,
Where you may have your nose made less and slit,
Your eyes thrust out.
  Mons.   Peace, peace, I pray thee peace.
Who dares do that? The brother of his King?   80
  Bus. Were your King brother in you; all your
    powers
(Stretch'd in the arms of great men and their bawds),
Set close down by you; all your stormy laws
Spouted with lawyers' mouths, and gushing blood,
Like to so many torrents; all your glories   85
(Making you terrible, like enchanted flames)
Fed with bare cockscombs and with crooked hams,
All your prerogatives, your shames and tortures;
All daring heaven, and opening hell about you—
Were I the man ye wrong'd so and provok'd,   90
Though ne'er so much beneath you, like a box-tree
I would, out of the roughness of my root,
Ram hardness in my lowness and, like Death
Mounted on earthquakes, I would trot through all
Honours and horrors, thorough foul and fair,   95
And from your whole strength toss you into the air.
  Mons. Go, th'art a devil! Such another spirit
Could not be still'd from all th' Armenian dragons.
O my love's glory, heir to all I have

98 still'd] distilled

63

(That's all I can say, and that all I swear)   100
If thou outlive me, as I know thou must,
Or else hath Nature no proportion'd end
To her great labours; she hath breathed a mind
Into thy entrails, of desert to swell
Into another great Augustus Cæsar,   105
Organs and faculties fitted to her greatness;
And should that perish like a common spirit,
Nature's a courtier and regards no merit.
   Hen. Here's nought but whispering with us; like a
    calm
Before a tempest, when the silent air   110
Lays her soft ear close to the earth to hearken
For that she fears steals on to ravish her;
Some fate doth join our ears to hear it coming.
Come, my brave eagle, let's to covert fly;
I see Almighty Æther in the smoke   115
Of all his clouds descending, and the sky
Hid in the dim ostents of tragedy.
               [*Exit* Henry *with* D'Ambois *and Ladies.*
   Guise [*aside to* Monsieur]. Now stir the humour, and
    begin the brawl.
   Mont. The King and D'Ambois now are grown all
    one.
   Mons. [*making horns at* Montsurry]. Nay, they are two,
    my lord.
   Mont.   How's that?
   Mons.   No more.   120
   Mont. I must have more, my lord.
   Mons.   What, more than two?
   Mont. How monstrous is this!
   Mons.   Why?
   Mont.   You make me horns!
   Mons. Not I, it is a work without my power;
Married men's ensigns are not made with fingers;

Of divine fabric they are, not men's hands;   125
Your wife, you know, is a mere Cynthia.
And she must fashion horns out of her nature.
  Mont. But doth she? Dare you charge her? Speak,
    false prince.
  Mons. I must not speak, my lord; but if you'll use
The learning of a nobleman, and read,   130
Here's something to those points; soft, you must pawn
Your honour having read it to return it.

                Enter Tamyra, Pero.

  Mont. Not I! I pawn mine honour for a paper?
  Mons. You must not buy it under.
                              [*Exeunt* Guise *and* Monsieur.
  Mont.   Keep it then,
And keep fire in your bosom.
  Tam.   What says he?   135
  Mont. You must make good the rest.
  Tam.   How fares my lord?
Takes my love anything to heart he says?
  Mont. Come y'are a—
  Tam.   What, my lord?
  Mont.   The plague of Herod
Feast in his rotten entrails.
  Tam.   Will you wreak
Your anger's just cause given by him, on me?   140
  Mont. By him?
  Tam.   By him, my lord; I have admir'd
You could all this time be at concord with him,
That still hath play'd such discords on your honour.
  Mont. Perhaps 'tis with some proud string of my
    wife's.
  Tam. How's that, my lord?
  Mont.   Your tongue will still admire, 145

              141 admir'd] wondered

Till my head be the miracle of the world.
   Tam. Oh, woe is me!

                        [*She seems to swound.*
   Pero.   What does your lordship mean?
Madam, be comforted; my lord but tries you.
Madam! Help, good my lord, are you not mov'd?
Do your set looks print in your words your thoughts? 150
Sweet lord, clear up those eyes, for shame of noblesse,
Unbend that masking forehead; whence is it
You rush upon her with these Irish wars,
More full of sound than hurt? But it is enough,
You have shot home, your words are in her heart;   155
She has not liv'd to bear a trial now.
   Mont. Look up, my love, and by this kiss receive
My soul amongst thy spirits, for supply
To thine chas'd with my fury.
   Tam.   Oh, my lord,
I have too long liv'd to hear this from you.   160
   Mont. 'Twas from my troubled blood, and not from
      me.
—I know not how I fare; a sudden night
Flows through my entrails, and a headlong chaos
Murmurs within me, which I must digest,
And not drown her in my confusions,   165
That was my life's joy, being best inform'd.—
Sweet, you must needs forgive me, that my love
(Like to a fire disdaining his suppression) ·
Rag'd being discourag'd; my whole heart is wounded
When any least thought in you is but touch'd,   170
And shall be till I know your former merits,
Your name and memory, altogether crave
In just oblivion their eternal grave;
And then, you must hear from me, there's no mean
In any passion I shall feel for you;   175

147 s.d. swound] swoon

Love is a razor cleansing, being well us'd,
But fetcheth blood still, being the least abus'd;
To tell you briefly all—the man that left me
When you appear'd, did turn me worse than woman,
And stabb'd me to the heart thus [*making horns*], with
   his fingers.   180
   Tam. Oh, happy woman! Comes my stain from him?
It is my beauty, and that innocence proves
That slew Chimæra, rescued Peleus
From all the savage beasts in Pelion,
And rais'd the chaste Athenian prince from hell: 185
All suffering with me, they for women's lusts,
I for a man's, that the Augean stable
Of his foul sin would empty in my lap;
How his guilt shunn'd me! Sacred Innocence,
That where thou fear'st art dreadful, and his face   190
Turn'd in flight from thee, that had thee in chase;
Come, bring me to him; I will tell the serpent
Even to his venom'd teeth (from whose curs'd seed
A pitch'd field starts up 'twixt my lord and me)
That his throat lies, and he shall curse his fingers,   195
For being so govern'd by his filthy soul.
   Mont. I know not if himself will vaunt t'have been
The princely author of the slavish sin,
Or any other; he would have resolv'd me,
Had you not come, not by his word, but writing,   200
Would I have sworn to give it him again,
And pawn'd mine honour to him for a paper.
   Tam. See how he flies me still! 'Tis a foul heart
That fears his own hand. Good, my lord, make haste
To see the dangerous paper; papers hold   205
Oft-times the forms and copies of our souls,
And, though the world despise them, are the prizes
Of all our honours; make your honour then

191 had . . . in chase] was hunting

67

A hostage for it, and with it confer
My nearest woman here, in all she knows;   210
Who (if the sun or Cerberus could have seen
Any stain in me) might as well as they;
And, Pero, here I charge thee by my love,
And all proofs of it (which I might call bounties),
By all that thou hast seen seem good in me,   215
And all the ill which thou shouldst spit from thee,
By pity of the wound this touch hath given me,
Not as thy mistress now, but a poor woman,
To death given over, rid me of my pains;
Pour on thy powder; clear thy breast of me: 220
My lord is only here; here speak thy worst,
Thy best will do me mischief; if thou spar'st me,
Never shine good thought on thy memory!
Resolve my lord, and leave me desperate.
   Pero. My lord!—My lord hath play'd a prodigal's
     part,   225
To break his stock for nothing; and an insolent,
To cut a Gordian when he could not loose it:
What violence is this, to put true fire
To a false train, to blow up long-crown'd peace
With sudden outrage, and believe a man   230
Sworn to the shame of women, gainst a woman
Born to their honours! But I will to him.
   Tam. No, I will write (for I shall never more
Meet with the fugitive) where I will defy him,
Were he ten times the brother of my king.   235
To him, my lord, and I'll to cursing him.
                         [Exeunt.

   209 confer] compare   217 touch] accusation

ACTUS QUARTI, SCENA SECUNDA

Enter D'Ambois *and* Friar.

Bus. I am suspicious, my most honour'd father,
By some of Monsieur's cunning passages,
That his still ranging and contentious nostrils,
To scent the haunts of Mischief have so us'd
The vicious virtue of his busy sense,   5
That he trails hotly of him, and will rouse him,
Driving him all enrag'd and foaming on us;
And therefore have entreated your deep skill
In the command of good aërial spirits,
To assume these magic rites, and call up one   10
To know if any have reveal'd unto him
Anything touching my dear love and me.
   Friar. Good son, you have amaz'd me but to make
The least doubt of it, it concerns so nearly
The faith and reverence of my name and order.   15
Yet will I justify, upon my soul,
All I have done; if any spirit i' th' earth or air
Can give you the resolve, do not despair.

Music: *and* Tamyra *enters with* Pero, *her maid, bearing a
letter.*

   Tam. Away, deliver it: [*Exit* Pero.
                Oh, may my lines,
Fill'd with the poison of a woman's hate,   20
When he shall open them, shrink up his curs'd eyes
With torturous darkness, such as stands in hell,
Stuck full of inward horrors, never lighted,
With which are all things to be fear'd, affrighted—
   Bus. How is it with my honour'd mistress?   25
   Tam. O servant, help, and save me from the gripes
Of shame and infamy. Our love is known;

2 cunning passages] sly innuendoes

Your Monsieur hath a paper where is writ
Some secret tokens that decipher it.

    Bus. What cold dull Northern brain, what fool but he 30
Durst take into his Epimethean breast
A box of such plagues as the danger yields
Incurr'd in this discovery? He had better
Ventur'd his breast in the consuming reach
Of the hot surfeits cast out of the clouds,   35
Or stood the bullets that (to wreak the sky)
The Cyclops ram in Jove's artillery.

    Friar. We soon will take the darkness from his face
That did that deed of darkness; we will know
What now the Monsieur and your husband do,   40
What is contain'd within the secret paper
Offer'd by Monsieur, and your love's events:
To which ends, honour'd daughter, at your motion,
I have put on these exorcising rites,
And, by my power of learned holiness   45
Vouchsaf'd me from above, I will command
Our resolution of a raised spirit.

    Tam. Good father, raise him in some beauteous form,
That with least terror I may brook his sight.

    Friar. Stand sure together, then, whate'er you see, 50
And stir not, as ye tender all our lives.

He puts on his robes.

*Occidentalium legionum spiritualium imperator (magnus
ille Behemoth) veni, veni, comitatus cum Astaroth locotenente
invicto. Adjuro te per Stygis inscrutabilia arcana, per ipsos
irremeabiles anfractus Averni: adesto ô Behemoth, tu cui* 55
*pervia sunt Magnatum scrinia; veni, per Noctis & tenebrarum
abdita profundissima; per labentia sidera; per ipsos motus*

31] *Epimetheus opened Pandora's box of mischief*
47 resolution] information

horarum furtivos, Hecatesque altum silentium! Appare in
forma spiritali, lucente, splendida & amabili.

    Thunder. Ascendit Behemoth. *Enter* Cartophylax, *&c.*

    Beh. What would the holy Friar?
    Friar.   I would see   60
What now the Monsieur and Montsurry do,
And see the secret paper that the Monsieur
Offer'd to Count Montsurry, longing much
To know on what events the secret loves
Of these two honour'd persons shall arrive.   65
    Beh. Why call'dst thou me to this accursed light,
To these light purposes? I am Emperor
Of that inscrutable darkness where are hid
All deepest truths, and secrets never seen,
All which I know, and command legions   70
Of knowing spirits that can do more than these.
Any of this my guard that circle me
In these blue fires, and out of whose dim fumes
Vast murmurs use to break, and from their sounds
Articulate voices, can do ten parts more   75
Than open such slight truths as you require.
    Friar. From the last night's black depth I call'd up
        one
Of the inferior ablest ministers,
And he could not resolve me; send one then
Out of thine own command, to fetch the paper   80
That Monsieur hath to show to Count Montsurry.
    Beh. I will. Cartophylax, thou that properly
Hast in thy power all papers so inscrib'd,
Glide through all bars to it and fetch that paper.
    Car. I will.   *[A torch removes.*
    Friar.   Till he returns, great Prince of Darkness, 85
Tell me if Monsieur and the Count Montsurry
Are yet encounter'd?

Beh.   Both them and the Guise
Are now together.
    Friar.   Show us all their persons,
And represent the place, with all their actions.
    Beh. The spirit will straight return, and then I'll
    show thee.   90
                            [*The torch returns.*
See, he is come. Why brought'st thou not the paper?
    Car. He hath prevented me, and got a spirit
Rais'd by another great in our command,
To take the guard of it before I came.
    Beh. This is your slackness, not t' invoke our powers 95
When first your acts set forth to their effects;
Yet shall you see it and themselves: behold
They come here, and the Earl now holds the paper.

Enter above Monsieur, Guise, Montsurry, *with a paper*

    Bus. May we not hear them?
    Friar.   No, be still and see.
    Bus. I will go fetch the paper.
    Friar.   Do not stir;   100
There's too much distance and too many locks
'Twixt you and them (how near soe'er they seem),
For any man to interrupt their secrets.
    Tam. O honour'd spirit, fly into the fancy
Of my offended lord, and do not let him   105
Believe what there the wicked man hath written.
    Beh. Persuasion hath already enter'd him
Beyond reflection; peace till their departure.
    Mons. There is a glass of ink where you may see
How to make ready black-fac'd tragedy: 110
You now discern, I hope, through all her paintings,
Her gasping wrinkles and fame's sepulchres.

                92 prevented] forestalled

Guise. Think you he feigns, my lord? What hold you
    now?
Do we malign your wife, or honour you?
Mons. What, stricken dumb! Nay fie, lord, be not
    daunted;   115
Your case is common; were it ne'er so rare,
Bear it as rarely! Now to laugh were manly;
A worthy man should imitate the weather
That sings in tempests, and, being clear, is silent.
Guise. Go home, my lord, and force your wife to
    write   120
Such loving lines to D'Ambois as she us'd
When she desir'd his presence.
Mons.   Do, my lord,
And make her name her conceal'd messenger,
That close and most inenarrable pander,
That passeth all our studies to exquire;   125
By whom convey the letter to her love;
And so you shall be sure to have him come
Within the thirsty reach of your revenge;
Before which, lodge an ambush in her chamber
Behind the arras, of your stoutest men   130
All close and soundly arm'd; and let them share
A spirit amongst them that would serve a thousand.

Enter above Pero *with a letter.*

Guise. Yet stay a little; see, she sends for you.
Mons. Poor, loving lady; she'll make all good yet,
Think you not so, my lord?

             [Montsurry *stabs* Pero *and exit.*

Guise.   Alas, poor soul!   135
Mons. This was cruelly done, i' faith.
Pero.   'Twas nobly done.

124 inenarrable] unspeakable   125 exquire] seek out

73

And I forgive his lordship from my soul.

   Mons. Then much good do't thee, Pero! Hast a
   letter?

   Pero. I hope it rather be a bitter volume

Of worthy curses for your perjury.   140

   Guise. To you, my lord.

   Mons.   To me? Now, out upon her.

   Guise. Let me see, my lord,

   Mons. You shall presently. How fares my Pero?

Who's there?

Enter Servant.

             Take in this maid, sh'as caught a clap,

And fetch my surgeon to her; come, my lord,   145

We'll now peruse our letter.

Exeunt Monsieur, Guise.

   Pero.   Furies rise

Out of the black lines, and torment his soul.

[*Lead her out.*

   Tam. Hath my lord slain my woman?

   Beh.   No, she lives.

   Friar. What shall become of us?

   Beh.   All I can say,

Being call'd thus late, is brief, and darkly this: 150

If D'Ambois' mistress dye not her white hand

In his forc'd blood, he shall remain untouch'd;

So, father, shall yourself, but by yourself:

To make this augury plainer, when the voice

Of D'Ambois shall invoke me, I will rise,   155

Shining in greater light, and show him all

That will betide ye all; meantime be wise,

And curb his valour with your policies.

[*Descendit cum suis.*

   Bus. Will he appear to me when I invoke him?

158 s.d.] he descends with his attendants

Friar. He will, be sure.

Bus.   It must be shortly then: 160
For his dark words have tied my thoughts on knots
Till he dissolve, and free them.

Tam.   In meantime,
Dear servant, till your powerful voice revoke him,
Be sure to use the policy he advis'd;
Lest fury in your too quick knowledge taken   165
Of our abuse, and your defence of me,
Accuse me more than any enemy;
And, father, you must on my lord impose
Your holiest charges, and the Church's power
To temper his hot spirit and disperse   170
The cruelty and the blood, I know his hand
Will shower upon our heads, if you put not
Your finger to the storm, and hold it up,
As my dear servant here must do with Monsieur.

Bus. I'll soothe his plots, and strow my hate with
      smiles,   175
Till all at once the close mines of my heart
Rise at full date, and rush into his blood:
I'll bind his arm in silk, and rub his flesh,
To make the vein swell, that his soul may gush
Into some kennel where it longs to lie,   180
And policy shall be flank'd with policy.
Yet shall the feeling centre where we meet
Groan with the weight of my approaching feet;
I'll make th' inspired thresholds of his court
Sweat with the weather of my horrid steps,   185
Before I enter; yet will I appear
Like calm security before a ruin;
A politician must like lightning melt
The very marrow, and not taint the skin:

180 kennel] gutter   182, 191 centre] earth
            187 security] confidence

His ways must not be seen; the superficies
Of the green centre must not taste his feet,
When hell is plow'd up with his wounding tracts,
And all his harvest reap'd by hellish facts.   [*Exeunt.*

FINIS ACTUS QUARTI

ACTUS QUINTI, SCENA PRIMA

Montsurry, *bare, unbraced, pulling* Tamyra *in by the hair,*
     Friar. *One bearing light, a standish and paper, which*
     sets a table.

Tam. Oh, help me, father!
Friar.   Impious earl, forbear.
Take violent hand from her, or, by mine order,
The King shall force thee.
     Mont.   'Tis not violent;
Come you not willingly?
     Tam.   Yes, good my lord.
     Friar. My lord, remember that your soul must seek   5
Her peace, as well as your revengeful blood;
You ever to this hour have prov'd yourself
A noble, zealous, and obedient son,
T'our holy mother; be not an apostate:
Your wife's offence serves not (were it the worst   10
You can imagine) without greater proofs
To sever your eternal bonds and hearts;
Much less to touch her with a bloody hand:
Nor is it manly, much less husbandly,
To expiate any frailty in your wife   15
With churlish strokes or beastly odds of strength:
The stony birth of clouds will touch no laurel,
Nor any sleeper; your wife is your laurel,

     192 tracts] traces, footprints   v. i. heading *bare*] bareheaded
unbraced] not fully dressed   *standish*] writing-stand   17 stony
birth] thunderbolt

And sweetest sleeper; do not touch her then;
Be not more rude than the wild seed of vapour   20
To her that is more gentle than that rude;
In whom kind nature suffer'd one offence
But to set off her other excellence.
  Mont. Good father, leave us; interrupt no more
The course I must run for mine honour sake.   25
Rely on my love to her, which her fault
Cannot extinguish; will she but disclose
Who was the secret minister of her love,
And through what maze he serv'd it, we are friends.
  Friar. It is a damn'd work to pursue those secrets, 30
That would ope more sin, and prove springs of slaughter;
Nor is't a path for Christian feet to tread,
But out of all way to the health of souls,
A sin impossible to be forgiven;
Which he that dares commit—
  Mont.   Good father, cease your terrors. 35
Tempt not a man distracted; I am apt
To outrages that I shall ever rue!
I will not pass the verge that bounds a Christian,
Nor break the limits of a man nor husband.
  Friar. Then God inspire you both with thoughts
      and deeds
                                                          40
Worthy his high respect, and your own souls.
  Tam. Father!
  Friar.   I warrant thee, my dearest daughter,
He will not touch thee; think'st thou him a pagan?
His honour and his soul lies for thy safety.   [*Exit.*
  Mont. Who shall remove the mountain from my
      breast.
                                                          45
Stand the opening furnace of my thoughts,
And set fit outcries for a soul in hell?
                              [Montsurry *turns a key.*
    44 lies] *in pawn, as a pledge*

77

For now it nothing fits my woes to speak
But thunder, or to take into my throat
The trump of Heaven, with whose determinate blasts 50
The winds shall burst, and the devouring seas
Be drunk up in his sounds; that my hot woes
(Vented enough) I might convert to vapour,
Ascending from my infamy unseen,
Shorten the world, preventing the last breath   55
That kills the living, and regenerates death.
    Tam. My lord, my fault (as you may censure it
With too strong arguments) is past your pardon:
But how the circumstances may excuse me
God knows, and your more temperate mind hereafter 60
May let my penitent miseries make you know.
    Mont. Hereafter? 'Tis a suppos'd infinite,
That from this point will rise eternally:
Fame grows in going; in the scapes of virtue
Excuses damn her: they be fires in cities   65
Enrag'd with those winds that less lights extinguish.
Come, Siren, sing, and dash against my rocks
Thy ruffian galley, rigg'd with quench for lust!
Sing, and put all the nets into thy voice
With which thou drew'st into thy strumpet's lap   70
The spawn of Venus, and in which ye danced;
That, in thy lap's stead, I may dig his tomb,
And quit his manhood with a woman's sleight,
Who never is deceiv'd in her deceit.
Sing (that is, write), and then take from mine eyes 75
The mists that hide the most inscrutable pander
That ever lapp'd up an adulterous vomit;
That I may see the devil, and survive
To be a devil, and then learn to wive:
That I may hang him, and then cut him down,   80
Then cut him up, and with my soul's beams search

57 censure] judge

The cranks and caverns of his brain, and study
The errant wilderness of a woman's face,
Where men cannot get out, for all the comets
That have been lighted at it: though they know   85
That adders lie a-sunning in their smiles,
That basilisks drink their poison from their eyes,
And no way there to coast out to their hearts;
Yet still they wander there, and are not stay'd
Till they be fetter'd, nor secure before   90
All cares devour them, nor in human consort
Till they embrace within their wife's two breasts
All Pelion and Cythaeron with their beasts.
Why write you not?
    Tam.   O, good my lord, forbear
In wreak of great faults to engender greater,   95
And make my love's corruption generate murther.
    Mont. It follows needfully as child and parent;
The chain-shot of thy lust is yet aloft,
And it must murther; 'tis thine own dear twin:
No man can add height to a woman's sin.   100
Vice never doth her just hate so provoke,
As when she rageth under virtue's cloak.
Write! For it must be; by this ruthless steel,
By this impartial torture, and the death
Thy tyrannies have invented in my entrails,   105
To quicken life in dying, and hold up
The spirit in fainting, teaching to preserve
Torments in ashes, that will ever last.
Speak! Will you write?
    Tam.   Sweet lord, enjoin my sin
Some other penance than what makes it worse: 110
Hide in some gloomy dungeon my loath'd face,
And let condemned murtherers let me down
(Stopping their noses) my abhorred food.
Hang me in chains, and let me eat these arms

That have offended: bind me face to face   115
To some dead woman, taken from the cart
Of execution, till death and time
In grains of dust dissolve me; I'll endure:
Or any torture that your wrath's invention
Can fright all pity from the world withal: 120
But to betray a friend with show of friendship,
That is too common for the rare revenge
Your rage affecteth; here then are my breasts,
Last night your pillows; here my wretched arms,
As late the wished confines of your life: 125
Now break them as you please, and all the bounds
Of manhood, noblesse, and religion.

    Mont. Where all these have been broken, they are kept
In doing their justice there with any show
Of the like cruelty; thine arms have lost   130
Their privilege in lust, and in their torture
Thus they must pay it.   [*Stabs her.*

    Tam.   O Lord!

    Mont.   Till thou writ'st,
I'll write in wounds (my wrong's fit characters)
Thy right of sufferance. Write!

    Tam.   Oh, kill me, kill me!
Dear husband, be not crueller than death;   135
You have beheld some Gorgon; feel, oh, feel
How you are turn'd to stone; with my heart-blood
Dissolve yourself again, or you will grow
Into the image of all tyranny.

    Mont. As thou are of adultery; I will ever   140
Prove thee my parallel, being most a monster;
Thus I express thee yet.   [*Stabs her again.*

    Tam.   And yet I live.

    Mont. Ay, for thy monstrous idol is not done yet:
This tool hath wrought enough; now, Torture, use
                    [*Sheaths his dagger.*

This other engine on th' habituate powers   145
Of her thrice-damn'd and whorish fortitude:

Enter Servants [*and place* Tamyra *on the rack*].

Use the most madding pains in her that ever
Thy venoms soak'd through, making most of death,
That she may weigh her wrongs with them, and then
Stand, Vengeance, on thy steepest rock, a victor!   150
    Tam. Oh, who is turn'd into my lord and husband?
Husband! My lord! None but my lord and husband!
Heaven, I ask thee remission of my sins,
Not of my pains; husband, oh, help me, husband!

Ascendit Friar *with a sword drawn.*

    Friar. What rape of honour and religion!   155
Oh, wrack of nature!   [*Falls and dies.*
    Tam.   Poor man! Oh, my father!
Father, look up! Oh, let me down, my lord,
And I will write.
    Mont.   Author of prodigies!
What new flame breaks out of the firmament,
That turns up counsels never known before?   160
Now is it true, earth moves, and heaven stands still;
Even heaven itself must see and suffer ill:
The too huge bias of the world hath sway'd
Her back-part upwards, and with that she braves
This hemisphere, that long her mouth hath mock'd!   165
The gravity of her religious face,
(Now grown too weighty with her sacrilege
And here discern'd sophisticate enough)
Turns to th' Antipodes; and all the forms
That her illusions have impress'd in her,   170
Have eaten through her back; and now all see,
How she is riveted with hypocrisy.
Was this the way? Was he the mean betwixt you?

Tam. He was, he was, kind worthy man, he was.

Mont. Write, write a word or two.

Tam.   I will, I will.   175
I'll write, but with my blood, that he may see
These lines come from my wounds, and not from me.
                                        [*Writes.*

Mont. Well might he die for thought: methinks the
       frame
And shaken joints of the whole world should crack
To see her parts so disproportionate;   180
And that his general beauty cannot stand
Without these stains in the particular man.
Why wander I so far? Here, here was she
That was a whole world without spot to me,
Though now a world of spots; oh, what a lightning   185
Is man's delight in women! What a bubble,
He builds his state, fame, life on, when he marries!
Since all earth's pleasures are so short and small,
The way t'enjoy it, is t'abjure it all.
Enough! I must be messenger myself,   190
Disguis'd like this strange creature: in, I'll after,
To see what guilty light gives this cave eyes,
And to the world sing new impieties.

Exeunt [Servants]. *He puts the* Friar *in the vault and
        follows. She wraps herself in the arras.*

ACTUS QUINTI, SCENA SECUNDA

Enter Monsieur *and* Guise.

Mons. Now shall we see that Nature hath no end
In her great works responsive to their worths;
That she, that makes so many eyes and souls
To see and foresee, is stark blind herself;

193 s.d. *arras*] curtain

And as illiterate men say Latin prayers   5
By rote of heart and daily iteration,
Not knowing what they say, so Nature lays
A deal of stuff together, and by use,
Or by the mere necessity of matter,
Ends such a work, fills it, or leaves it empty   10
Of strength or virtue, error or clear truth,
Not knowing what she does; but usually
Gives that which we call merit to a man,
And believe should arrive him on huge riches,
Honour, and happiness, that effects his ruin;   15
Right as in ships of war whole lasts of powder
Are laid, men think, to make them last, and guard
      them,
When a disorder'd spark that powder taking,
Blows up with sudden violence and horror
Ships that (kept empty) had sail'd long with terror.   20
  Guise. He that observes but like a worldly man
That which doth oft succeed, and by th' events
Values the worth of things, will think it true
That Nature works at random, just with you:
But with as much proportion she may make   25
A thing that from the feet up to the throat
Hath all the wondrous fabric man should have,
And leave it headless, for a perfect man,
As give a full man valour, virtue, learning,
Without an end more excellent than those   30
On whom she no such worthy part bestows.
  Mons. Yet shall you see it here; here will be one
Young, learned, valiant, virtuous, and full mann'd·
One on whom Nature spent so rich a hand
That with an ominous eye she wept to see   35
So much consum'd her virtuous treasury.
Yet as the winds sing through a hollow tree

  16 lasts] *A last was a large measure of quantity (O.E.D.)*

And (since it lets them pass through) let it stand;
But a tree solid (since it gives no way
To their wild rage) they rend up by the root: 40
So this whole man
(That will not wind with every crooked way,
Trod by the servile world) shall reel and fall
Before the frantic puffs of blind-born chance,
That pipes through empty men, and makes them
    dance.   45
Not so the sea raves on the Lybian sands,
Tumbling her billows in each others' neck;
Not so the surges of the Euxine sea
(Near to the frosty pole, where free Boötes
From those dark deep waves turns his radiant team)   50
Swell, being enrag'd, even from their inmost drop,
As Fortune swings about the restless state
Of virtue, now thrown into all men's hate.

      Enter Montsurry *disguised* [*as the* Friar] *with the*
                  Murtherers.

Away, my lord; you are perfectly disguis'd,
Leave us to lodge your ambush.
    Mont.   Speed me, vengeance! [*Exit.* 55
    Mons. Resolve, my masters, you shall meet with one
Will try what proofs your privy coats are made on:
When he is enter'd, and you hear us stamp,
Approach, and make all sure.
    Murtherers.   We will, my lord. [*Exeunt.*

ACTUS QUINTI, SCENA TERTIA

      D'Ambois *with two* Pages *with tapers.*

    Bus. Sit up to-night, and watch; I'll speak with none
But the old Friar, who bring to me.

Pages.   We will, sir.   [*Exeunt.*
 Bus. What violent heat is this? Methinks the fire
Of twenty lives doth on a sudden flash
Through all my faculties: the air goes high   5
In this close chamber, and the frighted earth

                                        [*Thunder.*

Trembles, and shrinks beneath me; the whole house
Nods with his shaken burthen.

                    Enter Umbra Friar.

                              Bless me, heaven!
 Umbra. Note what I want, dear son, and be fore-
        warn'd:
Oh, there are bloody deeds past and to come.   10
I cannot stay; a fate doth ravish me;
I'll meet thee in the chamber of thy love.   [*Exit.*
 Bus. What dismal change is here! The good old
        Friar
Is murther'd, being made known to serve my love;
And now his restless spirit would forewarn me   15
Of some plot dangerous and imminent.
Note what he wants? He wants his upper weed,
He wants his life and body: which of these
Should be the want he means, and may supply me
With any fit forewarning? This strange vision   20
(Together with the dark prediction
Us'd by the Prince of Darkness that was rais'd
By this embodied shadow) stir my thoughts
With reminiscion of the Spirit's promise,
Who told me that by any invocation   25
I should have power to raise him, though it wanted
The powerful words and decent rites of art:
Never had my set brain such need of spirit
T'instruct and cheer it; now then I will claim
Performance of his free and gentle vow   30

 8 s.d. Umbra] ghost   24 reminiscion] reminiscence

T'appear in greater light, and make more plain
His rugged oracle: I long to know
How my dear mistress fares, and be inform'd
What hand she now holds on the troubled blood
Of her incensed lord: methought the Spirit   35
(When he had utter'd his perplex'd presage)
Threw his chang'd countenance headlong into clouds;
His forehead bent, as it would hide his face,
He knock'd his chin against his darken'd breast,
And struck a churlish silence through his powers.   40
Terror of darkness! O thou King of flames!
That with thy music-footed horse dost strike
The clear light out of crystal on dark earth,
And hurl'st instructive fire about the world,
Wake, wake the drowsy and enchanted night,   45
That sleeps with dead eyes in this heavy riddle!
Or thou great Prince of shades where never sun
Sticks his far-darted beams, whose eyes are made
To shine in darkness, and see ever best
Where men are blindest, open now the heart   50
Of thy abashed oracle, that, for fear,
Of some ill it includes, would fain lie hid,
And rise thou with it in thy greater light.

[*Thunders. Surgit* Spiritus *cum suis.*

Beh. Thus, to observe my vow of apparition
In greater light, and explicate thy fate,   55
I come; and tell thee that, if thou obey
The summons that thy mistress next will send thee,
Her hand shall be thy death.
      Bus.   When will she send?
      Beh. Soon as I set again, where late I rose.
      Bus. Is the old Friar slain?
      Beh.   No, and yet lives not. 60

53 s.d.] Behemoth rises with his attendants

86

Bus. Died he a natural death?

Beh.   He did.

Bus.   Who then
Will my dear mistress send?

Beh.   I must not tell thee.

Bus. Who lets thee?

Beh.   Fate.

Bus.   Who are Fate's ministers?

Beh. The Guise and Monsieur.

Bus.   A fit pair of shears
To cut the threads of kings and kingly spirits,   65
And consorts fit to sound forth harmony
Set to the falls of kingdoms! Shall the hand
Of my kind mistress kill me?

Beh.   If thou yield
To her next summons. Y'are fair-warn'd; farewell!

                                   [*Thunders. Exit.*

Bus. I must fare well, however, though I die,   70
My death consenting with his augury:
Should not my powers obey when she commands,
My motion must be rebel to my will,
My will to life. If, when I have obey'd,
Her hand should so reward me, they must arm it,   75
Bind me, or force it; or, I lay my life,
She rather would convert it many times
On her own bosom, even to many deaths:
But were there danger of such violence,
I know 'tis far from her intent to send: 80
And who she should send is as far from thought,
Since he is dead, whose only mean she us'd.

                                   [*One knocks.*

Who's there? Look to the door, and let him in,
Though politic Monsieur or the violent Guise.

                  63 lets] prevents

Enter Montsurry, *like the* Friar, *with a letter written in blood.*

Mont. Hail to my worthy son.

Bus.   Oh, lying Spirit,   85
To say the Friar was dead! I'll now believe
Nothing of all his forg'd predictions.
My kind and honour'd father, well reviv'd!
I have been frighted with your death and mine,
And told my mistress' hand should be my death,   90
If I obey'd this summons.

Mont.   I believ'd
Your love had been much clearer than to give
Any such doubt a thought, for she is clear,
And having freed her husband's jealousy
(Of which her much abus'd hand here is witness)   95
She prays, for urgent cause, your instant presence.

Bus. Why, then your Prince of Spirits may be call'd
The Prince of liars.

Mont.   Holy Writ so calls him.

Bus. What! Writ in blood?   [*Opening the letter.*

Mont.   Ay, 'tis the ink of lovers.

Bus. Oh, 'tis a sacred witness of her love.   100
So much elixir of her blood as this,
Dropt in the lightest dame, would make her firm
As heat to fire; and, like to all the signs,
Commands the life confin'd in all my veins;
Oh, how it multiplies my blood with spirit,   105
And makes me apt t'encounter Death and Hell.
But come, kind father, you fetch me to heaven,
And to that end your holy weed was given.   [*Exeunt.*

ACTUS QUINTI, SCENA QUARTA

Thunder. Intrat Umbra Friar, *and discovers* Tamyra.

Umbra. Up with these stupid thoughts, still loved
   daughter,
And strike away this heartless trance of anguish.
Be like the sun, and labour in eclipses;
Look to the end of woes: oh, can you sit
Mustering the horrors of your servant's slaughter   5
Before your contemplation, and not study
How to prevent it? Watch when he shall rise,
And with a sudden outcry of his murther,
Blow his retreat before he be revenged.

Tam. O father, have my dumb woes wak'd your
   death?   10
When will our human griefs be at their height?
Man is a tree that hath no top in cares,
No root in comforts; all his power to live
Is given to no end, but t'have power to grieve.

Umbra. It is the misery of our creation,   15
Your true friend,
Led by your husband, shadow'd in my weed,
Now enters the dark vault.

Tam.   But, my dearest father,
Why will not you appear to him yourself,
And see that none of these deceits annoy him?   20

Umbra. My power is limited; alas! I cannot.
All that I can do—See, the cave opens!   [*Exit.*

   D'Ambois [*appears*] *at the Gulf.*

Tam. Away, my love, away! Thou wilt be
   murther'd.

   Enter Monsieur *and* Guise *above.*

17 shadow'd in my weed] disguised in my dress

89

Bus. Murther'd? I know not what that Hebrew
    means:
That word had ne'er been nam'd had all been
    D'Ambois.   25
Murther'd? By heaven, he is my murtherer
That shows me not a murtherer; what such bug
Abhorreth not the very sleep of D'Ambois?
Murther'd? Who dares give all the room I see
To D'Ambois' reach, or look with any odds   30
His fight i'th' face, upon whose hand sits death,
Whose sword hath wings, and every feather pierceth?
If I scape Monsieur's 'pothecary shops,
Foutre for Guise's shambles! 'Twas ill plotted;
They should have maul'd me here, when I was rising. 35
I am up and ready.
Let in my politic visitants, let them in,
Though entering like so many moving armours.
Fate is more strong than arms, and sly than treason,
And I at all parts buckled in my fate.   40

    Mons. } Why enter not the coward villains?
    Guise. }
    Bus. Dare they not come?

Enter Murtherers *with* [Umbra] Friar *at the other door.*

    Tam.   They come.
    First Mur.   Come all at once.
    Umbra. Back, coward murtherers, back!
    Omnes.   Defend us, heaven!

                        [*Exeunt all but the first.*

    First Mur. Come ye not on?
    Bus.   No, slave, nor goest thou off.
Stand you so firm?—Will it not enter here?   45
You have a face yet. So! In thy life's flame [*Kills him.*
I burn the first rites to my mistress' fame.

    27 bug] bugbear   40 buckled] armoured

Umbra. Breathe thee, brave son, against the other
    charge.

Bus. Oh, is it true then that my sense first told me?
Is my kind father dead?

Tam.   He is, my love.   50
'Twas the Earl, my husband, in his weed, that brought
    thee.

Bus. That was a speeding sleight, and well re-
    sembled.

Where is that angry Earl? My lord, come forth
And show your own face in your own affair;
Take not into your noble veins the blood   55
Of these base villains, nor the light reports
Of blister'd tongues for clear and weighty truth,
But me against the world, in pure defence
Of your rare lady, to whose spotless name
I stand here as a bulwark, and project   60
A life to her renown, that ever yet
Hath been untainted, even in envy's eye,
And, where it would protect, a sanctuary.
Brave Earl, come forth, and keep your scandal in:
'Tis not our fault, if you enforce the spot   65
Nor the wreak yours, if you perform it not.

Enter Montsurry, *with all the* Murtherers.

Mont. Cowards, a fiend or spirit beat ye off?
They are your own faint spirits that have forg'd
The fearful shadows that your eyes deluded:
The fiend was in you; cast him out then, thus.   70
        [*They fight.* D'Ambois *hath* Montsurry *down.*

Tam. Favour my lord, my love, oh, favour him!

Bus. I will not touch him: take your life, my lord,
And be appeas'd. [*Pistols shot within.* Bussy *is wounded.*
                 Oh, then the coward Fates

52 speeding sleight] successful trick   resembled] imitated

91

Have maim'd themselves, and ever lost their honour.
  Umbra. What have ye done, slaves? Irreligious lord! 75
  Bus. Forbear them, father; 'tis enough for me
That Guise and Monsieur, Death and Destiny,
Come behind D'Ambois. Is my body, then,
But penetrable flesh? And must my mind
Follow my blood? Can my divine part add   80
No aid to th' earthly in extremity?
Then these divines are but for form, not fact:
Man is of two sweet courtly friends compact,
A mistress and a servant: let my death
Define life nothing but a courtier's breath.   85
Nothing is made of nought, of all things made,
Their abstract being a dream but of a shade.
I'll not complain to earth yet, but to heaven,
And, like a man, look upwards even in death.
And if Vespasian thought in majesty   90
An emperor might die standing, why not I?

                                      [*She offers to help him.*

Nay, without help, in which I will exceed him;
For he died splinted with his chamber grooms.
Prop me, true sword, as thou hast ever done!
The equal thought I bear of life and death   95
Shall make me faint on no side; I am up;
Here like a Roman statue I will stand
Till death hath made me marble. Oh, my fame,
Live in despite of murther! Take thy wings
And haste thee where the grey ey'd Morn perfumes   100
Her rosy chariot with Sabæan spices!
Fly, where the Evening from th' Iberian vales
Takes on her swarthy shoulders Hecate,
Crown'd with a grove of oaks: fly where men feel
The burning axletree, and those that suffer   105
Beneath the chariot of the snowy Bear:

And tell them all that D'Ambois now is hasting
To the eternal dwellers; that a thunder
Of all their sighs together (for their frailties
Beheld in me) may quit my worthless fall   110
With a fit volley for my funeral.
   Umbra. Forgive thy murtherers.
   Bus.   I forgive them all;
And you, my lord, their fautor; for true sign
                   [*To* Montsurry.
Of which unfeign'd remission take my sword;
Take it, and only give it motion,   115
And it shall find the way to victory
By his own brightness, and th' inherent valour
My fight hath still'd into't with charms of spirit.
Now let me pray you that my weighty blood
Laid in one scale of your impartial spleen,   120
May sway the forfeit of my worthy love
Weigh'd in the other; and be reconcil'd
With all forgiveness to your matchless wife.
   Tam. Forgive thou me, dear servant, and this hand
That led thy life to this unworthy end;   125
Forgive it, for the blood with which 'tis stain'd,
In which I writ the summons of thy death—
The forced summons—by this bleeding wound,
By this here in my bosom, and by this
That makes me hold up both my hands imbru'd   130
For thy dear pardon.
   Bus.   Oh, my heart is broken!
Fate nor these murtherers, Monsieur nor the Guise,
Have any glory in my death, but this,
This killing spectacle, this prodigy:
My sun is turn'd to blood, in whose red beams   135
Pindus and Ossa (hid in drifts of snow,
Laid on my heart and liver) from their veins

   113 fautor] patron   118 still'd] instilled

93

Melt like two hungry torrents, eating rocks,
Into the ocean of all human life,
And make it bitter, only with my blood.   140
Oh, frail condition of strength, valour, virtue,
In me (like warning fire upon the top
Of some steep beacon, on a steeper hill)
Made to express it: like a falling star
Silently glanc'd, that like a thunderbolt   145
Look'd to have stuck and shook the firmament.
                                        [*Moritur.*

Umbra. Farewell, brave relics of a complete man,
Look up and see thy spirit made a star;
Join flames with Hercules, and when thou sett'st
Thy radiant forehead in the firmament,   150
Make the vast crystal crack with thy receipt;
Spread to a world of fire, and the aged sky
Cheer with new sparks of old humanity.
—Son of the earth, whom my unrested soul,
                                  [*To* Montsurry.
Rues t'have begotten in the faith of heaven,   155
Assay to gratulate and pacify
The soul fled from this worthy by performing
The Christian reconcilement he besought
Betwixt thee and thy lady; let her wounds
Manlessly digg'd in her, be eas'd and cur'd   160
With balm of thine own tears; or be assur'd
Never to rest free from my haunt and horror.
Mont. See how she merits this; still kneeling by,
And mourning his fall more than her own fault!
Umbra. Remove, dear daughter, and content thy
     husband;   165
So piety wills thee, and thy servant's peace.
                                   [*Exit* Umbra.
Tam. O wretched piety, that art so distract
     146 s.d. *Moritur*] he dies

94

In thine own constancy, and in thy right
Must be unrighteous: if I right my friend
I wrong my husband; if his wrong I shun,   170
The duty of my friend I leave undone:
Ill plays on both sides; here and there, it riseth;
No place, no good, so good, but ill compriseth;
Oh, had I never married but for form,
Never vow'd faith but purpos'd to deceive,   175
Never made conscience of any sin,
But cloak'd it privately and made it common;
Nor never honour'd been in blood or mind;
Happy had I been then, as others are
Of the like licence; I had then been honour'd;   180
Liv'd without envy; custom had benumb'd
All sense of scruple and all note of frailty;
My fame had been untouch'd, my heart unbroken:
But (shunning all) I strike on all offence,
O husband! Dear friend! O my conscience!   185
  Mons. Come, let's away; my senses are not proof
Against those plaints.
      [*Exeunt* Guise *and* Monsieur. D'Ambois *is borne off*.
  Mont. I must not yield to pity, nor to love
So servile and so traitorous: cease, my blood,
To wrestle with my honour, fame, and judgment: 190
Away, forsake my house, forbear complaints
Where thou hast bred them: here [are] all things
Of their own shame and sorrow; leave my house.
  Tam. Sweet lord, forgive me, and I will be gone,
And till these wounds (that never balm shall close   19f
Till death hath enter'd at them, so I love them,
Being open'd by your hands) by death be cur'd,
I never more will grieve you with my sight,
Never endure that any roof shall part
Mine eyes and heaven; but to the open deserts   200
(Like to a hunted tigress) I will fly,

Eating my heart, shunning the steps of men,
And look on no side till I be arriv'd.
    Mont. I do forgive thee, and upon my knees,
With hands held up to heaven, wish that mine honour 205
Would suffer reconcilement to my love;
But since it will not, honour never serve
My love with flourishing object, till it sterve!
And as this taper, though it upwards look,
Downwards must needs consume, so let our love!   210
As, having lost his honey, the sweet taste
Runs into savour, and will needs retain
A spice of his first parents, till, like life,
It sees and dies; so let our love! And lastly,
As when the flame is suffer'd to look up,   215
It keeps his lustre, but, being thus turn'd down,
(His natural course of useful light inverted),
His own stuff puts it out, so let our love!
Now turn from me, as here I turn from thee,
And may both points of heaven's straight axle-tree   220
Conjoin in one, before thyself and me.
                        [*Exeunt severally.*

FINIS ACTUS QUINTI ET ULTIMI.

EPILOGUE

WITH many hands you have seen D'Ambois slain,
Yet by your grace he may revive again,
And every day grow stronger in his skill
To please, as we presume he is in will.
The best deserving actors of the time   5
Had their ascents; and by degrees did climb

208 sterve] starve

To their full height, a place to study due.
To make him tread in their path lies in you;
He'll not forget his makers, but still prove
His thankfulness, as you increase your love.   10

FINIS

7 to study due] achieved by hard work

The Maid's Tragedy

BY

FRANCIS BEAUMONT

AND

JOHN FLETCHER

FRANCIS BEAUMONT (1584–1616)
JOHN FLETCHER (1579–1625)

The Maid's Tragedy

Acted in or soon before 1611; printed in 1619, second
quarto 'Newly perused, augmented, and inlarged' 1622,
and the present text taken from the latter.

[*Works*, ed. A. Dyce, 11 vols., is in modernized spelling;
Works, ed. A. Glover and A. R. Waller, 10 vols., Cambridge, 1905–12, reprints the second folio (1679) in the
spelling of that date with collations of earlier printed
editions; *The Dramatic Works in the Beaumont and
Fletcher Canon*, ed. Fredson Bowers, Cambridge, 1966– ,
contains *The Maid's Tragedy*, ed. Robert K. Turner, in
Vol. II, 1970; the present text is a reprint of P. A. Daniel's
edition in *Works*, Variorum edn. A. H. Bullen, Vol. I,
1904.]

The Maids Tragedie.

AS IT HATH BEENE

diuers times Acted at the *Black-Friers* by
the Kings Maiesties Seruants.

Newly perused, augmented, and inlarged, This second Impression.

ASPATIA.   AMINTOR.

LONDON,

Printed for *Francis Constable,* and are
to besold at the White Lion in
Pauls Church-yard. 1622.

DRAMATIS PERSONAE

KING.

LYSIPPUS, *brother to the* KING.

AMINTOR, *a noble gentleman.*

MELANTIUS,⎱ brothers to
DIPHILUS, ⎰ EVADNE.

CALIANAX, *an old humorous lord and father to* ASPATIA.

CLEON,⎱ *Gentlemen.*
STRATO,⎰

DIAGORAS, *a Servant.*

Lords, Gentlemen, Servants, &c.

EVADNE, *wife to* AMINTOR.

ASPATIA, *troth-plight wife to* AMINTOR.

ANTIPHILA,⎱ *waiting gentle-women to*
OLYMPIAS, ⎰ ASPATIA.

DULA, *a Lady.*

Ladies.

NIGHT,
CYNTHIA,
NEPTUNE, ⎰ *Masquers.*
AEOLUS,
Sea-gods,
& Winds,

SCENE, *Rhodes.*

THE STATIONER'S CENSURE

GOOD wine requires no bush, they say,
And I, no prologue such a play:
The makers therefore did forbear
To have that grace prefixed here.
But cease here, censure, lest the buyer
Hold thee in this a vain supplyer.
My office is to set it forth,
Where fame applauds its real worth.

CENSURE] opinion, judgement   8 Where] Whereas

ACT I

Scene I

Enter Lysippus, Diphilus, Cleon, *and* Strato.

Cle. The rest are making ready, sir.

Lys.   So let them;
There's time enough.

Diph. You are the brother to the King, my lord;
We'll take your word.

Lys. Strato, thou hast some skill in poetry;   5
What think'st thou of the masque? will it be well?

Stra. As well as masques can be.

Lys.   As masques can be?

Stra. Yes; they must commend their king, and
    speak in praise
Of the assembly, bless the bride and bridegroom
In person of some god; they're tied to rules   10
Of flattery.

Cle. See, good my lord, who is return'd!

Enter Melantius.

Lys. Noble Melantius!
The land by me welcomes thy virtues home;
Thou that with blood abroad buyest us our peace!   15
The breath of kings is like the breath of gods;
My brother wish'd thee here, and thou art here:
He will be too-too kind, and weary thee
With often welcomes; but the time doth give thee
A welcome above his or all the world's.   20

Mel. My lord, my thanks; but these scratch'd limbs
    of mine
Have spoke my love and truth unto my friends,
More than my tongue e'er could. My mind's the same

103

It ever was to you: where I find worth,
I love the keeper till he let it go,   25
And then I follow it.
    Diph.   Hail, worthy brother!
He that rejoices not at your return
In safety is mine enemy for ever.
    Mel. I thank thee, Diphilus. But thou art faulty:
I sent for thee to exercise thine arms   30
With me at Patria; thou camest not, Diphilus;
'Twas ill.
    Diph.   My noble brother, my excuse
Is my king's straight command,—which you, my lord,
Can witness with me.
    Lys.   'Tis most true, Melantius;
He might not come till the solemnities   35
Of this great match were past.
    Diph.   Have you heard of it?
    Mel. Yes, and have given cause to those that here
Envy my deeds abroad to call me gamesome;
I have no other business here at Rhodes.
    Lys. We have a masque to-night, and you must tread   40
A soldier's measure.
    Mel. These soft and silken wars are not for me:
The music must be shrill and all confused
That stirs my blood; and then I dance with arms.
But is Amintor wed?
    Diph.   This day.   45
    Mel. All joys upon him! for he is my friend.
Wonder not that I call a man so young my friend:
His worth is great; valiant he is and temperate;
And one that never thinks his life his own,
If his friend need it. When he was a boy,   50
As oft as I return'd (as, without boast,

      33 straight] strict   38 gamesome] wanton

I brought home conquest), he would gaze upon me
And view me round, to find in what one limb
The virtue lay to do those things he heard;
Then would he wish to see my sword, and feel   55
The quickness of the edge, and in his hand
Weigh it: he oft would make me smile at this.
His youth did promise much, and his ripe years
Will see it all performed.——

      Enter Aspatia, *passing with attendance.*

                       Hail, maid and wife!
Thou fair Aspatia, may the holy knot,   60
That thou hast tied to-day, last till the hand
Of age undo it! may'st thou bring a race
Unto Amintor, that may fill the world
Successively with soldiers!
   Asp.   My hard fortunes
Deserve not scorn, for I was never proud   65
When they were good.   [*Exit* Aspatia.
   Mel.   How's this?
   Lys. You are mistaken, sir; she is not married.
   Mel. You said Amintor was.
   Diph. 'Tis true; but——
   Mel.   Pardon me; I did receive
Letters at Patria from my Amintor,   70
That he should marry her.
   Diph.   And so it stood
In all opinion long; but your arrival
Made me imagine you had heard the change.
   Mel. Who has he taken then?
   Lys.   A lady, sir,
That bears the light above her, and strikes dead   75
With flashes of her eye; the fair Evadne,

   75 bears the light above her] *perhaps* wears a halo of light. *Both text and meaning are uncertain*

Your virtuous sister.

    Mel.   Peace of heart betwixt them!
But this is strange.

    Lys.   The King, my brother, did it
To honour you; and these solemnities
Are at his charge.   80

    Mel. 'Tis royal, like himself. But I am sad
My speech bears so unfortunate a sound
To beautiful Aspatia. There is rage
Hid in her father's breast, Calianax,
Bent long against me; and he should not think,   85
Could I but call it back, that I would take
So base revenges, as to scorn the state
Of his neglected daughter. Holds he still
His greatness with the King?

    Lys.   Yes. But this lady
Walks discontented, with her watery eyes   90
Bent on the earth. The unfrequented woods
Are her delight; where, when she sees a bank
Stuck full of flowers, she with a sigh will tell
Her servants what a pretty place it were
To bury lovers in; and make her maids   95
Pluck 'em, and strow her over like a corse.
She carries with her an infectious grief,
That strikes all her beholders: she will sing
The mournful'st things that ever ear hath heard,
And sigh, and sing again; and when the rest   100
Of our young ladies, in their wanton blood,
Tell mirthful tales in course, that fill the room
With laughter, she will, with so sad a look,
Bring forth a story of the silent death
Of some forsaken virgin, which her grief   105
Will put in such a phrase, that, ere she end,
She'll send them weeping one by one away.

       96 corse] corpse   102 in course] in turn

Mel. She has a brother under my command,
Like her; a face as womanish as hers,
But with a spirit that hath much out-grown   110
The number of his years.

Enter Amintor.

Cle.   My lord the bridegroom!
Mel. I might run fiercely, not more hastily,
Upon my foe. I love thee well, Amintor;
My mouth is much too narrow for my heart;
I joy to look upon those eyes of thine;   115
Thou art my friend, but my disorder'd speech
Cuts off my love.
Amin.   Thou art Melantius;
All love is spoke in that. A sacrifice,
To thank the gods Melantius is return'd
In safety! Victory sits on his sword,   120
As she was wont: may she build there and dwell;
And may thy armour be, as it hath been,
Only thy valour and thine innocence!
What endless treasures would our enemies give,
That I might hold thee still thus!
Mel.   I am poor   125
In words; but credit me, young man, thy mother
Could do no more but weep for joy to see thee
After long absence: all the wounds I gave
Fetch'd not so much away, nor all the cries
Of widowed mothers. But this is peace,   130
And that was war.
Amin.   Pardon, thou holy god
Of marriage-bed, and frown not, I am forced,
In answer of such noble tears as those,
To weep upon my wedding-day!
Mel. I fear thou art grown too fickle; for I hear   135
A lady mourns for thee; men say, to death;

107

Forsaken of thee; on what terms I know not.

Amin. She had my promise; but the King forbad it,
And made me make this worthy change, thy sister,
Accompanied with graces above her;   140
With whom I long to lose my lusty youth,
And grow old in her arms.

Mel.   Be prosperous!

Enter Messenger.

Mess. My lord, the masquers rage for you.

Lys.   We are gone.—
Cleon, Strato, Diphilus!

Amin. We'll all attend you.—

          [*Exeunt* Lysippus, Cleon, Strato, Diphilus.

                    We shall trouble you 145
With our solemnities.

Mel.   Not so, Amintor:
But if you laugh at my rude carriage
In peace, I'll do as much for you in war,
When you come thither. Yet I have a mistress
To bring to your delights; rough though I am,   150
I have a mistress, and she has a heart
She says; but, trust me, it is stone, no better;
There is no place that I can challenge in't.
But you stand still, and here my way lies.   [*Exeunt.*

Scene II

Enter Calianax *with* Diagoras.

Cal. Diagoras, look to the doors better, for shame!
you let in all the world, and anon the King will rail at

140 above her] *The quartos read* about her, *perhaps rightly*
147 rude carriage] rough behaviour

me. Why, very well said. By Jove, the King will have
the show i' th' court.

Diag. Why do you swear so, my lord? you know 5
he'll have it here.

Cal. By this light, if he be wise, he will not.

Diag. And if he will not be wise, you are forsworn.

Cal. One must sweat out his heart with swearing,
and get thanks on no side. I'll be gone, look to't who 10
will.

Diag. My lord, I shall never keep them out. Pray,
stay; your looks will terrify them.

Cal. My looks terrify them, you coxcombly ass, you!
I'll be judged by all the company whether thou hast 15
not a worse face than I.

Diag. I mean, because they know you and your office.

Cal. Office! I would I could put it off! I am sure I
sweat quite through my office.—I might have made
room at my daughter's wedding: they ha' near killed 20
her amongst them; and now I must do service for him
that hath forsaken her.—Serve that will!

[*Exit* Calianax.

Diag. He's so humorous since his daughter was forsaken! [*Knock within.*] Hark, hark! there, there! so,
so! codes, codes! What now?   25

Mel. [*within.*] Open the door.

Diag. Who's there?

Mel. [*within.*] Melantius.

Diag. I hope your lordship brings no troop with
you; for, if you do, I must return them.   30

[*Opens the door.*

Enter Melantius *and a Lady.*

Mel. None but this lady, sir.

Diag. The ladies are all placed above, save those

23 humorous] crotchety   25 codes] Gods (*Bullen*)

that come in the King's troop: the best of Rhodes sit
there, and there's room.

Mel. I thank you, sir.—When I have seen you 35
placed, madam, I must attend the King; but, the
masque done, I'll wait on you again.

Diag. [*opening another door.*] Stand back there!—
Room for my lord Melantius! [*Exeunt* Melantius *and*
Lady.]—Pray, bear back—this is no place for such 40
youths and their trulls—let the doors shut again.—
No!—do your heads itch? I'll scratch them for you.
[*Shuts the door.*]—So, now thrust and hang! [*Knocking*
within.]—Again! who is't now?—I cannot blame my
lord Calianax for going away: would he were here! he 45
would run raging amongst them, and break a dozen
wiser heads than his own in the twinkling of an eye.—
What's the news now?

[*Within.*] I pray you, can you help me to the speech
of the master-cook?   50

Diag. If I open the door, I'll cook some of your
calves-heads. Peace, rogues! [*Knocking within.*]—
Again!—who is't?

Mel. [*within.*] Melantius.

Re-enter Calianax.

Cal. Let him not in.   55

Diag. Oh, my lord, a' must.—Make room there for
my lord!

Re-enter Melantius.

Is your lady placed?

Mel.   Yes, sir, I thank you.—
My lord Calianax, well met:
Your causeless hate to me I hope is buried.   60

Cal. Yes, I do service for your sister here,

56 a' must] he must (*sc. be admitted*)

That brings mine own poor child to timeless death:
She loves your friend Amintor; such another
False-hearted lord as you.

   Mel.   You do me wrong,
A most unmanly one; and I am slow   65
In taking vengeance: but be well advised.

   Cal. It may be so.—Who placed the lady there,
So near the presence of the King?

   Mel.   I did.

   Cal. My lord, she must not sit there.

   Mel.   Why?

   Cal.   The place
Is kept for women of more worth.   70

   Mel. More worth than she! It misbecomes your age
And place to be thus womanish: forbear!
What you have spoke, I am content to think
The palsy shook your tongue to.

   Cal.   Why, 'tis well:
If I stand here to place men's wenches—

   Mel.   I   75
Shall quite forget this place, thy age, my safety,
And, through all, cut that poor sickly week
Thou hast to live away from thee!

   Cal. Nay, I know you can fight for your whore.

   Mel. Bate me the King, and, be he flesh and blood, 80
A' lies that says it! Thy mother at fifteen
Was black and sinful to her.

   Diag.   Good my lord—

   Mel. Some god pluck threescore years from that
     fond man,
That I may kill him, and not stain mine honour!
It is the curse of soldiers, that in peace   85
They shall be braved by such ignoble men,

  62 timeless] untimely (*as below*, II. i. 43, v. iv. 92)   **81 A']**
he   **83 fond]** foolish

As, if the land were troubled, would with tears
And knees beg succour from 'em. Would the blood,
That sea of blood, that I have lost in fight,
Were running in thy veins, that it might make thee   90
Apt to say less, or able to maintain,
Should'st thou say more!—This Rhodes, I see, is
    nought
But a place privileged to do men wrong.
    Cal. Ay, you may say your pleasure.

Enter Amintor.

    Amin. What vild injury   95
Has stirr'd my worthy friend, who is as slow
To fight with words as he is quick of hands?
    Mel. That heap of age, which I should reverence
If it were temperate; but testy years
Are most contemptible.
    Amin.   Good sir, forbear.   100
    Cal. There is just such another as yourself.
    Amin. He will wrong you, or me, or any man,
And talk as if he had no life to lose,
Since this our match. The King is coming in;
I would not for more wealth than I enjoy   105
He should perceive you raging: he did hear
You were at difference now, which hasten'd him.
                    [Hautboys play within.
    Cal. Make room there!

Enter King, Evadne, Aspatia, *Lords and Ladies.*

    King. Melantius, thou art welcome, and my love
Is with thee still: but this is not a place   110
To brabble in.—Calianax, join hands.
    Cal. He shall not have mine hand.
    King.   This is no time

    95 vild] vile (*the usual spelling in this period*)

To force you to't. I do love you both:—
Calianax, you look well to your office;—
And you, Melantius, are welcome home.—   115
Begin the masque.
    Mel. Sister, I joy to see you and your choice;
You look'd with my eyes when you took that man:
Be happy in him!   [*Recorders.*
    Evad.   Oh, my dearest brother,
Your presence is more joyful than this day   120
Can be unto me!

The Masque.

Night *rises in mists.*

    Night. Our reign is come; for in the quenching sea
The sun is drown'd, and with him fell the Day.
Bright Cynthia, hear my voice! I am the Night,
For whom thou bear'st about thy borrow'd light;   125
Appear! no longer thy pale visage shroud,
But strike thy silver horns quite through a cloud,
And send a beam upon my swarthy face,
By which I may discover all the place
And persons, and how many longing eyes   130
Are come to wait on our solemnities.

Enter Cynthia.

How dull and black am I! I could not find
This beauty without thee, I am so blind:
Methinks they shew like to those eastern streaks,
That warn us hence before the morning breaks.   135
Back, my pale servant! for these eyes know how
To shoot far more and quicker rays than thou.
    Cynth. Great queen, they be a troop for whom alone
One of my clearest moons I have put on;

    119 s.d. *Recorders*] wind instruments of the flute type
      133 This beauty] the ladies, the 'troop' of l. 138

A troop, that looks as if thyself and I   140
Had pluck'd our reins in and our whips laid by,
To gaze upon these mortals, that appear
Brighter than we.

Night.   Then let us keep 'em here;
And never more our chariots drive away,
But hold our places and outshine the Day.   145

   Cynth. Great queen of shadows, you are pleased to
     speak
Of more than may be done: we may not break
The gods' decrees; but when our time is come,
Must drive away, and give the Day our room.
Yet, whilst our reign lasts, let us stretch our power   150
To give our servants one contented hour,
With such unwonted solemn grace and state,
As may for ever after force them hate
Our brother's glorious beams, and wish the Night,
Crown'd with a thousand stars and our cold light: 155
For almost all the world their service bend
To Phœbus, and in vain my light I lend,
Gazed on unto my setting from my rise
Almost of none but of unquiet eyes.

   Night. Then shine at full, fair queen, and by thy
     power   160
Produce a birth, to crown this happy hour,
Of nymphs and shepherds; let their songs discover,
Easy and sweet, who is a happy lover;
Or, if thou woo't, thine own Endymion
From the sweet flowery bank he lies upon,   165
On Latmus' brow, thy pale beams drawn away,
And of his long night let him make this day.

   Cynth. Thou dream'st, dark queen; that fair boy
     was not mine,

  154 brother] Phoebus Apollo, the sun   162 discover] reveal
164 woo't] will it

Nor went I down to kiss him. Ease and wine
Have bred these bold tales: poets, when they rage,   170
Turn gods to men, and make an hour an age.
But I will give a greater state and glory,
And raise to time a nobler memory
Of what these lovers are.—Rise, rise, I say,
Thou power of deeps, thy surges laid away,   175
Neptune, great king of waters, and by me
Be proud to be commanded!

Neptune rises.

  Nept.   Cynthia, see,
Thy word hath fetch'd me hither: let me know
Why I ascend.
  Cynth.   Doth this majestic show
Give thee no knowledge yet?
  Nept.   Yes, now I see   180
Something intended, Cynthia, worthy thee.
Go on; I'll be a helper.
  Cynth.   Hie thee, then,
And charge the Wind fly from this rocky den,
Let loose his subjects; only Boreas,
Too foul for our intention, as he was,   185
Still keep him fast chain'd: we must have none here
But vernal blasts and gentle winds appear,
Such as blow flowers, and through the glad boughs
    sing
Many soft welcomes to the lusty spring;
These are our music: next, thy watery race   190
Bring on in couples; we are pleased to grace
This noble night, each in their richest things
Your own deeps or the broken vessel brings:
Be prodigal, and I shall be as kind
And shine at full upon you.

Nept.   Ho, the Wind!   195
Commanding Æolus!   [*Enter Æolus out of a Rock.*
  Æol.   Great Neptune!
  Nept.   He.
  Æol. What is thy will?
  Nept.   We do command thee free
Favonius and thy milder winds, to wait
Upon our Cynthia; but tie Boreas strait,
He's too rebellious.
  Æol.   I shall do it.
  Nept.   Do.   [*Exit Æolus.* 200
  Æol. [*within.*]Great master of the flood and all below,
Thy full command has taken.——Ho, the Main!
Neptune!   [*Re-enter Æolus, followed by* Favonius *and
                                       other Winds.*

  Nept.   Here.
  Æol.   Boreas has broke his chain,
And struggling with the rest, has got away.
  Nept. Let him alone, I'll take him up at sea;   205
I will not long be thence. Go once again,
And call out of the bottoms of the main
Blue Proteus and the rest; charge them put on
Their greatest pearls, and the most sparkling stone
The beaten rock breeds; tell this night is done   210
By me a solemn honour to the Moon:
Fly, like a full sail.
  Æol.   I am gone.   [*Exit.*
  Cynth.   Dark Night,
Strike a full silence, do a thorough right
To this great chorus that our music may
Touch high as heaven, and make the east break day   215
At mid-night.   [*Music.*

195–6] Wind! | Commanding *Daniel and others read* Wind-|
Commanding, *but cf. ll.* 202–3   198 Favonius] zephyr, west
wind   205 take . . . up] arrest

116

FIRST SONG

During which Proteus *and other sea-deities enter.*

Cynthia, to thy power and thee
        We obey.
Joy to this great company!
        And no day   220
Come to steal this night away,
    Till the rites of love are ended,
And the lusty bridegroom say,
    Welcome, light, of all befriended!

Pace out, you watery powers below,   225
        Let your feet,
Like the galleys when they row,
        Even beat:
Let your unknown measures, set
    To the still winds, tell to all,   230
That gods are come, immortal, great,
    To honour this great nuptial.

                          [The measure.

SECOND SONG

Hold back thy hours, dark Night, till we have done;
    The Day will come too soon:
Young maids will curse thee, if thou steal'st away,   235
And leavest their losses open to the day:
        Stay, stay, and hide
        The blushes of the bride.

Stay, gentle Night, and with thy darkness cover
        The kisses of her lover;   240
Stay, and confound her tears and her shrill cryings,
Her weak denials, vows, and often-dyings;
        Stay, and hide all:
        But help not, though she call.

                      [Another measure.

Nept. Great Queen of us and heaven, hear what I
   bring   245
To make this hour a full one.
   Cynth.   Speak, sea's king.
   Nept. The tunes my Amphitrite joys to have,
When she will dance upon the rising wave,
And court me as she sails. My Tritons, play
Music to lay a storm! I'll lead the way.   250
                          [*Masquers dance; Neptune leads it.*

THIRD SONG

To bed, to bed! Come, Hymen, lead the bride,
   And lay her by her husband's side;
      Bring in the virgins every one,
      That grieve to lie alone,
That they may kiss while they may say a maid;   255
To-morrow 'twill be other kiss'd and said.
      Hesperus, be long a-shining,
      Whilst these lovers are a-twining.

   Æol. [*within.*] Ho, Neptune!
   Nept.   Æolus!
               Re-enter Æolus.

   Æol.   The sea goes high,
Boreas hath raised a storm: go and apply   260
Thy trident; else, I prophesy, ere day
Many a tall ship will be cast away.
Descend with all the gods and all their power,
To strike a calm.   [*Exit.*
   Cynth.   We thank you for this hour:
My favour to you all. To gratulate   265
So great a service, done at my desire,
Ye shall have many floods, fuller and higher
Than you have wish'd for; and no ebb shall dare

            265 gratulate] reward

To let the Day see where your dwellings are.
Now back unto your governments in haste,   270
Lest your proud charge should swell above the waste,
And win upon the island.
  Nept.   We obey.

                    [Neptune *descends and the Sea-gods.*

  Cynth. Hold up thy head, dead Night; see'st thou
    not Day?
The east begins to lighten: I must down,
And give my brother place.
  Night.   Oh, I could frown   275
To see the Day, the Day that flings his light
Upon my kingdom and contemns old Night!
Let him go on and flame! I hope to see
Another wild-fire in his axletree,
And all fall drench'd. But I forget; speak, queen: 280
The Day grows on; I must no more be seen.
  Cynth. Heave up thy drowsy head again, and see
A greater light, a greater majesty,
Between our set and us! whip up thy team:
The day breaks here, and yon sun-flaring stream   285
Shot from the south. Which way wilt thou go? say.
  Night. I'll vanish into mists.
  Cynth.   I into Day.
                              [*Exeunt.*
          Finis Masque.

  King. Take lights there!—Ladies, get the bride to
    bed.—
We will not see you laid; good night, Amintor;
We'll ease you of that tedious ceremony: 290
Were it my case, I should think time run slow.
If thou be'st noble, youth, get me a boy,
That may defend my kingdom from my foes.

Amin. All happiness to you!
King.   Good-night Melantius.
                                          [*Exeunt.*

ACT II

SCENE I

Enter Evadne, Aspatia, Dula, *and other Ladies.*

Dula. Madam, shall we undress you for this fight?
The wars are nak'd that you must make to-night.
  Evad. You are very merry, Dula.
  Dula.   I should be
Far merrier, madam, if it were with me
As it is with you.
  Evad.   How's that?
  Dula.   That I might go   5
To bed with him wi' th' credit that you do.
  Evad. Why, how now, wench?
  Dula. Come, ladies, will you help?
  Evad. I am soon undone.
  Dula. And as soon done: 10
Good store of clothes will trouble you at both.
  Evad. Art thou drunk, Dula?
  Dula.   Why, here's none but we.
  Evad. Thou think'st belike there is no modesty
When we're alone.
  Dula. Ay, by my troth, you hit my thoughts aright. 15
  Evad. You prick me, lady.
  1. Lady.   'Tis against my will.
  Dula. Anon you must endure more and lie still;
You're best to practise.
  Evad.   Sure, this wench is mad.
  Dula. No, faith, this is a trick that I have had

120

Since I was fourteen.

  Evad.   'Tis high time to leave it. 20
  Dula. Nay, now I'll keep it till the trick leave me.
A dozen wanton words, put in your head,
Will make you livelier in your husband's bed.
  Evad. Nay, faith, then take it.
  Dula.   Take it, madam! where?
We all, I hope, will take it that are here. 25
  Evad. Nay, then, I'll give thee o'er.
  Dula.   So I will make
The ablest man in Rhodes, or his heart ache.
  Evad. Wilt take my place to-night?
  Dula. I'll hold your cards against any two I know.
  Evad. What wilt thou do? 30
  Dula. Madam, we'll do't, and make 'em leave play
  too.
  Evad. Aspatia, take her part.
  Dula.   I will refuse it:
She will pluck down a side; she does not use it.
  Evad. Why, do, I prithee.
  Dula.   You will find the play
Quickly, because your head lies well that way. 35
  Evad. I thank thee, Dula. Would thou couldst instil
Some of thy mirth into Aspatia!
Nothing but sad thoughts in her breast do dwell:
Methinks, a mean betwixt you would do well.
  Dula. She is in love: hang me, if I were so, 40
But I could run my country. I love too
To do those things that people in love do.
  Asp. It were a timeless smile should prove my
  cheek:

29–35] *doubles entendres on the terms of card games were common*
32 take her part] be her partner 33 pluck down] 'let down'
does not use] is not used to 41 run my country] drive my
country at a hot pace (*Thorndike*)

It were a fitter hour for me to laugh,
When at the altar the religious priest   45
Were pacifying the offended powers
With sacrifice, than now. This should have been
My rite; and all your hands have been employed
In giving me a spotless offering
To young Amintor's bed, as we are now   50
For you. Pardon, Evadne: would my worth
Were great as yours, or that the King, or he,
Or both, thought so! Perhaps he found me worthless:
But till he did so, in these ears of mine,
These credulous ears, he pour'd the sweetest words   55
That art or love could frame. If he were false,
Pardon it, Heaven! and, if I did want
Virtue, you safely may forgive that too;
For I have lost none that I had from you.
   Evad. Nay, leave this sad talk, madam.
   Asp.   Would I could! 60
Then I should leave the cause.
   Evad. See, if you have not spoil'd all Dula's mirth!
   Asp. Thou think'st thy heart hard; but, if thou be'st
    caught,
Remember me; thou shalt perceive a fire
Shot suddenly into thee.   65
   Dula. That's not so good; let 'em shoot anything
but fire, and I fear 'em not.
   Asp. Well, wench, thou may'st be taken.
   Evad. Ladies, good-night: I'll do the rest myself.
   Dula. Nay, let your lord do some.   70

   Asp.   *Lay a garland on my hearse*
               Of the dismal yew—

   Evad. That's one of your sad songs, madam.
   Asp. Believe me, 'tis a very pretty one.
   Evad. How is it, madam?   75

SONG

Asp.   *Lay a garland on my hearse*
              Of the dismal yew;
      Maidens, willow-branches bear;
              Say I died true.
      My love was false, but I was firm   80
              From my hour of birth:
      Upon my buried body lay
              Lightly, gentle earth!

Evad. Fie on't, madam! the words are so strange,
they are able to make one dream of hobgoblins.— 85
I could never have the power—sing that, Dula.

Dula. *I could never have the power*
      To love one above an hour,
      But my heart would prompt mine eye
      On some other man to fly.   90
        Venus, fix mine eyes fast,
        Or, if not, give me all that I shall see at last!

Evad. So, leave me now.
Dula.   Nay, we must see you laid.
Asp. Madam, good night. May all the marriage-joys
That longing maids imagine in their beds   95
Prove so unto you! May no discontent
Grow 'twixt your love and you! but, if there do,
Inquire of me, and I will guide your moan;
Teach you an artificial way to grieve,
To keep your sorrow waking. Love your lord   100
No worse than I: but, if you love so well,
Alas, you may displease him! so did I.
This is the last time you shall look on me.—
Ladies, farewell. As soon as I am dead,

  82 *lay*] *cf. l. 76; the familiar 'lie' is an 'improvement' by Theo-*
bald (1750)   99 *artifical*] artistic, ingenious

Come all and watch one night about my hearse;   105
Bring each a mournful story and a tear,
To offer at it when I go to earth;
With flattering ivy clasp my coffin round;
Write on my brow my fortune; let my bier
Be borne by virgins, that shall sing by course   110
The truth of maids and perjuries of men.

    Evad. Alas, I pity thee.   [*Exit* Evadne.
    Omnes.   Madam, good night.
    1. *Lady.* Come, we'll let in the bridegroom.
    Dula.   Where's my lord?

Enter Amintor.

    1. *Lady.* Here, take this light.
    Dula.   He'll find her in the dark.
    1. *Lady.* Your lady's scarce a-bed yet; you must
      help her.   115
    Asp. Go, and be happy in your lady's love.
May all the wrongs that you have done to me
Be utterly forgotten in my death!
I'll trouble you no more; yet I will take
A parting kiss, and will not be denied.—   120
You'll come, my lord, and see the virgins weep
When I am laid in earth, though you yourself
Can know no pity. Thus I wind myself
Into this willow-garland, and am prouder
That I was once your love, though now refused,   125
Than to have had another true to me.
So with my prayers I leave you, and must try
Some yet unpractised way to grieve and die.
                        [*Exit* Aspatia.

    Dula. Come, ladies, will you go?
    Omnes.   Good night, my lord.

110 by course] in **turns**

124

Amin. Much happiness unto you all!—   130

[*Exeunt* Ladies.

I did that lady wrong. Methinks, I feel
A grief shoot suddenly through all my veins;
Mine eyes rain: this is strange at such a time.
It was the King first moved me to't; but he
Has not my will in keeping. Why do I   135
Perplex myself thus? Something whispers me,
Go not to bed. My guilt is not so great
As mine own conscience, too sensible,
Would make me think; I only brake a promise,
And 'twas the King enforced me. Timorous flesh,   140
Why shakest thou so? Away, my idle fears!

Re-enter Evadne.

Yonder she is, the lustre of whose eye
Can blot away the sad remembrance
Of all these things.—Oh, my Evadne, spare
That tender body; let it not take cold!   145
The vapours of the night shall not fall here.
To bed, my love: Hymen will punish us
For being slack performers of his rites.
Camest thou to call me?

Evad.   No.

Amin.   Come, come, my love,
And let us lose ourselves to one another.   150
Why art thou up so long?

Evad.   I am not well.

Amin. To bed then; let me wind thee in these arms
Till I have banish'd sickness.

Evad.   Good my lord,
I cannot sleep.

Amin.   Evadne, we will watch;
I mean no sleeping.

138 sensible] sensitive

Evad.   I'll not go to bed.   155

Amin. I prithee, do.

Evad.   I will not for the world.

Amin. Why, my dear love?

Evad.   Why! I have sworn I will not.

Amin. Sworn!

Evad.   Ay.

Amin.   How? sworn, Evadne!

Evad. Yes, sworn, Amintor; and will swear again,
If you will wish to hear me.   160

Amin. To whom have you sworn this?

Evad. If I should name him, the matter were not
   great.

Amin. Come, this is but the coyness of a bride.

Evad. The coyness of a bride!

Amin.   How prettily
That frown becomes thee!

Evad.   Do you like it so?   165

Amin. Thou can'st not dress thy face in such a look
But I shall like it.

Evad. What look will like you best?

Amin.   Why do you ask?

Evad. That I may show you one less pleasing to you.

Amin. How's that?   170

Evad. That I may show you one less pleasing to you.

Amin. I prithee, put thy jests in milder looks;
It shows as thou wert angry.

Evad.   So perhaps
I am indeed.

Amin.   Why, who has done thee wrong?
Name me the man, and by thyself I swear,   175
Thy yet-unconquer'd self, I will revenge thee!

Evad. Now I shall try thy truth. If thou dost love me,
Thou weigh'st not any thing compared with me:

168 like] please

126

Life, honour, joys eternal, all delights
This world can yield, or hopeful people feign,   180
Or in the life to come, are light as air
To a true lover when his lady frowns,
And bids him *do this*. Wilt thou kill this man?
Swear, my Amintor, and I'll kiss the sin
Off from thy lips.
 Amin.   I wonnot swear, sweet love,   185
Till I do know the cause.
 Evad.   I would thou wouldst.
Why, it is thou that wrong'st me; I hate thee;
Thou should'st have kill'd thyself.
 Amin. If I should know that, I should quickly kill
The man you hated.
 Evad.   Know it, then, and do't.   190
 Amin. Oh, no! what look soe'er thou shalt put on
To try my faith, I shall not think thee false;
I cannot find one blemish in thy face,
Where falsehood should abide. Leave, and to bed.
If you have sworn to any of the virgins   195
That were your old companions to preserve
Your maidenhead a night, it may be done
Without this means.
 Evad.   A maidenhead, Amintor,
At my years!
 Amin. Sure she raves; this cannot be
Her natural temper.—Shall I call thy maids?   200
Either thy healthful sleep hath left thee long,
Or else some fever rages in thy blood.
 Evad. Neither, Amintor: think you I am mad,
Because I speak the truth?
 Amin.   Is this the truth?
Will you not lie with me to-night?
 Evad.   To-night!   205

185 wonnot] won't

You talk as if you thought I would hereafter.
  Amin. Hereafter! yes, I do.
  Evad.   You are deceived.
Put off amazement, and with patience mark
What I shall utter, for the oracle
Knows nothing truer: 'tis not for a night   210
Or two that I forbear thy bed, but ever.
  Amin. I dream. Awake, Amintor!
  Evad.   You hear right:
I sooner will find out the beds of snakes,
And with my youthful blood warm their cold flesh,
Letting them curl themselves about my limbs,   215
Than sleep one night with thee. This is not feign'd,
Nor sounds it like the coyness of a bride.
  Amin. Is flesh so earthly to endure all this?
Are these the joys of marriage?—Hymen, keep
This story (that will make succeeding youth   220
Neglect thy ceremonies) from all ears;
Let it not rise up, for thy shame and mine
To after-ages: we will scorn thy laws,
If thou no better bless them. Touch the heart
Of her that thou hast sent me, or the world   225
Shall know this: not an altar then will smoke
In praise of thee; we will adopt us sons;
Then virtue shall inherit, and not blood.
If we do lust, we'll take the next we meet,
Serving ourselves as other creatures do;   230
And never take note of the female more,
Nor of her issue. I do rage in vain;
She can but jest.—Oh, pardon me, my love!
So dear the thoughts are that I hold of thee,
That I must break forth. Satisfy my fear;   235
It is a pain, beyond the hand of death,
To be in doubt: confirm it with an oath,
If this be true.

Evad.   Do you invent the form:
Let there be in it all the binding words
Devils and conjurors can put together,   240
And I will take it. I have sworn before,
And here by all things holy do again,
Never to be acquainted with thy bed!
Is your doubt over now?
    Amin. I know too much: would I had doubted still! 245
Was ever such a marriage-night as this!
You powers above, if you did ever mean
Man should be used thus, you have thought a way
How he may bear himself, and save his honour:
Instruct me in it; for to my dull eyes   250
There is no mean, no moderate course to run;
I must live scorn'd, or be a murderer:
Is there a third? Why is this night so calm?
Why does not Heaven speak in thunder to us,
And drown her voice?
    Evad.   This rage will do no good.   255
    Amin. Evadne, hear me. Thou hast ta'en an oath,
But such a rash one, that to keep it were
Worse than to swear it: call it back to thee;
Such vows as that never ascend the Heaven;
A tear or two will wash it quite away.   260
Have mercy on my youth, my hopeful youth,
If thou be pitiful! for, without boast,
This land was proud of me: what lady was there,
That men call'd fair and virtuous in this isle,
That would have shunn'd my love? It is in thee   265
To make me hold this worth.—Oh, we vain men,
That trust out all our reputation
To rest upon the weak and yielding hand
Of feeble woman! But thou art not stone;
Thy flesh is soft, and in thine eyes doth dwell   270
The spirit of love; thy heart cannot be hard.

Come, lead me from the bottom of despair
To all the joys thou hast; I know thou wilt;
And make me careful lest the sudden change
O'ercome my spirits.

    Evad.   When I call back this oath,   275
The pains of hell environ me!

    Amin. I sleep, and am too temperate. Come to bed!
Or by those hairs, which, if thou hadst a soul
Like to thy locks, were threads for kings to wear
About their arms——

    Evad.   Why, so perhaps they are.   280

    Amin. I'll drag thee to my bed, and make thy tongue
Undo this wicked oath, or on thy flesh
I'll print a thousand wounds to let out life!

    Evad. I fear thee not: do what thou darest to me!
Every ill-sounding word or threatening look   285
Thou shewest to me will be reveng'd at full.

    Amin. It will not sure, Evadne.

    Evad. Do not you hazard that.

    Amin. Ha' ye your champions?

    Evad. Alas, Amintor, think'st thou I forbear   290
To sleep with thee, because I have put on
A maiden's strictness? Look upon these cheeks,
And thou shalt find the hot and rising blood
Unapt for such a vow. No; in this heart
There dwells as much desire and as much will   295
To put that wished act in practice as ever yet
Was known to woman; and they have been shown
Both. But it was the folly of thy youth
To think this beauty, to what hand soe'er
It shall be call'd, shall stoop to any second.   300
I do enjoy the best, and in that height
Have sworn to stand or die: you guess the man.

    Amin. No; let me know the man that wrongs me so,

274 careful] anxious   288 hazard] 'bet on'

That I may cut his body into motes,
And scatter it before the northern wind.   305
 Evad. You dare not strike him.
 Amin.   Do not wrong me so:
Yes, if his body were a poisonous plant
That it were death to touch, I have a soul
Will throw me on him.
 Evad. Why, 'tis the King.
 Amin.   The King!
 Evad.   What will you do now? 310
 Amin. It is not the King!
 Evad. What did he make this match for, dull
  Amintor?
 Amin. Oh, thou hast named a word, that wipes
  away
All thoughts revengeful! In that sacred word,
'The King,' there lies a terror: what frail man   315
Dares lift his hand against it? Let the gods
Speak to him when they please: till when, let us
Suffer and wait.
 Evad. Why should you fill yourself so full of heat,
And haste so to my bed? I am no virgin.   320
 Amin. What devil put it in thy fancy, then,
To marry me?
 Evad. Alas, I must have one
To father children, and to bear the name
Of husband to me, that my sin may be
More honourable!
 Amin.   What strange thing am I!   325
 Evad. A miserable one; one that myself
Am sorry for.
 Amin. Why, show it then in this:
If thou hast pity, though thy love be none,
Kill me; and all true lovers, that shall live

328 none] *sc.* non-existent

In after ages cross'd in their desires,   330
Shall bless thy memory, and call thee good,
Because such mercy in thy heart was found,
To rid a lingering wretch.
    Evad.   I must have one
To fill thy room again, if thou wert dead;
Else, by this night, I would! I pity thee.   335
    Amin. These strange and sudden injuries have fallen
So thick upon me, that I lose all sense
Of what they are. Methinks, I am not wrong'd;
Nor is it aught, if from the censuring world
I can but hide it. Reputation,   340
Thou art a word, no more!—But thou hast shown
An impudence so high, that to the world
I fear thou wilt betray or shame thyself.
    Evad. To cover shame, I took thee; never fear
That I would blaze myself.
    Amin.   Nor let the King   345
Know I conceive he wrongs me; then mine honour
Will thrust me into action: that my flesh
Could bear with patience. And it is some ease
To me in these extremes, that I knew this
Before I touch'd thee; else, had all the sins   350
Of mankind stood betwixt me and the King,
I had gone through 'em to his heart and thine.
I have left one desire: 'tis not his crown
Shall buy me to thy bed, now I resolve
He has dishonour'd thee. Give me thy hand: 355
Be careful of thy credit, and sin close;
'Tis all I wish. Upon thy chamber-floor
I'll rest to-night, that morning visitors
May think we did as married people use:
And, prithee, smile upon me when they come,   360

333 rid] despatch (*Daniel*)   334 fill . . . room] take . . .
place   345 blaze] blazon   356 close] secretly

And seem to toy, as if thou hadst been pleased
With what we did.
   Evad.   Fear not; I will do this.
   Amin. Come, let us practise; and, as wantonly
As ever longing bride and bridegroom met,
Let's laugh and enter here.
   Evad.   I am content.   365
   Amin. Down all the swellings of my troubled heart!
When we walk thus intwined, let all eyes see
If ever lovers better did agree.   [*Exeunt.*

SCENE II

Enter Aspatia, Antiphila, *and* Olympias.

   Asp. Away, you are not sad! force it no further.
Good gods, how well you look! Such a full colour
Young bashful brides put on: sure, you are new
    married!
   Ant. Yes, madam, to your grief.
   Asp.   Alas, poor wenches!
Go learn to love first; learn to lose yourselves;   5
Learn to be flatter'd, and believe and bless
The double tongue that did it; make a faith
Out of the miracles of ancient lovers,
Such as spake truth, and died in't; and, like me,
Believe all faithful, and be miserable.   10
Did you ne'er love yet, wenches? Speak, Olympias:
Thou hast an easy temper, fit for stamp.
   Olym. Never.
   Asp.   Nor you, Antiphila?
   Ant.   Nor I.
   Asp. Then, my good girls, be more than women,
    wise;

   12 fit for stamp] impressionable

At least be more than I was; and be sure   15
You credit any thing the light gives life to,
Before a man. Rather believe the sea
Weeps for the ruin'd merchant, when he roars;
Rather, the wind courts but the pregnant sails,
When the strong cordage cracks; rather, the sun   20
Comes but to kiss the fruit in wealthy autumn,
When all falls blasted. If you needs must love,
(Forced by ill fate,) take to your maiden-bosoms
Two dead-cold aspics, and of them make lovers:
They cannot flatter nor forswear; one kiss   25
Makes a long peace for all. But man,—
Oh, that beast man! Come, let's be sad, my girls:
That down-cast of thine eye, Olympias,
Shows a fine sorrow.—Mark, Antiphila;
Just such another was the nymph Œnone's,   30
When Paris brought home Helen.—Now, a tear;
And then thou art a piece expressing fully
The Carthage-queen, when from a cold sea-rock,
Full with her sorrow, she tied fast her eyes
To the fair Trojan ships; and, having lost them,   35
Just as thine eyes do, down stole a tear.—Antiphila,
What would this wench do, if she were Aspatia?
Here she would stand, till some more pitying god
Turn'd her to marble.—'Tis enough, my wench.—
Show me the piece of needlework you wrought.   40
 Ant. Of Ariadne, madam?
 Asp.   Yes, that piece.—
This should be Theseus; h'as a cozening face.—
You meant him for a man?
 Ant.   He was so, madam.
 Asp. Why, then, 'tis well enough.—Never look
 back;
You have a full wind and a false heart, Theseus.—   45

24 aspics] asps

Does not the story say, his keel was split,
Or his masts spent, or some kind rock or other
Met with his vessel?
    Ant.   Not as I remember.
    Asp. It should ha' been so. Could the gods know this,
And not, of all their number, raise a storm?   50
But they are all as evil. This false smile
Was well express'd; just such another caught me.—
You shall not go so.—
Antiphila, in this place work a quicksand,
And over it a shallow smiling water,   55
And his ship ploughing it; and then a Fear:
Do that Fear bravely, wench.
    Ant.   'Twill wrong the story.
    Asp. 'Twill make the story, wrong'd by wanton poets,
Live long and be believed. But where's the lady?
    Ant. There, madam.   60
    Asp. Fie, you have miss'd it here, Antiphila;
You are much mistaken, wench:
These colours are not dull and pale enough
To show a soul so full of misery
As this sad lady's was. Do it by me,   65
Do it again by me, the lost Aspatia;
And you shall find all true but the wild island.
Suppose I stand upon the sea-beach now,
Mine arms thus, and mine hair blown with the wind,
Wild as that desert; and let all about me   70
Tell that I am forsaken. Do my face
(If thou hadst ever feeling of a sorrow)
Thus, thus, Antiphila: strive to make me look
Like Sorrow's monument; and the trees about me,
Let them be dry and leafless; let the rocks   75
Groan with continual surges; and behind me,

Make all a desolation. See, see, wenches,
A miserable life of this poor picture!
   Olym. Dear madam!
   Asp.   I have done. Sit down; and let us
Upon that point fix all our eyes, that point there.   80
Make a dull silence, till you feel a sudden sadness
Give us new souls.

Enter Calianax.

   Cal. The King may do this, and he may not do it:
My child is wrong'd, disgraced.—Well, how now, hus-
     wives?
What, at your ease! is this a time to sit still?   85
Up, you young lazy whores, up, or I'll swinge you!
   Olym. Nay, good my lord—
   Cal. You'll lie down shortly. Get you in, and work!
What are you grown so rusty you want heats?
We shall have some of the court-boys heat you shortly. 90
   Ant. My lord, we do no more than we are charged:
It is the lady's pleasure we be thus;
In grief she is forsaken.
   Cal.   There's a rogue too.
A young dissembling slave!—Well, get you in.—
I'll have a bout with that boy. 'Tis high time   95
Now to be valiant: I confess my youth
Was never prone that way. What, made an ass!
A court-stale! Well, I will be valiant,
And beat some dozen of these whelps; I will!
And there's another of 'em, a trim cheating soldier;   100
I'll maul that rascal; h'as out-braved me twice:
But now, I thank the gods, I am valiant.—
Go, get you in.—I'll take a course with all.

                        [*Exeunt Omnes.*

ACT III

SCENE I

Enter Cleon, Strato, Diphilus.

Cle. Your sister is not up yet.

Diph. Oh, brides must take their morning's rest; the
night is troublesome.

Stra. But not tedious.

Diph. What odds, he has not my sister's maidenhead 5
to-night?

Stra. None; it's odds against any bridegroom living,
he ne'er gets it while he lives.

Diph. Y'are merry with my sister; you'll please to
allow me the same freedom with your mother.   10

Stra. She's at your service.

Diph. Then she's merry enough of herself; she needs
no tickling. Knock at the door.

Stra. We shall interrupt them.

Diph. No matter; they have the year before them.— 15
Good morrow, sister! Spare yourself to-day; the night
will come again.

Enter Amintor.

Amin. Who's there? my brother! I am no readier yet.
Your sister is but now up.

Diph. You look as you had lost your eyes to-night: 20
I think you ha' not slept.

Amin. I'faith I have not.

Diph. You have done better, then.

Amin. We ventured for a boy: when he is twelve,
A' shall command against the foes of Rhodes.   25
Shall we be merry?

18, 81 readier, ready] dressed for the day

Stra. You cannot; you want sleep.

Amin.   'Tis true;—[*Aside.*] but she,
As if she had drunk Lethe, or had made
Even with Heaven, did fetch so still a sleep,
So sweet and sound——

    Diph.   What's that?

    Amin.   Your sister frets 30
This morning, and does turn her eyes upon me,
As people on their headsman. She does chafe,
And kiss, and chafe again, and clap my cheeks!
She's in another world.

    Diph. Then I had lost: I was about to lay   35
You had not got her maidenhead to-night.

    Amin. [*aside.*] Ha! does he not mock me?—Y'ad lost
      indeed;
I do not use to bungle.

    Cle. You do deserve her.

    Amin. [*aside.*] I laid my lips to hers, and that wild
      breath,   40
That was so rude and rough to me last night,
Was sweet as April. I'll be guilty too,
If these be the effects.—

Enter Melantius.

    Mel. Good day, Amintor; for to me the name
Of brother is too distant: we are friends,   45
And that is nearer.

    Amin.   Dear Melantius!
Let me behold thee.—Is it possible?

    Mel. What sudden gaze is this?

    Amin.   'Tis wondrous strange!

    Mel. Why does thine eye desire so strict a view
Of that it knows so well? There's nothing here   50
That is not thine.

    Amin.   I wonder much, Melantius,

138

To see those noble looks, that make me think
How virtuous thou art: and, on the sudden,
'Tis strange to me thou shouldst have worth and
    honour;
Or not be base, and false, and treacherous,   55
And every ill. But——
    Mel.   Stay, stay, my friend;
I fear this sound will not become our loves:
No more; embrace me.
    Amin.   Oh, mistake me not!
I know thee to be full of all those deeds
That we frail men call good; but by the course   60
Of nature thou shouldst be as quickly changed
As are the winds; dissembling as the sea,
That now wears brows as smooth as virgins' be,
Tempting the merchant to invade his face,
And in an hour calls his billows up,   65
And shoots 'em at the sun, destroying all
A' carries on him.—[*Aside.*] Oh, how near am I
To utter my sick thoughts!—
    Mel. But why, my friend, should I be so by nature?
    Amin. I have wed thy sister, who hath virtuous
    thoughts   70
Enough for one whole family; and it is strange
That you should feel no want.
    Mel. Believe me, this is compliment too cunning
    for me.
    Diph. What should I be then by the course of nature,
They having both robb'd me of so much virtue?   75
    Stra. Oh, call the bride, my lord, Amintor,
That we may see her blush, and turn her eyes down:
It is the prettiest sport.
    Amin. Evadne!
    Evad. [*within.*] My lord?
    Amin.   Come forth, my love:

Your brothers do attend to wish you joy.   80
  Evad. [*within.*] I am not ready yet.
  Amin.   Enough, enough.
  Evad. [*within.*] They'll mock me.
  Amin.   Faith, thou shalt come in.

Enter Evadne.

  Mel. Good morrow, sister. He that understands
Whom you have wed, need not to wish you joy;
You have enough: take heed you be not proud.   85
  Diph. Oh, sister, what have you done?
  Evad. I done! why, what have I done?
  Stra. My lord Amintor swears you are no maid now.
  Evad. Push!
  Stra. I'faith, he does.   90
  Evad. I knew I should be mock'd.
  Diph. With a truth.
  Evad. If 'twere to do again, in faith I would not
marry.
  Amin. [*aside.*] Nor I, by Heaven!—   95
  Diph. Sister, Dula swears she heard you cry two
rooms off.
  Evad. Fie, how you talk!
  Diph. Let's see you walk, Evadne. By my troth,
y'are spoil'd.   100
  Mel. Amintor—
  Amin. Ha!
  Mel. Thou art sad.
  Amin. Who, I? I thank you for that. Shall Diphilus,
thou, and I, sing a catch?   105
  Mel. How!
  Amin. Prithee, let's.
  Mel. Nay, that's too much the other way.
  Amin. I am so lighten'd with my happiness!—
How dost thou, love? kiss me.   110

Evad. I cannot love you, you tell tales of me.

Amin. Nothing but what becomes us.—Gentlemen,
Would you had all such wives,—[*Aside.*] and all the
    world,
That I might be no wonder!—Y'are all sad:
What, do you envy me? I walk, methinks,   115
On water, and ne'er sink, I am so light.

Mel. 'Tis well you are so.

Amin. Well! how can I be other, when she looks
    thus?
Is there no music there? Let's dance.

Mel. Why, this is strange, Amintor!   120

Amin. I do not know myself; yet I could wish
My joy were less.

Diph. I'll marry too, if it will make one thus.

Evad. Amintor, hark.

Amin. What says my love?—[*Aside.*] I must obey.— 125

Evad. [*aside to Amin.*] You do it scurvily, 'twill be
    perceived.

Cle. My lord, the King is here.

Amin. Where?

Stra. And his brother.

Enter King and Lysippus.

King. Good morrow, all.—   130
Amintor, joy on joy fall thick upon thee!—
And, madam, you are alter'd since I saw you,
(I must salute you) you are now another's.
How liked you your night's rest?

Evad. Ill, sir.   135

Amin. Indeed she took but little.

Lys. You'll let her take more, and thank her too,
shortly.

King. Amintor, wert thou truly honest till thou
wert married?   140

141

Amin. Yes, sir.

King. Tell me, then, how shews the sport unto thee?

Amin. Why, well.

King. What did you do?

Amin. No more, nor less, than other couples use;   145
You know what 'tis; it has but a coarse name.

   King. But, prithee, I should think, by her black eye,
And her red cheek, she would be quick and stirring
In this same business; ha?

   Amin.   I cannot tell;
I ne'er tried other, sir; but I perceive   150
She is as quick as you delivered.

   King. Well, you'll trust me then, Amintor,
To choose a wife for you again?

   Amin. No, never, sir.

   King. Why, like you this so ill?

   Amin.   So well I like her,   155
For this I bow my knee in thanks to you,
And unto Heaven will pay my grateful tribute
Hourly; and do hope we shall draw out
A long contented life together here,
And die both, full of grey hairs, in one day;   160
For which the thanks is yours. But if the powers
That rule us please to call her first away,
Without pride spoke, this world holds not a wife
Worthy to take her room.

   King [*aside*].   I do not like this.—
All forbear the room, but you, Amintor,   165
And your lady. I have some speech with you,
That may concern your after living well.

     Exeunt all but the King, Amintor, *and* Evadne.

   Amin. [*aside.*] A' will not tell me that he lies with
    her?
If he do, something heavenly stay my heart,

For I shall be apt to thrust this arm of mine   170
To acts unlawful!—

   King.   You will suffer me
To talk with her, Amintor, and not have
A jealous pang?

   Amin.   Sir, I dare trust my wife
With whom she dares to talk, and not be jealous.—

   King. How do you like Amintor?

   Evad.   As I did, sir.   175

   King. How's that?

   Evad. As one that, to fulfil your will and pleasure,
I have given leave to call me wife and love.

   King. I see there is no lasting faith in sin;
They that break word with Heaven will break again   180
With all the world, and so dost thou with me.

   Evad. How, sir?

   King.   This subtle woman's ignorance
Will not excuse you: thou hast taken oaths,
So great, methought they did not well become
A woman's mouth, that thou wouldst ne'er enjoy   185
A man but me.

   Evad.   I never did swear so;
You do me wrong.

   King.   Day and night have heard it.

   Evad. I swore indeed that I would never love
A man of lower place; but, if your fortune
Should throw you from this height, I bade you trust   190
I would forsake you, and would bend to him
That won your throne: I love with my ambition,
Not with my eyes. But, if I ever yet
Touch'd any other, leprosy light here
Upon my face! which for your royalty   195
I would not stain.

   King. Why, thou dissemblest, and it is in me
To punish thee.

Evad.   Why, it is in me, then,
Not to love you, which will more afflict
Your body than your punishment can mine.   200
  King. But thou hast let Amintor lie with thee.
  Evad. I ha' not.
  King.   Impudence! he says himself so.
  Evad. A' lies.
  King.   A' does not.
  Evad.   By this light, he does,
Strangely and basely! and I'll prove it so:
I did not only shun him for a night,   205
But told him I would never close with him.
  King. Speak lower; 'tis false.
  Evad.   I am no man
To answer with a blow; or, if I were,
You are the King. But urge me not; 'tis most true.
  King. Do not I know the uncontrolled thoughts   210
That youth brings with him, when his blood is high
With expectation and desire of that
He long hath waited for? Is not his spirit,
Though he be temperate, of a valiant strain
As this our age hath known? What could he do,   215
If such a sudden speech had met his blood,
But ruin thee for ever, if he had not kill'd thee?
He could not bear it thus; he is as we,
Or any other wrong'd man.
  Evad.   It is dissembling.
  King. Take him! farewell: henceforth I am thy foe;   220
And what disgraces I can blot thee with look for.
  Evad. Stay,   sir!—Amintor!—You   shall   hear.—
    Amintor!
  Amin. What, my love?
  Evad. Amintor, thou hast an ingenious look,
And shouldst be virtuous: it amazeth me   225

224 ingenious] ingenuous

That thou canst make such base malicious lies!
   Amin. What, my dear wife?
   Evad.   Dear wife! I do despise thee.
Why, nothing can be baser than to sow
Dissention amongst lovers.
   Amin.   Lovers! who?
   Evad. The King and me—
   Amin.   Oh, God!   230
   Evad. Who should live long, and love without dis-
      taste,
Were it not for such pickthanks as thyself.
Did you lie with me? swear now, and be punish'd
In hell for this!
   Amin.   The faithless sin I made
To fair Aspatia is not yet revenged;   235
It follows me.—I will not lose a word
To this vild woman; but to you, my king,
The anguish of my soul thrusts out this truth,
Y'are a tyrant! and not so much to wrong
An honest man thus, as to take a pride   240
In talking with him of it.
   Evad.   Now, sir, see
How loud this fellow lied!
   Amin. You that can know to wrong, should know
      how men
Must right themselves. What punishment is due
From me to him that shall abuse my bed?   245
Is it not death? nor can that satisfy,
Unless I send your lives through all the land,
To shew how nobly I have freed myself.
   King. Draw not thy sword; thou knowest I cannot
      fear
A subject's hand; but thou shalt feel the weight   250
Of this, if thou dost rage.

    243 to] to do   **247 send . . . land]** broadcast your lives

Amin.   The weight of that!
If you have any worth, for heaven's sake, think
I fear not swords; for, as you are mere man,
I dare as easily kill you for this deed,
As you dare think to do it. But there is   255
Divinity about you, that strikes dead
My rising passions: as you are my king,
I fall before you, and present my sword
To cut mine own flesh, if it be your will.
Alas, I am nothing but a multitude   260
Of walking griefs! Yet, should I murder you,
I might before the world take the excuse
Of madness; for, compare my injuries,
And they will well appear too sad a weight
For reason to endure: but, fall I first   265
Amongst my sorrows, ere my treacherous hand
Touch holy things! But why (I know not what
I have to say), why did you choose out me
To make thus wretched? there were thousands, fools,
Easy to work on, and of state enough,   270
Within the island.
    Evad.   I would not have a fool;
It were no credit for me.
    Amin.   Worse and worse!
Thou, that darest talk unto thy husband thus,
Profess thyself a whore, and, more than so,
Resolve to be so still!——It is my fate   275
To bear and bow beneath a thousand griefs,
To keep that little credit with the world.—
But there were wise ones too; you might have ta'en
Another.
    King. No; for I believed thee honest,
As thou wert valiant.
    Amin.   All the happiness   280
        277 that little] such little! (*Thorndike*)

146

Bestow'd upon me turns into disgrace.
Gods, take your honesty again, for I
Am loaden with it!—Good my lord the King,
Be private in it.

King.   Thou mayst live, Amintor,
Free as thy king, if thou wilt wink at this,   285
And be a means that we may meet in secret.

Amin. A bawd! Hold, hold, my breast! A bitter
      curse
Seize me, if I forget not all respects
That are religious, on another word
Sounded like that; and through a sea of sins   290
Will wade to my revenge, though I should call
Pains here and after life upon my soul!

King. Well, I am resolute you lay not with her;
And so I leave you.   [*Exit* King.

Evad.   You must needs be prating;
And see what follows!

Amin.   Prithee, vex me not: 295
Leave me; I am afraid some sudden start
Will pull a murther on me.

Evad.   I am gone;
I love my life well.   [*Exit* Evadne.

Amin.   I hate mine as much.
This 'tis to break a troth! I should be glad,
If all this tide of grief would make me mad.   [*Exit.* 300

SCENE II

Enter Melantius.

Mel. I'll know the cause of all Amintor's griefs,
Or friendship shall be idle.

Enter Calianax.

293 resolute] convinced

147

Cal.   Oh, Melantius,
My daughter will die!
Mel.   Trust me, I am sorry:
Would thou hadst ta'en her room!
Cal.   Thou art a slave,
A cut-throat slave, a bloody treacherous slave!   5
    Mel. Take heed, old man; thou wilt be heard to
        rave,
And lose thine offices.
    Cal.   I am valiant grown
At all these years, and thou art but a slave!
    Mel. Leave!
Some company will come, and I respect   10
Thy years, not thee, so much, that I could wish
To laugh at thee alone.
    Cal.   I'll spoil your mirth:
I mean to fight with thee. There lie, my cloak.
This was my father's sword, and he durst fight.
Are you prepared?
    Mel.   Why wilt thou dote thyself   15
Out of thy life? Hence, get thee to bed;
Have careful looking-to, and eat warm things,
And trouble not me: my head is full of thoughts
More weighty than thy life or death can be.
    Cal. You have a name in war, where you stand safe 20
Amongst a multitude; but I will try
What you dare do unto a weak old man
In single fight. You'll give ground, I fear.
Come draw.
    Mel. I will not draw, unless thou pull'st thy death 25
Upon thee with a stroke. There's no one blow
That thou canst give hath strength enough to kill me.
Tempt me not so far, then: the power of earth
Shall not redeem thee.—
    Cal. [*aside.*]   I must let him alone;

He's stout and able; and, to say the truth,   30
However I may set a face and talk,
I am not valiant. When I was a youth,
I kept my credit with a testy trick
I had 'mongst cowards, but durst never fight.—
    Mel. I will not promise to preserve your life,   35
If you do stay.—
    Cal. [*aside.*]   I would give half my land
That I durst fight with that proud man a little:
If I had men to hold him, I would beat him
Till he ask'd me mercy.—
    Mel.   Sir, will you be gone?—
    Cal. [*aside.*] I dare not stay; but I will go home, and
        beat   40
My servants all over for this.   [*Exit* Calianax.
    Mel. This old fellow haunts me.
But the distracted carriage of mine Amintor
Takes deeply on me. I will find the cause:
I fear his conscience cries, he wrong'd Aspatia.   45

Enter Amintor.

    Amin. [*aside.*] Men's eyes are not so subtle to per-
        ceive
My inward misery: I bear my grief
Hid from the world. How art thou wretched then?
For aught I know, all husbands are like me;
And every one I talk with of his wife   50
Is but a well dissembler of his woes,
As I am. Would I knew it! for the rareness
Afflicts me now.—
    Mel. Amintor, we have not enjoy'd our friendship
of late; for we were wont to change our souls in talk. 55
    Amin. Melantius, I can tell thee a good jest of Strato
and a lady the last day.

55 change] exchange

Mel. How was't?

Amin. Why, such an odd one!

Mel. I have long'd to speak with you; not of an idle 60
jest that's forced, but of matter you are bound to utter
to me.

Amin. What is that, my friend?

Mel. I have observed your words fall from your
    tongue

Wildly; and all your carriage   65
Like one that strove to show his merry mood,
When he were ill-disposed: you were not wont
To put such scorn into your speech, or wear
Upon your face ridiculous jollity.
Some sadness sits here, which your cunning would   70
Cover o'er with smiles, and 'twill not be. What is it?

  Amin. A sadness here! what cause
Can fate provide for me to make me so?
Am I not loved through all this isle? The King
Rains greatness on me. Have I not received   75
A lady to my bed, that in her eye
Keeps mounting fire, and on her tender cheeks
Inevitable colour, in her heart
A prison for all virtue? Are not you,
Which is above all joys, my constant friend?   80
What sadness can I have? No; I am light,
And feel the courses of my blood more warm
And stirring than they were. Faith, marry too;
And you will feel so unexpress'd a joy
In chaste embraces, that you will indeed   85
Appear another.

  Mel.   You may shape, Amintor,
Causes to cozen the whole world withal,
And yourself too; but 'tis not like a friend
To hide your soul from me. 'Tis not your nature

78 inevitable] irresistible

150

To be thus idle: I have seen you stand   90
As you were blasted 'midst of all your mirth;
Call thrice aloud, and then start, feigning joy
So coldly!—World, what do I here? a friend
Is nothing. Heaven, I would ha' told that man
My secret sins! I'll search an unknown land,   95
And there plant friendship; all is wither'd here.
Come with a compliment! I would have fought,
Or told my friend a' lied, ere sooth'd him so.
Out of my bosom!
    Amin. But there is nothing.
    Mel.   Worse and worse! farewell: 100
From this time have acquaintance, but no friend.
    Amin. Melantius, stay: you shall know what that is.
    Mel. See, how you play'd with friendship! be advised
How you give cause unto yourself to say
You ha' lost a friend.
    Amin.   Forgive what I ha' done;   105
For I am so o'ergone with injuries
Unheard of, that I lose consideration
Of what I ought to do,—oh!—oh!
    Mel. Do not weep. What is't?
May I once but know the man   110
Hath turn'd my friend thus!
    Amin.   I had spoke at first,
But that——
    Mel.   But what?
    Amin.   I held it most unfit
For you to know. Faith, do not know it yet.
    Mel. Thou see'st my love, that will keep company
With thee in tears; hide nothing, then, from me;   115
For when I know the cause of thy distemper,
With mine old armour I'll adorn myself,
My resolution, and cut through thy foes,
Unto thy quiet, till I place thy heart

As peaceable as spotless innocence.   120
What is it?
   Amin.   Why, 'tis this——it is too big
To get out—let my tears make way awhile.
   Mel. Punish me strangely, Heaven, if he scape
Of life or fame, that brought this youth to this!
   Amin. Your sister——
   Mel.   Well said.   125
   Amin. You'll wish't unknown, when you have heard
    it.
   Mel. No.
   Amin. Is much to blame,
And to the King has given her honour up,
And lives in whoredom with him.
   Mel.   How is this?   130
Thou art run mad with injury indeed;
Thou couldst not utter this else. Speak again;
For I forgive it freely; tell thy griefs.
   Amin. She's wanton; I am loath to say, a whore,
Though it be true.   135
   Mel. Speak yet again, before mine anger grow
Up beyond throwing down: what are thy griefs?
   Amin. By all our friendship, these.
   Mel.   What, am I tame?
After mine actions, shall the name of friend
Blot all our family, and stick the brand   140
Of whore upon my sister, unrevenged?
My shaking flesh, be thou a witness for me,
With what unwillingness I go to scourge
This railer, whom my folly hath call'd friend!—
I will not take thee basely: thy sword   145
Hangs near thy hand; draw it, that I may whip
Thy rashness to repentance; draw thy sword!
   Amin. Not on thee, did thine anger swell as high
As the wild surges. Thou shouldst do me ease

Here and eternally, if thy noble hand   150
Would cut me from my sorrows.
    Mel.   This is base
And fearful. They that use to utter lies
Provide not blows but words to qualify
The men they wrong'd. Thou hast a guilty cause.
    Amin. Thou pleasest me; for so much more like this 155
Will raise my anger up above my griefs,
(Which is a passion easier to be borne,)
And I shall then be happy.
    Mel.   Take, then, more
To raise thine anger: 'tis mere cowardice
Makes thee not draw; and I will leave thee dead,   160
However. But if thou art so much press'd
With guilt and fear as not to dare to fight,
I'll make thy memory loath'd, and fix a scandal
Upon thy name for ever.
    Amin.   Then I draw,
As justly as our magistrates their swords   165
To cut offenders off. I knew before
'Twould grate your ears; but it was base in you
To urge a weighty secret from your friend,
And then rage at it. I shall be at ease,
If I be kill'd; and, if you fall by me,   170
I shall not long outlive you.
    Mel.   Stay awhile.—
The name of friend is more than family,
Or all the world besides: I was a fool.
Thou searching human nature, that didst wake
To do me wrong, thou art inquisitive,   175
And thrusts me upon questions that will take
My sleep away! Would I had died, ere known
This sad dishonour!—Pardon me, my friend.
If thou wilt strike, here is a faithful heart;
Pierce it, for I will never heave my hand   180

To thine. Behold the power thou hast in me!
I do believe my sister is a whore,
A leprous one. Put up thy sword, young man.
  Amin. How should I bear it, then, she being so?
I fear, my friend, that you will lose me shortly;   185
And I shall do a foul act on myself
Through these disgraces.
  Mel.   Better half the land
Were buried quick together. No, Amintor;
Thou shalt have ease. Oh, this adulterous king,
That drew her to't; where got he the spirit   190
To wrong me so?
  Amin.   What is it, then, to me,
If it be wrong to you?
  Mel.   Why, not so much:
The credit of our house is thrown away.
But from his iron den I'll waken Death,
And hurl him on this king: my honesty   195
Shall steel my sword; and on its horrid point
I'll wear my cause, that shall amaze the eyes
Of this proud man, and be too glittering
For him to look on.
  Amin. I have quite undone my fame.   200
  Mel. Dry up thy watery eyes,
And cast a manly look upon my face;
For nothing is so wild as I thy friend
Till I have freed thee: still this swelling breast.
I go thus from thee, and will never cease   205
My vengeance till I find thy heart at peace.
  Amin. It must not be so. Stay. Mine eyes would tell
How loath I am to this; but, love and tears,
Leave me awhile! for I have hazarded
All that this world calls happy.—Thou hast wrought 210
A secret from me, under name of friend,
Which art could ne'er have found, nor torture wrung

From out my bosom. Give it me again;
For I will find it, wheresoe'er it lies,
Hid in the mortal'st part: invent a way   215
To give it back.
    Mel.   Why would you have it back?
I will to death pursue him with revenge.
    Amin. Therefore I call it back from thee; for I know
Thy blood so high, that thou wilt stir in this,
And shame me to posterity. Take to thy weapon.   220
    Mel. Hear thy friend, that bears more years than
       thou.
    Amin. I will not hear: but draw, or I——
    Mel.   Amintor!
    Amin. Draw, then; for I am full as resolute
As fame and honour can enforce me be:
I cannot linger. Draw!
    Mel.   I do. But is not   225
My share of credit equal with thine,
If I do stir?
    Amin.   No; for it will be call'd
Honour in thee to spill thy sister's blood,
If she her birth abuse, and on the King
A brave revenge; but on me, that have walk'd   230
With patience in it, it will fix the name
Of fearful cuckold. Oh, that word! Be quick.
    Mel. Then, join with me.
    Amin. I dare not do a sin, or else I would.
Be speedy.   235
    Mel. Then, dare not fight with me; for that's a sin.—
His grief distracts him.—Call thy thoughts again,
And to thyself pronounce the name of friend,
And see what that will work. I will not fight.
    Amin. You must.
    Mel.   I will be kill'd first. Though my passions 240

232 fearful] cowardly

Offer'd the like to you, 'tis not this earth
Shall buy my reason to it. Think awhile,
For you are (I must weep when I speak that)
Almost besides yourself.
    Amin.   Oh, my soft temper!
So many sweet words from thy sister's mouth,   245
I am afraid would make me take her to
Embrace, and pardon her. I am mad indeed,
And know not what I do. Yet have a care.
Of me in what thou dost.
    Mel.   Why, thinks my friend
I will forget his honour? or, to save   250
The bravery of our house, will lose his fame,
And fear to touch the throne of majesty?
    Amin. A curse will follow that; but rather live
And suffer with me.
    Mel.   I will do what worth
Shall bid me, and no more.
    Amin.   Faith, I am sick,   255
And desperately, I hope; yet, leaning thus,
I feel a kind of ease.
    Mel.   Come, take again
Your mirth about you.
    Amin.   I shall never do't.
    Mel. I warrant you; look up; we'll walk together;
Put thine arm here; all shall be well again.   260
    Amin. Thy love (oh, wretched!), ay, thy love,
      Melantius;
Why, I have nothing else.
    Mel.   Be merry, then.   [*Exeunt.*

Enter Melantius *again.*

    Mel. This worthy young man may do violence
Upon himself; but I have cherish'd him

244 besides] beside

To my best power, and sent him smiling from me,   265
To counterfeit again. Sword, hold thine edge;
My heart will never fail me.—   [*Enter* Diphilus.
                                    Diphilus!
Thou com'st as sent.
    Diph.   Yonder has bin such laughing.
    Mel. Betwixt whom?
    Diph.   Why, our sister and the King;
I thought their spleens would break; they laugh'd us all   270
Out of the room.
    Mel. They must weep, Diphilus.
    Diph.   Must they?
    Mel.   They must.
Thou art my brother; and, if I did believe
Thou hadst a base thought, I would rip it out,
Lie where it durst.
    Diph.   You should not; I would first   275
Mangle myself and find it.
    Mel.   That was spoke
According to our strain. Come, join thy hands,
And swear a firmness to what project I
Shall lay before thee.
    Diph.   You do wrong us both;
People hereafter shall not say, there pass'd   280
A bond, more than our loves, to tie our lives
And deaths together.
    Mel. It is as nobly said as I would wish.
Anon I'll tell you wonders: we are wrong'd.
    Diph. But I will tell you now, we'll right ourselves.   285
    Mel. Stay not: prepare the armour in my house;
And what friends you can draw unto our side,
Not knowing of the cause, make ready too.
Haste, Diphilus, the time requires it, haste!—
                                    [*Exit* Diphilus.
I hope my cause is just; I know my blood   290

Tells me it is; and I will credit it.
To take revenge, and lose myself withal,
Were idle; and to scape impossible,
Without I had the fort, which (misery!)
Remaining in the hands of my old enemy   295
Calianax——but I must have it. See,

Enter Calianax.

Where he comes shaking by me!—Good my lord,
Forget your spleen to me; I never wrong'd you,
But would have peace with every man.
    Cal.   'Tis well;
If I durst fight, your tongue would lie at quiet.   300
    Mel. Y'are touchy without all cause.
    Cal.   Do, mock me.
    Mel. By mine honour, I speak truth.
    Cal.   Honour! where is't?
    Mel. See, what starts you make
Into your idle hatred to my love
And freedom to you.   305
I come with resolution to obtain
A suit of you.
    Cal.   A suit of me!
'Tis very like it should be granted, sir.
    Mel. Nay, go not hence:
'Tis this; you have the keeping of the fort,   310
And I would wish you, by the love you ought
To bear unto me, to deliver it
Into my hands.
    Cal. I am in hope thou art mad to talk to me thus.
    Mel. But there is a reason to move you to it: 315
I would kill the King, that wrong'd you and your
    daughter.
    Cal. Out, traitor!
    Mel.   Nay, but stay: I cannot scape,

The deed once done, without I have this fort.

   Cal. And should I help thee?

Now thy treacherous mind betrays itself.   320

   Mel. Come, delay me not;

Give me a sudden answer, or already

Thy last is spoke! refuse not offer'd love,

When it comes clad in secrets.

   Cal. [*aside.*]   If I say

I will not, he will kill me; I do see't   325

Writ in his looks; and should I say I will,

He'll run and tell the King.—I do not shun

Your friendship, dear Melantius; but this cause

Is weighty: give me but an hour to think.

   Mel. Take it.—[*Aside.*] I know this goes unto the

   King;   330

But I am arm'd.—   [*Exit* Melantius.

   Cal.   Methinks I feel myself

But twenty now again. This fighting fool

Wants policy: I shall revenge my girl,

And make her red again. I pray my legs

Will last that pace that I will carry them: 335

I shall want breath before I find the King.   [*Exit.*

ACT IV

Scene I

   Enter Evadne *and Ladies: to them* Melantius.

Mel. Save you!

Evad.   Save you, sweet brother!

Mel. In my blunt eye, methinks you look Evadne.

Evad. Come, you would make me blush.

      2 look] seem, look like

Mel.   I would, Evadne;
I shall displease my ends else.

Evad. You shall, if you commend me; I am bashful. 5
Come, sir, how do I look?

Mel. I would not have your women hear me
Break into commendation of you; 'tis not seemly.

Evad. Go wait me in the gallery.— [*Exeunt Ladies.*
                              Now speak.

Mel. I'll lock your doors first.

Evad.   Why?   10

Mel. I will not have your gilded things, that dance
In visitation with their Milan skins,
Choke up my business.

Evad. You are strangely disposed, sir.

Mel. Good madam, not to make you merry.   15

Evad. No; if you praise me, 'twill make me sad.

Mel. Such a sad commendation I have for you.

Evad. Brother, the court has made you witty,
And learn to riddle.

Mel. I praise the court for't; has it learnt you
    nothing?   20

Evad. Me!

Mel. Ay, Evadne; thou art young and handsome,
A lady of a sweet complexion,
And such a flowing carriage, that it cannot
Choose but inflame a kingdom.   25

Evad. Gentle brother!

Mel. 'Tis yet in thy repentance, foolish woman,
To make me gentle.

Evad.   How is this?

Mel.   'Tis base;
And I could blush, at these years, thorough all
My honour'd scars, to come to such a parley.   30

Evad. I understand ye not.

12 Milan skins] gloves from Milan

Mel.   You dare not, fool!
They that commit thy faults fly the remembrance.
    Evad. My faults, sir! I would have you know, I care
        not
If they were written here, here in my forehead.
    Mel. Thy body is too little for the story;   35
The lusts of which would fill another woman,
Though she had twins within her.
    Evad.   This is saucy:
Look you intrude no more; there lies your way.
    Mel. Thou art my way, and I will tread upon thee,
Till I find truth out.
    Evad.   What truth is that you look for? 40
    Mel. Thy long-lost honour. Would the gods had
        set me
Rather to grapple with the plague, or stand
One of their loudest bolts! Come, tell me quickly,
Do it without enforcement, and take heed
You swell me not above my temper.
    Evad.   How, sir!   45
Where got you this report?
    Mel.   Where there was people,
In every place.
    Evad. They and the seconds of it are base people:
Believe them not, they lied.
    Mel. Do not play with mine anger, do not, wretch! 50
I come to know that desperate fool that drew thee
From thy fair life: be wise, and lay him open.
    Evad. Unhand me, and learn manners! such another
Forgetfulness forfeits your life.
    Mel. Quench me this mighty humour, and then tell
        me   55
Whose whore you are; for you are one, I know it.
Let all mine honours perish but I'll find him,
Though he lie lock'd up in thy blood! Be sudden;

There is no facing it; and be not flatter'd;
The burnt air, when the Dog reigns, is not fouler   60
Than thy contagious name, till thy repentance
(If the gods grant thee any) purge thy sickness.

    Evad. Begone! you are my brother; that's your
      safety.

    Mel. I'll be a wolf first: 'tis, to be thy brother,
An infamy below the sin of coward.   65
I am as far from being part of thee
As thou art from thy virtue: seek a kindred
'Mongst sensual beasts, and make a goat thy brother;
A goat is cooler. Will you tell me yet?

    Evad. If you stay here and rail thus, I shall tell you 70
I'll ha' you whipp'd. Get you to your command,
And there preach to your sentinels, and tell them
What a brave man you are: I shall laugh at you.

    Mel. Y'are grown a glorious whore! Where be your
      fighters?
What mortal fool durst raise thee to this daring,   75
And I alive! By my just sword, h'ad safer
Bestrid a billow when the angry North
Ploughs up the sea, or made Heaven's fire his foe!
Work me no higher. Will you discover yet?

    Evad. The fellow's mad. Sleep, and speak sense.   80

    Mel. Force my swoln heart no further: I would save
      thee.
Your great maintainers are not here, they dare not:
Would they were all, and armed! I would speak loud;
Here's one should thunder to 'em. Will you tell me?—
Thou hast no hope to scape: he that dares most,   85
And damns away his soul to do thee service,
Will sooner snatch meat from a hungry lion
Than come to rescue thee; thou hast death about
    thee;—

    60 Dog] Sirius, the Dog-star   74 glorious] ostentatious

He has undone thine honour, poison'd thy virtue,
And, of a lovely rose, left thee a canker.   90
    Evad. Let me consider.
    Mel.   Do, whose child thou wert,
Whose honour thou hast murder'd, whose grave
    open'd
And so pull'd on the gods, that in their justice
They must restore him flesh again and life,
And raise his dry bones to revenge this scandal.   95
    Evad. The gods are not of my mind: they had better
Let 'em lie sweet still in the earth; they'll stink here.
    Mel. Do you raise mirth out of my easiness?
Forsake me, then, all weaknesses of nature,
That make men women! Speak, you whore, speak
    truth,   100
Or, by the dear soul of thy sleeping father,
This sword shall be thy lover! tell, or I'll kill thee;
And, when thou hast told all, thou wilt deserve it.
    Evad. You will not murder me?
    Mel. No; 'tis justice, and a noble one,   105
To put the light out of such base offenders.
    Evad. Help!
    Mel. By thy foul self, no human help shall help thee,
If thou criest! When I have kill'd thee, as I
Have vow'd to do if thou confess not, naked,   110
As thou hast left thine honour, will I leave thee;
That on thy branded flesh the world may read
Thy black shame and my justice. Wilt thou bend yet?
    Evad. Yes.
    Mel.   Up, and begin your story.
    Evad.   Oh, I
Am miserable!
    Mel.   'Tis true, thou art. Speak truth still.   115
    Evad. I have offended: noble sir, forgive me!
    Mel. With what secure slave?

Evad.   Do not ask me, sir;
Mine own remembrance is a misery
Too mighty for me.
    Mel. Do not fall back again; my sword's unsheathed
      yet.   120
    Evad. What shall I do?
    Mel.   Be true, and make your fault less.
    Evad. I dare not tell.
    Mel. Tell, or I'll be this day a-killing thee.
    Evad. Will you forgive me, then?
    Mel. Stay; I must ask mine honour first.   125
I have too much foolish nature in me: speak.
    Evad. Is there none else here?
    Mel. None but a fearful conscience; that's too many.
Who is't?
    Evad.   Oh, hear me gently! It was the King.
    Mel. No more. My worthy father's and my services 130
Are liberally rewarded! King, I thank thee!
For all my dangers and my wounds thou hast paid me
In my own metal: these are soldiers' thanks!—
How long have you lived thus, Evadne?
    Evad.   Too long.
    Mel. Too late you find it. Can you be sorry?   135
    Evad. Would I were half as blameless!
    Mel. Evadne, thou wilt to thy trade again.
    Evad. First to my grave.
    Mel.   Would gods thou hadst been so blest!
Dost thou not hate this King now? prithee hate him:
Couldst thou not curse him? I command thee, curse
      him;   140
Curse till the gods hear, and deliver him
To thy just wishes. Yet I fear, Evadne,
You had rather play your game out.
    Evad.   No; I feel
Too many sad confusions here, to let in

Any loose flame hereafter.   145
　Mel. Dost thou not feel, amongst all those, one
　　brave anger,
That breaks out nobly and directs thine arm
To kill this base king?
　Evad.　　　　　　All the gods forbid it!
　Mel. No, all the gods require it; they are
Dishonour'd in him.   150
　Evad. 'Tis too fearful.
　Mel. Y'are valiant in his bed, and bold enough
To be a stale whore, and have your madam's name
Discourse for grooms and pages; and hereafter,
When his cool majesty hath laid you by,   155
To be at pension with some needy sir
For meat and coarser clothes: thus far you know
No fear. Come, you shall kill him.
　Evad.　　　　　　　Good sir!
　Mel. An 'twere to kiss him dead, thou'dst smother
　　him:
Be wise, and kill him. Canst thou live, and know   160
What noble minds shall make thee, see thyself
Found out with every finger, made the shame
Of all successions, and in this great ruin
Thy brother and thy noble husband broken?
Thou shalt not live thus. Kneel, and swear to help me, 165
When I shall call thee to it; or, by all
Holy in Heaven and earth, thou shalt not live
To breathe a full hour longer; not a thought!
Come, 'tis a righteous oath. Give me thy hands,
And, both to Heaven held up, swear, by that wealth 170
This lustful thief stole from thee, when I say it,
To let his foul soul out.
　Evad.　　　　　Here I swear it;
And, all you spirits of abused ladies,
Help me in this performance!

Mel. Enough. This must be known to none   175
But you and I, Evadne; not to your lord,
Though he be wise and noble, and a fellow
Dares step as far into a worthy action
As the most daring, ay, as far as justice.
Ask me not why. Farewell.   [*Exit* Melantius. 180
   Evad. Would I could say so to my black disgrace!
Oh, where have I been all this time? how friended,
That I should lose myself thus desperately,
And none for pity shew me how I wander'd?
There is not in the compass of the light   185
A more unhappy creature: sure, I am monstrous;
For I have done those follies, those mad mischiefs,
Would dare a woman. Oh, my loaded soul,
Be not so cruel to me; choke not up
The way to my repentance!

Enter Amintor.

                       Oh, my lord!   190

Amin. How now?
Evad.   My much-abused lord!   [*Kneels.*
Amin.   This cannot be!
   Evad. I do not kneel to live; I dare not hope it;
The wrongs I did are greater. Look upon me,
Though I appear with all my faults.
   Amin.   Stand up.
This is a new way to beget more sorrows: 195
Heaven knows I have too many. Do not mock me:
Though I am tame, and bred up with my wrongs,
Which are my foster-brothers, I may leap,
Like a hand-wolf, into my natural wildness,
And do an outrage: prithee, do not mock me: 200
   Evad. My whole life is so leprous, it infects

188 dare] amaze, terrify, daunt   199 hand-wolf] tamed
wolf

166

All my repentance. I would buy your pardon,
Though at the highest set; even with my life:
That slight contrition, that's no sacrifice
For what I have committed.
    Amin.   Sure, I dazzle: 205
There cannot be a faith in that foul woman,
That knows no god more mighty than her mischiefs.
Thou dost still worse, still number on thy faults,
To press my poor heart thus. Can I believe
There's any seed of virtue in that woman   210
Left to shoot up, that dares go on in sin
Known, and so known as thine is? Oh, Evadne,
Would there were any safety in thy sex,
That I might put a thousand sorrows off,
And credit thy repentance! but I must not: 215
Thou hast brought me to that dull calamity,
To that strange misbelief of all the world
And all things that are in it, that I fear
I shall fall like a tree, and find my grave,
Only remembering that I grieve.
    Evad.   My lord,   220
Give me your griefs: you are an innocent,
A soul as white as Heaven; let not my sins
Perish your noble youth. I do not fall here
To shadow by dissembling with my tears,
(As all say women can,) or to make less   225
What my hot will hath done, which Heaven and you
Knows to be tougher than the hand of time
Can cut from man's remembrance; no, I do not;
I do appear the same, the same Evadne,
Drest in the shames I lived in, the same monster.   230
But these are names of honour to what I am;
I do present myself the foulest creature,
Most poisonous, dangerous, and despised of men,

203 set] stake

Lerna e'er bred or Nilus. I am hell,
Till you, my dear lord, shoot your light into me,   235
The beams of your forgiveness; I am soul-sick,
And wither with the fear of one condemn'd,
Till I have got your pardon.
    Amin.   Rise, Evadne.
Those heavenly powers that put this good into thee
Grant a continuance of it! I forgive thee: 240
Make thyself worthy of it; and take heed,
Take heed, Evadne, this be serious.
Mock not the powers above, that can and dare
Give thee a great example of their justice
To all ensuing ages, if thou play'st   245
With thy repentance, the best sacrifice.
    Evad. I have done nothing good to win belief,
My life hath been so faithless. All the creatures,
Made for Heaven's honours, have their ends, and good
    ones,
All but the cozening crocodiles, false women: 250
They reign here like those plagues, those killing sores,
Men pray against; and when they die, like tales
Ill told and unbelieved, they pass away,
And go to dust forgotten. But, my lord,
Those short days I shall number to my rest   255
(As many must not see me) shall, though too late,
Though in my evening, yet perceive a will,
Since I can do no good, because a woman,
Reach constantly at something that is near it:
I will redeem one minute of my age,   260
Or, like another Niobe, I'll weep,
Till I am water.
    Amin.   I am now dissolved;
My frozen soul melts. May each sin thou hast,
Find a new mercy! Rise; I am at peace.
Hadst thou been thus, thus excellently good,   265

Before that devil-king tempted thy frailty,
Sure thou hadst made a star. Give me thy hand:
From this time I will know thee; and, as far
As honour gives me leave, be thy Amintor.
When we meet next, I will salute thee fairly,   270
And pray the gods to give thee happy days:
My charity shall go along with thee,
Though my embraces must be far from thee.
I should ha' kill'd thee, but this sweet repentance
Locks up my vengeance; for which thus I kiss thee—   275
The last kiss we must take: and would to heaven
The holy priest that gave our hands together
Had given us equal virtues! Go, Evadne;
The gods thus part our bodies. Have a care
My honour falls no farther: I am well, then.   280
    Evad. All the dear joys here, and above hereafter,
Crown thy fair soul! Thus I take leave, my lord;
And never shall you see the foul Evadne,
Till she have tried all honour'd means, that may
Set her in rest and wash her stains away.   285

                                    [*Exeunt.*

SCENE II

Hautboys play within.

Banquet. Enter King *and* Calianax.

    King. I cannot tell how I should credit this
From you, that are his enemy.
    Cal.   I am sure
He said it to me; and I'll justify it
What way he dares oppose—but with my sword.
    King. But did he break, without all circumstance,   5
To you his foe, that he would have the fort,

heading *Banquet*] dessert and wines   3 justify] prove

                         169

To kill me, and then scape?
 Cal.   If he deny it,
I'll make him blush.
 King.   It sounds incredibly.
 Cal. Ay, so does every thing I say of late.
 King. Not so, Calianax.
 Cal.   Yes, I should sit 10
Mute whilst a rogue with strong arms cuts your
  throat.
 King. Well, I will try him: and, if this be true,
I'll pawn my life I'll find it; if 't be false,
And that you clothe your hate in such a lie,
You shall hereafter dote in your own house, 15
Not in the court.
 Cal.   Why, if it be a lie,
Mine ears are false, for I'll be sworn I heard it.
Old men are good for nothing: you were best
Put me to death for hearing, and free him
For meaning it. You would a trusted me 20
Once, but the time is alter'd.
 King. .   And will still,
Where I may do with justice to the world:
You have no witness.
 Cal.   Yes, myself.
 King.   No more,
I mean, there were that heard it.
 Cal.   How? no more!
Would you have more? why, am not I enough 25
To hang a thousand rogues?
 King.   But so you may
Hang honest men too, if you please.
 Cal.   I may!
'Tis like I will do so: there are a hundred
Will swear it for a need too, if I say it——

20 a] have (*cf.* v. iii. 24)

King. Such witnesses we need not.
Cal.   And 'tis hard   30
If my word cannot hang a boisterous knave.
King. Enough.—Where's Strato?

Enter Strato.

Stra. Sir?
King. Why, where's all the company? Call Amintor
  in;
Evadne. Where's my brother, and Melantius?   35
Bid him come too; and Diphilus. Call all
That are without there.—   [*Exit* Strato.
              If he should desire
The combat of you, 'tis not in the power
Of all our laws to hinder it, unless
We mean to quit 'em.
Cal.   Why, if you do think   40
'Tis fit an old man and a councillor
To fight for what he says, then you may grant it.

Enter Amintor, Evadne, Melantius, Diphilus,
      Lysippus, Cleon, Strato, *and* Diagoras.

King. Come, sirs!—Amintor, thou art yet a bride-
  groom,
And I will use thee so; thou shalt sit down.—
Evadne, sit;—and you, Amintor, too;   45
This banquet is for you, sir.—Who has brought
A merry tale about him, to raise laughter
Amongst our wine? Why, Strato, where art thou?
Thou wilt chop out with them unseasonably,
When I desire 'em not.   50
Stra. 'Tis my ill luck, sir, so to spend them, then.
King. Reach me a bowl of wine.—Melantius, thou
Art sad.
Mel. I should be, sir, the merriest here,

40 quit] desert

171

But I ha' ne'er a story of mine own
Worth telling at this time.
    King.   Give me the wine.—   55
Melantius, I am now considering
How easy 'twere for any man we trust
To poison one of us in such a bowl.
    Mel. I think it were not hard, sir, for a knave.
    Cal. [*aside.*] Such as you are.   60
    King. I'faith, 'twere easy. It becomes us well
To get plain-dealing men about ourselves;
Such as you all are here.—Amintor, to thee;
And to thy fair Evadne!   [*Drinks.*
    Mel. [*apart to Cal.*]   Have you thought
Of this, Calianax?
    Cal.   Yes, marry, have I.   65
    Mel. And what's your resolution?
    Cal.   Ye shall have it,—
[*Aside.*] Soundly, I warrant you.
    King. Reach to Amintor, Strato.
    Amin.   Here, my love;
        [*Drinks, and then hands the cup to* Evadne.
This wine will do thee wrong, for it will set
Blushes upon thy cheeks; and, till thou dost   70
A fault, 'twere pity.
    King.   Yet I wonder much
At the strange desperation of these men,
That dare attempt such acts here in our state:
He could not scape that did it.
    Mel. Were he known, unpossible.   75
    King. It would be known, Melantius.
    Mel. It ought to be. If he got then away,
He must wear all our lives upon his sword:
He need not fly the island; he must leave
No one alive.

    66 have it] *pun on* (*a*) have the fort *and* (*b*) 'catch it'

King.   No; I should think no man   80
Could kill me, and scape clear, but that old man.
   Cal. But I! heaven bless me! I! should I, my liege?
   King. I do not think thou wouldst; but yet thou
    mightst,
For thou hast in thy hands the means to scape,
By keeping of the fort.—He has, Melantius,   85
And he has kept it well.
   Mel.   From cobwebs, sir,
'Tis clean swept: I can find no other art
In keeping of it now; 'twas ne'er besieged
Since he commanded.
   Cal.   I shall be sure
Of your good word: but I have kept it safe   90
From such as you.
   Mel.   Keep your ill temper in:
I speak no malice; had my brother kept it,
I should ha' said as much.
   King.   You are not merry,
Brother, drink wine. Sit you all still.—Calianax,
                        [*Apart to him.*
I cannot trust this: I have thrown out words,   95
That would have fetch'd warm blood upon the cheeks
Of guilty men, and he is never moved;
He knows no such thing.
   Cal.   Impudence may scape,
When feeble virtue is accused.
   King.   A' must,
If he were guilty, feel an alteration   100
At this our whisper, whilst we point at him:
You see he does not.
   Cal.   Let him hang himself:
What care I what he does? this he did say.
   King. Melantius, you can easily conceive
What I have meant; for men that are in fault   105

Can subtiy apprehend when others aim
At what they do amiss: but I forgive
Freely before this man,—Heaven do so too!
I will not touch thee, so much as with shame
Of telling it. Let it be so no more.   110
  Cal. Why, this is very fine!
  Mel.   I cannot tell
What 'tis you mean; but I am apt enough
Rudely to thrust into an ignorant fault.
But let me know it: happily 'tis nought
But misconstruction; and, where I am clear,   115
I will not take forgiveness of the gods,
Much less of you.
  King.   Nay, if you stand so stiff,
I shall call back my mercy.
  Mel.   I want smoothness
To thank a man for pardoning of a crime
I never knew.   120
  King. Not to instruct your knowledge, but to shew
    you
My ears are every where; you meant to kill me,
And get the fort to scape.
  Mel.   Pardon me, sir;
My bluntness will be pardon'd. You preserve
A race of idle people here about you,   125
Facers and talkers, to defame the worth
Of those that do things worthy. The man that utter'd
    this
Had perish'd without food, be't who it will,
But for this arm, that fenced him from his foe:
And if I thought you gave a faith to this,   130
The plainness of my nature would speak more.
Give me a pardon (for you ought to do't)
To kill him that spake this.

     126 Facers] shameless people

Cal. [*aside.*]   Ay, that will be
The end of all: then I am fairly paid
For all my care and service.—

Mel.   That old man,   135
Who calls me enemy, and of whom I
(Though I will never match my hate so low)
Have no good thought, would yet, I think, excuse me,
And swear he thought me wrong'd in this.

Cal.   Who, I?
Thou shameless fellow! didst thou not speak to me   140
Of it thyself?

Mel.   Oh, then, it came from him!

Cal. From me! who should it come from but from
    me?

Mel. Nay, I believe your malice is enough:
But I ha' lost my anger.—Sir, I hope
You are well satisfied.

King.   Lysippus, cheer   145
Amintor and his lady: there's no sound
Comes from you; I will come and do't myself.

Amin. [*aside.*] You have done already, sir, for me, I
    thank you.

King. Melantius, I do credit this from him,
How slight soe'er you make't.

Mel.   'Tis strange you should. 150

Cal. 'Tis strange he should believe an old man's
    word,
That never lied in's life!

Mel.   I talk not to thee.—
Shall the wild words of this distemper'd man,
Frantic with age and sorrow, make a breach
Betwixt your majesty and me? 'Twas wrong   155
To hearken to him; but to credit him,
As much at least as I have power to bear.
But pardon me—whilst I speak only truth,

I may commend myself—I have bestow'd
My careless blood with you, and should be loath   160
To think an action that would make me lose
That and my thanks too. When I was a boy,
I thrust myself into my country's cause,
And did a deed that pluck'd five years from time,
And styled me man then. And for you, my king,   165
Your subjects all have fed by virtue of
My arm: this sword of mine hath plough'd the ground,
And reapt the fruit in peace;
And you yourself have lived at home in ease.
So terrible I grew, that without swords   170
My name hath fetch'd you conquest: and my heart
And limbs are still the same; my will as great
To do you service. Let me not be paid
With such a strange distrust.

    King.   Melantius,
I held it great injustice to believe   175
Thine enemy, and did not; if I did,
I do not; let that satisfy.—What, struck
With sadness all? More wine!

    Cal.   A few fine words
Have overthrown my truth. Ah, th'art a villain!

    Mel. Why, thou wert better let me have the fort: 180
                                [*Apart to him.*
Dotard, I will disgrace thee thus for ever;
There shall no credit lie upon thy words:
Think better, and deliver it.

    Cal.   My liege,
He's at me now again to do it.—Speak;
Deny it, if thou canst.—Examine him   185
Whilst he is hot, for, if he cool again,
He will forswear it.

    King.   This is lunacy,
I hope, Melantius.

Mel.   He hath lost himself
Much, since his daughter miss'd the happiness
My sister gain'd; and, though he call me foe,   190
I pity him.
   Cal.   Pity! a pox upon you!
   Mel. Mark his disorder'd words: and at the masque
Diagoras knows he raged and rail'd at me,
And call'd a lady whore, so innocent
She understood him not. But it becomes   195
Both you and me too to forgive distraction:
Pardon him, as I do.
   Cal.   I'll not speak for thee,
For all thy cunning.—If you will be safe,
Chop off his head; for there was never known
So impudent a rascal.
   King.   Some, that love him,   200
Get him to bed. Why, pity should not let
Age make itself contemptible; we must be
All old. Have him away.
   Mel.   Calianax,
The King believes you: come, you shall go home,
And rest; you ha' done well.—[*Apart to him.*] You'll
    give it up,   205
When I have used you thus a month, I hope.—
   Cal. Now, now, 'tis plain, sir; he does move me still:
He says, he knows I'll give him up the fort,
When he has used me thus a month. I am mad,
Am I not still?
   Omnes.   Ha, ha, ha!   210
   Cal. I shall be mad indeed, if you do thus.
Why should you trust a sturdy fellow there,
That has no virtue in him, (all's in his sword)
Before me? Do but take his weapons from him,
And he's an ass; and I am a very fool,   215
Both with 'em and without 'em, as you use me.

Omnes. Ha, ha, ha!

King. 'Tis well, Calianax: but if you use
This once again, I shall entreat some other
To see your offices be well discharged.—   220
Be merry, gentlemen.—It grows somewhat late.—
Amintor, thou wouldst be a-bed again.

Amin. Yes, sir.

King.   And you, Evadne.—Let me take
Thee in my arms, Melantius, and believe
Thou art, as thou deservest to be, my friend   225
Still and for ever.—Good Calianax,
Sleep soundly; it will bring thee to thyself.

                    [*Exeunt all except* Melantius *and* Calianax.

Cal. Sleep soundly! I sleep soundly now, I hope;
I could not be thus else.—How darest thou stay
Alone with me, knowing how thou hast used me?   230

Mel. You cannot blast me with your tongue, and
         that's
The strongest part you have about you.

Cal.   I
Do look for some great punishment for this;
For I begin to forget all my hate,
And take't unkindly that mine enemy   235
Should use me so extraordinarily scurvily.

Mel. I shall melt too, if you begin to take
Unkindnesses: I never meant you hurt.

Cal. Thou'lt anger me again. Thou wretched rogue,
Meant me no hurt! disgrace me with the King!   240
Lose all my offices! This is no hurt,
Is it? I prithee, what dost thou call hurt?

Mel. To poison men, because they love me not;
To call the credit of men's wives in question;
To murder children betwixt me and land;   245
This I call hurt.

Cal.   All this thou think'st is sport;

For mine is worse: but use thy will with me;
For betwixt grief and anger I could cry.
   Mel. Be wise, then, and be safe; thou may'st revenge.
   Cal. Ay, o' the King: I would revenge of thee.   250
   Mel. That you must plot yourself.
   Cal.   I am a fine plotter.
   Mel. The short is, I will hold thee with the King
In this perplexity, till peevishness
And thy disgrace have laid thee in thy grave:
But if thou wilt deliver up the fort,   255
I'll take thy trembling body in my arms,
And bear thee over dangers; thou shalt hold
Thy wonted state.
   Cal.   If I should tell the King,
Canst thou deny 't again?
   Mel.   Try, and believe.
   Cal. Nay, then, thou canst bring any thing about.   260
Melantius, thou shalt have the fort.
   Mel.   Why, well.
Here let our hate be buried; and this hand
Shall right us both. Give me thy aged breast
To compass.
   Cal.   Nay, I do not love thee yet;
I cannot well endure to look on thee;   265
And if I thought it were a courtesy,
Thou shouldst not have it. But I am disgraced;
My offices are to be ta'en away;
And, if I did but hold this fort a day,
I do believe the King would take it from me,   270
And give it thee, things are so strangely carried.
Ne'er thank me for't; but yet the King shall know
There was some such thing in't I told him of,
And that I was an honest man.
   Mel.   He'll buy
That knowledge very dearly.—   [*Re-enter* Diphilus.

Diphilus,   275

What news with thee?

Diph.   This were a night indeed
To do it in: the King hath sent for her.

Mel. She shall perform it, then.—Go, Diphilus,
And take from this good man, my worthy friend,
The fort; he'll give it thee.

Diph.   Ha' you got that?   280

Cal. Art thou of the same breed? canst thou deny
This to the King too?

Diph.   With a confidence
As great as his.

Cal.   Faith, like enough.

Mel. Away, and use him kindly.

Cal.   Touch not me;
I hate the whole strain. If thou follow me   285
A great way off, I'll give thee up the fort;
And hang yourselves.

Mel.   Begone.

Diph.   He's finely wrought.

            [*Exeunt* Calianax *and* Diphilus.

Mel. This is a night, spite of astronomers,
To do the deed in. I will wash the stain
That rests upon our house off with his blood.   290

Re-enter Amintor.

Amin. Melantius, now assist me; if thou be'st
That which thou say'st, assist me. I have lost
All my distempers, and have found a rage
So pleasing! Help me.

Mel. [*aside.*]   Who can see him thus,
And not swear vengeance?—What's the matter,
    friend?   295

Amin. Out with thy sword; and, hand in hand with
    me,

180

Rush to the chamber of this hated king,
And sink him with the weight of all his sins
To hell for ever.

Mel.   'Twere a rash attempt,
Not to be done with safety. Let your reason   300
Plot your revenge, and not your passion.

Amin. If thou refusest me in these extremes,
Thou art no friend. He sent for her to me;
By heaven, to me, myself! and, I must tell ye,
I love her as a stranger: there is worth   305
In that vild woman, worthy things, Melantius;
And she repents. I'll do't myself alone,
Though I be slain. Farewell.

Mel. [*aside.*]   He'll overthrow
My whole design with madness.—Amintor,
Think what thou dost: I dare as much as valour;   310
But 'tis the King, the King, the King, Amintor,
With whom thou fightest!—[*Aside.*] I know he's
      honest,
And this will work with him.—

Amin.   I cannot tell
What thou hast said; but thou hast charm'd my sword
Out of my hand, and left me shaking here   315
Defenceless.

Mel.   I will take it up for thee.

Amin. What a wild beast is uncollected man!
The thing that we call honour bears us all
Headlong unto sin, and yet itself is nothing.

Mel. Alas, how variable are thy thoughts!   320

Amin. Just like my fortunes. I was run to that
I purposed to have chid thee for. Some plot,
I did distrust, thou hadst against the King,
By that old fellow's carriage. But take heed;
There's not the least limb growing to a king,   325
But carries thunder in it.

Mel.   I have none
Against him.
Amin.   Why, come, then; and still remember
We may not think revenge.
Mel.   I will remember. [*Exeunt.*

ACT V

SCENE I

Enter Evadne *and a* Gentleman of the Bed-chamber.

Evad. Sir, is the King a-bed?
Gent. Madam, an hour ago.
Evad. Give me the key, then; and let none be near;
'Tis the King's pleasure.
Gent. I understand you, madam; would 'twere mine! 5
I must not wish good rest unto your ladyship.
Evad. You talk, you talk.
Gent. 'Tis all I dare do, madam; but the King
Will wake, and then, methinks—
Evad. Saving your imagination, pray, good night,
     sir.   10
Gent. A good night be it, then, and a long one,
     madam.
I am gone.   [*Exit.*

[SCENE II]

The King discovered in bed asleep.

Evad. The night grows horrible; and all about me
Like my black purpose. Oh, the conscience

[SCENE II] *As Daniel notes there is no fresh scene, but the older editors' wrong division cannot now be dropped without disturbing the numbering of scenes and lines.*

Of a lost virtue, whither wilt thou pull me?
To what things dismal as the depth of hell
Wilt thou provoke me? Let no woman dare   5
From this hour be disloyal, if her heart be flesh,
If she have blood, and can fear. 'Tis a daring
Above that desperate fool's that left his peace,
And went to sea to fight: 'tis so many sins,
An age cannot repent 'em; and so great,   10
The gods want mercy for. Yet I must through 'em:
I have begun a slaughter on my honour,
And I must end it there.—A' sleeps. Oh God,
Why give you peace to this untemperate beast,
That hath so long transgress'd you? I must kill him,   15
And I will do it bravely: the mere joy
Tells me, I merit in it. Yet I must not
Thus tamely do it, as he sleeps—that were
To rock him to another world; my vengeance
Shall take him waking, and then lay before him   20
The number of his wrongs and punishments:
I'll shape his sins like Furies, till I waken
His evil angel, his sick conscience,
And then I'll strike him dead. King, by your leave;
                      [*Ties his arms to the bed.*
I dare not trust your strength; your grace and I   25
Must grapple upon even terms no more.
So, if he rail me not from my resolution,
I shall be strong enough.—
My lord the King!—My lord!—A' sleeps,
As if he meant to wake no more.—My lord!—   30
Is he not dead already?—Sir! my lord!
   King. Who's that?
   Evad.   Oh, you sleep soundly, sir.
   King.   My dear Evadne,
I have been dreaming of thee: come to bed.
   Evad. I am come at length, sir; but how welcome?

King. What pretty new device is this, Evadne?   35
What, do you tie me to you? By my love,
This is a quaint one. Come, my dear, and kiss me;
I'll be thy Mars; to bed, my queen of love:
Let us be caught together, that the gods may see
And envy our embraces.
    Evad.   Stay, sir, stay;   40
You are too hot, and I have brought you physic
To temper your high veins.
    King. Prithee, to bed, then; let me take it warm;
There thou shalt know the state of my body better.
    Evad. I know you have a surfeited foul body;   45
And you must bleed.
    King.   Bleed!
    Evad. Ay, you shall bleed. Lie still; and, if the devil,
Your lust, will give you leave, repent. This steel
Comes to redeem the honour that you stole,
King, my fair name; which nothing but thy death   50
Can answer to the world.
    King.   How's this, Evadne?
    Evad. I am not she; nor bear I in this breast
So much cold spirit to be call'd a woman:
I am a tiger; I am any thing
That knows not pity. Stir not: if thou dost,   55
I'll take thee unprepared, thy fears upon thee,
That make thy sins look double, and so send thee
(By my revenge, I will!) to look those torments
Prepared for such black souls.
    King. Thou dost not mean this; 'tis impossible;   60
Thou art too sweet and gentle.
    Evad.   No, I am **not:**
I am as foul as thou art, and can number
As many such hells here. I was once fair,
Once I was lovely; not a blowing rose
More chastely sweet, till thou, thou, thou, foul canker, 65

(Stir not) didst poison me. I was a world of virtue,
Till your cursed court and you (Hell bless you for't!)
With your temptations on temptations
Made me give up mine honour; for which, King,
I am come to kill thee.
    King.   No!
    Evad.   I am.
    King.   Thou art not!   70
I prithee speak not these things: thou art gentle,
And wert not meant thus rugged.
    Evad.   Peace, and hear me.
Stir nothing but your tongue, and that for mercy
To those above us; by whose lights I vow,
Those blessed fires that shot to see our sin,   75
If thy hot soul had substance with thy blood,
I would kill that too; which, being past my steel,
My tongue shall reach. Thou art a shameless villain;
A thing out of the overcharge of nature,
Sent, like a thick cloud, to disperse a plague   80
Upon weak catching women; such a tyrant,
That for his lust would sell away his subjects,
Ay, all his Heaven hereafter!
    King.   Hear, Evadne,
Thou soul of sweetness, hear! I am thy king.
    Evad. Thou art my shame! Lie still; there's none
        about you,   85
Within your cries; all promises of safety
Are but deluding dreams. Thus, thus, thou foul man,
Thus I begin my vengeance!   [*Stabs him.*
    King.   Hold, Evadne!
I do command thee hold!
    Evad.   I do not mean, sir,
To part so fairly with you; we must change   90
More of these love-tricks yet.

75 fires] meteors

King.   What bloody villain
Provoked thee to this murder?
     Evad.   Thou, thou monster!
     King. Oh!
     Evad. Thou kept'st me brave at court, and whored
     me, King;
Then married me to a young noble gentleman,   95
And whored me still.
     King.   Evadne, pity me!
     Evad. Hell take me, then! This for my lord Amintor!
This for my noble brother! and this stroke
For the most wrong'd of women!   [*Kills him.*
     King.   Oh! I die.
     Evad. Die all our faults together! I forgive thee.   100
                              [*Exit.*

               Enter two of the Bed-chamber.

     1. Come, now she's gone, let's enter; the King
expects it, and will be angry.
     2. 'Tis a fine wench: we'll have a snap at her one of
these nights, as she goes from him.
     1. Content. How quickly he had done with her! I   105
see kings can do no more that way than other mortal
people.
     2. How fast he is! I cannot hear him breathe.
     1. Either the tapers give a feeble light,
Or he looks very pale.
     2.   And so he does: 110
Pray Heaven he be well! let's look.—Alas!
He's stiff, wounded, and dead! Treason, treason!
     1. Run forth and call.
     2. Treason, treason!   [*Exit.*
     1. This will be laid on us: who can believe   115
A woman could do this?

               Enter Cleon *and* Lysippus.

                              186

Cle. How now! where's the traitor?

1. Fled, fled away; but there her woeful act
Lies still.

Cle.   Her act! a woman!

Lys.   Where's the body?

1. There.   120

Lys. Farewell, thou worthy man! There were two
    bonds
That tied our loves, a brother and a king,
The least of which might fetch a flood of tears;
But such the misery of greatness is,
They have no time to mourn; then, pardon me!   125

Enter Strato.

Sirs, which way went she?

Stra.   Never follow her;
For she, alas! was but the instrument.
News is now brought in, that Melantius
Has got the fort, and stands upon the wall,
And with a loud voice calls those few that pass   130
At this dead time of night, delivering
The innocence of this act.

Lys. Gentlemen, I am your king.

Stra. We do acknowledge it.

Lys. I would I were not! Follow, all; for this   135
Must have a sudden stop.   [*Exeunt.*

SCENE III

Enter Melantius, Diphilus, *and* Calianax, *on the walls.*

Mel. If the dull people can believe I am arm'd,
(Be constant, Diphilus,) now we have time
Either to bring our banish'd honours home,
Or create new ones in our ends.

Diph.   I fear not;
My spirit lies not that way.—Courage, Calianax!   5
    Cal. Would I had any! you should quickly know it.
    Mel. Speak to the people; thou art eloquent.
    Cal. 'Tis a fine eloquence to come to the gallows:
You were born to be my end; the devil take you!
Now must I hang for company. 'Tis strange,   10
I should be old, and neither wise nor valiant.

    Enter Lysippus, Cleon, Strato, Diagoras, *and Guard.*

    Lys. See where he stands, as boldly confident
As if he had his full command about him!
    Stra. He looks as if he had the better cause, sir;
Under your gracious pardon, let me speak it.   15
Though he be mighty-spirited, and forward
To all great things, to all things of that danger
Worse men shake at the telling of, yet certainly
I do believe him noble, and this action
Rather pull'd on than sought: his mind was ever   20
As worthy as his hand.
    Lys.   'Tis my fear too.
Heaven forgive all!—Summon him, lord Cleon.
    Cle. Ho, from the walls there!
    Mel.   Worthy Cleon, welcome:
We could a wish'd you here, lord; you are honest.
    Cal. [*aside.*] Well, thou art as flattering a knave, 25
though I dare not tell thee so—
    Lys. Melantius!
    Mel. Sir?
    Lys. I am sorry that we meet thus; our old love
Never required such distance. Pray to Heaven,   30
You have not left yourself, and sought this safety
More out of fear than honour! You have lost
A noble master; which your faith, Melantius,

24 a] have *cf.* iv. ii. 20

Some think might have preserved: yet you know best.
    Cal. [*aside.*] When time was, I was mad: some that
       dares fight,   35
I hope will pay this rascal.
    Mel. Royal young man, those tears look lovely on
       thee:
Had they been shed for a deserving one,
They had been lasting monuments. Thy brother,
Whilst he was good, I call'd him King, and served him 40
With that strong faith, that most unwearied valour,
Pull'd people from the farthest sun to seek him,
And beg his friendship: I was then his soldier.
But since his hot pride drew him to disgrace me,
And brand my noble actions with his lust,   45
(That never-cured dishonour of my sister,
Base stain of whore, and, which is worse,
The joy to make it still so,) like myself,
Thus I have flung him off with my allegiance;
And stand here mine own justice, to revenge   50
What I have suffer'd in him, and this old man
Wronged almost to lunacy.
    Cal.   Who, I?
You would draw me in. I have had no wrong;
I do disclaim ye all.
    Mel.   The short is this.
'Tis no ambition to lift up myself   55
Urgeth me thus; I do desire again
To be a subject, so I may be free:
If not, I know my strength, and will unbuild
This goodly town. Be speedy, and be wise,
In a reply.
    Stra.   Be sudden, sir, to tie   60
All up again. What's done is past recall,
And past you to revenge; and there are thousands
That wait for such a troubled hour as this.

Throw him the blank.

Lys.   Melantius, write in that thy choice:
My seal is at it.   65
    Mel. It was our honours drew us to this act,
Not gain; and we will only work our pardons.
    Cal. Put my name in too.
    Diph. You disclaim'd us all, but now, Calianax.
    Cal. That's all one;   70
I'll not be hang'd hereafter by a trick:
I'll have it in.
    Mel. You shall, you shall.—
Come to the back gate, and we'll call you King,
And give you up the fort.
    Lys.   Away, away!   75

                              [*Exeunt Omnes.*

Scene IV

Enter Aspatia *in man's apparel.*

    Asp. This is my fatal hour. Heaven may forgive
My rash attempt, that causelessly hath laid
Griefs on me that will never let me rest,
And put a woman's heart into my breast.
It is more honour for you that I die;   5
For she that can endure the misery
That I have on me, and be patient too,
May live and laugh at all that you can do.

Enter Servant.

God save you, sir!
    Serv.   And you sir! What's your business?
    Asp. With you, sir, now; to do me the fair office   10
To help me to your lord.
    Serv.   What, would you serve him?

Asp. I'll do him any service; but, to haste,
For my affairs are earnest, I desire
To speak with him.
    Serv. Sir, because you are in such haste, I would be
      loath   15
Delay you longer: you can not.
    Asp. It shall become you, though, to tell your lord.
    Serv. Sir, he will speak with nobody;
But in particular, I have in charge,
About no weighty matters.
    Asp.   This is most strange.   20
Art thou gold-proof? there's for thee; help me to him.
                                      [*Gives money.*
    Serv. Pray be not angry, sir: I'll do my best.   [*Exit.*
    Asp. How stubbornly this fellow answer'd me!
There is a vild dishonest trick in man,
More than in woman. All the men I meet   25
Appear thus to me, are harsh and rude,
And have a subtilty in every thing,
Which love could never know; but we fond women
Harbour the easiest and the smoothest thoughts,
And think all shall go so. It is unjust   30
That men and women should be match'd together.

Enter Amintor *and his* Man.

    Amin. Where is he?
    Serv.   There, my lord.
    Amin.   What would you, sir?
    Asp. Please it your lordship to command your man
Out of the room, I shall deliver things
Worthy your hearing.
    Amin.   Leave us.   [*Exit* Servant.
    Asp. [*aside.*]   Oh, that that shape 35
Should bury falsehood in it!—

24 vild] vile

Amin.   Now your will, sir.

Asp. When you know me, my lord, you needs must
   guess
My business; and I am not hard to know;
For, till the chance of war mark'd this smooth face
With these few blemishes, people would call me   40
My sister's picture, and her mine. In short,
I am the brother to the wrong'd Aspatia.

   Amin. The wrong'd Aspatia! Would thou wert so
   too
Unto the wrong'd Amintor! Let me kiss
                         [*Kisses her hand.*
That hand of thine, in honour that I bear   45
Unto the wrong'd Aspatia. Here I stand
That did it.—Would he could not!—Gentle youth,
Leave me; for there is something in thy looks
That calls my sins in a most hideous form
Into my mind; and I have grief enough   50
Without thy help.

   Asp.   I would I could with credit!
Since I was twelve years old, I had not seen
My sister till this hour I now arrived:
She sent for me to see her marriage;
A woeful one! but they that are above   55
Have ends in every thing. She used few words,
But yet enough to make me understand
The baseness of the injuries you did her.
That little training I have had is war:
I may behave myself rudely in peace;   60
I would not, though. I shall not need to tell you,
I am but young, and would be loath to lose
Honour, that is not easily gain'd again.
Fairly I mean to deal: the age is strict

   47 Would . . . not] *Perhaps corrupt; or may mean* Would this
youth could not stand here (to reproach me)

For single combats; and we shall be stopp'd,   65
If it be publish'd. If you like your sword,
Use it; if mine appear a better to you,
Change; for the ground is this, and this the time,
To end our difference.
Amin.   Charitable youth,
If thou be'st such, think not I will maintain   70
So strange a wrong: and, for thy sister's sake,
Know, that I could not think that desperate thing
I durst not do; yet, to enjoy this world,
I would not see her; for, beholding thee,
I am I know not what. If I have aught   75
That may content thee, take it, and begone,
For death is not so terrible as thou;
Thine eyes shoot guilt into me.
Asp.   Thus, she swore,
Thou wouldst behave thyself, and give me words
That would fetch tears into mine eyes; and so   80
Thou dost indeed. But yet she bade me watch,
Lest I were cozen'd, and be sure to fight
Ere I return'd.
Amin.   That must not be with me.
For her I'll die directly; but against her
Will never hazard it.
Asp.   You must be urged: 85
I do not deal uncivilly with those
That dare to fight; but such a one as you
Must be used thus.   *[She strikes him.*
Amin.   I prithee, youth, take heed.
Thy sister is a thing to me so much
Above mine honour, that I can endure   90
All this—Good gods! a blow I can endure;
But stay not, lest thou draw a timeless death
Upon thyself.

   65 single combats] duels   **92** timeless] untimely

Asp.   Thou art some prating fellow;
One that has studied out a trick to talk,
And move soft-hearted people; to be kick'd,   95
                                        [*She kicks him.*
Thus to be kick'd.—[*Aside.*] Why should he be so slow
In giving me my death?—
      Amin.   A man can bear
No more, and keep his flesh. Forgive me, then!
I would endure yet, if I could. Now shew
The spirit thou pretendest, and understand   100
Thou hast no hour to live.
                    [*They fight*, Aspatia *is wounded.*
                          What dost thou mean?
Thou canst not fight: the blows thou mak'st at me
Are quite besides; and those I offer at thee,
Thou spread'st thine arms, and tak'st upon thy breast,
Alas, defenceless!
      Asp.   I have got enough,   105
And my desire. There is no place so fit
For me to die as here.   [*Falls.*

      Enter Evadne, *her hands bloody, with a knife.*

      Evad. Amintor, I am loaden with events,
That fly to make thee happy; I have joys,
That in a moment can call back thy wrongs,   110
And settle thee in thy free state again.
It is Evadne still that follows thee,
But not her mischiefs.
      Amin. Thou canst not fool me to believe again;
But thou hast looks and things so full of news,   115
That I am stay'd.
      Evad. Noble Amintor, put off thy amaze;
Let thine eyes loose, and speak. Am I not fair?
Looks not Evadne beauteous with these rites now?

  103 besides] wide of the mark   117 amaze] stupor

194

Were those hours half so lovely in thine eyes   120
When our hands met before the holy man?
I was too foul within to look fair then:
Since I knew ill, I was not free till now.
    Amin. There is presage of some important thing
About thee, which, it seems, thy tongue hath lost: 125
Thy hands are bloody, and thou hast a knife.
    Evad. In this consists thy happiness and mine:
Joy to Amintor! for the King is dead.
    Amin. Those have most power to hurt us, that we
       love;
We lay our sleeping lives within their arms.   130
Why, thou hast raised up mischief to his height,
And found one to outname thy other faults;
Thou hast no intermission of thy sins,
But all thy life is a continued ill:
Black is thy colour now, disease thy nature.   135
Joy to Amintor! Thou hast touch'd a life,
The very name of which had power to chain
Up all my rage, and calm my wildest wrongs.
    Evad. 'Tis done; and, since I could not find a way
To meet thy love so clear as through his life,   140
I cannot now repent it.
    Amin. Couldst thou procure the gods to speak to me,
To bid me love this woman and forgive,
I think I should fall out with them. Behold,
Here lies a youth whose wounds bleed in my breast,   145
Sent by his violent fate to fetch his death
From my slow hand! And, to augment my woe,
You now are present, stain'd with a king's blood
Violently shed. This keeps night here,
And throws an unknown wilderness about me.   150
    Asp. Oh, oh, oh!
    Amin. No more; pursue me not.
    Evad.   Forgive me, then,

And take me to thy bed: we may not part.
  Amin. Forbear, be wise, and let my rage go this way.
  Evad. 'Tis you that I would stay, not it.
  Amin.   Take heed; 155
It will return with me.
  Evad.   If it must be,
I shall not fear to meet it: take me home.
  Amin. Thou monster of all cruelty, forbear!
  Evad. For Heaven's sake, look more calm: thine eyes
    are sharper
Than thou canst make thy sword.
  Amin.   Away, away!   160
Thy knees are more to me than violence;
I am worse than sick to see knees follow me
For that I must not grant. For Heaven's sake, stand.
  Evad. Receive me, then.
  Amin.   I dare not stay thy language:
In midst of all my anger and my grief,   165
Thou dost awake something that troubles me,
And says, I loved thee once. I dare not stay;
There is no end of woman's reasoning.   *[Leaves her.*
  Evad. Amintor, thou shalt love me now again:
Go; I am calm. Farewell, and peace for ever!   170
Evadne, whom thou hatest, will die for thee.
                    [Kills herself.
  Amin. I have a little human nature yet,
That's left for thee, that bids me stay thy hand. *[Returns.*
  Evad. Thy hand was welcome, but it came too late.
Oh, I am lost! the heavy sleep makes haste. *[She dies.* 175
  Asp. Oh, oh, oh!
  Amin. This earth of mine doth tremble, and I feel
A stark affrighted motion in my blood;
My soul grows weary of her house, and I

161 knees] kneelings   164 stay ... language] endure ...
argument

All over am a trouble to myself.   180
There is some hidden power in these dead things,
That calls my flesh unto 'em; I am cold:
Be resolute, and bear 'em company.
There's something yet, which I am loath to leave:
There's man enough in me to meet the fears   185
That death can bring; and yet would it were done!
I can find nothing in the whole discourse
Of death, I durst not meet the boldest way;
Yet still, betwixt the reason and the act,
The wrong I to Aspatia did stands up;   190
I have not such another fault to answer:
Though she may justly arm herself with scorn
And hate of me, my soul will part less troubled,
When I have paid to her in tears my sorrow:
I will not leave this act unsatisfied,   195
If all that's left in me can answer it.
    Asp. Was it a dream? there stands Amintor still;
Or I dream still.
    Amin. How dost thou? speak; receive my love and
        help.
Thy blood climbs up to his old place again;   200
There's hope of thy recovery.
    Asp. Did you not name Aspatia?
    Amin.   I did.
    Asp. And talk'd of tears and sorrow unto her?
    Amin. 'Tis true; and, till these happy signs in thee
Did stay my course, 'twas thither I was going.   205
    Asp. Thou art there already, and these wounds are
        hers:
Those threats I brought with me sought not revenge,
But came to fetch this blessing from thy hand:
I am Aspatia yet.
    Amin. Dare my soul ever look abroad again?   210
    Asp. I shall sure live, Amintor; I am well;

A kind of healthful joy wanders within me.

Amin. The world wants lives to expiate thy loss;
Come, let me bear thee to some place of help.

Asp. Amintor, thou must stay; I must rest here;   215
My strength begins to disobey my will.
How dost thou, my best soul? I would fain live
Now, if I could: wouldst thou have loved me, then?

Amin. Alas,
All that I am's not worth a hair from thee!   220

Asp. Give me thine hand; mine hands grope up and
    down,
And cannot find thee; I am wondrous sick:
Have I thy hand, Amintor?

Amin. Thou greatest blessing of the world, thou hast.

Asp. I do believe thee better than my sense.   225
Oh, I must go! farewell!   [*Dies.*

Amin. She sounds.—Aspatia!—Help! for Heaven's
    sake, water,
Such as may chain life ever to this frame!—
Aspatia, speak!—What, no help yet? I fool;
I'll chafe her temples. Yet there's nothing stirs: 230
Some hidden power tell her, Amintor calls,
And let her answer me!—Aspatia, speak!—
I have heard, if there be any life, but bow
The body thus, and it will shew itself.
Oh, she is gone! I will not leave her yet.   235
Since out of justice we must challenge nothing,
I'll call it mercy, if you'll pity me,
You heavenly powers, and lend forth some few years
The blessed soul to this fair seat again!
No comfort comes; the gods deny me too.   240
I'll bow the body once again.—Aspatia!—
The soul is fled for ever; and I wrong
Myself, so long to lose her company.

227 sounds] swoons   233 bow] bend

Must I talk now? Here's to be with thee, love!

[*Kills himself.*

Enter Servant.

Serv. This is a great grace to my lord, to have the   245
new king come to him: I must tell him he is entering.
—Oh, God!—Help, help!

Enter Lysippus, Melantius, Calianax, Cleon,
Diphilus, Strato.

Lys. Where's Amintor?
Serv. Oh, there, there!
Lys. How strange is this!   250
Cal. What should we do here?
Mel. These deaths are such acquainted things with
    me,
That yet my heart dissolves not. May I stand
Stiff here for ever! Eyes, call up your tears!
This is Amintor: heart, he was my friend;   255
Melt! now it flows.—Amintor, give a word
To call me to thee.
Amin. Oh!
Mel. Melantius calls his friend Amintor. Oh,
Thy arms are kinder to me than thy tongue!   260
Speak, speak!
Amin. What?
Mel. That little word was worth all the sounds
That ever I shall hear again.
Diph.   Oh, brother,
Here lies your sister slain! you lose yourself   265
In sorrow there.
Mel.   Why, Diphilus, it is
A thing to laugh at, in respect of this:
Here was my sister, father, brother, son;
All that I had.—Speak once again; what youth
Lies slain there by thee?

Amin.   'Tis Aspatia.   270
My last is said. Let me give up my soul
Into thy bosom.   [*Dies.*

   Cal. What's that? what's that? Aspatia!

   Mel. I never did
Repent the greatness of my heart till now;   275
It will not burst at need.

   Cal. My daughter dead here too! And you have all
fine new tricks to grieve; but I ne'er knew any but
direct crying.

   Mel. I am a prattler: but no more.
                              [*Offers to kill himself.*
   Diph.   Hold, brother! 280

   Lys. Stop him.

   Diph. Fie, how unmanly was this offer in you!
Does this become our strain?

   Cal. I know not what the matter is, but I am grown
very kind, and am friends with you all now. You have 285
given me that among you will kill me quickly; but
I'll go home, and live as long as I can.   [*Exit.*

   Mel. His spirit is but poor that can be kept
From death for want of weapons.
Is not my hands a weapon good enough   290
To stop my breath? or, if you tie down those,
I vow, Amintor, I will never eat,
Or drink, or sleep, or have to do with that
That may preserve life! This I swear to keep.

   Lys. Look to him, though, and bear those bodies in. 295
May this a fair example be to me,
To rule with temper; for on lustful kings
Unlook'd-for sudden deaths from Heaven are sent;
But cursed is he that is their instrument.

FINIS

282 offer] attempt.

The Duchess of Malfi

BY

JOHN WEBSTER

JOHN WEBSTER (1580?–1635)

The Duchess of Malfi

Acted perhaps in 1613 or 1614; printed in 1623, second
quarto 1640 and third quarto 1678, both with amend-
ments and mistakes, and the present text taken from the
first quarto.

[*Complete Works*, ed. F. L. Lucas, 4 vols., 1927, 1967;
The Duchess of Malfi, ed. F. L. Lucas with some revisions,
printed separately 1958; ed. Elizabeth Brennan, 1964
(New Mermaid); ed. J. R. Brown, 1964 (Revels Plays);
the first quarto reprinted in facsimile 1968 (Scolar Press).]

THE
TRAGEDY

OF THE DVTCHESSE
Of Malfy.

As it was Presented priuatly, at the Black-
Friers; and publiquely at the Globe, By the
Kings Maiesties Seruants.

The perfect and exact Coppy, with diuerse
things Printed, that the length of the Play would
not beare in the Presentment.

VVritten by *John Webster.*

Hora.——— *Si quid*----
———*Candidus Imperti si non his vtere mecum.*

LONDON:

Printed by N I C H O L A S O K E S, for I O H N
W A T E R S O N, and are to be sold at the
signe of the Crowne, in *Paules*
Church-yard, 1 6 2 3.

THE ACTORS' NAMES

BOSOLA, *J. Lowin.*
FERDINAND, 1 *R. Burbage.* 2 *J. Taylor*
CARDINAL, 1 *H. Condell.* 2 *R. Robinson.*
ANTONIO, 1 *W. Ostler.* 2 *R. Benfeild.*
DELIO, *J. Underwood.*
FOROBOSCO, *N. Tooley.*
MALATESTE.
The Marquess of PESCARA, *J. Rice.*
CASTRUCHIO.
RODERIGO.
GRISOLAN.
The several mad men, N. Tooley, J. Underwood, &c.
The DUCHESS, *R. Sharpe.*
The CARDINAL's *Mistress, J. Tomson.*
The DOCTOR,   ⎫
CARIOLA,   ⎬ *R. Pallant.*
COURT OFFICERS.   ⎭
Old Lady.
Three young Children.
Two Pilgrims.
Ladies, Executioners, and Attendants.

Actors' Names] *From the original, completed by Lucas. Where two actors are given the first was presumably the creator of the part and the second replaced him at a revival. All are well-known members of the King's Players, and many appear again in the list of* The Roman Actor

TO THE RIGHT
HONORABLE, *GEORGE*
HARDING, *Baron* Berkeley *of* Berkeley
Castle, and Knight of the Order of the *Bath*
to the Illustrious Prince CHARLES   5

My Noble Lord,

That I may present my excuse why, being a stranger
to your Lordship, I offer this poem to your patronage,
I plead this warrant: men who never saw the sea, yet
desire to behold that regiment of waters, choose some   10
eminent river to guide them thither, and make that,
as it were, their conduct or postilion. By the like
ingenious means has your fame arrived at my knowledge, receiving it from some of worth who both in
contemplation and practice owe to your Honour their   15
clearest service. I do not altogether look up at your
title, the ancien'st nobility being but a relic of time
past, and the truest honour indeed being for a man to
confer honour on himself, which your learning strives
to propagate, and shall make you arrive at the dignity   20
of a great example. I am confident this work is not
unworthy your Honour's perusal, for by such poems
as this poets have kiss'd the hands of great princes, and
drawn their gentle eyes to look down upon their sheets
of paper, when the poets themselves were bound up   25
in their winding-sheets. The like courtesy from your
Lordship shall make you live in your grave, and laurel

Dedication. 2–3 *George Harding*] 13th Baron Berkeley (1601–
58), a discriminating patron of letters, to whom Burton dedicated
The Anatomy of Melancholy in 1621 and Massinger *The Renegado*
in 1630   17 ancien'st nobility] *The Complete Peerage
traces the descent from* 1066

spring out of it, when the ignorant scorners of the Muses (that like worms in libraries seem to live only to destroy learning) shall wither, neglected and for- 30 gotten. This work and myself I humbly present to your approved censure, it being the utmost of my wishes to have your Honorable self my weighty and perspicuous comment; which grace so done me shall ever be acknowledged 35

> By your Lordship's
> in all duty and
> observance,
> *John Webster.*

32 approved censure] tried judgement

The dedication is followed by complimentary verses signed by the dramatists Thomas Middleton, William Rowley, and John Ford, with all of whom Webster wrote plays in collaboration.

ACTUS PRIMUS, SCENA PRIMA

Enter Antonio *and* Delio.

Delio. You are welcome to your country, dear
    Antonio;
You have been long in France, and you return
A very formal Frenchman, in your habit.
How do you like the French court?

Ant.   I admire it—
In seeking to reduce both state and people   5
To a fix'd order, their judicious king
Begins at home; quits first his royal palace
Of flatt'ring sycophants, of dissolute
And infamous persons,—which he sweetly terms
His Master's master-piece, the work of heaven;   10
Considering duly that a prince's court
Is like a common fountain, whence should flow
Pure silver drops in general, but if't chance
Some curs'd example poison't near the head,
Death and diseases through the whole land spread.   15
And what is't makes this blessed government
But a most provident Council, who dare freely
Inform him the corruption of the times?
Though some o' th' court hold it presumption
To instruct princes what they ought to do,   20
It is a noble duty to inform them
What they ought to foresee.—Here comes Bosola,
                          [*Enter* Bosola.
The only court-gall; yet I observe his railing
Is not for simple love of piety:
Indeed, he rails at those things which he wants;   25
Would be as lecherous, covetous, or proud,

3 formal] punctilious   habit] dress   13 in general] everywhere   23 gall] sore

207

Bloody, or envious, as any man,
If he had means to be so.—Here's the cardinal.

[*Enter* Cardinal.

Bos. I do haunt you still.

Card. So.   30

Bos. I have done you better service than to be slighted thus. Miserable age, where only the reward of doing well is the doing of it!

Card. You enforce your merit too much.

Bos. I fell into the galleys in your service, where, for   35
two years together, I wore two towels instead of a shirt, with a knot on the shoulder, after the fashion of a Roman mantle. Slighted thus! I will thrive some way: black-birds fatten best in hard weather; why not I, in these dog-days?   40

Card. Would you could become honest!

Bos. With all your divinity, do but direct me the way to it. I have known many travel far for it, and yet return as arrant knaves as they went forth, because they carried themselves always along with them.   45

[*Exit* Cardinal.

Are you gone? Some fellows, they say, are possessed with the devil, but this great fellow were able to possess the greatest devil, and make him worse.

Ant. He hath denied thee some suit?

Bos. He and his brother are like plum-trees that   50
grow crooked over standing pools; they are rich and o'erladen with fruit, but none but crows, pies, and caterpillars feed on them. Could I be one of their flatt'ring panders, I would hang on their ears like a horseleech, till I were full, and then drop off. I pray,   55
leave me.

Who would rely upon these miserable dependences,

34 enforce] praise, insist on   57 dependences] ap-
pointments in reversion (*on the death of the holder*)

in expectation to be advanc'd to-morrow? what creature
ever fed worse than hoping Tantalus? nor ever died
any man more fearfully than he that hop'd for a pardon. 60
There are rewards for hawks and dogs when they have
done us service; but for a soldier, that hazards his
limbs in a battle, nothing but a kind of geometry is his
last supportation.

Delio. Geometry?   65

Bos. Ay, to hang in a fair pair of slings, take his latter
swing in the world upon an honourable pair of crutches,
from hospital to hospital—Fare ye well, sir. And yet
do not you scorn us, for places in the court are but like
beds in the hospital, where this man's head lies at that 70
man's foot, and so lower and lower.   [*Exit.*

Delio. I knew this fellow seven years in the galleys
For a notorious murther, and 'twas thought
The cardinal suborn'd it: he was releas'd
By the French general, Gaston de Foix,   75
When he recover'd Naples.

Ant.   'Tis great pity
He should be thus neglected: I have heard
He's very valiant. This foul melancholy
Will poison all his goodness, for (I'll tell you)
If too immoderate sleep be truly said   80
To be an inward rust unto the soul,
It then doth follow want of action
Breeds all black malcontents, and their close rearing
(Like moths in cloth) do hurt for want of wearing.

Enter Silvio, Castruchio, Roderigo, *and* Grisolan.

Delio. The presence 'gins to fill; you promis'd me   85
To make me the partaker of the natures
Of some of your great courtiers.

Ant.   The Lord Cardinal's

83 close] secret

And other strangers' that are now in court?
I shall.—Here comes the great Calabrian Duke.

                                     [Enter Ferdinand.

Ferd. Who took the ring oftenest?   90
Sil. Antonio Bologna, my lord.
Ferd. Our sister duchess' great-master of her household? give him the jewel.—When shall we leave this sportive action, and fall to action indeed?
Cast. Methinks, my lord, you should not desire to 95 go to war in person.
Ferd. Now for some gravity!—why, my lord?
Cast. It is fitting a soldier arise to be a prince, but not necessary a prince descend to be a captain.
Ferd. No?   100
Cast. No, my lord, he were far better do it by a deputy.
Ferd. Why should he not as well sleep, or eat, by a deputy? This might take idle, offensive, and base office from him, whereas the other deprives him of honour. 105
Cast. Believe my experience: that realm is never long in quiet, where the ruler is a soldier.
Ferd. Thou told'st me thy wife could not endure fighting.
Cast. True, my lord.   110
Ferd. And of a jest she broke, of a captain she met full of wounds—I have forgot it.
Cast. She told him, my lord, he was a pitiful fellow, to lie, like the children of Ismael, all in tents.
Ferd. Why, there's a wit were able to undo all the 115 chirurgeons o' the city, for although gallants should quarrel, and had drawn their weapons, and were ready to go to it, yet her persuasions would make them put up.

   111 broke, of] made about   114 tents] *pun on (a)* ordinary sense *and (b)* surgical dressings   116 chirurgeons] surgeons 118 put up] sheath *(their weapons)*

Cast. That she would, my lord.—How do you like
my Spanish jennet?   120

Rod. He is all fire.

Ferd. I am of Pliny's opinion, I think he was begot
by the wind; he runs as if he were ballass'd with quick-
silver.

Sil. True, my lord, he reels from the tilt often.   125

Rod., Gris. Ha, ha, ha!

Ferd. Why do you laugh? methinks you that are
courtiers should be my touch-wood, take fire when I
give fire; that is, laugh when I laugh, were the subject
never so witty—   130

Cast. True, my lord, I myself have heard a very good
jest, and have scorn'd to seem to have so silly a wit
as to understand it.

Ferd. But I can laugh at your fool, my lord.

Cast. He cannot speak, you know, but he makes 135
faces: my lady cannot abide him.

Ferd. No?

Cast. Nor endure to be in merry company; for she
says too much laughing, and too much company, fills
her too full of the wrinkle.   140

Ferd. I would, then, have a mathematical instrument made for her face, that she might not laugh out
of compass.—I shall shortly visit you at Milan, Lord
Silvio.

Sil. Your grace shall arrive most welcome.   145

Ferd. You are a good horseman, Antonio: you have
excellent riders in France: what do you think of good
horsemanship?

Ant. Nobly, my lord: as out of the Grecian horse
issued many famous princes, so out of brave horseman- 150
ship arise the first sparks of growing resolution, that
raise the mind to noble action.

123 ballass'd] ballasted   129 when I laugh] *sc. and only then*

Ferd. You have bespoke it worthily.

Sil. Your brother, the Lord Cardinal, and sister Duchess.   155

Enter Cardinal, Duchess, Cariola, *and* Julia.

Card. Are the galleys come about?

Gris. They are, my lord.

Ferd. Here's the Lord Silvio is come to take his leave.

Delio. Now, sir, your promise: what's that Cardinal? 160
I mean his temper? they say he's a brave fellow,
Will play his five thousand crowns at tennis, dance,
Court ladies, and one that hath fought single combats.

Ant. Some such flashes superficially hang on him,
for form; but, observe his inward character, he is a 165
melancholy churchman; the spring in his face is
nothing but the engend'ring of toads; where he is
jealous of any man, he lays worse plots for them than
ever was impos'd on Hercules, for he strews in his
way flatterers, panders, intelligencers, atheists, and a 170
thousand such political monsters. He should have been
Pope; but instead of coming to it by the primitive
decency of the church, he did bestow bribes so largely
and so impudently as if he would have carried it away
without heaven's knowledge. Some good he hath 175
done——

Delio. You have given too much of him. What's his
      brother?

Ant. The Duke there? a most perverse and turbu-
      lent nature:
What appears in him mirth is merely outside;
If he laught heartily, it is to laugh   180
All honesty out of fashion.

Delio.   Twins?

168 jealous (*a common spelling*)

Ant. In quality.
He speaks with others' tongues, and hears men's suits
With others' ears; will seem to sleep o' th' bench
Only to entrap offenders in their answers;
Dooms men to death by information;   185
Rewards by hearsay.
    Delio. Then the law to him
Is like a foul black cobweb to a spider—
He makes it his dwelling and a prison
To entangle those shall feed him.
    Ant. Most true:
He ne'er pays debts, unless they be shrewd turns,   190
And those he will confess that he doth owe.
Last, for his brother there, the Cardinal,
They that do flatter him most say oracles
Hang at his lips; and verily I believe them,
For the devil speaks in them.   195
But for their sister, the right noble Duchess,
You never fix'd your eye on three fair medals
Cast in one figure, of so different temper.
For her discourse, it is so full of rapture,
You only will begin then to be sorry   200
When she doth end her speech, and wish, in wonder,
She held it less vain-glory to talk much,
Than your penance to hear her: whilst she speaks,
She throws upon a man so sweet a look,
That it were able to raise one to a galliard   205
That lay in a dead palsy, and to dote
On that sweet countenance; but in that look
There speaketh so divine a continence
As cuts off all lascivious and vain hope.
Her days are practis'd in such noble virtue,   210
That sure her nights, nay, more, her very sleeps,
Are more in heaven than other ladies' shrifts.

         205 galliard] lively dance

Let all sweet ladies break their flatt'ring glasses,
And dress themselves in her.
  Delio.   Fie, Antonio,
You play the wire-drawer with her commendations. 215
  Ant. I'll case the picture up: only thus much—
All her particular worth grows to this sum:
She stains the time past, lights the time to come.
  Cari. You must attend my lady in the gallery,
Some half an hour hence.   220
  Ant. I shall.   [*Exeunt* Antonio *and* Delio.
  Ferd. Sister, I have a suit to you.
  Duch.   To me, sir?
  Ferd. A gentleman here, Daniel de Bosola,
One that was in the galleys——
  Duch.   Yes, I know him.—
  Ferd. A worthy fellow he is: pray, let me entreat for 225
The provisorship of your horse.
  Duch.   Your knowledge of him
Commends him and prefers him.
  Ferd.   Call him hither.
           [*Exit* Attendant.
We now are upon parting. Good Lord Silvio,
Do us commend to all our noble friends
At the leaguer.
  Sil.   Sir, I shall.
  Ferd.   You are for Milan? 230
  Sil. I am.
  Duch. Bring the caroches.—We'll bring you down
to the haven.
      [*Exeunt except* Cardinal *and* Ferdinand.
  Card. Be sure you entertain that Bosola
For your intelligence: I would not be seen in't; 235
And therefore many times I have slighted him
When he did court our furtherance, as this morning.

 230 leaguer] camp 232 caroches] coaches bring] escort

Ferd. Antonio, the great-master of her household,
Had been far fitter.

Card.   You are deceiv'd in him
His nature is too honest for such business.—   240
He comes: I'll leave you.   [*Exit.*

Enter Bosola.

Bos.   I was lur'd to you.
Ferd. My brother, here, the Cardinal could never
Abide you.

Bos.   Never since he was in my debt.
Ferd. May be some oblique character in your face
Made him suspect you?

Bos.   Doth he study physiognomy? 245
There's no more credit to be given to th' face
Than to a sick man's urine, which some call
The physician's whore because she cozens him.
He did suspect me wrongfully.

Ferd.   For that
You must give great men leave to take their times.   250
Distrust doth cause us seldom be deceiv'd;
You see the oft shaking of the cedar-tree
Fastens it more at root.

Bos.   Yet, take heed;
For to suspect a friend unworthily
Instructs him the next way to suspect you,   255
And prompts him to deceive you.

Ferd.   There's gold.
Bos.   So:
What follows? (never rain'd such show'rs as these
Without thunderbolts i' th' tail of them;) whose throat
    must I cut?
Ferd. Your inclination to shed blood rides post
Before my occasion to use you. I give you that   260

255 next] nearest

215

To live i' th' court here, and observe the duchess:
To note all the particulars of her haviour,
What suitors do solicit her for marriage,
And whom she best affects. She's a young widow:
I would not have her marry again.

  Bos.   No, sir?   265
  Ferd. Do not you ask the reason; but be satisfied,
I say I would not.
  Bos.   It seems you would create me
One of your familiars.
  Ferd.   Familiar! what's that?
  Bos. Why, a very quaint invisible devil in flesh,—
An intelligencer.
  Ferd.   Such a kind of thriving thing   270
I would wish thee; and ere long thou mayst arrive
At a higher place by't.
  Bos.   Take your devils,
Which hell calls angels: these curs'd gifts would make
You a corrupter, me an impudent traitor:
And should I take these, they'ld take me to hell.   275
  Ferd. Sir, I'll take nothing from you that I have
     given:
There is a place that I procur'd for you
This morning, the provisorship o' the horse;
Have you heard on't?
  Bos.   No.
  Ferd.   'Tis yours, is't not worth thanks?
  Bos. I would have you curse yourself now, that your
     bounty   280
(Which makes men truly noble) e'er should make me
A villain. Oh, that to avoid ingratitude
For the good deed you have done me, I must do
All the ill man can invent! Thus the devil
Candies all sins o'er; and what heaven terms vild,   285

    273 angels] *gold coins*   285 vild] vile

That names he complimental.

Ferd.   Be yourself;
Keep your old garb of melancholy; 'twill express
You envy those that stand above your reach,
Yet strive not to come near 'em: this will gain
Access to private lodgings, where yourself   290
May, like a politic dormouse——

Bos.   As I have seen some
Feed in a lord's dish, half asleep, not seeming
To listen to any talk; and yet these rogues
Have cut his throat in a dream. What's my place?
The provisorship o' the horse? say, then, my corrup-
   tion   295
Grew out of horse-dung: I am your creature.

Ferd. Away!

Bos. Let good men, for good deeds, covet good fame,
Since place and riches oft are bribes of shame:
Sometimes the devil doth preach.   [*Exit* Bosola. 300

Enter Cardinal, Duchess, *and* Cariola.

Card. We are to part from you; and your own discretion
Must now be your director.

Ferd.   You are a widow:
You know already what man is; and therefore
Let not youth, high promotion, eloquence——

Card. No, nor anything without the addition,
   honour,   305
Sway your high blood.

Ferd.   Marry! they are most luxurious
Will wed twice.

Card.   Oh, fie!

Ferd.   Their livers are more spotted
Than Laban's sheep.

306 luxurious] lustful

Duch.   Diamonds are of most value,
They say, that have pass'd through most jewellers'
    hands.
Ferd. Whores, by that rule, are precious.
Duch.   Will you hear me? 310
I'll never marry—
Card.   So most widows say;
But commonly that motion lasts no longer
Than the turning of an hour-glass—the funeral sermon
And it, end both together.
Ferd.   Now hear me:
You live in a rank pasture here, i' th' court;   315
There is a kind of honey-dew that's deadly;
'Twill poison your fame; look to't: be not cunning;
For they whose faces do belie their hearts
Are witches, ere they arrive at twenty years,
Ay, and give the devil suck.
Duch.   This is terrible good counsel— 320
Ferd. Hypocrisy is woven of a fine small thread,
Subtler than Vulcan's engine: yet, believe't,
Your darkest actions, nay, your privat'st thoughts,
Will come to light—
Card.   You may flatter yourself,
And take your own choice; privately be married   325
Under the eaves of night——
Ferd.   Think't the best voyage
That e'er you made; like the irregular crab,
Which, though't goes backward, thinks that it goes
    right,
Because it goes its own way: but observe,
Such weddings may more properly be said   330
To be executed than celebrated.
Card.   The marriage night

322 Vulcan's engine] *the net in which he caught Mars and
Venus in adultery*

Is the entrance into some prison.

Ferd.   And those joys,
Those lustful pleasures, are like heavy sleeps
Which do fore-run man's mischief.

Card.   Fare you well.
Wisdom begins at the end: remember it.   [*Exit.* 335

  Duch. I think this speech between you both was
    studied,
It came so roundly off.

  Ferd.   You are my sister;
This was my father's poniard, do you see?
I'ld be loth to see't look rusty, 'cause 'twas his.
I would have you give o'er these chargeable revels: 340
A visor and a mask are whispering-rooms
That were never built for goodness;—fare ye
    well;—
And women like that part which, like the lamprey,
Hath ne'er a bone in't.

  Duch.   Fie, sir!

  Ferd.   Nay,
I mean the tongue; variety of courtship: 345
What cannot a neat knave with a smooth tale
Make a woman believe? Farewell, lusty widow.
                                              [*Exit.*

  Duch. Shall this move me? If all my royal kindred
Lay in my way unto this marriage,
I'ld make them my low footsteps: and even now,   350
Even in this hate, (as men in some great battles,
By apprehending danger, have achiev'd
Almost impossible actions—I have heard soldiers say
    so),
So I, through frights and threat'nings, will assay
This dangerous venture. Let old wives report   355
I wink'd and chose a husband.—Cariola,

    350 footsteps] step-ladder   356 wink'd] slept

To thy known secrecy I have given up
More than my life, my fame—
  Cari.   Both shall be safe;
For I'll conceal this secret from the world
As warily as those that trade in poison   360
Keep poison from their children.
  Duch.   Thy protestation
Is ingenious and hearty: I believe it.
Is Antonio come?
  Cari.   He attends you.
  Duch.   Good dear soul,
Leave me; but place thyself behind the arras,
Where thou mayst overhear us. Wish me good speed; 365
            [Cariola *withdraws behind the arras.*
For I am going into a wilderness,
Where I shall find nor path nor friendly clew
To be my guide.
                              [*Enter* Antonio.
            I sent for you: sit down;
Take pen and ink, and write: are you ready?
  Ant.   Yes.
  Duch. What did I say?
  Ant.   That I should write somewhat. 370
  Duch. Oh, I remember—
After these triumphs and this large expense
It's fit, like thrifty husbands, we inquire
What's laid up for to-morrow.
  Ant. So please your beauteous excellence—
  Duch.   Beauteous! 375
Indeed, I thank you: I look young for your sake;
You have ta'en my cares upon you.
  Ant.   I'll fetch your grace
The particulars of your revenue, and expense.

362 ingenious] ingenuous, candid   373 husbands] heads
of the household

Duch. Oh, you are an upright treasurer: but you
    mistook;
For when I said I meant to make inquiry   380
What's laid up for to-morrow, I did mean
What's laid up yonder for me.
    Ant.   Where?
    Duch.   In heaven.
I am making my will (as 'tis fit princes should,
In perfect memory), and, I pray, sir, tell me,
Were not one better make it smiling, thus,   385
Than in deep groans and terrible ghastly looks,
As if the gifts we parted with procur'd
That violent distraction?
    Ant.   Oh, much better.
    Duch. If I had a husband now, this care were quit:
But I intend to make you overseer.   390
What good deed shall we first remember? say.
    Ant. Begin with that first good deed began i' th'
    world
After man's creation, the sacrament of marriage—
I'ld have you first provide for a good husband;
Give him all.
    Duch.   All?
    Ant.   Yes, your excellent self.   395
    Duch. In a winding-sheet?
    Ant.   In a couple.
    Duch. Saint Winifred, that were a strange will!
    Ant. 'Twere strange
If there were no will in you to marry again.
    Duch. What do you think of marriage?   400
    Ant. I take't, as those that deny purgatory—
It locally contains, or heaven, or hell;
There's no third place in't.
    Duch.   How do you affect it?

396 couple] marriage   403 affect] like

Ant. My banishment, feeding my melancholy,
Would often reason thus—   405
    Duch. Pray, let's hear it.
    Ant. Say a man never marry, nor have children,
What takes that from him? only the bare name
Of being a father, or the weak delight
To see the little wanton ride a-cock-horse   410
Upon a painted stick, or hear him chatter
Like a taught starling.
    Duch.   Fie, fie, what's all this?
One of your eyes is blood-shot; use my ring to't,
They say 'tis very sovereign: 'twas my wedding-ring,
And I did vow never to part with it   415
But to my second husband.
    Ant. You have parted with it now.
    Duch. Yes, to help your eye-sight.
    Ant. You have made me stark blind.
    Duch. How?   420
    Ant. There is a saucy and ambitious devil
Is dancing in this circle.
    Duch.   Remove him.
    Ant.   How?
    Duch. There needs small conjuration, when your
    finger
May do it: thus; is it fit?
                     [*She puts the ring upon his finger: he kneels.*
    Ant.   What said you?
    Duch.   Sir,
This goodly roof of yours is too low built;   425
I cannot stand upright in't, nor discourse,
Without I raise it higher: raise yourself,
Or, if you please, my hand to help you: so.
                                 [*Raises him.*
    Ant. Ambition, madam, is a great man's madness,
That is not kept in chains and close-pent rooms,   430

But in fair lightsome lodgings, and is girt
With the wild noise of prattling visitants,
Which makes it lunatic beyond all cure.
Conceive not I am so stupid but I aim
Whereto your favours tend: but he's a fool   435
That, being a-cold, would thrust his hands i' th' fire
To warm them.
    Duch.   So, now the ground's broke,
You may discover what a wealthy mine
I make you lord of.
    Ant.   Oh, my unworthiness!
    Duch. You were ill to sell yourself: 440
This dark'ning of your worth is not like that
Which tradesmen use i' th' city: their false lights
Are to rid bad wares off: and I must tell you,
If you will know where breathes a complete man
(I speak it without flattery), turn your eyes,   445
And progress through yourself.
    Ant. Were there nor heaven nor hell,
I should be honest: I have long serv'd virtue,
And ne'er ta'en wages of her.
    Duch.   Now she pays it.
The misery of us that are born great!   450
We are forc'd to woo, because none dare woo us;
And as a tyrant doubles with his words,
And fearfully equivocates, so we
Are forc'd to express our violent passions
In riddles and in dreams, and leave the path   455
Of simple virtue, which was never made
To seem the thing it is not. Go, go brag
You have left me heartless—mine is in your bosom,
I hope 'twill multiply love there. You do tremble:
Make not your heart so dead a piece of flesh   460
To fear, more than to love me. Sir, be confident:

444 complete] *pronounced* cómplete

223

What is't distracts you? This is flesh and blood, sir;
'Tis not the figure cut in alabaster
Kneels at my husband's tomb. Awake, awake, man!
I do here put off all vain ceremony,   465
And only do appear to you a young widow
That claims you for her husband, and, like a widow,
I use but half a blush in't.

    Ant.   Truth speak for me;
I will remain the constant sanctuary
Of your good name.

    Duch.   I thank you, gentle love: 470
And 'cause you shall not come to me in debt,
Being now my steward, here upon your lips
I sign your *Quietus est*. This you should have begg'd
    now:
I have seen children oft eat sweetmeats thus,
As fearful to devour them too soon.   475

    Ant. But for your brothers?

    Duch.   Do not think of them:
All discord, without this circumference,
Is only to be pitied, and not fear'd:
Yet, should they know it, time will easily
Scatter the tempest.

    Ant.   These words should be mine,   480
And all the parts you have spoke, if some part of it
Would not have savour'd flattery.

    Duch. Kneel.

                [Cariola *comes from behind the arras.*

    Ant. Ha!

    Duch. Be not amaz'd, this woman's of my counsel: 485
I have heard lawyers say, a contract in a chamber
Per verba de presenti is absolute marriage.

---

    477 without this circumference] outside this circle (*embracing
him*)   487 Per verba de presenti] by words about the present
(sc. *recognizing a fact as opposed to making a promise*)

Bless, heaven, this sacred Gordian, which let violence
Never untwine!

Ant. And may our sweet affections, like the spheres, 490
Be still in motion!

Duch.   Quickening, and make
The life soft music!

Ant. That we may imitate the loving palms,
Best emblem of a peaceful marriage,
That never bore fruit, divided!   495

Duch. What can the church force more?

Ant. That fortune may not know an accident,
Either of joy or sorrow, to divide
Our fixed wishes!

Duch.   How can the church build faster?
We now are man and wife, and 'tis the church   500
That must but echo this.—Maid, stand apart:
I now am blind.

Ant.   What's your conceit in this?

Duch. I would have you lead your fortune by the
     hand
Unto your marriage-bed:
(You speak in me this, for we now are one:)   505
We'll only lie, and talk together, and plot
To appease my humorous kindred; and if you please,
Like the old tale in Alexander and Lodowick,
Lay a naked sword between us, keep us chaste.
Oh, let me shroud my blushes in your bosom,   510
Since 'tis the treasury of all my secrets!

Cari. Whether the spirit of greatness or of woman
Reign most in her, I know not, but it shows
A fearful madness: I owe her much of pity.   [*Exeunt.*

488 Gordian] *the knot which could not be untied, cut with his
sword by Alexander*   499 faster] more firmly   501
echo this] *such marriages required confirmation later*   502
conceit] idea   507 humorous] crotchety, 'difficult'

ACTUS II, SCENA I

Enter Bosola *and* Castruchio.

Bos. You say you would fain be taken—for an
eminent courtier?

Cast. 'Tis the very main of my ambition.

Bos. Let me see, you have a reasonable good face
for't already, and your night-cap expresses your ears 5
sufficiently largely—I would have you learn to twirl
the strings of your band with a good grace, and in a
set speech, at the end of every sentence, to hum three
or four times, or blow your nose (till it smart again) to
recover your memory. When you come to be a presi- 10
dent in criminal causes, if you smile upon a prisoner,
hang him; but if you frown upon him and threaten
him, let him be sure to 'scape the gallows.

Cast. I would be a very merry president.

Bos. Do not sup a nights; 'twill beget you an ad- 15
mirable wit.

Cast. Rather it would make me have a good stomach
to quarrel, for they say, your roaring boys eat meat
seldom, and that makes them so valiant. But how shall
I know whether the people take me for an eminent 20
fellow?

Bos. I will teach a trick to know it: give out you lie
a-dying, and if you hear the common people curse you,
be sure you are taken for one of the prime night-caps.—
                              [*Enter* Old Lady.

You come from painting now?   25

Old Lady. From what?

---

5 night-cap] *A white skull-cap worn by Serjeants at Law*
7 band] *Barristers' white tabs*   15 a nights] at night   18
roaring boys] braggart bullies   24 night-caps] lawyers; *cf.*
l. 5; (Lucas, controverting O.E.D.)

Bos. Why, from your scurvy face-physic. To behold
thee not painted inclines somewhat near a miracle:
these, in thy face here, were deep ruts and foul sloughs
the last progress. There was a lady in France that, 30
having had the small-pox, flayed the skin off her face
to make it more level; and whereas before she look'd
like a nutmeg-grater, after she resembled an abortive
hedge-hog.

Old Lady. Do you call this painting?   35

Bos. No, no, but careening of an old morphewed
lady, to make her disembogue again: there's rough-
cast phrase to your plastic.

Old Lady. It seems you are well acquainted with my
closet.   40

Bos. One would suspect it for a shop of witchcraft,
to find in it the fat of serpents, spawn of snakes, Jews'
spittle, and their young children's ordure; and all these
for the face. I would sooner eat a dead pigeon taken
from the soles of the feet of one sick of the plague, than 45
kiss one of you fasting. Here are two of you, whose sin
of your youth is the very patrimony of the physician,
makes him renew his footcloth with the spring, and
change his high-priced courtezan with the fall of the
leaf. I do wonder you do not loathe yourselves. Observe 50
my meditation now:
What thing is in this outward form of man
To be belov'd? We account it ominous,
If nature do produce a colt, or lamb,
A fawn, or goat, in any limb resembling   55
A man, and fly from 't as a prodigy.

---

30 progress] *formal royal tour*   36 morphewed] scurfy;
(*'careening' suggests weed and barnacles*)   37 disembogue]
put to sea   37–38 rough-cast . . . plastic] coarse plaster . . .
finished plaster   44–5 pigeon . . . plague] *A recognized*
treatment   48 footcloth] housings of his mule or horse

Man stands amaz'd to see his deformity,
In any other creature but himself.
But in our own flesh though we bear diseases
Which have their true names only ta'en from beasts,— 60
As the most ulcerous wolf and swinish measle,—
Though we are eaten up of lice and worms,
And though continually we bear about us
A rotten and dead body, we delight
To hide it in rich tissue: all our fear,   65
(Nay, all our terror) is, lest our physician
Should put us in the ground to be made sweet.—
Your wife's gone to Rome: you two couple, and get
    you
To the wells at Lucca to recover your aches.
I have other work on foot.

> [*Exeunt* Castruchio *and* Old Lady.

                              I observe our duchess   70
Is sick a-days, she pukes, her stomach seethes,
The fins of her eye-lids look most teeming blue,
She wanes i' the cheek, and waxes fat i' th' flank,
And (contrary to our Italian fashion)
Wears a loose-bodied gown: there's somewhat in't.   75
I have a trick may chance discover it,
A pretty one; I have bought some apricocks,
The first our spring yields.

> *Enter* Antonio *and* Delio *talking together apart.*

Delio.   And so long since married?
You amaze me.
  Ant.   Let me seal your lips for ever:
For, did I think that anything but th' air   80
Could carry these words from you, I should wish

69 wells] thermal springs   aches] *pronounced* aitches   72
fins] *Meaning disputed; perhaps* ends, edges (*from the French*)

You had no breath at all.—Now, sir, in your contemplation?
You are studying to become a great wise fellow?

Bos. Oh, sir, the opinion of wisdom is a foul tetter
that runs all over a man's body: if simplicity direct us 85
to have no evil, it directs us to a happy being; for the
subtlest folly proceeds from the subtlest wisdom: let
me be simply honest.

Ant. I do understand your inside.

Bos.   Do you so?

Ant. Because you would not seem to appear to th'
world   90
Puff'd up with your preferment, you continue
This out-of-fashion melancholy: leave it, leave it.

Bos. Give me leave to be honest in any phrase, in any
compliment whatsoever. Shall I confess myself to you?
I look no higher than I can reach: they are the gods 95
that must ride on winged horses, a lawyer's mule of a
slow pace will both suit my disposition and business;
for, mark me, when a man's mind rides faster than his
horse can gallop, they quickly both tire.

Ant. You would look up to heaven, but I think   100
The devil, that rules i' th' air, stands in your light.

Bos. Oh, sir, you are lord of the ascendant, chief man
with the duchess: a duke was your cousin-german
remov'd. Say you were lineally descended from King
Pepin, or he himself, what of this? search the heads of 105
the greatest rivers in the world, you shall find them
but bubbles of water. Some would think the souls of
princes were brought forth by some more weighty
cause than those of meaner persons: they are deceiv'd,
there's the same hand to them: the like passions sway 110
them, the same reason that makes a vicar to go to law
for a tithe-pig, and undo his neighbours, makes them

102 lord of the ascendant] ruling planet (*in astrology*)

spoil a whole province, and batter down goodly cities
with the cannon.

Enter Duchess *and* Ladies.

Duch. Your arm, Antonio: do I not grow fat?   115
I am exceeding short-winded.—Bosola,
I would have you, sir, provide for me a litter;
Such a one as the Duchess of Florence rode in.
   Bos. The Duchess us'd one when she was great with
     child.
   Duch. I think she did.—Come hither, mend my ruff: 120
Here, when? thou art such a tedious lady; and
Thy breath smells of lemon pills: would thou hadst
     done!
Shall I sound under thy fingers? I am
So troubled with the mother!
   Bos. [*aside.*]   I fear too much
   Duch. I have heard you say that the French courtiers 125
Wear their hats on 'fore the king.
   Ant. I have seen it.
   Duch. In the presence?
   Ant. Yes.
   Duch. Why should not we bring up that fashion?   130
'Tis ceremony more than duty, that consists
In the removing of a piece of felt:
Be you the example to the rest o' th' court;
Put on your hat first.
   Ant.   You must pardon me:
I have seen, in colder countries than in France,   135
Nobles stand bare to th' prince; and the distinction
Methought show'd reverently.
   Bos. I have a present for your grace.
   Duch.   For me, sir?

121 tedious] slow   123 sound] swoon   124 the
mother] hysteria

Bos. Apricocks, madam

Duch.   Oh, sir, where are they?
I have heard of none to-year.

Bos. [*aside.*]   Good; her colour rises.   140

Duch. Indeed, I thank you: they are wondrous fair
    ones.
What an unskilful fellow is our gardener!
We shall have none this month.

Bos. Will not your grace pare them?

Duch. No: they taste of musk, methinks; indeed
    they do.   145

Bos. I know not: yet I wish your grace had par'd 'em.

Duch. Why?

Bos.   I forgot to tell you, the knave gardener,
Only to raise his profit by them the sooner,
Did ripen them in horse-dung.

Duch.   Oh, you jest.—
You shall judge: pray, taste one.

Ant.   Indeed, madam,   150
I do not love the fruit.

Duch.   Sir, you are loth
To rob us of our dainties: 'tis a delicate fruit;
They say they are restorative.

Bos.   'Tis a pretty art,
This grafting.

Duch.   'Tis so; a bett'ring of nature.

Bos. To make a pippin grow upon a crab,   155
A damson on a black-thorn.—[*Aside.*] How greedily
    she eats them!
A whirlwind strike off these bawd farthingales!
For, but for that, and the loose-bodied gown,
I should have discover'd apparently
The young springal cutting a caper in her belly.   160

---

139 apricocks] apricots. *The significance of this episode appears
at* II. ii. 1 *sq.*   157 farthingales] hooped petticoats

Duch. I thank you, Bosola: they were right good
    ones,
If they do not make me sick.
    Ant.   How now, madam!
    Duch. This green fruit and my stomach are not
    friends:
How they swell me!
    Bos. [*aside.*] Nay, you are too much swell'd already. 165
    Duch. Oh, I am in an extreme cold sweat!
    Bos.   I am very sorry. [*Exit.*
    Duch. Lights to my chamber!—O good Antonio,
I fear I am undone!
    Delio.   Lights there, lights!
                                   [*Exit* Duchess.
    Ant. O my most trusty Delio, we are lost!
I fear she's fall'n in labour; and there's left   170
No time for her remove.
    Delio.   Have you prepar'd
Those ladies to attend her? and procur'd
That politic safe conveyance for the midwife
Your duchess plotted?
    Ant. I have.
    Delio.   Make use, then, of this forc'd occasion: 175
Give out that Bosola hath poison'd her
With these apricocks; that will give some colour
For her keeping close.
    Ant.   Fie, fie, the physicians
Will then flock to her.
    Delio.   For that you may pretend
She'll use some prepar'd antidote of her own,   180
Lest the physicians should re-poison her.
    Ant. I am lost in amazement: I know not what to
    think on't.   [*Exeunt.*

SCENA II

Enter Bosola *and* Old Lady.

Bos. So, so, there's no question but her tetchiness and most vulturous eating of the apricocks are apparent signs of breeding.—Now?

Old Lady. I am in haste, sir.

Bos. There was a young waiting-woman had a 5 monstrous desire to see the glass-house——

Old Lady. Nay, pray, let me go.

Bos. And it was only to know what strange instrument it was, should swell up a glass to the fashion of a woman's belly.   10

Old Lady. I will hear no more of the glass-house. You are still abusing women!

Bos. Who, I? no; only, by the way now and then, mention your frailties. The orange-tree bears ripe and green fruit and blossoms all together; and some of you 15 give entertainment for pure love, but more for more precious reward. The lusty spring smells well; but drooping autumn tastes well. If we have the same golden showers that rained in the time of Jupiter the Thunderer, you have the same Danäes still, to hold up 20 their laps to receive them. Didst thou never study the mathematics?

Old Lady. What's that, sir?

Bos. Why, to know the trick how to make a many lines meet in one centre. Go, go, give your foster- 25 daughters good counsel: tell them, that the devil takes delight to hang at a woman's girdle, like a false rusty watch, that she cannot discern how the time passes.

[*Exit* Old Lady. *Enter* Antonio, Roderigo, *and* Grisolan.

6 glass-house] *A glass factory near the Blackfriars theatre attracted much attention; so below,* IV. ii. 88.

Ant. Shut up the court-gates.

Rod.   Why, sir? what's the danger? 30

Ant. Shut up the posterns presently, and call
All the officers o' th' court.

Gris.   I shall instantly.   [*Exit.*

Ant. Who keeps the key o' th' park-gate?

Rod.   Forobosco.

Ant. Let him bring't presently.

                    [*Re-enter* Grisolan *with* Servants.

First Serv. Oh, gentleman o' th' court, the foulest
    treason!   35

Bos. [*aside.*] If that these apricocks should be poison'd
    now,
Without my knowledge?

First Serv.   There was taken even now
A Switzer in the duchess' bed-chamber——

Second Serv. A Switzer?

First Serv.   With a pistol in his great cod-piece.

Bos. Ha, ha, ha!   40

First Serv. The cod-piece was the case for't.

Second Serv.   There was a cunning traitor:
Who would have search'd his cod-piece?

First Serv. True, if he had kept out of the ladies'
    chambers:
And all the moulds of his buttons were leaden bullets.

Second Serv. Oh wicked cannibal! a fire-lock in's cod-
    piece!   45

First Serv. 'Twas a French plot, upon my life.

Second Serv. To see what the devil can do!

Ant. All the officers here?

Servants. We are.

Ant. Gentlemen,   50

39 cod-piece] '*a bag-like appendage attached to the front*' of
form-fitting breeches, sometimes useful as a pocket (*Linthicum*)
45 cannibal] savage

We have lost much plate you know; and but this even-
    ing
Jewels, to the value of four thousand ducats,
Are missing in the duchess' cabinet.
Are the gates shut?
    Serv.   Yes.
    Ant.   'Tis the duchess' pleasure
Each officer be lock'd into his chamber   55
Till the sun-rising; and to send the keys
Of all their chests and of their outward doors
Into her bed-chamber. She is very sick.
    Rod. At her pleasure.
    Ant. She entreats you take't not ill: the innocent   60
Shall be the more approv'd by it.
    Bos. Gentleman o' th' wood-yard, where's your
        Switzer now?
    First Serv. By this hand, 'twas credibly reported by
one o' th' black guard.
                 [*Exeunt all except* Antonio *and* Delio.
    Delio. How fares it with the duchess?
    Ant.   She's expos'd 65
Unto the worst of torture, pain and fear.
    Delio. Speak to her all happy comfort.
    Ant. How I do play the fool with mine own danger!
You are this night, dear friend, to post to Rome:
My life lies in your service.
    Delio.   Do not doubt me.   70
    Ant. Oh, 'tis far from me: and yet fear presents me
Somewhat that looks like danger.
    Delio.   Believe it,
'Tis but the shadow of your fear, no more:
How superstitiously we mind our evils!
The throwing down salt, or crossing of a hare,   75

61 approv'd] proved innocent   64 black guard] kitchen
servants

Bleeding at nose, the stumbling of a horse,
Or singing of a cricket, are of power
To daunt whole man in us. Sir, fare you well:
I wish you all the joys of a bless'd father;
And, for my faith, lay this unto your breast,—   80
Old friends, like old swords, still are trusted best.

[*Exit. **Enter** Cariola.*

Cari. Sir, you are the happy father of a son:
Your wife commends him to you.

Ant.   Blessed comfort!—
For heaven-sake, tend her well: I'll presently
Go set a figure for's nativity.   [*Exeunt.* 85

SCENA III

Enter Bosola, *with a dark lantern.*

Bos. Sure I did hear a woman shriek: list, ha!
And the sound came, if I receiv'd it right,
From the duchess' lodgings. There's some stratagem
In the confining all our courtiers
To their several wards: I must have part of it;   5
My intelligence will freeze else. List, again!
It may be 'twas the melancholy bird,
Best friend of silence and of solitariness,
The owl, that scream'd so.—Ha! Antonio!

Enter Antonio.

Ant. I heard some noise.—Who's there? what art
      thou? speak.   10
Bos. Antonio? Put not your face nor body
To such a forc'd expression of fear:
I am Bosola, your friend

Ant.   Bosola!

84 presently] now   85 figure] *sc. for a horoscope*

—This mole does undermine me.—Heard you not
A noise even now?

Bos.   From whence?

Ant.   From the duchess' lodging. 15

Bos. Not I: did you?

Ant.   I did, or else I dream'd.

Bos. Let's walk towards it.

Ant.   No: it may be 'twas
But the rising of the wind—

Bos.   Very likely.
Methinks 'tis very cold, and yet you sweat:
You look wildly.

Ant.   I have been setting a figure   20
For the duchess' jewels.

Bos.   Ah, and how falls your question?
Do you find it radical?

Ant.   What's that to you?
'Tis rather to be question'd what design,
When all men were commanded to their lodgings,
Makes you a night-walker.

Bos.   In sooth I'll tell you: 25
Now all the court's asleep, I thought the devil
Had least to do here; I came to say my prayers;
And if it do offend you I do so,
You are a fine courtier.

Ant. [*aside.*]   This fellow will undo me.—
You gave the duchess apricocks to-day: 30
Pray heaven they were not poison'd!

Bos.   Poison'd! a Spanish fig
For the imputation.

Ant.   Traitors are ever confident
Till they are discover'd. There were jewels stol'n too—
In my conceit, none are to be suspected
More than yourself.

22 radical] *answerable by astrology*   34 conceit] opinion

Bos.   You are a false steward.   35
Ant. Saucy slave! I'll pull thee up by the roots.
Bos. May be the ruin will crush you to pieces.
Ant. You are an impudent snake indeed, sir:
Are you scarce warm, and do you show your sting?

        *   *   *   *   *   *   *   40

Ant. You libel well, sir.
Bos.   No, sir: copy it out,
And I will set my hand to't.
Ant. [*aside.*]   My nose bleeds.
One that were superstitious would count
This ominous, when it merely comes by chance:
Two letters, that are wrote here for my name,   45
Are drown'd in blood!
Mere accident.—For you, sir, I'll take order
I' th' morn you shall be safe:—[*aside*] 'tis that must
    colour
Her lying-in:—sir, this door you pass not:
I do not hold it fit that you come near   50
The duchess' lodgings, till you have quit yourself.—
[*Aside.*] The great are like the base, nay, they are the
    same,
When they seek shameful ways to avoid shame.
                                        [*Exit.*

Bos. Antonio hereabout did drop a paper—
Some of your help, false friend:—Oh, here it is.   55
What's here? a child's nativity calculated!
*The duchess was deliver'd of a son, 'tween the hours twelve
and one in the night, Anno Dom.* 1504,—that's this year—
decimo nono Decembris,—that's this night—*taken accord-*

___

40 ***&c.] *The original gives two successive speeches to Antonio,
and imperfect sense shows that something is missing. No satisfactory
emendation has been proposed.*   55 false friend] *sc.* the dark
lantern

ing to the meridian of Malfi,—that's our duchess: happy 60
discovery!—*The lord of the first house being combust in the*
ascendant, signifies short life; and Mars being in a human
sign, join'd to the tail of the Dragon, in the eight house, doth
threaten a violent death. Cætera non scrutantur.
Why, now 'tis most apparent; this precise fellow   65
Is the duchess' bawd:—I have it to my wish!
This is a parcel of intelligency
Our courtiers were cas'd up for: it needs must follow
That I must be committed on pretence
Of poisoning her; which I'll endure, and laugh at.   70
If one could find the father now! but that
Time will discover. Old Castruchio
I' th' morning posts to Rome: by him I'll send
A letter that shall make her brothers' galls
O'erflow their livers. This was a thrifty way.   75
Though lust do mask in ne'er so strange disguise,
She's oft found witty, but is never wise.   [*Exit.*

SCENA IV

Enter Cardinal *and* Julia.

  Card. Sit: thou art my best of wishes. Prithee, tell me
What trick didst thou invent to come to Rome
Without thy husband?
  Julia.   Why, my lord, I told him
I came to visit an old anchorite
Here, for devotion.
  Card.   Thou art a witty false one,—   5
I mean, to him.
  Julia.   You have prevail'd with me
Beyond my strongest thoughts: I would not now

  65 precise] Puritanical   67 parcel of intelligency] piece of
information

Find you inconstant.
  Card.   Do not put thyself
To such a voluntary torture, which proceeds
Out of your own guilt.
  Julia.   How, my lord!
  Card.   You fear 10
My constancy, because you have approv'd
Those giddy and wild turnings in yourself.
  Julia. Did you e'er find them?
  Card.   Sooth, generally for women,
A man might strive to make glass malleable,
Ere he should make them fixed.
  Julia.   So, my lord! 15
  Card. We had need go borrow that fantastic glass
Invented by Galileo the Florentine,
To view another spacious world i' th' moon,
And look to find a constant woman there.
  Julia. This is very well, my lord.
  Card.   Why do you weep? 20
Are tears your justification? the self-same tears
Will fall into your husband's bosom, lady,
With a loud protestation that you love him
Above the world.—Come, I'll love you wisely,
That's jealously; since I am very certain 25
You cannot make me cuckold.
  Julia.   I'll go home
To my husband.
  Card.   You may thank me, lady,
I have taken you off your melancholy perch,
Bore you upon my fist, and show'd you game,
And let you fly at it.—I pray thee, kiss me.— 30
When thou wast with thy husband, thou wast watch'd
Like a tame elephant:—still you are to thank me:—
Thou hadst only kisses from him, and high feeding;

   28–30 perch . . . fist . . . fly] *Terms of falconry*

But what delight was that? 'twas just like one
That hath a little fing'ring on the lute,   35
Yet cannot tune it:—still you are to thank me.
   Julia. You told me of a piteous wound i' th' heart,
And a sick liver, when you woo'd me first,
And spake like one in physic.
   Card. Who's that?——

                         [*Enter* Servant.
            Rest firm—for my affection to thee, 40
Lightning moves slow to't.
   Serv.   Madam, a gentleman,
That's come post from Malfi, desires to see you.
   Card. Let him enter: I'll withdraw.   [*Exit.*
   Serv.   He says
Your husband, old Castruchio, is come to Rome,
Most pitifully tir'd with riding post.   45
                  [*Exit.   Enter* Delio.
   Julia. [*aside.*] Signior Delio! 'tis one of my old suitors.
   Delio. I was bold to come and see you.
   Julia.   Sir, you are welcome.
   Delio. Do you lie here?
   Julia.   Sure, your own experience
Will satisfy you no: our Roman prelates
Do not keep lodging for ladies.
   Delio.   Very well: 50
I have brought you no commendations from your
   husband,
For I know none by him.
   Julia.   I hear he's come to Rome.
   Delio. I never knew man and beast, of a horse and a
   knight,
So weary of each other: if he had had a good back,
He would have undertook to have borne his horse,   55
His breech was so pitifully sore.
            40 for] as for

Julia.   Your laughter
Is my pity.
    Delio.   Lady, I know not whether
You want money, but I have brought you some.
    Julia. From my husband?
    Delio.   No, from mine own allowance.
    Julia. I must hear the condition, ere I be bound to
      take it.   60
    Delio. Look on't, 'tis gold: hath it not a fine colour?
    Julia. I have a bird more beautiful.
    Delio.   Try the sound on't.
    Julia. A lute-string far exceeds it:
It hath no smell, like cassia or civet;
Nor is it physical, though some fond doctors   65
Persuade us seethe't in cullises. I'll tell you,
This is a creature bred by——
                              [*Enter* Servant.
    Serv.   Your husband's come,
Hath deliver'd a letter to the Duke of Calabria
That, to my thinking, hath put him out of his wits.
                                                  [*Exit.*

    Julia. Sir, you hear: 70
Pray, let me know your business and your suit
As briefly as can be.
    Delio.   With good speed: I would wish you,
At such time as you are non-resident
With your husband, my mistress.
    Julia. Sir, I'll go ask my husband if I shall,   75
And straight return your answer.   [*Exit.*
    Delio.   Very fine!
Is this her wit, or honesty, that speaks thus?
I heard one say the Duke was highly mov'd
With a letter sent from Malfi. I do fear

  65 physical] medicinal, curative   fond] foolish   66 cullises] broths

Antonio is betray'd: how fearfully   80
Shows his ambition now! unfortunate fortune!
They pass through whirl-pools, and deep woes do
    shun,
Who the event weigh, ere the action's done.   [*Exit.*

SCENA V

Enter Cardinal *and* Ferdinand *with a letter.*

Ferd. I have this night digg'd up a mandrake.
Card.   Say you?
Ferd. And I am grown mad with't.
Card.   What's the prodigy?
Ferd. Read there,—a sister damn'd: she's loose i' th'
    hilts;
Grown a notorious strumpet.
Card.   Speak lower.
Ferd.   Lower!
Rogues do not whisper't now, but seek to publish't   5
(As servants do the bounty of their lords)
Aloud; and with a covetous searching eye,
To mark who note them. Oh, confusion seize her!
She hath had most cunning bawds to serve her turn,
And more secure conveyances for lust   10
Than towns of garrison for service.
Card.   Is't possible?
Can this be certain?
Ferd.   Rhubarb, Oh, for rhubarb
To purge this choler! here's the cursed day
To prompt my memory; and here't shall stick
Till of her bleeding heart I make a sponge   15
To wipe it out.

    1 Say you?] How say you? What do you say?
    10 secure conveyances] safe passages

Card.   Why do you make yourself
So wild a tempest?
Ferd.   Would I could be one,
That I might toss her palace 'bout her ears,
Root up her goodly forests, blast her meads,
And lay her general territory as waste   20
As she hath done her honours.
Card.   Shall our blood,
The royal blood of Arragon and Castile,
Be thus attainted?
Ferd.   Apply desperate physic:
We must not now use balsamum, but fire,
The smarting cupping-glass, for that's the mean   25
To purge infected blood, such blood as hers.
There is a kind of pity in mine eye,—
I'll give it to my handkercher; and now 'tis here,
I'll bequeath this to her bastard.
Card.   What to do?
Ferd. Why, to make soft lint for his mother's
    wounds,   30
When I have hew'd her to pieces.
Card.   Curs'd creature!
Unequal nature, to place women's hearts
So far upon the left side!
Ferd.   Foolish men,
That e'er will trust their honour in a bark
Made of so slight weak bulrush as is woman,   35
Apt every minute to sink it!
Card. Thus ignorance, when it hath purchas'd
    honour,
It cannot wield it.
Ferd.   Methinks I see her laughing,—
Excellent hyena! Talk to me somewhat, quickly,

32 unequal] unjust   33 upon the left side] inclined to folly
(*Lucas*)   39 Talk ... somewhat] say something or other

Or my imagination will carry me   40
To see her in the shameful act of sin.
   Card. With whom?
   Ferd. Happily with some strong-thigh'd bargeman,
Or one o' th' wood-yard that can quoit the sledge,
Or toss the bar, or else some lovely squire   45
That carries coals up to her privy lodgings.
   Card. You fly beyond your reason.
   Ferd.   Go to, mistress!
'Tis not your whore's milk that shall quench my wild-
    fire,
But your whore's blood.
   Card. How idly shows this rage, which carries you, 50
As men convey'd by witches through the air,
On violent whirlwinds! this intemperate noise
Fitly resembles deaf men's shrill discourse,
Who talk aloud, thinking all other men
To have their imperfection.
   Ferd.   Have not you   55
My palsy?
   Card. Yes, yet I can be angry
Without this rupture: there is not in nature
A thing that makes man so deform'd, so beastly,
As doth intemperate anger. Chide yourself.   60
You have divers men who never yet express'd
Their strong desire of rest but by unrest,
By vexing of themselves. Come, put yourself
In tune.
   Ferd. So, I will only study to seem
The thing I am not. I could kill her now,   65
In you, or in myself; for I do think
It is some sin in us heaven doth revenge
By her.

   43 Happily] haply, perhaps   44 quoit the sledge] throw
the hammer

Card.   Are you stark mad?

Ferd.   I would have their bodies
Burnt in a coal-pit with the ventage stopp'd,
That their curs'd smoke might not ascend to heaven; 70
Or dip the sheets they lie in in pitch or sulphur,
Wrap them in't, and then light them like a match;
Or else to-boil their bastard to a cullis,
And give't his lecherous father to renew
The sin of his back.

Card.   I'll leave you.

Ferd.   Nay, I have done. 75
I am confident, had I been damn'd in hell,
And should have heard of this, it would have put me
Into a cold sweat. In, in; I'll go sleep.
Till I know who leaps my sister, I'll not stir:
That known, I'll find scorpions to string my whips, 80
And fix her in a general eclipse.   [*Exeunt.*

ACTUS III, SCENA I

Enter Antonio *and* Delio.

Ant. Our noble friend, my most beloved Delio!
Oh, you have been a stranger long at court;
Came you along with the Lord Ferdinand?

Delio. I did, sir; and how fares your noble duchess?

Ant. Right fortunately well: she's an excellent   5
Feeder of pedigrees; since you last saw her,
She hath had two children more, a son and daughter.

Delio. Methinks 'twas yesterday: let me but wink,
And not behold your face, which to mine eye
Is somewhat leaner, verily I should dream   10
It were within this half hour.

Ant. You have not been in law, friend Delio,
Nor in prison, nor a suitor at the court,

Nor begg'd the reversion of some great man's place,
Nor troubled with an old wife, which doth make   15
Your time so insensibly hasten.

Delio.   Pray, sir, tell me,
Hath not this news arriv'd yet to the ear
Of the Lord Cardinal?

Ant.   I fear it hath:
The Lord Ferdinand, that's newly come to court,
Doth bear himself right dangerously.

Delio.   Pray, why?   20

Ant. He is so quiet that he seems to sleep
The tempest out, as dormice do in winter:
Those houses that are haunted are most still,
Till the devil be up.

Delio.   What say the common people?

Ant. The common rabble do directly say   25
She is a strumpet.

Delio.   And your graver heads,
Which would be politic, what censure they?

Ant. They do observe I grow to infinite purchase,
The left-hand way; and all suppose the duchess
Would amend it, if she could; for, say they,   30
Great princes, though they grudge their officers
Should have such large and unconfined means
To get wealth under them, will not complain,
Lest thereby they should make them odious
Unto the people—for other obligation   35
Of love, or marriage, between her and me
They never dream of.

> *Enter* Ferdinand, Duchess, *and* Bosola.

Delio.   The Lord Ferdinand
Is going to bed.

    25 directly] explicitly   27 censure] judge   28 pur-
chase] wealth   29 left-hand] sinister

Ferd.   I'll instantly to bed,
For I am weary.—I am to bespeak
A husband for you.
    Duch.   For me, sir! pray, who is't?   40
    Ferd. The great Count Malateste.
    Duch.   Fie upon him!
A count! he's a mere stick of sugar-candy;
You may look quite thorough him!—When I choose
A husband, I will marry for your honour.
    Ferd. You shall do well in't.—How is't, worthy
    Antonio?   45
    Duch. But, sir, I am to have private conference with
    you
About a scandalous report, is spread
Touching mine honour.
    Ferd.   Let me be ever deaf to't:
One of Pasquil's paper-bullets, court-calumny,
A pestilent air, which princes' palaces   50
Are seldom purg'd of. Yet, say that it were true,
I pour it in your bosom, my fix'd love
Would strongly excuse, extenuate, nay, deny
Faults, were they apparent in you. Go, be safe
In your own innocency.
    Duch. [*aside.*]   Oh bless'd comfort!   55
This deadly air is purg'd.
              [*Exeunt* Duchess, Antonio, Delio.
    Ferd.   Her guilt treads on
Hot-burning coulters.—Now, Bosola,
How thrives our intelligence?
    Bos.   Sir, uncertainly:
'Tis rumour'd she hath had three bastards, but
By whom we may go read i' th' stars.

43 thorough] through   49 Pasquil's paper-bullets] Pas-
quinades, satirical pamphlets   57 coulters] plough-shares.
To walk over red-hot ones was a form of trial by ordeal

248

Ferd.   Why, some   60
Hold opinion, all things are written there.

Bos. Yes, if we could find spectacles to read them—
I do suspect there hath been some sorcery
Us'd on the duchess.

Ferd.   Sorcery! To what purpose?

Bos. To make her dote on some desertless fellow   65
She shames to acknowledge.

Ferd.   Can your faith give way
To think there's power in potions, or in charms,
To make us love whether we will or no?

Bos. Most certainly.

Ferd. Away! these are mere gulleries, horrid things, 70
Invented by some cheating mountebanks
To abuse us. Do you think that herbs or charms
Can force the will? Some trials have been made
In this foolish practice, but the ingredients
Were lenative poisons, such as are of force   75
To make the patient mad; and straight the witch
Swears, by equivocation, they are in love.
The witch-craft lies in her rank blood. This night
I will force confession from her. You told me
You had got, within these two days, a false key   80
Into her bed-chamber.

Bos. I have.

Ferd. As I would wish.

Bos. What do you intend to do?

Ferd. Can you guess?   85

Bos. No.

Ferd. Do not ask, then:
He that can compass me, and know my drifts,
May say he hath put a girdle 'bout the world,
And sounded all her quick-sands.

72 abuse] deceive   75 lenative poisons] *perhaps* love-potions
(*Lucas*)

Bos.   I do not   90
Think so.
    Ferd.   What do you think, then, pray?
    Bos.   That you
Are your own chronicle too much, and grossly
Flatter yourself.
    Ferd.   Give me thy hand; I thank thee:
I never gave pension but to flatterers,
Till I entertained thee. Farewell.   95
That friend a great man's ruin strongly checks,
Who rails into his belief all his defects.   [*Exeunt.*

SCENA II

Enter Duchess, Antonio, *and* Cariola.

    Duch. Bring me the casket hither, and the glass.—
You get no lodging here to-night, my lord.
    Ant. Indeed, I must persuade one.
    Duch.   Very good!
I hope in time 'twill grow into a custom,
That noblemen shall come with cap and knee   5
To purchase a night's lodging of their wives.
    Ant. I must lie here.
    Duch.   Must! you are a lord of mis-rule.
    Ant. Indeed, my rule is only in the night.
    Duch. To what use will you put me?
    Ant.   We'll sleep together.
    Duch. Alas, what pleasure can two lovers find in
        sleep!   10
    Cari. My lord, I lie with her often; and I know
She'll much disquiet you.
    Ant.   See, you are complain'd of.
    Cari. For she's the sprawling'st bedfellow

Ant.   I shall like her
The better for that.
    Cari.   Sir, shall I ask you a question?
    Ant. Ay, pray thee, Cariola.   15
    Cari. Wherefore still, when you lie with my lady,
Do you rise so early?
    Ant.   Labouring men
Count the clock oft'nest, Cariola,
Are glad when their task's ended.
    Duch.   I'll stop your mouth.
                                [*Kisses him.*

    Ant. Nay, that's but one; Venus had two soft doves 20
To draw her chariot; I must have another.—
                                [*Kisses her.*

When wilt thou marry, Cariola?
    Cari.   Never, my lord.
    Ant. Oh, fie upon this single life! forgo it!
We read how Daphne, for her peevish flight,
Became a fruitless bay-tree; Syrinx turn'd   25
To the pale empty reed; Anaxarete
Was frozen into marble: whereas those
Which married, or prov'd kind unto their friends,
Were by a gracious influence transhap'd
Into the olive, pomegranate, mulberry,   30
Became flow'rs, precious stones, or eminent stars.
    Cari. This is a vain poetry: but I pray you, tell me,
If there were propos'd me, wisdom, riches, and beauty,
In three several young men, which should I choose?
    Ant. 'Tis a hard question: this was Paris' case, 35
And he was blind in't, and there was great cause;
For how was't possible he could judge right,
Having three amorous goddesses in view,
And they stark naked? 'twas a motion

  16 still] always   24 peevish] perverse   39 motion]
show

Were able to benight the apprehension   40
Of the severest counsellor of Europe.
Now I look on both your faces so well form'd,
It puts me in mind of a question I would ask.
  Cari. What is't?
  Ant.   I do wonder why hard-favour'd ladies,
For the most part, keep worse-favour'd waiting-
     women   45
To attend them, and cannot endure fair ones.
  Duch. Oh, that's soon answer'd.
Did you ever in your life know an ill painter
Desire to have his dwelling next door to the shop
Of an excellent picture-maker? 'twould disgrace   50
His face-making, and undo him. I prithee,
When were we so merry?—My hair tangles.
  Ant. Pray thee, Cariola, let's steal forth the room,
And let her talk to herself: I have divers times
Serv'd her the like, when she hath chaf'd extremely.   55
I love to see her angry. Softly, Cariola.
                    [*Exeunt* Antonio *and* Cariola.
  Duch. Doth not the colour of my hair 'gin to change?
When I wax gray, I shall have all the court
Powder their hair with arras, to be like me.
You have cause to love me; I enter'd you into my heart 60
Before you would vouchsafe to call for the keys.

                Enter Ferdinand *behind.*

We shall one day have my brothers take you napping:
Methinks his presence, being now in court,
Should make you keep your own bed; but you'll say
Love mix'd with fear is sweetest. I'll assure you,   65
You shall get no more children till my brothers
Consent to be your gossips. Have you lost your
     tongue?
        59 arras] orris-root (*a white powder*)

                    252

'Tis welcome: [Ferdinand *advances.*
For know, whether I am doom'd to live or die,
I can do both like a prince.

                          [Ferdinand *gives her a poniard.*
   Ferd.   Die, then quickly!   70
Virtue, where art thou hid? what hideous thing
Is it that doth eclipse thee?
   Duch.   Pray, sir, hear me.
   Ferd. Or is it true, thou art but a bare name,
And no essential thing?
   Duch.   Sir——
   Ferd.   Do not speak.
   Duch. No, sir: I will plant my soul in mine ears, to
     hear you.   75
   Ferd. Oh most imperfect light of human reason,
That mak'st us so unhappy, to foresee
What we can least prevent! Pursue thy wishes,
And glory in them: there's in shame no comfort
But to be past all bounds and sense of shame.   80
   Duch. I pray, sir, hear me: I am married.
   Ferd.   So!
   Duch. Happily, not to your liking: but for that,
Alas, your shears do come untimely now
To clip the bird's wings that's already flown!
Will you see my husband?
   Ferd.   Yes, if I could change   85
Eyes with a basilisk.
   Duch.   Sure, you came hither
By his confederacy.
   Ferd.   The howling of a wolf
Is music to thee, screech-owl: prithee, peace.—
Whate'er thou art that hast enjoy'd my sister,
(For I am sure thou hear'st me,) for thine own sake   90

   82 Happily] haply, perhaps   86 basilisk] *sc. to kill him*
with a look

Let me not know thee. I came hither prepar'd
To work thy discovery; yet am now persuaded
It would beget such violent effects
As would damn us both. I would not for ten millions
I had beheld thee: therefore use all means   95
I never may have knowledge of thy name;
Enjoy thy lust still, and a wretched life,
On that condition.—And for thee, vild woman,
If thou do wish thy lecher may grow old
In thy embracements, I would have thee build   100
Such a room for him as our anchorites
To holier use inhabit. Let not the sun
Shine on him till he's dead; let dogs and monkeys
Only converse with him, and such dumb things
To whom nature denies use to sound his name;   105
Do not keep a paraquito, lest she learn it;
If thou do love him, cut out thine own tongue,
Lest it bewray him.
    Duch.   Why might not I marry?
I have not gone about, in this, to create
Any new world or custom.
    Ferd.   Thou art undone;   110
And thou hast ta'en that massy sheet of lead
That hid thy husband's bones, and folded it
About my heart.
    Duch.   Mine bleeds for't.
    Ferd.   Thine? thy heart?
What should I name't, unless a hollow bullet
Fill'd with unquenchable wild-fire?
    Duch.   You are in this   115
Too strict; and were you not my princely brother,
I would say, too wilful: my reputation
Is safe.
    Ferd. Dost thou know what reputation is?
I'll tell thee,—to small purpose, since the instruction

254

Comes now too late—
Upon a time Reputation, Love, and Death,
Would travel o'er the world; and it was concluded
That they should part, and take three several ways.
Death told them, they should find him in great battles,
Or cities plagu'd with plagues: Love gives them
      counsel   125
To inquire for him 'mongst unambitious shepherds,
Where dowries were not talk'd of, and sometimes
'Mongst quiet kindred that had nothing left
By their dead parents: 'Stay,' quoth Reputation,
'Do not forsake me; for it is my nature,   130
If once I part from any man I meet,
I am never found again.' And so for you:
You have shook hands with Reputation,
And made him invisible. So, fare you well:
I will never see you more.
    Duch.   Why should only I,   135
Of all the other princes of the world,
Be cas'd up, like a holy relic? I have youth
And a little beauty.
    Ferd.   So you have some virgins
That are witches. I will never see thee more.
        [*Exit. Enter* Antonio *with a pistol, and* Cariola.
    Duch. You saw this apparition?
    Ant.   Yes: we are   140
Betray'd. How came he hither? I should turn
This to thee, for that.
    Cari.   Pray, sir, do; and when
That you have cleft my heart, you shall read there
Mine innocence.
    Duch.   That gallery gave him entrance.
    Ant. I would this terrible thing would come again, 145
That, standing on my guard, I might relate

    142 This to thee, for that] *sc. pistol to Cariola for betrayal*

My warrantable love.—   [*She shows the poniard.*
                          Ha! what means this?
   Duch. He left this with me.
   Ant.   And it seems did wish
You would use it on yourself?
   Duch.   His action seem'd
To intend so much.
   Ant.   This hath a handle to't,   150
As well as a point: turn it towards him, and
So fasten the keen edge in his rank gall—
                             [*Knocking within.*
How now? who knocks? more earthquakes?
   Duch.   I stand
As if a mine beneath my feet were ready
To be blown up.
   Cari.   'Tis Bosola.
   Duch.   Away!   155
Oh, misery! methinks unjust actions
Should wear these marks and curtains, and not we.
You must instantly part hence: I have fashion'd it
   already.   [*Exit* Antonio. *Enter* Bosola.
   Bos. The duke your brother is ta'en up in a whirl-
   wind;
Hath took horse, and's rid post to Rome.
   Duch.   So late?   160
   Bos. He told me, as he mounted into th' saddle,
You were undone.
   Duch.   Indeed, I am very near it.
   Bos. What's the matter?
   Duch. Antonio, the master of our household,
Hath dealt so falsely with me in's accounts: 165
My brother stood engag'd with me for money
Ta'en up of certain Neapolitan Jews,
And Antonio lets the bonds be forfeit.

167 ta'en up] borrowed

Bos. Strange!—[*Aside.*] This is cunning.
Duch.   And hereupon
My brother's bills at Naples are protested   170
Against.—Call up our officers.
Bos.   I shall.

                              [*Exit. Enter* Antonio.

Duch. The place that you must fly to is Ancona:
Hire a house there; I'll send after you
My treasure and my jewels. Our weak safety
Runs upon enginous wheels: short syllables   175
Must stand for periods. I must now accuse you
Of such a feigned crime as Tasso calls
Magnanima menzogna, a noble lie,
'Cause it must shield our honours.—Hark! they are
    coming.

                              [*Enter* Bosola *and* Officers.

Ant. Will your grace hear me?   180
Duch. I have got well by you; you have yielded me
A million of loss: I am like to inherit
The people's curses for your stewardship.
You had the trick in audit-time to be sick,
Till I had sign'd your quietus; and that cur'd you   185
Without help of the doctor.—Gentlemen,
I would have this man be an example to you all;
So shall you hold my favour; I pray, let him;
For h'as done that, alas, you would not think of,
And, because I intend to be rid of him,   190
I mean not to publish.—Use your fortune elsewhere.
Ant. I am strongly arm'd to brook my overthrow,

---

175 enginous wheels] *The hands of a clock mark a long period
for a short movement of the main gear-wheel*   **188** let him] *sc.
'be an example', with ironical ambiguity (continued in the next
phrase) whether to follow or to avoid. Lucas suggests further
deliberate ambiguities*

As commonly men bear with a hard year:
I will not blame the cause on't; but do think
The necessity of my malevolent star   195
Procures this, not her humour. Oh, the inconstant
And rotten ground of service! you may see,
'Tis e'en like him, that in a winter night,
Takes a long slumber o'er a dying fire,
As loth to part from 't; yet parts thence as cold   200
As when he first sat down.
    Duch.   We do confiscate,
Towards the satisfying of your accounts,
All that you have.
    Ant.   I am all yours; and 'tis very fit
All mine should be so.
    Duch.   So, sir, you have your pass.
    Ant. You may see, gentlemen, what 'tis to serve   205
A prince with body and soul.   [*Exit.*
    Bos. Here's an example for extortion: what moisture
is drawn out of the sea, when foul weather comes,
pours down, and runs into the sea again.
    Duch. I would know what are your opinions   210
Of this Antonio.
    Sec. Off. He could not abide to see a pig's head
      gaping:
I thought your grace would find him a Jew.
    Third Off. I would you had been his officer, for your
own sake.   215
    Fourth Off. You would have had more money.
    First Off. He stopp'd his ears with black wool, and,
to those came to him for money, said he was thick of
hearing.
    Sec. Off. Some said he was an hermaphrodite, for he 220
could not abide a woman.

   217 black] *See Marlowe,* 1 *Tamburlaine,* IV. i. 48–64, *for
black as the symbol of utter ruthlessness.*

Fourth Off. How scurvy proud he would look, when
the treasury was full! Well, let him go.

First Off. Yes, and the chippings of the buttery fly
after him, to scour his gold chain.   225

Duch. Leave us.—What think you of these?

                                [*Exeunt* Officers.

Bos. That these are rogues, that in's prosperity,
But to have waited on his fortune, could have wish'd
His dirty stirrup riveted through their noses,
And follow'd after's mule, like a bear in a ring;   230
Would have prostituted their daughters to his lust;
Made their first-born, intelligencers; thought none
    happy
But such as were born under his blest planet,
And wore his livery: and do these lice drop off now?
Well, never look to have the like again: 235
He hath left a sort of flatt'ring rogues behind him;
Their doom must follow. Princes pay flatterers
In their own money: flatterers dissemble their vices,
And they dissemble their lies; that's justice.
Alas, poor gentleman!   240

Duch. Poor! he hath amply fill'd his coffers.

Bos. Sure, he was too honest. Pluto, the god of
    riches,
When he's sent, by Jupiter, to any man,
He goes limping, to signify that wealth
That comes on God's name comes slowly; but when
    he's sent   245
On the devil's errand, he rides post, and comes in by
    scuttles.
Let me show you what a most unvalu'd jewel
You have in a wanton humour thrown away,
To bless the man shall find him. He was an excellent

    230 in a ring] with a ring in its nose   236 sort] set, gang
246 by scuttles] scuttling   247 unvalu'd] invaluable

Courtier, and most faithful; a soldier, that thought it 250
As beastly to know his own value too little
As devilish to acknowledge it too much.
Both his virtue and form deserv'd a far better fortune:
His discourse rather delighted to judge itself than show
    itself.
His breast was fill'd with all perfection, 255
And yet it seem'd a private whisp'ring-room,
It made so little noise of't
   Duch.   But he was basely descended.
   Bos. Will you make yourself a mercenary herald,
Rather to examine men's pedigrees than virtues?
You shall want him: 260
For know an honest statesman to a prince
Is like a cedar, planted by a spring.
The spring bathes the tree's root, the grateful tree
Rewards **it** with his shadow: you have not done so.
I would sooner swim to the Bermoothes on 265
Two politicians' rotten bladders, tied
Together with an intelligencer's heart-string,
Than depend on so changeable a prince's favour.
Fare thee well, Antonio! since the malice of the world
Would needs down with thee, it cannot be said yet 270
That any ill happened unto thee,
Considering thy fall was accompanied with virtue.
   Duch. Oh, you render me excellent music!
   Bos.   Say you?
   Duch. This good one that you speak of is my hus-
band.
   Bos. Do I not dream? can this ambitious age 275
Have so much goodness in't, as to prefer
A man merely for worth, without these shadows
Of wealth and painted honours? possible?
   Duch. I have had three children by him.

254 discourse] reason   265 Bermoothes] Bermudas

Bos.   Fortunate lady!
For you have made your private nuptial bed   280
The humble and fair seminary of peace.
No question but many an unbenefic'd scholar
Shall pray for you for this deed, and rejoice
That some preferment in the world can yet
Arise from merit. The virgins of your land   285
That have no dowries shall hope your example
Will raise them to rich husbands. Should you want
Soldiers, 'twould make the very Turks and Moors
Turn Christians, and serve you for this act.
Last, the neglected poets of your time,   290
In honour of this trophy of a man,
Rais'd by that curious engine, your white hand,
Shall thank you, in your grave, for't; and make that
More reverend than all the cabinets
Of living princes. For Antonio,   295
His fame shall likewise flow from many a pen,
When heralds shall want coats to sell to men.
    Duch. As I taste comfort in this friendly speech,
So would I find concealment.
    Bos. Oh, the secret of my prince,   300
Which I will wear on th' inside of my heart!
    Duch. You shall take charge of all my coin and
        jewels,
And follow him; for he retires himself
To Ancona.
    Bos.   So.
    Duch.   Whither, within few days,
I mean to follow thee.
    Bos.   Let me think: 305
I would wish your grace to feign a pilgrimage
To our Lady of Loretto, scarce seven leagues
From fair Ancona; so may you depart
Your country with more honour, and your flight

Will seem a princely progress, retaining   310
Your usual train about you.
 Duch.   Sir, your direction
Shall lead me by the hand.
 Cari.   In my opinion,
She were better progress to the baths at Lucca,
Or go visit the Spa
In Germany; for, if you will believe me,   315
I do not like this jesting with religion,
This feigned pilgrimage.
 Duch.   Thou art a superstitious fool:
Prepare us instantly for our departure.
Past sorrows, let us moderately lament them,
For those to come, seek wisely to prevent them.   320
        [*Exit* Duchess, *with* Cariola.
 Bos. A politician is the devil's quilted anvil;
He fashions all sins on him, and the blows
Are never heard: he may work in a lady's chamber,
(As here for proof.) What rests, but I reveal
All to my lord? Oh, this base quality   325
Of intelligencer! why, every quality i' th' world
Prefers but gain or commendation:
Now, for this act I am certain to be rais'd,
And men that paint weeds to the life are prais'd.
           [*Exit.*

SCENA III

Enter Cardinal, Ferdinand, Malateste, Pescara,
Delio, *and* Silvio.

 Card. Must we turn soldier, then?
 Mal.   The Emperor,
Hearing your worth that way, ere you attain'd
This reverend garment, joins you in commission

With the right fortunate soldier the Marquis of
    Pescara,
And the famous Lannoy.

Card.   He that had the honour   5
Of taking the French king prisoner?

Mal.   The same.
Here's a plot drawn for a new fortification
At Naples.

Ferd. This great Count Malateste, I perceive,
Hath got employment?

Delio.   No employment, my lord;   10
A marginal note in the muster-book, that he is
A voluntary lord.

Ferd.   He's no soldier?

Delio. He has worn gun-powder in's hollow tooth
for the tooth-ache.

Sil. He comes to the leaguer with a full intent   15
To eat fresh beef and garlic, means to stay
Till the scent be gone, and straight return to court.

Delio. He hath read all the late service
As the City-Chronicle relates it;
And keeps two painters going, only to express   20
Battles in model.

Sil.   Then he'll fight by the book.

Delio. By the almanac, I think,
To choose good days, and shun the critical.
That's his mistress' scarf.

Sil.   Yes, he protests
He would do much for that taffeta—   25

Delio. I think he would run away from a battle,
To save it from taking prisoner.

Sil.   He is horribly afraid
Gun-powder will spoil the perfume on't.

Delio. I saw a Dutchman break his pate once

       7 plot] plan   15 leaguer] camp

For calling him pot-gun; he made his head   30
Have a bore in't like a musket.
   Sil. I would he had made a touch-hole to't.
He is indeed a guarded sumpter-cloth,
Only for the remove of the court.   [*Enter* Bosola.
   Pes. Bosola arriv'd! what should be the business?   35
Some falling-out amongst the cardinals.
These factions amongst great men, they are like
Foxes, when their heads are divided,
They carry fire in their tails, and all the country
About them goes to wreck for't.
   Sil.   What's that Bosola? 40
   Delio. I knew him in Padua,—a fantastical scholar,
like such who study to know how many knots was in
Hercules' club, of what colour Achilles' beard was, or
whether Hector were not troubled with the tooth-
ache. He hath studied himself half blear-ey'd to know 45
the true symmetry of Cæsar's nose by a shoeing-horn;
and this he did to gain the name of a speculative man.
   Pes. Mark Prince Ferdinand:
A very salamander lives in's eye,
To mock the eager violence of fire.   50
   Sil. That cardinal hath made more bad faces with
his oppression than ever Michael Angelo made good
ones: he lifts up's nose, like a foul porpoise before a
storm.
   Pes. The Lord Ferdinand laughs.   55
   Delio. Like a deadly cannon that lightens ere it
smokes.
   Pes. These are your true pangs of death,
The pangs of life, that struggle with great statesmen—
   Delio. In such a deformed silence witches whisper 60
their charms.

   30 pot-gun] popgun   33 guarded sumpter-cloth] fringed
saddle-cloth

Card. Doth she make religion her riding-hood
To keep her from the sun and tempest?
    Ferd.   That,
That damns her.—Methinks her fault and beauty,
Blended together, show like leprosy,   65
The whiter, the fouler. I make it a question
Whether her beggarly brats were ever christen'd.
    Card. I will instantly solicit the state of Ancona
To have them banish'd.
    Ferd.   You are for Loretto:
I shall not be at your ceremony; fare you well.—   70
Write to the Duke of Malfi, my young nephew
She had by her first husband, and acquaint him
With 's mother's honesty.
    Bos.   I will.
    Ferd.   Antonio!
A slave that only smell'd of ink and counters,
And ne'er in 's life look'd like a gentleman,   75
But in the audit-time.—Go, go presently,
Draw me out an hundred and fifty of our horse,
And meet me at the fort-bridge.   [*Exeunt.*

SCENA IV

Enter Two Pilgrims to the Shrine of our Lady of Loretto.

    1 *Pil.* I have not seen a goodlier shrine than this,
Yet I have visited many.
    2 *Pil.*   The Cardinal of Arragon
Is this day to resign his cardinal's hat:
His sister duchess likewise is arriv'd
To pay her vow of pilgrimage. I expect   5
A noble ceremony.
    1 *Pil.*   No question.—They come.

Here the ceremony of the Cardinal's instalment, in the habit of a soldier, perform'd in delivering up his cross, hat, robes, and ring, at the shrine, and investing him with sword, helmet, shield, and spurs; then Antonio, the Duchess, and their children, having presented themselves at the shrine, are (by a form of banishment in dumb-show expressed towards them by the Cardinal and the state of Ancona) banished: during all which ceremony, this ditty is sung, to very solemn music, by divers churchmen: and then exeunt all except the Two Pilgrims.

Arms and honours deck thy story,
To thy fame's eternal glory!
Adverse fortune ever fly thee;
No disastrous fate come nigh thee!

The author disclaims this ditty to be his.   10

I alone will sing thy praises,
Whom to honour virtue raises,
And thy study, that divine is,
Bent to martial discipline is;
Lay aside all those robes lie by thee;   15
Crown thy arts with arms, they'll beautify thee.

O worthy of worthiest name, adorn'd in this manner,
Lead bravely thy forces on under war's warlike banner!
Oh, mayst thou prove fortunate in all martial courses!
Guide thou still, by skill, in art and forces!   20
Victory attend thee nigh, whilst fame sings loud thy powers;
Triumphant conquest crown thy head, and blessings pour down
*   showers!*

 1 *Pil.* Here's a strange turn of state! who would
    have thought
So great a lady would have match'd herself

   7-22] *The authorship of this ditty is not known*

Unto so mean a person! yet the cardinal   25
Bears himself much too cruel.
   2 Pil.   They are banish'd.
   1 Pil. But I would ask what power hath this state
Of Ancona to determine of a free prince?
   2 Pil. They are a free state, sir, and her brother
     show'd
How that the Pope, fore-hearing of her looseness,   30
Hath seiz'd into th' protection of the church
The dukedom which she held as dowager.
   1 Pil. But by what justice?
   2 Pil.   Sure, I think by none,
Only her brother's instigation.
   1 Pil. What was it with such violence he took   35
Off from her finger?
   2 Pil.   'Twas her wedding-ring;
Which he vow'd shortly he would sacrifice
To his revenge.
   1 Pil.   Alas, Antonio!
If that a man be thrust into a well,
No matter who sets hand to't, his own weight   40
Will bring him sooner to th' bottom. Come, let's hence.
Fortune makes this conclusion general,
All things do help th' unhappy man to fall.   [*Exeunt.*

SCENA V

Enter Antonio, Duchess, Children, Cariola, Servants.

   Duch. Banish'd Ancona!
   Ant.   Yes, you see what pow'r
Lightens in great men's breath.
   Duch.   Is all our train
Shrunk to this poor remainder?
   Ant.   These poor men.

Which have got little in your service, vow
To take your fortune: but your wiser buntings,   5
Now they are fledg'd, are gone.

    Duch.   They have done wisely.
This puts me in mind of death; physicians thus,
With their hands full of money, use to give o'er
Their patients.

    Ant.   Right the fashion of the world
From decay'd fortunes every flatterer shrinks;   10
Men cease to build, where the foundation sinks.

    Duch. I had a very strange dream to-night.

    Ant.   What was't?

    Duch. Methought I wore my Coronet of State,
And on a sudden all the diamonds
Were chang'd to pearls.

    Ant.   My interpretation   15
Is, you'll weep shortly; for, to me, the pearls
Do signify your tears.

    Duch.   The birds that live i' th' field,
On the wild benefit of nature, live
Happier than we; for they may choose their mates,
And carol their sweet pleasures to the spring.   20

                      [*Enter* Bosola *with a letter.*

    Bos. You are happily o'erta'en.

    Duch.   From my brother?

    Bos. Yes, from the Lord Ferdinand, your brother,
All love and safety—

    Duch.   Thou dost blanch mischief,
Would'st make it white. See, see, like to calm weather
At sea before a tempest, false hearts speak fair   25
To those they intend most mischief.

A Letter.

Send Antonio to me; I want his head in a business:
         9 Right] just, exactly

A politic equivocation!
He doth not want your counsel, but your head;
That is, he cannot sleep till you be dead.   30
And here's another pitfal that's strew'd o'er
With roses; mark it, 'tis a cunning one:
I stand engaged for your husband for several debts at Naples:
let not that trouble him, I had rather have his heart than his
money.   35
And I believe so too.

   Bos.   What do you believe?

   Duch. That he so much distrusts my husband's love,
He will by no means believe his heart is with him
Until he see it: the devil is not cunning enough
To circumvent us in riddles.   40

   Bos. Will you reject that noble and free league
Of amity and love which I present you?

   Duch. Their league is like that of some politic kings,
Only to make themselves of strength and pow'r
To be our after-ruin; tell them so.   45

   Bos. And what from you?

   Ant.   Thus tell him; I will not come.

   Bos. And what of this?

   Ant.   My brothers have dispers'd
Bloodhounds abroad; which till I hear are muzzl'd,
No truce, though hatch'd with ne'er such politic skill,
Is safe, that hangs upon our enemies' will.   50
I'll not come at them.

   Bos.   This proclaims your breeding:
Every small thing draws a base mind to fear,
As the adamant draws iron. Fare you well, sir:
You shall shortly hear from's.   [*Exit.*

   Duch.   I suspect some ambush:
Therefore by all my love I do conjure you   55
To take your eldest son, and fly towards Milan.
Let us not venture all this poor remainder

In one unlucky bottom.

Ant.   You counsel safely.
Best of my life, farewell, since we must part:
Heaven hath a hand in't; but no otherwise   60
Than as some curious artist takes in sunder
A clock or watch, when it is out of frame,
To bring't in better order.

Duch.   I know not which is best,
To see you dead, or part with you.—Farewell, boy:
Thou art happy, that thou has not understanding   65
To know thy misery; for all our wit
And reading brings us to a truer sense
Of sorrow.—In the eternal church, sir,
I do hope we shall not part thus.

Ant.   Oh, be of comfort!
Make patience a noble fortitude,   70
And think not how unkindly we are us'd:
Man, like to cassia, is prov'd best, being bruis'd.

Duch. Must I, like to a slave-born Russian,
Account it praise to suffer tyranny?
And yet, O Heaven, thy heavy hand is in't!   75
I have seen my little boy oft scourge his top,
And compar'd myself to't: naught made me e'er
Go right but heaven's scourge-stick.

Ant.   Do not weep:
Heaven fashion'd us of nothing; and we strive
To bring ourselves to nothing.—Farewell, Cariola,   80
And thy sweet armful.—If I do never see thee more,
Be a good mother to your little ones,
And save them from the tiger: fare you well.

Duch. Let me look upon you once more, for that speech
Came from a dying father: your kiss is colder   85
Than that I have seen an holy anchorite
Give to a dead man's skull.

58 bottom] ship, cargo

Ant. My heart is turn'd to a heavy lump of lead,
With which I sound my danger: fare you well.

                                    [*Exit with son.*

Duch. My laurel is all withered.   90
Cari. Look, madam, what a troop of armed men
Make toward us!

              [*Enter* Bosola *with a Guard, with visards.*

Duch.   Oh, they are very welcome:
When Fortune's wheel is over-charg'd with princes,
The weight makes it move swift: I would have my ruin
Be sudden.—I am your adventure, am I not?   95
Bos. You are: you must see your husband no more.
Duch. What devil art thou that counterfeits heaven's
    thunder?
Bos. Is that terrible? I would have you tell me whether
Is that note worse that frights the silly birds
Out of the corn, or that which doth allure them   100
To the nets? you have heark'ned to the last too much.
Duch. O misery! like to a rusty o'ercharg'd cannon,
Shall I never fly in pieces?—Come, to what prison?
Bos. To none.
Duch. Whither, then?
Bos.   To your palace.
Duch.   I have heard 105
That Charon's boat serves to convey all o'er
The dismal lake, but brings none back again.
Bos. Your brothers mean you safety and pity.
Duch.   Pity!
With such a pity men preserve alive
Pheasants and quails, when they are not fat enough   110
To be eaten.
Bos. These are your children?
Duch.   Yes.
Bos.   Can they prattle?
Duch.   No:

But I intend, since they were born accurs'd,
Curses shall be their first language.
    Bos.   Fie, madam!
Forget this base, low fellow——
    Duch.   Were I a man,   115
I'd beat that counterfeit face into thy other.
    Bos. One of no birth——
    Duch.   Say that he was born mean,
Man is most happy when's own actions
Be arguments and examples of his virtue.
    Bos. A barren, beggarly virtue.   120
    Duch. I prithee, who is greatest? can you tell?
Sad tales befit my woe: I'll tell you one.
A salmon, as she swam unto the sea,
Met with a dog-fish, who encounters her
With this rough language: 'Why art thou so bold 125
To mix thyself with our high state of floods,
Being no eminent courtier, but one
That for the calmest and fresh time o' th' year
Dost live in shallow rivers, rank'st thyself
With silly smelts and shrimps? and darest thou 130
Pass by our dog-ship without reverence?'
'O,' quoth the salmon, 'sister, be at peace:
Thank Jupiter we both have pass'd the net!
Our value never can be truly known,
Till in the fisher's basket we be shown: 135
I' th' market then my price may be the higher,
Even when I am nearest to the cook and fire.'
So, to great men, the moral may be stretched:
Men oft are valu'd high, when th'are most wretched.——
But come, whither you please. I am arm'd 'gainst
    misery;   140
Bent to all sways of the oppressor's will:
There's no deep valley, but near some great hill.
                                 [*Exeunt.*

ACTUS IV, SCENA I

Enter Ferdinand *and* Bosola.

Ferd. How doth our sister duchess bear herself
In her imprisonment?
Bos.   Nobly: I'll describe her:
She's sad, as one long us'd to't: and she seems
Rather to welcome the end of misery
Than shun it; a behaviour so noble   5
As gives a majesty to adversity:
You may discern the shape of loveliness
More perfect in her tears than in her smiles:
She will muse for hours together; and her silence,
Methinks, expresseth more than if she spake.   10
Ferd. Her melancholy seems to be fortifi'd
With a strange disdain.
Bos.   'Tis so; and this restraint,
(Like English mastives, that grow fierce with tying,)
Makes her too passionately apprehend
Those pleasures she's kept from.
Ferd.   Curse upon her!   15
I will no longer study in the book
Of another's heart. Inform her what I told you.
                    [*Exit. Enter* Duchess.
Bos. All comfort to your grace!
Duch.   I will have none.
Pray thee, why dost thou wrap thy poison'd pills
In gold and sugar?   20
Bos. Your elder brother, the Lord Ferdinand,
Is come to visit you, and sends you word,
'Cause once he rashly made a solemn vow
Never to see you more, he comes i' th' night;
And prays you, gently, neither torch nor taper   25
Shine in your chamber: he will kiss your hand,

And reconcile himself; but, for his vow,
He dares not see you—
 Duch.   At his pleasure.—
Take hence the lights.—He's come.

     [*Exeunt with lights. Enter* Ferdinand.

 Ferd.   Where are you?
 Duch.   Here, sir.
 Ferd. This darkness suits you well.
 Duch.   I would ask you pardon. 30
 Ferd. You have it;
For I account it the honorabl'st revenge,
Where I may kill, to pardon.—Where are your cubs?
 Duch. Whom?
 Ferd. Call them your children;   35
For though our national law distinguish bastards
From true legitimate issue, compassionate nature
Makes them all equal.
 Duch.   Do you visit me for this?
You violate a sacrament o' th' church
Shall make you howl in hell for't.
 Ferd.   It had been well, 40
Could you have liv'd thus always; for, indeed,
You were too much i' th' light:—but no more;
I come to seal my peace with you. Here's a hand

    [*Gives her a dead man's hand.*

To which you have vow'd much love; the ring upon't
You gave.
 Duch. I affectionately kiss it.   45
 Ferd. Pray, do, and bury the print of it in your
  heart.
I will leave this ring with you, for a love-token;
And the hand as sure as the ring; and do not doubt
But you shall have the heart too: when you need a
  friend,

Send it to him that ow'd it; you shall see
Whether he can aid you.
    Duch.   You are very cold:
I fear you are not well after your travel.—
Ha! lights!——Oh, horrible!
    Ferd.   Let her have lights enough.   [*Exit.*
    Duch. What witchcraft doth he practise, that he
       hath left
A dead man's hand here?——   55
      [*Here is discovered, behind a traverse, the artificial
      figures of Antonio and his children, appearing as if
      they were dead.*
    Bos. Look you, here's the piece from which 'twas
       ta'en.
He doth present you this sad spectacle,
That, now you know directly they are dead,
Hereafter you may wisely cease to grieve
For that which cannot be recovered.   60
    Duch. There is not between heaven and earth one
       wish
I stay for after this: it wastes me more
Than were't my picture, fashion'd out of wax,
Stuck with a magical needle, and then buried
In some foul dunghill; and yond's an excellent property 65
For a tyrant, which I would account mercy.
    Bos. What's that?
    Duch. If they would bind me to that lifeless trunk,
And let me freeze to death.
    Bos.   Come, you must live.
    Duch. That's the greatest torture souls feel in
       hell——   70
In hell, that they must live, and cannot die.
Portia, I'll new kindle thy coals again,
And revive the rare and almost dead example

        50 ow'd] owned

Of a loving wife.

Bos.   Oh, fie! despair? remember
You are a Christian.

Duch.   The Church enjoins fasting: 75
I'll starve myself to death.

Bos.   Leave this vain sorrow.
Things being at the worst begin to mend: the bee
When he hath shot his sting into your hand,
May then play with your eye-lid.

Duch.   Good comfortable fellow,
Persuade a wretch that's broke upon the wheel   80
To have all his bones new set; entreat him live
To be executed again. Who must despatch me?
I account this world a tedious theatre,
For I do play a part in 't 'gainst my will.

Bos. Come, be of comfort, I will save your life.   85

Duch. Indeed, I have not leisure to tend so small a
business.

Bos. Now, by my life, I pity you.

Duch.   Thou art a fool, then,
To waste thy pity on a thing so wretch'd
As cannot pity itself. I am full of daggers.
Puff, let me blow these vipers from me.

                              [*Enter* Servant.
                              What are you? 90

Serv. One that wishes you long life.

Duch. I would thou wert hang'd for the horrible
curse
Thou hast given me: I shall shortly grow one
Of the miracles of pity. I'll go pray;—No,
I'll go curse.

Bos.   Oh, fie!

Duch.   I could curse the stars.

Bos.   Oh, fearful! 95

Duch. And those three smiling seasons of the year

Into a Russian winter: nay, the world
To its first chaos.

Bos.   Look you, the stars shine still.

Duch. Oh, but you must remember, my curse hath
    a great way to go.—
Plagues, that make lanes through largest families,   100
Consume them!—

Bos.   Fie, lady!

Duch.   Let them, like tyrants,
Never be rememb'red but for the ill they have done;
Let all the zealous prayers of mortified
Churchmen forget them!—

Bos.   Oh, uncharitable!

Duch. Let heaven a little while cease crowning
    martyrs,   105
To punish them!—
Go, howl them this, and say, I long to bleed:
It is some mercy when men kill with speed.   [*Exit.*

Enter Ferdinand.

Ferd. Excellent, as I would wish; she's plagu'd in art:
These presentations are but fram'd in wax   110
By the curious master in that quality,
Vicentio Lauriola, and she takes them
For true substantial bodies.

Bos.   Why do you do this?

Ferd. To bring her to despair.

Bos.   Faith, end here,
And go no farther in your cruelty: 115
Send her a penitential garment to put on
Next to her delicate skin, and furnish her
With beads and prayer-books.

Ferd.   Damn her! that body of hers,
While that my blood ran pure in't, was more worth

111 curious] subtle   quality] craft

277

Than that which thou wouldst comfort, call'd a soul. 120
I will send her masks of common courtezans,
Have her meat serv'd up by bawds and ruffians,
And, 'cause she'll needs be mad, I am resolv'd
To remove forth the common hospital
All the mad-folk, and place them near her lodging;   125
There let them practise together, sing and dance,
And act their gambols to the full o' th' moon:
If she can sleep the better for it, let her.
Your work is almost ended.

    Bos.   Must I see her again?
    Ferd.   Yes.
    Bos. Never.
    Ferd.   You must.
    Bos.   Never in mine own shape; 130
That's forfeited by my intelligence
And this last cruel lie: when you send me next,
The business shall be comfort.
    Ferd.   Very likely;
Thy pity is nothing of kin to thee. Antonio
Lurks about Milan: thou shalt shortly thither,   135
To feed a fire as great as my revenge,
Which nev'r will slack till it have spent his fuel:
Intemperate agues make physicians cruel.   [*Exeunt.*

SCENA II

Enter Duchess *and* Cariola.

    Duch. What hideous noise was that?
    Cari.   'Tis the wild consort
Of madmen, lady, which your tyrant brother
Hath plac'd about your lodging—this tyranny,
I think, was never practis'd till this hour.

          124 forth] from

Duch. Indeed, I thank him: nothing but noise and
   folly   5
Can keep me in my right wits, whereas reason
And silence make me stark mad. Sit down;
Discourse to me some dismal tragedy.
   Cari. Oh, 'twill increase your melancholy!
   Duch.   Thou art deceiv'd:
To hear of greater grief would lessen mine.   10
This is a prison?
   Cari.   Yes, but you shall live
To shake this durance off.
   Duch.   Thou art a fool:
The robin-red-breast and the nightingale
Never live long in cages.
   Cari.   Pray, dry your eyes.
What think you of, madam?   15
   Duch. Of nothing;
When I muse thus, I sleep.
   Cari. Like a madman, with your eyes open?
   Duch. Dost thou think we shall know one another
In the other world?
   Cari.   Yes, out of question.   20
   Duch. Oh, that it were possible we might
But hold some two days' conference with the dead!
From them I should learn somewhat, I am sure,
I never shall know here. I'll tell thee a miracle:
I am not mad yet, to my cause of sorrow: 25
Th' heaven o'er my head seems made of molten brass,
The earth of flaming sulphur, yet I am not mad.
I am acquainted with sad misery,
As the tann'd galley-slave is with his oar;
Necessity makes me suffer constantly,   30
And custom makes it easy. Who do I look like now?
   Cari. Like to your picture in the gallery,
A deal of life in show, but none in practice;

Or rather like some reverend monument
Whose ruins are even pitied.
  Duch.   Very proper;   35
And Fortune seems only to have her eye-sight
To behold my tragedy.—
How now! What noise is that?
            [*Enter* Servant.
  Serv.   I am come to tell you
Your brother hath intended you some sport.
A great physician, when the Pope was sick   40
Of a deep melancholy, presented him
With several sorts of madmen, which wild object
Being full of change and sport, forc'd him to laugh,
And so th' imposthume broke: the self-same cure
The duke intends on you.
  Duch.   Let them come in.   45
  Serv. There's a mad lawyer, and a secular priest,
A doctor that hath forfeited his wits
By jealousy, an astrologian
That in his works said such a day o' th' month
Should be the day of doom, and, failing of't,   50
Ran mad; an English tailor craz'd i' th' brain
With the study of new fashion; a gentleman usher
Quite beside himself with care to keep in mind
The number of his lady's salutations
Or 'How do you' she employ'd him in each morning; 55
A farmer, too, an excellent knave in grain,
Mad 'cause he was hind'red transportation:
And let one broker that's mad loose to these,
You'ld think the devil were among them.
  Duch. Sit, Cariola.—Let them loose when you
   please,   60
For I am chain'd to endure all your tyranny.
            [*Enter* Madmen.

 42 sorts] collections   **57** transportation] export permit

Here by a Madman this song is sung, to a dismal
kind of music.

    Oh, let us howl some heavy note,
      Some deadly dogged howl,
    Sounding as from the threat'ning throat
      Of beasts and fatal fowl!   65
    As ravens, screech-owls, bulls, and bears,
      We'll bell, and bawl our parts,
    Till irksome noise have cloy'd your ears
      And corrosiv'd your hearts.
    At last, whenas our quire wants breath,   70
      Our bodies being blest,
    We'll sing, like swans, to welcome death,
      And die in love and rest.

1 *Madman.* Doom's-day not come yet? I'll draw it
nearer by a perspective, or make a glass that shall set 75
all the world on fire upon an instant. I cannot sleep;
my pillow is stuff'd with a litter of porcupines.

2 *Madman.* Hell is a mere glass-house, where the
devils are continually blowing up women's souls on
hollow irons, and the fire never goes out.   80

3 *Madman.* I will lie with every woman in my parish
the tenth night; I will tythe them over like hay-cocks.

4 *Madman.* Shall my pothecary out-go me because
I am a cuckold? I have found out his roguery; he makes
allum out of his wife's urine, and sells it to Puritans 85
that have sore throats with over-straining.

1 *Madman.* I have skill in heraldry.

2 *Madman.* Hast?

1 *Madman.* You do give for your crest a woodcock's
head with the brains pick'd out on't; you are a very 90
ancient gentleman.

    69 corrosiv'd] (*pronounced* córrosived) treated with corrosive
75 perspective] telescope   78 glass-house] glass factory (*as
at* II. ii. 6)

3 *Madman.* Greek is turn'd Turk: we are only to be saved by the Helvetian translation.

1 *Madman.* Come on, sir, I will lay the law to you.

2 *Madman.* Oh, rather lay a corrosive: the law will 95 eat to the bone.

3 *Madman.* He that drinks but to satisfy nature is damn'd.

4 *Madman.* If I had my glass here, I would show a sight should make all the women here call me mad 100 doctor.

1 *Madman.* What's he? a rope-maker?

[*Pointing at* 3 Madman

2 *Madman.* No, no, no, a snuffling knave that while he shows the tombs will have his hand in a wench's placket.   105

3 *Madman.* Woe to the caroche that brought home my wife from the mask at three o'clock in the morning! it had a large featherbed in it.

4 *Madman.* I have pared the devil's nails forty times, roasted them in raven's eggs, and cured agues with 110 them.

3 *Madman.* Get me three hundred milch-bats, to make possets to procure sleep.

4 *Madman.* All the college may throw their caps at me: I have made a soap-boiler costive; it was my 115 masterpiece.

[*Here the dance, consisting of* 8 Madmen, *with music answerable thereunto; after which,* Bosola, *like an old man, enters.*

Duch. Is he mad too?

---

93 Helvetian translation] Geneva Bible (*of* 1560)   105
placket] '*a short opening . . . at the top of a woman's petticoat . . .
in front . . . with indelicate suggestion*' (*Linthicum*)   114
throw their caps at] compete in vain with (*Lucas*)   116 s.d.
answerable] appropriate.

Serv.   Pray, question him. I'll leave you.
                    [*Exeunt* Servant *and* Madmen.
Bos. I am come to make thy tomb—
Duch.   Ha! my tomb!
Thou speak'st, as if I lay upon my death-bed,
Gasping for breath: dost thou perceive me sick?   120
Bos. Yes, and the more dangerously, since thy sickness is insensible.
Duch. Thou art not mad, sure: dost know me?
Bos. Yes.
Duch. Who am I?   125
Bos. Thou art a box of worm-seed, at best, but a salvatory of green mummy. What's this flesh? a little cruded milk, fantastical puff-paste. Our bodies are weaker than those paper prisons boys use to keep flies in; more contemptible, since ours is to preserve earth- 130 worms. Didst thou ever see a lark in a cage? Such is the soul in the body: this world is like her little turf of grass, and the heaven o'er our heads like her looking-glass, only gives us a miserable knowledge of the small compass of our prison.   135
Duch. Am not I thy duchess?
Bos. Thou are some great woman, sure, for riot begins to sit on thy forehead (clad in gray hairs) twenty years sooner than on a merry milk-maid's. Thou sleep'st worse than if a mouse should be forc'd 140 to take up her lodging in a cat's ear: a little infant that breeds its teeth, should it lie with thee, would cry out, as if thou wert the more unquiet bedfellow.
Duch. I am Duchess of Malfi still.
Bos. That makes thy sleep so broken: 145
Glories, like glow-worms, afar off shine bright,

122 insensible] unperceived   127 salvatory] ointment-
box   mummy] *a medical preparation from the substance of mum-
mies (O.E.D.)*   128 cruded] curdled

But, look'd to near, have neither heat nor light.

Duch. Thou art very plain.

Bos. My trade is to flatter the dead, not the living;
I am a tomb-maker.   150

Duch. And thou com'st to make my tomb?

Bos. Yes.

Duch. Let me be a little merry:—of what stuff wilt
thou make it?

Bos. Nay, resolve me first, of what fashion?   155

Duch. Why, do we grow fantastical on our death-
bed?

Do we affect fashion in the grave?

Bos. Most ambitiously. Princes' images on their
tombs

Do not lie, as they were wont, seeming to pray

Up to heaven; but with their hands under their cheeks, 160

As if they died of the tooth-ache: they are not carved

With their eyes fix'd upon the stars; but as

Their minds were wholly bent upon the world,

The self-same way they seem to turn their faces.

Duch. Let me know fully therefore the effect   165

Of this thy dismal preparation,

This talk fit for a charnel.

Bos.   Now I shall:—

[*Enter* Executioners, *with a coffin, cords, and a bell.*

Here is a present from your princely brothers;

And may it arrive welcome, for it brings

Last benefit, last sorrow.

Duch.   Let me see it: 170

I have so much obedience in my blood,

I wish it in their veins, to do them good.

Bos. This is your last presence-chamber.

Cari. O my sweet lady!

Duch.   Peace; it affrights not me.

155 resolve] tell

284

Bos. I am the common bellman   175
That usually is sent to condemn'd persons
The night before they suffer.
 Duch.   Even now thou said'st
Thou wast a tomb-maker.
 Bos.   'Twas to bring you
By degrees to mortification. Listen.

   Hark, now every thing is still,   180
   The screech-owl and the whistler shrill
   Call upon our dame, aloud,
   And bid her quickly don her shroud!
   Much you had of land and rent;
   Your length in clay's now competent: 185
   A long war disturb'd your mind;
   Here your perfect peace is sign'd.
   Of what is't fools make such vain keeping?
   Sin their conception, their birth weeping,
   Their life a general mist of error,   190
   Their death a hideous storm of terror.
   Strew your hair with powders sweet,
   Don clean linen, bathe your feet,
   And (the foul fiend more to check)
   A crucifix let bless your neck   195
   'Tis now full tide 'tween night and day;
   End your groan, and come away.

 Cari. Hence, villains, tyrants, murderers! alas!
What will you do with my lady?—Call for help.
 Duch. To whom? to our next neighbours? they are
  mad-folks.   200
 Bos. Remove that noise.
 Duch.   Farewell, Cariola.
In my last will I have not much to give:

    185 competent] sufficient

      285

A many hungry guests have fed upon me,
Thine will be a poor reversion.

Cari.   I will die with her.

Duch. I pray thee, look thou giv'st my little boy   205
Some syrup for his cold, and let the girl
Say her prayers ere she sleep.

[Cariola *is forced off.*
Now what you please:

What death?

Bos. Strangling; here are your executioners.

Duch. I forgive them: 210
The apoplexy, catarrh, or cough o' th' lungs,
Would do as much as they do.

Bos. Doth not death fright you.

Duch.   Who would be afraid on't,
Knowing to meet such excellent company
In th' other world?   215

Bos. Yet, methinks,
The manner of your death should much afflict you:
This cord should terrify you.

Duch.   Not a whit:
What would it pleasure me to have my throat cut
With diamonds? or to be smothered   220
With cassia? or to be shot to death with pearls?
I know death hath ten thousand several doors
For men to take their exits; and 'tis found
They go on such strange geometrical hinges,
You may open them both ways: anyway, for heaven-sake, 225
So I were out of your whispering. Tell my brothers
That I perceive death, now I am well awake,
Best gift is they can give or I can take,
I would fain put off my last woman's-fault,
I'ld not be tedious to you.

First Execut.   We are ready.   230

Duch. Dispose my breath how please you; but my body

Bestow upon my women, will you?

Execut.   Yes.

Duch. Pull, and pull strongly, for your able strength
Must pull down heaven upon me:—
Yet stay; heaven-gates are not so highly arch'd   235
As princes' palaces; they that enter there
Must go upon their knees.—Come, violent death,

                                        [*Kneels.*

Serve for mandragora to make me sleep!—
Go tell my brothers, when I am laid out,
They then may feed in quiet.

                              [*They strangle her.*

Bos.   Where's the waiting-woman? 240
Fetch her: some other strangle the children.

                    [*Enter Executioners with* Cariola.

Look you, there sleeps your mistress.

Cari.   Oh, you are damn'd
Perpetually for this! My turn is next;
Is't not so order'd?

Bos.   Yes, and I am glad
You are so well prepar'd for't.

Cari.   You are deceiv'd, sir,   245
I am not prepar'd for't, I will not die,
I will first come to my answer; and know
How I have offended.

Bos.   Come, despatch her.—
You kept her counsel, now you shall keep ours.

Cari. I will not die, I must not, I am contracted   250
To a young gentleman.

Execut.   Here's your wedding-ring.

Cari. Let me but speak with the duke. I'll discover
Treason to his person.

Bos.   Delays:—throttle her.

Execut. She bites and scratches.

Cari.   If you kill me now,

I am damn'd; I have not been at confession   255
This two years.

    Bos. When?

    Cari.   I am quick with child.

    Bos.   Why, then,

            [*They strangle* Cariola *and bear her off.*

Your credit's sav'd. Bear her into the next room;
Let this lie still.

                        [*Enter* Ferdinand.

    Ferd.   Is she dead?

    Bos.   She is what
You'd have her. But here begin your pity: 260

               [*Shows the Children strangled.*

Alas, how have these offended?—

    Ferd.   The death
Of young wolves is never to be pitied.

    Bos. Fix your eye here.

    Ferd.   Constantly.

    Bos.   Do you not weep?
Other sins only speak; murder shrieks out:
The element of water moistens the earth,   265
But blood flies upwards, and bedews the heavens.

    Ferd. Cover her face; mine eyes dazzle: she died
       young.

    Bos. I think not so; her infelicity
Seem'd to have years too many

    Ferd.   She and I were twins;
And should I die this instant, I had liv'd   270
Her time to a minute.

    Bos.   It seems she was born first:
You have bloodily approv'd the ancient truth,
That kindred commonly do worse agree
Than remote strangers.

    Ferd.   Let me see her face again.
Why didst thou not pity her? what an excellent   275

Honest man mightst thou have been,
If thou hadst borne her to some sanctuary!
Or, bold in a good cause, oppos'd thyself,
With thy advanced sword above thy head,
Between her innocence and my revenge!   280
I bade thee, when I was distracted of my wits,
Go kill my dearest friend, and thou hast done't.
For let me but examine well the cause:
What was the meanness of her match to me?
Only I must confess I had a hope,   285
Had she continu'd widow, to have gain'd
An infinite mass of treasure by her death:
And that was the main cause. Her marriage—
That drew a stream of gall quite through my heart.
For thee, (as we observe in tragedies   290
That a good actor many times is curs'd
For playing a villain's part,) I hate thee for't,
And, for my sake, say, thou hast done much ill
    well.
    Bos. Let me quicken your memory, for I perceive
You are falling into ingratitude: I challenge   295
The reward due to my service.
    Ferd.   I'll tell thee
What I'll give thee.
    Bos.   Do.
    Ferd.   I'll give thee a pardon
For this murther.
    Bos.   Ha!
    Ferd.   Yes, and 'tis
The largest bounty I can study to do thee.
By what authority didst thou execute   300
This bloody sentence?
    Bos.   By yours.
    Ferd.   Mine! was I her judge?
Did any ceremonial form of law

Doom her to not-being? did a complete jury
Deliver her conviction up i' th' court?
Where shalt thou find this judgment register'd,   305
Unless in hell? See, like a bloody fool,
Th'hast forfeited thy life, and thou shalt die for't.

   Bos. The office of justice is perverted quite
When one thief hangs another. Who shall dare
To reveal this?

   Ferd.   Oh, I'll tell thee;   310
The wolf shall find her grave, and scrape it up,
Not to devour the corpse, but to discover
The horrid murther.

   Bos.   You, not I, shall quake for't.

   Ferd. Leave me.

   Bos.   I will first receive my pension.

   Ferd. You are a villain.

   Bos.   When your ingratitude   315
Is judge, I am so.

   Ferd.   O horror,
That not the fear of him which binds the devils
Can prescribe man's obedience!—
Never look upon me more.

   Bos.   Why, fare thee well.
Your brother and yourself are worthy men: 320
You have a pair of hearts, are hollow graves,
Rotten, and rotting others; and your vengeance,
Like two chain'd bullets, still goes arm in arm:
You may be brothers; for treason, like the plague,
Doth take much in a blood. I stand like one   325
That long hath ta'en a sweet and golden dream:
I am angry with myself, now that I wake.

   Ferd. Get thee into some unknown part o' th' world,
That I may never see thee.

   303 complete] *pronounced* cómplete   321 You . . . hearts]
your hearts are alike

Bos.   Let me know
Wherefore I should be thus neglected. Sir,   330
I serv'd your tyranny, and rather strove
To satisfy yourself than all the world:
And though I loath'd the evil, yet I lov'd
You that did counsel it; and rather sought
To appear a true servant than an honest man.   335
  Ferd. I'll go hunt the badger by owl-light:
'Tis a deed of darkness.   [*Exit.*
  Bos. He's much distracted. Off, my painted honour!
While with vain hopes our faculties we tire,
We seem to sweat in ice and freeze in fire.   340
What would I do, were this to do again?
I would not change my peace of conscience
For all the wealth of Europe.—She stirs; here's life:—
Return, fair soul, from darkness, and lead mine
Out of this sensible hell:—she's warm, she breathes:— 345
Upon thy pale lips I will melt my heart,
To store them with fresh colour.—Who's there!
Some cordial drink!—Alas! I dare not call:
So pity would destroy pity.—Her eye opes,
And heaven in it seems to ope, that late was shut,   350
To take me up to mercy.
  Duch.   Antonio!
  Bos. Yes, madam, he is living;
The dead bodies you saw were but feign'd statues:
He's reconcil'd to your brothers; the Pope hath
    wrought
The atonement.
  Duch.   Mercy!   [*She dies.* 355
  Bos. Oh, she's gone again! there the cords of life
    broke.
O sacred innocence, that sweetly sleeps
On turtles' feathers, whilst a guilty conscience

345 sensible] palpable

291

Is a black register, wherein is writ
All our good deeds and bad, a perspective   360
That shows us hell! That we cannot be suffer'd
To do good when we have a mind to it!
This is manly sorrow;
These tears, I am very certain, never grew
In my mother's milk: my estate is sunk   365
Below the degree of fear: where were
These penitent fountains while she was living?
Oh, they were frozen up! Here is a sight
As direful to my soul as is the sword
Unto a wretch hath slain his father. Come,   370
I'll bear thee hence,
And execute thy last will; that's deliver
Thy body to the reverend dispose
Of some good women: that the cruel tyrant
Shall not deny me. Then I'll post to Milan,   375
Where somewhat I will speedily enact
Worth my dejection.   *Exit.*

ACTUS V, SCENA I

Enter Antonio *and* Delio.

Ant. What think you of my hope of reconcilement
To the Arragonian brethren?
    Delio.   I misdoubt it:
For though they have sent their letters of safe-conduct
For your repair to Milan, they appear
But nets to entrap you. The Marquis of Pescara,   5
Under whom you hold certain land in cheat,
Much 'gainst his noble nature, hath been mov'd
To seize those lands, and some of his dependants
Are at this instant making it their suit

373 dispose] disposal   v. i. 6 in cheat] subject to escheat

To be invested in your revenues.   10
I cannot think they mean well to your life
That do deprive you of your means of life,
Your living.

    Ant.   You are still an heretic
To any safety I can shape myself.

    Delio. Here comes the marquis: I will make myself   15
Petitioner for some part of your land,
To know whither it is flying.

    Ant.   I pray, do.

                    [*Enter* Pescara. Antonio *retires.*

    Delio. Sir, I have a suit to you.

    Pes.   To me?

    Delio.   An easy one:
There is the Citadel of Saint Bennet,
With some demesnes, of late in the possession   20
Of Antonio Bologna,—please you bestow them on me.

    Pes. You are my friend; but this is such a suit,
Nor fit for me to give, nor you to take.

    Delio. No, sir?

    Pes.   I will give you ample reason for't
Soon in private:—here's the cardinal's mistress.   25

                       [*Enter* Julia.

    Julia. My lord, I am grown your poor petitioner,
And should be an ill beggar, had I not
A great man's letter here, the Cardinal's,
To court you in my favour.   [*Gives a letter.*

    Pes.   He entreats for you
The Citadel of Saint Bennet, that belong'd   30
To the banish'd Bologna.

    Julia.   Yes.

    Pes. I could not have thought of a friend I could
Rather pleasure with it: 'tis yours.

    Julia.   Sir, I thank you;
And he shall know how doubly I am engag'd

Both in your gift, and speediness of giving   35
Which makes your grant the greater.   [*Exit.*
   Ant.   How they fortify
Themselves with my ruin!
   Delio.   Sir, I am
Little bound to you.
   Pes.   Why?
   Delio. Because you deni'd this suit to me, and gave't
To such a creature.
   Pes.   Do you know what it was?   40
It was Antonio's land; not forfeited
By course of law, but ravish'd from his throat
By the cardinal's entreaty: it were not fit
I should bestow so main a piece of wrong
Upon my friend; 'tis a gratification   45
Only due to a strumpet, for it is injustice.
Shall I sprinkle the pure blood of innocents
To make those followers I call my friends
Look ruddier upon me? I am glad
This land, ta'en from the owner by such wrong,   50
Returns again unto so foul an use
As salary for his lust. Learn, good Delio,
To ask noble things of me, and you shall find
I'll be a noble giver.
   Delio.   You instruct me well.
   Ant. Why, here's a man now, would fright impu-
    dence   55
From sauciest beggars.
   Pes.   Prince Ferdinand's come to Milan,
Sick, as they give out, of an apoplexy;
But some say 'tis a frenzy: I am going
To visit him.   [*Exit.*
   Ant.   'Tis a noble old fellow.
                   [Antonio *advances.*
   Delio. What course do you mean to take, Antonio? 60

Ant. This night I mean to venture all my fortune,
(Which is no more than a poor ling'ring life,)
To the cardinal's worst of malice: I have got
Private access to his chamber; and intend
To visit him about the mid of night,   65
(As once his brother did our noble duchess.)
It may be that the sudden apprehension
Of danger,—for I'll go in mine own shape,—
When he shall see it fraight with love and duty,
May draw the poison out of him, and work   70
A friendly reconcilement: if it fail,
Yet it shall rid me of this infamous calling;
For better fall once, than be ever falling.
    Delio. I'll second you in all danger; and howe'er,
My life keeps rank with yours.   75
    Ant. You are still my lov'd and best friend.
                                                            [*Exeunt.*

SCENA II

Enter Pescara *and* Doctor.

Pes. Now, doctor, may I visit your patient?
    Doc. If't please your lordship: but he's instantly
To take the air here in the gallery
By my direction.
    Pes.   Pray thee, what's his disease?
    Doc. A very pestilent disease, my lord,   5
They call lycanthropia.
    Pes.   What's that?
I need a dictionary to't.
    Doc.   I'll tell you.
In those that are possess'd with't there o'erflows
Such melancholy humour, they imagine
Themselves to be transformed into wolves,   10

69 fraight] fraught

Steal forth to church-yards in the dead of night,
And dig dead bodies up: as two nights since
One met the duke 'bout midnight in a lane
Behind Saint Mark's church, with the leg of a man
Upon his shoulder; and he howl'd fearfully;   15
Said he was a wolf, only the difference
Was, a wolf's skin was hairy on the outside,
His on the inside; bade them take their swords,
Rip up his flesh, and try: straight I was sent for,
And, having minister'd to him, found his grace   20
Very well recover'd.

    Pes.   I am glad on't.
    Doc. Yet not without some fear
Of a relapse. If he grow to his fit again,
I'll go a nearer way to work with him
Than ever Paracelsus dream'd of; if   25
They'll give me leave, I'll buffet his madness out of
    him.
Stand aside; he comes.

    Enter Ferdinand, Malateste, Cardinal, *and* Bosola.

    Ferd.   Leave me.
    Mal. Why doth your lordship love this solitariness?
    Ferd. Eagles commonly fly alone: they are crows,
daws, and starlings that flock together. Look, what's 30
that follows me?
    Mal. Nothing, my lord.
    Ferd. Yes.
    Mal. 'Tis your shadow.
    Ferd. Stay it; let it not haunt me.   35
    Mal. Impossible, if you move, and the sun shine.
    Ferd. I will throttle it.
              [*Throws himself down on his shadow.*
    Mal. Oh, my lord, you are angry with nothing.
    Ferd. You are a fool: how is't possible I should catch

my shadow, unless I fall upon't? When I go to hell, I 40
mean to carry a bribe; for, look you, good gifts ever-
more make way for the worst persons.

Pes. Rise, good my lord.

Ferd. I am studying the art of patience.

Pes. 'Tis a noble virtue.   45

Ferd. To drive six snails before me from this town to
Moscow; neither use goad nor whip to them, but let
them take their own time;—the patient'st man i' th'
world match me for an experiment:—and I'll crawl
after like a sheep-biter.   50

Card. Force him up.   [*They raise him.*

Ferd. Use me well, you were best.
What I have done, I have done: I'll confess nothing.

   Doc. Now let me come to him.—Are you mad, my
      lord?
Are you out of your princely wits?

   Ferd.   What's he?

   Pes.   Your doctor. 55

Ferd. Let me have his beard saw'd off, and his eye-
brows fil'd more civil.

Doc. I must do mad tricks with him, for that's the
only way on't.—I have brought your grace a salamander's skin to keep you from sun-burning.   60

Ferd. I have cruel sore eyes.

Doc. The white of a cockatrix's egg is present
remedy.

Ferd. Let it be a new-laid one, you were best.
Hide me from him: physicians are like kings,—   65
They brook no contradiction.

   Doc. Now he begins to fear me: now let me alone
      with him.

   Card. How now! put off your gown!

   Doc. Let me have some forty urinals fill'd with rose-
water: he and I'll go pelt one another with them.— 70

Now he begins to fear me.—Can you fetch a frisk, sir?
—Let him go, let him go, upon my peril: I find by his
eye he stands in awe of me; I'll make him as tame as a
dormouse.

Ferd. Can you fetch your frisks, sir!—I will stamp 75
him into a cullis, flay off his skin, to cover one of the
anatomies this rogue hath set i' th' cold yonder in
Barber-Chirurgeons' Hall.—Hence, hence! you are all
of you like beasts for sacrifice: there's nothing left of
you but tongue and belly, flattery and lechery. [*Exit.* 80

Pes. Doctor, he did not fear you throughly.

Doc. True, I was somewhat too forward.

Bos. Mercy upon me, what a fatal judgment
Hath fall'n upon this Ferdinand!

Pes.   Knows Your Grace
What accident hath brought unto the prince   85
This strange distraction?

Card. (I must feign somewhat.)—Thus they say it
    grew:
You have heard it rumour'd for these many years,
None of our family dies, but there is seen
The shape of an old woman, which is given   90
By tradition to us to have been murther'd
By her nephews, for her riches. Such a figure
One night, as the prince sat up late at's book,
Appear'd to him; when crying out for help,
The gentleman of's chamber found his grace   95
All on a cold sweat, alter'd much in face
And language: since which apparition,
He hath grown worse and worse, and I much fear
He cannot live.

---

71 fetch a frisk] cut a caper   76 cullis] broth (*made in
part from pounded meat*)   77 anatomies] anatomical specimens,
skeletons   78 Barber-Chirurgeons' Hall] *contained an
anatomical museum*

Bos. Sir, I would speak with you.

Pes.   We'll leave your grace, 100
Wishing to the sick prince, our noble lord,
All health of mind and body.

Card.   You are most welcome.
            [*Exeunt* Pescara, Malateste, *and* Doctor.
Are you come? so.—[*Aside.*] This fellow must not know
By any means I had intelligence
In our duchess' death; for, though I counsell'd it,   105
The full of all th' engagement seem'd to grow
From Ferdinand.—Now, sir, how fares our sister?
I do not think but sorrow makes her look
Like to an oft-dy'd garment: she shall now
Take comfort from me. Why do you look so wildly? 110
Oh, the fortune of your master here, the prince,
Dejects you; but be you of happy comfort:
If you'll do one thing for me I'll entreat,
Though he had a cold tomb-stone o'er his bones,
I'ld make you what you would be.

Bos.   Any thing;   115
Give it me in a breath, and let me fly to't:
They that think long small expedition win,
For musing much o' th' end cannot begin.

                                     [*Enter* Julia.

Julia. Sir, will you come in to supper?
Card.   I am busy, leave me.
Julia [*aside.*] What an excellent shape hath that
    fellow!   [*Exit.* 120
Card. 'Tis thus: Antonio lurks here in Milan;
Inquire him out, and kill him. While he lives,
Our sister cannot marry; and I have thought
Of an excellent match for her. Do this, and style me
Thy advancement.

Bos.   But by what means shall I find him out? 125

124–5 style . . . Thy advancement] name your own reward

Card. There is a gentleman call'd Delio
Here in the camp, that hath been long approv'd
His loyal friend. Set eye upon that fellow;
Follow him to mass; may be Antonio,
Although he do account religion   130
But a school-name, for fashion of the world
May accompany him; or else go inquire out
Delio's confessor, and see if you can bribe
Him to reveal it. There are a thousand ways
A man might find to trace him; as, to know   135
What fellows haunt the Jews for taking up
Great sums of money, for sure he's in want;
Or else to go to th' picture-makers, and learn
Who bought her picture lately: some of these
Happily may take.
    Bos.   Well, I'll not freeze i' th' business: 140
I would see that wretched thing, Antonio,
Above all sights i' th' world.
    Card.   Do, and be happy.
                               [Exit.

    Bos. This fellow doth breed basilisks in 's eyes,
He's nothing else but murder; yet he seems
Not to have notice of the Duchess' death.   145
'Tis his cunning: I must follow his example;
There cannot be a surer way to trace
Than that of an old fox.

                       [Enter Julia.

    Julia. So, sir! You are well met!
    Bos.   How now?
    Julia. Nay, the doors are fast enough: 150
Now, sir, I will make you confess your treachery.
    Bos. Treachery?
    Julia.   Yes; confess to me
Which of my women 'twas you hir'd to put

   136 taking up] borrowing   **140** Happily] haply, perhaps

Love-powder into my drink?

    Bos.   Love-powder!

    Julia.   Yes,

When I was at Malfi.   **155**

Why should I fall in love with such a face else?

I have already suffer'd for thee so much pain,

The only remedy to do me good

Is to kill my longing.

    Bos.   Sure, your pistol holds

Nothing but perfumes or kissing-comfits; Excellent

      lady!   **160**

You have a pretty way on't to discover

Your longing. Come, come, I'll disarm you,

And arm you thus—yet this is wondrous strange.

    Julia. Compare thy form and my eyes together,

You'll find my love no such great miracle.   **165**

Now you'll say

I am wanton: this nice modesty in ladies

Is but a troublesome familiar

That haunts them.

    Bos. Know you me, I am a blunt soldier.

    Julia.   The better: **170**

Sure, there wants fire where there are no lively sparks

Of roughness.

    Bos.   And I want compliment.

    Julia.   Why, ignorance

In courtship cannot make you do amiss,

If you have a heart to do well.

    Bos.   You are very fair.

    Julia. Nay, if you lay beauty to my charge,   **175**

I must plead unguilty.

    Bos.   Your bright eyes

Carry a quiver of darts in them sharper

  168 familiar] familiar spirit (*good or evil*)   172 compliment]
polish, *savoir-faire*

Than sun-beams.

Julia.   You will mar me with commendation,
Put yourself to the charge of courting me,
Whereas now I woo you.   180

    Bos. [*aside.*] I have it, I will work upon this creature.—
Let us grow most amorously familiar:
If the great cardinal now should see me thus,
Would he not count me a villain?

    Julia. No; he might count me a wanton,   185
Not lay a scruple of offence on you;
For if I see and steal a diamond,
The fault is not i' th' stone, but in me the thief
That purloins it. I am sudden with you:
We that are great women of pleasure use to cut off   190
These uncertain wishes and unquiet longings,
And in an instant join the sweet delight
And the pretty excuse together. Had you been i' th'
    street,
Under my chamber-window, even there
I should have courted you.

    Bos.   Oh, you are an excellent lady! 195
    Julia. Bid me do somewhat for you presently
To express I love you.

    Bos.   I will; and if you love me,
Fail not to effect it.
The cardinal is grown wondrous melancholy;
Demand the cause, let him not put you off   200
With feign'd excuse; discover the main ground on't.

    Julia. Why would you know this?

    Bos.   I have depended on him,
And I hear that he is fall'n in some disgrace
With the Emperor: if he be, like the mice
That forsake falling houses, I would shift   205
To other dependance.

196 presently] immediately

Julia. You shall not need follow the wars:
I'll be your maintenance.

Bos. And I your loyal servant:
But I cannot leave my calling.   210

Julia. Not leave an
Ungrateful general for the love of a sweet lady!
You are like some, cannot sleep in feather-beds,
But must have blocks for their pillows.

Bos.   Will you do this?

Julia. Cunningly.

Bos.   To-morrow I'll expect th' intelligence. 215

Julia. To-morrow! get you into my cabinet;
You shall have it with you. Do not delay me,
No more than I do you: I am like one
That is condemn'd; I have my pardon promis'd,
But I would see it seal'd. Go, get you in: 220
You shall see me wind my tongue about his heart
Like a skein of silk.

                         [*Exit* Bosola. *Enter* Cardinal.

Card.   Where are you?

                                    [*Enter* Servant.

Serv.   Here.

Card. Let none, upon your lives, have conference
With the Prince Ferdinand, unless I know it.—
[*Aside.*] In this distraction he may reveal   225
The murder.   [*Exit* Servant.
            Yond's my ling'ring consumption:
I am weary of her, and by any means
Would be quit of.

Julia.   How now, my lord! what ails you?

Card. Nothing.

Julia.   Oh, you are much alter'd:
Come, I must be your secretary, and remove   230
This lead from off your bosom, what's the matter?

230 secretary] confidant

303

Card. I may not tell you.

Julia.   Are you so far in love with sorrow
You cannot part with part of it? or think you
I cannot love your grace when you are sad
As well as merry? or do you suspect   235
I, that have a been a secret to your heart
These many winters, cannot be the same
Unto your tongue?

Card.   Satisfy thy longing,—
The only way to make thee keep my counsel
Is, not to tell thee.

Julia.   Tell your echo this,   240
Or flatterers, that like echoes still report
What they hear though most imperfect, and not me;
For if that you be true unto yourself,
I'll know.

Card.   Will you rack me?

Julia.   No, judgment shall
Draw it from you: it is an equal fault,   245
To tell one's secrets unto all, or none.

Card. The first argues folly.

Julia.   But the last tyranny.

Card. Very well; why, imagine I have committed
Some secret deed, which I desire the world
May never hear of.

Julia.   Therefore may not I know it?   250
You have conceal'd for me as great a sin
As adultery. Sir, never was occasion
For perfect trial of my constancy
Till now: sir, I beseech you——

Card.   You'll repent it.

Julia.   Never.

Card. It hurries thee to ruin: I'll not tell thee.   255
Be well advis'd, and think what danger 'tis
To receive a prince's secrets: they that do,

Had need have their breasts hoop'd with adamant
To contain them. I pray thee, yet be satisfi'd;
Examine thine own frailty; 'tis more easy   260
To tie knots, than unloose them: 'tis a secret
That, like a ling'ring poison, may chance lie
Spread in thy veins, and kill thee seven year hence.
 Julia. Now you dally with me.
 Card.   No more; thou shalt know it.
By my appointment, the great Duchess of Malfi   265
And two of her young children, four nights since,
Were strangled.
 Julia.   Oh heaven! sir, what have you done!
 Card. How now? how settles this? think you your
  bosom
Will be a grave dark and obscure enough
For such a secret?
 Julia.   You have undone yourself, sir.   270
 Card. Why?
 Julia.   It lies not in me to conceal it.
 Card.   No?
Come, I will swear you to't upon this book.
 Julia. Most religiously.
 Card.   Kiss it.   [*She kisses the book.*
Now you shall never utter it; thy curiosity
Hath undone thee: thou'rt poison'd with that book;   275
Because I knew thou couldst not keep my counsel,
I have bound thee to't by death.   [*Enter* Bosola.
 Bos. For pity-sake, hold!
 Card.   Ha, Bosola!
 Julia.   I forgive you
This equal piece of justice you have done;
For I betray'd your counsel to that fellow: 280
He over-heard it; that was the cause I said
It lay not in me to conceal it.
 Bos.   Oh foolish woman,

Couldst not thou have poison'd him?

Julia.   'Tis weakness,
Too much to think what should have been done.—I go,
I know not whither.   [*Dies.*

Card.   Wherefore com'st thou hither?   285

Bos. That I might find a great man like yourself,
Not out of his wits (as the Lord Ferdinand),
To remember my service.

Card.   I'll have thee hew'd in pieces.

Bos. Make not yourself such a promise of that life
Which is not yours to dispose of.

Card.   Who plac'd thee here? 290

Bos. Her lust, as she intended.

Card.   Very well:
Now you know me for your fellow-murderer.

Bos. And wherefore should you lay fair marble
   colours
Upon your rotten purposes to me?
Unless you imitate some that do plot great treasons, 295
And when they have done, go hide themselves i' th'
   graves
Of those were actors in't?

Card.   No more; there is
A fortune attends thee.

Bos. Shall I go sue to Fortune any longer?
'Tis the fool's pilgrimage.

Card.   I have honours in store for thee. 300

Bos. There are many ways that conduct to seeming
Honour, and some of them very dirty ones.

Card. Throw to the devil
Thy melancholy.—The fire burns well;
What need we keep a stirring of't, and make   305
A great smother? Thou wilt kill Antonio?

Bos. Yes.

Card.   Take up that body.

Bos.   I think I shall
Shortly grow the common bier for church-yards.

Card. I will allow thee some dozen of attendants
To aid thee in the murther.   310

Bos. Oh, by no means. Physicians that apply horse-
leeches to any rank swelling use to cut off their tails,
that the blood may run through them the faster: let
me have no train when I go to shed blood, lest it make
me have a greater when I ride to the gallows.   315

Card. Come to me after midnight, to help to remove
    that body
To her own lodging: I'll give out she died o' the plague;
'Twill breed the less inquiry after her death.

Bos. Where's Castruchio her husband?

Card. He's rode to Naples, to take possession   320
Of Antonio's citadel.

Bos. Believe me, you have done a very happy turn.

Card. Fail not to come: there is the master-key
Of our lodgings; and by that you may conceive
What trust I plant in you.

Bos.   You shall find me **ready.** 325
                            [*Exit* Cardinal.

O poor Antonio, though nothing be so needful
To thy estate as pity, yet I find
Nothing so dangerous! I must look to my footing:
In such slippery ice-pavements men had need
To be frost-nail'd well, they may break their necks
    else;   330
The precedent's here afore me. How this man
Bears up in blood! seems fearless! Why, 'tis well;
Security some men call the suburbs of hell,
Only a dead wall between. Well, good Antonio,
I'll seek thee out; and all my care shall be   335
To put thee into safety from the reach

333 security] over-confidence

Of these most cruel biters, that have got
Some of thy blood already. It may be,
I'll join with thee in a most just revenge:
The weakest arm is strong enough, that strikes   340
With the sword of justice. Still methinks the duchess
Haunts me: there, there!—'Tis nothing but my
    melancholy.
O Penitence, let me truly taste thy cup,
That throws men down only to raise them up!

                                        [*Exit.*

SCENA III

Enter Antonio *and* Delio.

(*Echo from the Duchess's grave.*)

  Delio. Yond's the cardinal's window. This fortifica-
    tion
Grew from the ruins of an ancient abbey;
And to yond side o' th' river lies a wall,
Piece of a cloister, which in my opinion
Gives the best echo that you ever heard,   5
So hollow and so dismal, and withal
So plain in the distinction of our words,
That many have suppos'd it is a spirit
That answers.
  Ant.   I do love these ancient ruins.
We never tread upon them but we set   10
Our foot upon some reverend history:
And, questionless, here in this open court,
Which now lies naked to the injuries
Of stormy weather, some men lie interr'd
Lov'd the church so well, and gave so largely to 't,   15
They thought it should have canopi'd their bones
Till dooms-day; but all things have their end:

Churches and cities, which have diseases like to men,
Must have like death that we have.
>   *Echo.*   *Like death that we have.*
>   *Delio.* Now the echo hath caught you.
>   *Ant.*   It groan'd methought, and gave 20
A very deadly accent.
>   *Echo.*   *Deadly accent.*
>   *Delio.* I told you 'twas a pretty one: you may make it
A huntsman, or a falconer, a musician,
Or a thing of sorrow.
>   *Echo.*   *A thing of sorrow.*
>   *Ant.* Ay, sure, that suits it best.
>   *Echo.*   *That suits it best.* 25
>   *Ant.* 'Tis very like my wife's voice.
>   *Echo.*   *Ay, wife's voice.*
>   *Delio.* Come, let us walk further from't.
I would not have you go to the cardinal's to-night:
Do not.
>   *Echo.* *Do not.*   30
>   *Delio.* Wisdom doth not more moderate wasting
>   sorrow
Than time: take time for't; be mindful of thy safety.
>   *Echo. Be mindful of thy safety.*
>   *Ant.*   Necessity compels me:
Make scrutiny through the passages
Of your own life, you'll find it impossible   35
To fly your fate.
>   *Echo.*   *Oh, fly your fate!*
>   *Delio.* Hark! the dead stones seem to have pity on
>   you,
And give you good counsel.
>   *Ant.*   Echo, I will not talk with thee,
For thou art a dead thing.
>   *Echo.*   *Thou art a dead thing.*
>   *Ant.* My duchess is asleep now,   40

And her little ones, I hope sweetly: oh heaven,
Shall I never see her more?
   Echo.   *Never see her more.*
   Ant. I mark'd not one repetition of the echo
But that; and on the sudden a clear light
Presented me a face folded in sorrow.   45
   Delio. Your fancy merely.
   Ant.   Come, I'll be out of this ague,
For to live thus is not indeed to live;
It is a mockery and abuse of life:
I will not henceforth save myself by halves;
Lose all, or nothing.
   Delio.   Your own virtue save you! 50
I'll fetch your eldest son, and second you:
It may be that the sight of his own blood
Spread in so sweet a figure may beget
The more compassion.
   Ant.   However, fare you well.
Though in our miseries Fortune have a part,   55
Yet in our noble sufferings she hath none:
Contempt of pain, that we may call our own.
                               [Exeunt.

SCENA IV

Enter Cardinal, Pescara, Malateste, Roderigo, *and*
Grisolan.

   Card. You shall not watch to-night by the sick
     prince;
His grace is very well recover'd.
   Mal. Good my lord, suffer us.
   Card.   Oh, by no means;
The noise, and change of object in his eye,
Doth more distract him: I pray, all to bed;   5
And though you hear him in his violent fit,

Do not rise, I entreat you.

Pes. So, sir; we shall not.

Card.   Nay, I must have you promise
Upon your honours, for I was enjoin'd to't
By himself; and he seem'd to urge it sensibly.   10

Pes. Let our honours bind this trifle.

Card. Nor any of your followers.

Mal. Neither.

Card. It may be, to make trial of your promise,
When he's asleep, myself will rise and feign   15
Some of his mad tricks, and cry out for help,
And feign myself in danger.

Mal.   If your throat were cutting,
I'ld not come at you, now I have protested against it.

Card. Why, I thank you.

                               [Withdraws.

Gris.   'Twas a foul storm to-night.

Rod. The Lord Ferdinand's chamber shook like an
    osier.   20

Mal. 'Twas nothing but pure kindness in the devil
To rock his own child.

                 [Exeunt all except the Cardinal.

Card. The reason why I would not suffer these
About my brother, is, because at midnight
I may with better privacy convey   25
Julia's body to her own lodging. Oh, my conscience!
I would pray now; but the devil takes away my heart
For having any confidence in prayer.
About this hour I appointed Bosola
To fetch the body: when he hath serv'd my turn,   30
He dies.

                 [Exit. Enter Bosola.

Bos. Ha! 'twas the cardinal's voice; I heard him
name Bosola and my death. Listen; I hear one's footing.

                    [Enter Ferdinand.

Ferd. Strangling is a very quiet death.

Bos.—Nay, then, I see I must stand upon my guard. 35

Ferd. What say' to that? whisper softly; do you
    agree to't?
So; it must be done i' th' dark: the Cardinal
Would not for a thousand pounds the doctor should
    see it.   [*Exit.*

Bos. My death is plotted; here's the consequence of
    murther.

We value not desert nor Christian breath,   40
When we know black deeds must be cur'd with death.

                   [*Enter* Antonio *and* Servant.

Serv. Here stay, sir, and be confident, I pray:
I'll fetch you a dark lanthorn.   [*Exit.*

Ant.   Could I take him
At his prayers, there were hope of pardon.

Bos.   Fall right, my sword!—
                      [*Stabs him.*

I'll not give thee so much leisure as to pray.   45

Ant. Oh, I am gone! Thou hast ended a long suit
In a minute.

Bos.   What art thou?

Ant.   A most wretched thing,
That only have thy benefit in death,
To appear myself.

               [*Enter* Servant *with light.*

Serv.   Where are you, sir?

Ant. Very near my home.—Bosola!

Serv.   Oh, misfortune! 50

Bos. Smother thy pity, thou art dead else.—Antonio!
The man I would have sav'd 'bove mine own life!
We are merely the stars' tennis-balls, struck and banded
Which way please them.—Oh, good Antonio,
I'll whisper one thing in thy dying ear   55

    36 say'] say you   53 banded] bandied

Shall make thy heart break quickly! thy fair duchess
And two sweet children——

Ant.   Their very names
Kindle a little life in me.

Bos.   Are murder'd.

Ant. Some men have wish'd to die
At the hearing of sad tidings; I am glad   60
That I shall do't in sadness: I would not now
Wish my wounds balm'd nor heal'd, for I have no use
To put my life to. In all our quest of greatness,
Like wanton boys whose pastime is their care,
We follow after bubbles blown in th' air.   65
Pleasure of life, what is't? only the good hours
Of an ague; merely a preparative to rest,
To endure vexation. I do not ask
The process of my death; only commend me
To Delio.   70

Bos. Break, heart!

Ant.   And let my son fly the courts of princes.
                                    [Dies.

Bos. Thou seem'st to have lov'd Antonio.

Serv.   I brought him hither,
To have reconcil'd him to the cardinal.

Bos. I do not ask thee that.
Take him up, if thou tender thine own life,   75
And bear him where the lady Julia
Was wont to lodge.—Oh, my fate moves swift!
I have this cardinal in the forge already;
Now I'll bring him to th' hammer. O direful mis-
    prision!
I will not imitate things glorious,   80
No more than base; I'll be mine own example.—
On, on, and look thou represent, for silence,
The thing thou bear'st.   *[Exeunt.*

    61 in sadness] in earnest   79 misprision] mistake

SCENA V

Enter Cardinal, *with a book.*

Card. I am puzzl'd in a question about hell;
He says, in hell there's one material fire,
And yet it shall not burn all men alike.
Lay him by. How tedious is a guilty conscience!
When I look into the fish-ponds in my garden,   5
Methinks I see a thing arm'd with a rake,
That seems to strike at me.

Enter Bosola, *and* Servant *bearing* Antonio's *body.*

                                    Now, art thou come?
Thou look'st ghastly:
There sits in thy face some great determination
Mix'd with some fear.
Bos.   Thus it lightens into action: 10
I am come to kill thee.
Card.   Ha!—Help! our guard!
Bos. Thou art deceiv'd;
They are out of thy howling.
Card. Hold; and I will faithfully divide
Revenues with thee.
Bos.   Thy prayers and proffers   15
Are both unseasonable.
Card.   Raise the watch!
We are betray'd!
Bos.   I have confin'd your flight:
I'll suffer your retreat to Julia's chamber,
But no further.
Card.   Help! we are betray'd!

Enter, above, Pescara, Malateste, Roderigo, *and*
Grisolan.

4 tedious] troublesome

314

Mal. Listen.   20

Card. My dukedom for rescue!

Rod.   Fie upon his counterfeiting!

Mal. Why, 'tis not the cardinal.

Rod.   Yes, yes, 'tis he:
But I'll see him hang'd, ere I'll go down to him.

Card. Here's a plot upon me; I am assaulted! I am
   lost,
Unless some rescue!

Gris.   He doth this pretty well;   25
But it will not serve to laugh me out of mine honour.

Card. The sword's at my throat!

Rod.   You would not bawl so loud then.

Mal. Come, come!
Let's go to bed: he told us this much aforehand.

Pes. He wish'd you should not come at him; but,
   believe't,   30
The accent of the voice sounds not in jest:
I'll down to him, howsoever, and with engines
Force ope the doors.   [*Exit above.*

Rod.   Let's follow him aloof,
And note how the Cardinal will laugh at him.
   [*Exeunt, above,* Malateste, Roderigo, *and* Grisolan.

Bos. There's for you first, 'cause you shall not un-
   barricade the door   35
To let in rescue.   [*He kills the* Servant.

Card. What cause hast thou to pursue my life?

Bos.   Look there.

Card. Antonio!

Bos.   Slain by my hand unwittingly.
Pray, and be sudden: when thou kill'd'st thy sister,
Thou took'st from Justice her most equal balance,   40
And left her naught but her sword.

Card. Oh, mercy!

34 'cause] because = in order that   39 sudden] quick

315

Bos. Now it seems thy greatness was only outward;
For thou fall'st faster of thyself, than calamity
Can drive thee. I'll not waste longer time; there!   45
                              [*Stabs him.*

Card. Thou hast hurt me.
Bos.   Again!   [*Stabs him again.*
Card.   Shall I die like a leveret,
Without any resistance?—Help, help, help!
I am slain!   [*Enter* Ferdinand.
Ferd.   The alarum! give me a fresh horse;
Rally the vaunt-guard, or the day is lost,
Yield, yield! I give you the honour of arms
Shake my sword over you; will you yield?   50
Card. Help me; I am your brother!
Ferd.   The devil!
My brother fight upon the adverse party!
          [*He wounds the* Cardinal, *and, in the scuffle, gives*
               Bosola *his death-wound.*
There flies your ransom.
Card.   O justice!
I suffer now for what hath former bin:
Sorrow is held the eldest child of sin.   55
Ferd. Now you're brave fellows. Cæsar's fortune was
harder than Pompey's; Cæsar died in the arms of pros-
perity, Pompey at the feet of disgrace. You both died
in the field. The pain's nothing: pain many times is
taken away with the apprehension of greater, as the   60
tooth-ache with the sight of a barber that comes to
pull it out: there's philosophy for you.
Bos. Now my revenge is perfect.—Sink, thou main
    cause
Of my undoing!—The last part of my life
                              [*He kills* Ferdinand.   65
Hath done me best service.

     55 bin] been (*a common spelling used to mark the rhyme*)

316

Ferd. Give me some wet hay; I am broken-winded.
I do account this world but a dog-kennel:
I will vault credit and affect high pleasures
Beyond death.
    Bos.   He seems to come to himself,   70
Now he's so near the bottom.
    Ferd. My sister, oh my sister! there's the cause on't.
Whether we fall by ambition, blood, or lust,
Like diamonds, we are cut with our own dust.
                                         [Dies.

    Card. Thou hast thy payment too.   75
    Bos. Yes, I hold my weary soul in my teeth;
'Tis ready to part from me. I do glory
That thou, which stood'st like a huge pyramid
Begun upon a large and ample base,
Shalt end in a little point, a kind of nothing.   80
        [Enter, below, Pescara, Malateste, Roderigo,
            and Grisolan.
    Pes. How now, my lord!
    Mal. Oh, sad disaster!
    Rod. How comes this?
    Bos. Revenge for the Duchess of Malfi murdered
By th' Arragonian brethren; for Antonio   85
Slain by his hand; for lustful Julia
Poison'd by this man; and lastly for myself,
That was an actor in the main of all
Much 'gainst mine own good nature, yet i' th' end
Neglected.
    Pes.   How now, my lord!
    Card.   Look to my brother: 90
He gave us these large wounds, as we were struggling
Here i' th' rushes. And now, I pray, let me
Be laid by and never thought of.   *[Dies.*
    Pes. How fatally, it seems, he did withstand
His own rescue!

Mal.   Thou wretched thing of blood,   95
How came Antonio by his death?

  Bos. In a mist; I know not how:
Such a mistake as I have often seen
In a play. Oh, I am gone!
We are only like dead walls or vaulted graves,   100
That, ruin'd, yields no echo. Fare you well.
It may be pain, but no harm, to me to die
In so good a quarrel. Oh, this gloomy world!
In what a shadow, or deep pit of darkness,
Doth womanish and fearful mankind live!   105
Let worthy minds ne'er stagger in distrust
To suffer death or shame for what is just:
Mine is another voyage.   [*Dies.*

  Pes. The noble Delio, as I came to th' palace,
Told me of Antonio's being here, and show'd me   110
A pretty gentleman, his son and heir.

              [*Enter* Delio *with* Antonio's *Son.*

  Mal. Oh sir, you come too late!
  Delio.   I heard so, and
Was arm'd for't ere I came. Let us make noble use
Of this great ruin; and join all our force
To establish this young hopeful gentleman   115
In's mother's right. These wretched eminent things
Leave no more fame behind 'em, than should one
Fall in a frost, and leave his print in snow;
As soon as the sun shines, it ever melts,
Both form and matter. I have ever thought   120
Nature doth nothing so great for great men
As when she's pleas'd to make them lords of truth:
Integrity of life is fame's best friend.
Which nobly, beyond death, shall crown the end.

                                        [*Exeunt.*

The Roman Actor

BY

PHILIP MASSINGER

PHILIP MASSINGER (1583–1640)

The Roman Actor

Licensed for acting 11 October 1626; printed in 1629.

[*Plays*, ed. W. Gifford, 4 vols., 1805 (second edition 1813), in modern spelling, is the foundation of all later collected editions, though *Plays*, ed. F. Cunningham, 1868, includes one play first printed from manuscript after Gifford's death. *The Roman Actor* was edited in the original spelling by W. L. Sandidge, Princeton, 1929.]

THE
ROMAN
ACTOR.
A
TRAGÆDIE.

As it hath diuers times beene, with
good allowance Acted, at the private
Play-houfe in the *Black-Friers*,
by the Kings Majeſties
Servants.

WRITTEN
By PHILIP MASSINGER.

LONDON.
Printed by *B. A.* and *T. F.* for ROBERT ALLOT, and
are to be ſold at his Shop at the ſigne of the *Beare*
in *Pauls* Church-yard. 1 6 2 9.

M

The persons presented.	The principal Actors.	
Domitianus Cæsar.	JOHN LOWIN.	
Paris the Tragedian.	JOSEPH TAYLOR.	
Parthenius a freeman of *Cæsar's.*	RICHARD SHARPE.	
		5
Ælius Lamia, and *Stephanos.*	THOMAS POLLARD.	
Junius Rusticus.	ROBERT BENFIELD.	
Aretinus Clemens, Cæsar's spy.	EYLLARDT SWANSTONE.	
Æsopus a Player.	RICHARD ROBINSON.	
Philargus a rich Miser.	ANTHONY SMITH.	10
Palphurius Sura a Senator.	WILLIAM PATTRICKE.	
Fulcinius a senator.		
Latinus a Player.	CURTISE GREVILL.	
3 Tribunes.	GEORGE VERNON.	
2 Lictors.	JAMES HORNE.	15
Ascletario an Astrologer.		
Sejeius } Conspirators. *Entellus*		
Domitia the wife of *Ælius Lamia.*	JOHN TOMPSON.	
		20
Domitilla cousin-german to *Cæsar.*	JOHN HUNNIEMAN.	
Julia, Titus' Daughter.	WILLIAM TRIGGE.	
Cænis, Vespasian's Concubine.	ALEXANDER GOUGH.	
A Lady.		
		25

Centurions, Soldiers, Hangmen, Servants, Captives.

persons . . . Actors] *From the original, completed by Gifford. All the actors are well-known King's players, and many had appeared in* The Duchess of Malfi. *J. Taylor wrote some of the complimentary verses mentioned below.* 4 freeman] *We should write* freedman *for the Latin* libertus, *but Massinger's usage is consistent and was common in his day.*

To my much honoured and most true Friends,
SIR PHILIP KNYVET, KNIGHT AND BARONET,
AND TO SIR THOMAS JAY, KNIGHT,
AND THOMAS BELLINGHAM,
of Newtimber in Sussex ESQUIRE.   5

How much I acknowledge myself bound for your
so many and extraordinary favours conferr'd upon
me (as far as it is in my power,) posterity shall take
notice; I were most unworthy of such noble friends,
if I should not, with all thankfulness, profess and own 10
them. In the composition of this Tragedy you were
my only supporters, and it being now by your principal encouragement to be turn'd into the world, it
cannot walk safer than under your protection. It hath
been happy in the suffrage of some learned and 15
judicious gentlemen when it was presented, nor shall
they find cause, I hope, in the perusal, to repent them
of their good opinion of it. If the gravity and height
of the subject distaste such as are only affected with
jigs and ribaldry (as I presume it will), their con- 20
demnation of me and my poem can no way offend me:
my reason teaching me such malicious and ignorant
detractors deserve rather contempt than satisfaction.

dedication] Sir Philip Knyvet, Bart. (1583–1655), of New
Buckenham, Norfolk. Massinger addressed a complimentary
poem, *The Virgin's Character*, to his eldest daughter.   Sir
Thomas Jay (or Jeay), Knt. (*c.* 1585–1636+), Keeper of the
King's Armoury at Greenwich 1628+, J.P. for Middlesex 1636;
author of complimentary verses on this play and others and of a
few occasional verses preserved in manuscript.   Thomas
Bellingham, Esq. (*d.* 1648 or 1649), son of Sir Edward Bellingham
(*d.* 1640); apparently not otherwise known in public life.   19
distaste] displease.

I ever held it the most perfect birth of my Minerva;
and therefore in justice offer it to those that have best 25
deserv'd of me, who I hope in their courteous accep-
tance will render it worth their receiving, and ever, in
their gentle construction of my imperfections, believe
they may at their pleasure dispose of him that is wholly
and sincerely   30

Devoted to their service,
PHILIP MASSINGER.

24. Minerva] *Goddess of wisdom and of arts.*

*The dedication is followed by complimentary verses signed by
T. J[ay], one of the patrons; Tho. G[offe]; Tho. May;
Robert Harvey; and Joseph Taylor, one of the actors.*

THE ROMAN ACTOR

A Tragedy

ACTUS I, SCÆNA I

Enter Paris, Latinus, *and* Æsopus.

Æsop. What do we act to-day?
Lat.   Agave's frenzy,
With Pentheus' bloody end.
Par.   It skills not what;
The times are dull, and all that we receive
Will hardly satisfy the day's expense.
The Greeks, (to whom we owe the first invention   5
Both of the buskin'd scene and humble sock,)
That reign in every noble family,
Declaim against us; and our amphitheatre,
Great Pompey's work, that hath giv'n full delight
Both to the eye and ear of fifty thousand   10
Spectators in one day, as if it were
Some unknown desert, or great Rome unpeopl'd,
Is quite forsaken.
Lat.   Pleasures of worse natures
Are gladly entertain'd, and they that shun us,
Practise in private sports the stews would blush at. 15
A litter borne by eight Liburnian slaves,
To buy diseases from a glorious strumpet,
The most censorious of our Roman gentry,
Nay, of the guarded robe, the senators,
Esteem an easy purchase.
Par.   Yet grudge us,   20
(That with delight join profit, and endeavour
To build their minds up fair, and on the stage

2 skills] matters   6 buskin'd . . . sock] tragic and comic
drama   17 glorious] ostentatious   19 guarded] bordered,
fringed

Decipher to the life what honours wait
On good and glorious actions, and the shame
That treads upon the heels of vice,) the salary   25
Of six sestertii!

  Æsop.   For the profit, Paris,
And mercenary gain, they are things beneath us;
Since, while you hold your grace and power with Cæsar,
We, from your bounty, find a large supply,
Nor can one thought of want ever approach us.   30

  Par. Our aim is glory, and to leave our names
To aftertimes.

  Lat.   And, would they give us leave,
There ends all our ambition.

  Æsop.   We have enemies,
And great ones too, I fear. 'Tis given out lately,
The consul Aretinus, Cæsar's spy,   35
Said at his table, ere a month expired,
For being gall'd in our last comedy,
He would silence us for ever.

  Par.   I expect
No favour from him; my strong Aventine is,
That great Domitian, whom we oft have cheer'd   40
In his most sullen moods, will once return,
Who can repair, with ease, the consul's ruins.

  Lat. 'Tis frequent in the city, he hath subdued
The Catti and the Daci, and, ere long,
The second time will enter Rome in triumph.   45

Enter two Lictors.

  Par. Jove hasten it!—With us?—I now believe
The consul's threats, Æsopus.

  1. *Lict.*   You are summon'd
T' appear to-day in Senate.

39 Aventine] refuge, sanctuary (*from a hill in Rome*)   43
frequent] common talk   44 Catti] *better spelled* Chatti

2. *Lict*.   And there to answer
What shall be urg'd against you.
    Par.   We obey you.
Nay, droop not, fellows; innocence should be bold.   50
We, that have personated in the scene
The ancient heroes, and the falls of princes,
With loud applause, being to act ourselves,
Must do it with undaunted confidence.
Whate'er our sentence be, think 'tis in sport;   55
And, though condemn'd, let's hear it without sorrow,
As if we were to live again to-morrow.
    1. *Lict*. 'Tis spoken like yourself.

        Enter Ælius Lamia, Junius Rusticus, *and*
                   Palphurius Sura.

    Lam.   Whither goes Paris?
    1. *Lict*. He's cited to the Senate.
    Lat.   I am glad the state is
So free from matters of more weight and trouble   60
That it has vacant time to look on us.
    Par. That reverend place, in which the affairs of
        kings
And provinces were determin'd, to descend
To the censure of a bitter word, or jest,
Dropp'd from a poet's pen! Peace to your lordships!   65
We are glad that you are safe.
        [*Exeunt* Lictors, Paris, Latinus, *and* Æsopus.
    Lam.   What times are these!
To what is Rome fall'n! may we being alone
Speak our thoughts freely of the prince and state,
And not fear the informer?
    Rust.   Noble Lamia,
So dangerous the age is, and such bad acts   70
Are practis'd everywhere, we hardly sleep,

64 censure] judgement

Nay, cannot dream, with safety. All our actions
Are call'd in question; to be nobly born
Is now a crime, and to deserve too well,
Held capital treason. Sons accuse their fathers,   75
Fathers their sons; and, but to win a smile
From one in grace at court, our chastest matrons
Make shipwreck of their honours. To be virtuous
Is to be guilty. They are only safe
That know to soothe the prince's appetite,   80
And serve his lusts.
   Sura.   'Tis true; and 'tis my wonder,
That two sons of so different a nature
Should spring from good Vespasian. We had a Titus,
Styl'd justly the delight of all mankind,
Who did esteem that day lost in his life   85
In which some one or other tasted not
Of his magnificent bounties; one that had
A ready tear, when he was forc'd to sign
The death of an offender; and so far
From pride that he disdain'd not the converse   90
Even of the poorest Roman.
   Lam.   Yet his brother,
Domitian, that now sways the power of things,
Is so inclin'd to blood that no day passes
In which some are not fasten'd to the hook,
Or thrown down from the Gemonies. His freemen   95
Scorn the nobility, and he himself,
As if he were not made of flesh and blood,
Forgets he is a man.
   Rust.   In his young years,
He show'd what he would be when grown to ripeness:
His greatest pleasure was, being a child,   100
With a sharp-pointed bodkin to kill flies,

94–95 hook . . . Gemonies] *Ignominious and painful execution*
95 &c. freemen] *See note on persons presented, above, p.* 322.

Whose rooms now men supply. For his escape
In the Vitellian war, he rais'd a temple
To Jupiter, and proudly plac'd his figure
In the bosom of the god: and in his edicts   105
He does not blush, or start, to style himself
(As if the name of emperor were base)
Great Lord and God Domitian.
    Sura.   I have letters
He's on his way to Rome, and purposes
To enter with all glory. The flattering Senate   110
Decrees him divine honours, and to cross it,
Were death with studied torments; for my part,
I will obey the time; it is in vain
To strive against the torrent.
    Rust.   Let's to the Curia.
And, though unwillingly, give our suffrages,   115
Before we are compell'd.
    Lam.   And since we cannot
With safety use the active, let's make use of
The passive fortitude, with this assurance,—
That the state, sick in him, the gods to friend,
Though at the worst, will now begin to mend.   120
                                        [Exeunt.

ACTUS I, SCÆNA 2

Enter Domitia *and* Parthenius, *with a letter.*

    Dom. To me this reverence!
    Parth.   I pay it, lady,
As a debt due to her that's Cæsar's mistress:
For understand with joy, he that commands
All that the sun gives warmth to is your servant.

    111 cross] thwart   114 Curia] Senate-house

Be not amaz'd, but fit you to your fortunes.   5
Think upon state, and greatness, and the honours
That wait upon Augusta, for that name
Ere long comes to you:—still you doubt your vassal:—
But, when you've read this letter, writ and sign'd
With his imperial hand, you will be freed   10
From fear and jealousy, and I beseech you
When all the beauties of the earth bow to you,
And senators shall take it for an honour,
As I do now, to kiss these happy feet;
When every smile you give is a preferment,   15
And you dispose of provinces to your creatures,
Think on Parthenius.

    Dom.   Rise. I am transported,
And hardly dare believe what is assur'd here.
The means, my good Parthenius, that wrought Cæsar,
Our god on earth, to cast an eye of favour   20
Upon his humble handmaid?

    Parth.   What but your beauty?
When Nature fram'd you for her masterpiece,
As the pure abstract of all rare in woman,
She had no other ends but to design you
To the most eminent place. I will not say   25
(For it would smell of arrogance, to insinuate
The service I have done you) with what zeal
I oft have made relation of your virtues,
Or how I have sung your goodness; or how Cæsar
Was fir'd with the relation of your story;   30
I am rewarded in the act, and happy
In that my project prosper'd.

    Dom.   You are modest;
And were it in my power I would be thankful.
If that, when I was mistress of myself,
And, in my way of youth, pure and untainted,   35

    15 preferment] promotion

330

The emperor had vouchsaf'd to seek my favours,
I had with joy given up my virgin fort,
At the first summons, to his soft embraces;
But I am now another's, not mine own.
You know I have a husband:—for my honour,   40
I would not be his strumpet; and how law
Can be dispens'd with to become his wife,
To me's a riddle.
    Parth.   I can soon resolve it:
When power puts in its plea the laws are silenc'd.
The world confesses one Rome, and one Cæsar,   45
And, as his rule is infinite, his pleasures
Are unconfin'd; this syllable, his will,
Stands for a thousand reasons.
    Dom.   But with safety,—
Suppose I should consent,—how can I do it?
My husband is a senator, of a temper   50
Not to be jested with.   [*Enter* Lamia.
    Parth.   As if he durst
Be Cæsar's rival!—here he comes; with ease
I will remove this scruple.
    Lam.   —How! so private!
My own house made a brothel! Sir, how durst you,
Though guarded with your power in court, and great-
    ness,   55
Hold conference with my wife? As for you, minion,
I shall hereafter treat—
    Parth.   You are rude and saucy
Nor know to whom you speak.
    Lam.   This is fine, i' faith!
    Parth. Your wife? But touch her, that respect for-
    gotten
That's due to her whom mightiest Cæsar favours,   60
And think what 'tis to die. Not to lose time,
She's Cæsar's choice. It is sufficient honour

You were his taster in this heavenly nectar,
But now must quit the office.
  Lam.   This is rare!   65
Cannot a man be master of his wife,
Because she's young and fair, without a patent?
I in mine own house am an emperor,
And will defend what's mine—where are my knaves?
If such an insolence escape unpunish'd—
  Parth. In yourself, Lamia.—Cæsar hath forgot 70
To use his power, and I, his instrument,
In whom, though absent, his authority speaks,
Have lost my faculties!   [*Stamps.*
       [*Enter a Centurion with Soldiers.*
  Lam.   The guard! why, am I
Design'd for death?
  Dom.   As you desire my favour,
Take not so rough a course.
  Parth.   All your desires 75
Are absolute commands. Yet give me leave
To put the will of Cæsar into act.
Here's a bill of divorce between your lordship
And this great lady. If you refuse to sign it,
And so as if you did it uncompell'd,   80
Won to it by reasons that concern yourself,
Her honour too untainted, here are clerks
Shall in your best blood write it new, till torture
Compel you to perform it.
  Lam.   Is this legal?
  Parth. Monarchs that dare not do unlawful things, 85
Yet bear them out, are constables, not kings.
Will you dispute?
  Lam.   I know not what to urge
Against myself, but too much dotage on her,
Love, and observance.

   89 observance] respectful treatment

 Parth.   Set it under your hand
That you are impotent, and cannot pay   90
The duties of a husband; or that you are mad;
(Rather than want just cause, we'll make you so.)
Dispatch, you know the danger else;—deliver it,—
Nay, on your knee.—Madam, you are now free,
And mistress of yourself.
 Lam.   Can you, Domitia,   95
Consent to this?
 Dom.   'Twould argue a base mind
To live a servant, when I may command.
I now am Cæsar's, and yet, in respect
I once was yours, when you come to the palace,
(Provided you deserve it in your service,)   100
You shall find me your good mistress. Wait me,
  Parthenius;
And now farewell, poor Lamia! [*Exeunt all but* Lamia.
 Lam.   To the gods
I bend my knees (for tyranny hath banish'd
Justice from men), and as they would deserve
Their altars, and our vows, humbly invoke 'em, 105
That this my ravish'd wife may prove as fatal
To proud Domitian, and her embraces
Afford him, in the end, as little joy,
As wanton Helen brought to him of Troy. [*Exit.*

ACTUS I, SCÆNA 3

Enter Lictors, Aretinus, Fulcinius, Rusticus, Sura,
Paris, Latinus, *and* Æsopus.

 Aret. Fathers conscript, may this our meeting be
Happy to Cæsar and the commonwealth!

   1 fathers conscript] *patres conscripti*, Senators

Lict. Silence!

Aret.   The purpose of this frequent Senate
Is first to give thanks to the gods of Rome
That, for the propagation of the empire,   5
Vouchsafe us one to govern it, like themselves.
In height of courage, depth of understanding,
And all those virtues, and remarkable graces,
Which make a prince most eminent, our Domitian
Transcends the ancient Romans. I can never   10
Bring his praise to a period. What good man
That is a friend to truth, dares make it doubtful
That he hath Fabius' staidness, and the courage
Of bold Marcellus, to whom Hannibal gave
The style of Target, and the Sword of Rome?   15
But he has more, and every touch more Roman;
As Pompey's dignity, Augustus' state,
Antony's bounty, and great Julius' fortune,
With Cato's resolution. I am lost
In th' ocean of his virtues. In a word,   20
All excellencies of good men in him meet,
But no part of their vices.

   Rust.   This is no flattery!

   Sura. Take heed, you'll be observ'd.

   Aret.   'Tis then most fit
That we, (as to the father of our country,
Like thankful sons, stand bound to pay true service   25
For all those blessings that he show'rs upon us,)
Should not connive, and see his government
Deprav'd and scandaliz'd by meaner men,
That to his favour and indulgence owe
Themselves and being.

   Par.   Now he points at us.   30

   Aret. Cite Paris, the tragedian.

   Par.   Here.

3 frequent] crowded

334

Aret.   Stand forth.
In thee, as being the chief of thy profession,
I do accuse the quality of treason,
As libellers against the state and Cæsar.
    Par. Mere accusations are not proofs, my lord: 35
In what are we delinquents?
    Aret.   You are they
That search into the secrets of the time,
And, under feign'd names, on the stage, present
Actions not to be touch'd at; and traduce
Persons of rank and quality of both sexes,   40
And, with satirical and bitter jests,
Make even the senators ridiculous
To the plebeians.
    Par.   If I free not myself,
(And in myself the rest of my profession)
From these false imputations, and prove   45
That they make that a libel, which the poet
Writ for a comedy, so acted too,
It is but justice that we undergo
The heaviest censure.
    Aret.   Are you on the stage,
You talk so boldly?
    Par.   The whole world being one,   50
This place is not exempted: and I am
So confident in the justice of our cause,
That I could wish Cæsar, (in whose great name
All kings are comprehended,) sat as judge,
To hear our plea, and then determine of us.   55
If to express a man sold to his lusts,
Wasting the treasure of his time and fortunes
In wanton dalliance, and to what sad end
A wretch that's so given over does arrive at;

    33 quality] acting profession   55 determine] judge,
decide

Deterring careless youth, by his example,   60
From such licentious courses; laying open
The snares of bawds, and the consuming arts
Of prodigal strumpets, can deserve reproof;
Why are not all your golden principles,
Writ down by grave philosophers to instruct us   65
To choose fair virtue for our guide, not pleasure,
Condemn'd unto the fire?
    Sura.   There's spirit in this.
    Par. Or if desire of honour was the base
On which the building of the Roman empire
Was rais'd up to this height; if to inflame   70
The noble youth with an ambitious heat
T' endure the frosts of danger, nay, of death,
To be thought worthy the triumphal wreath
By glorious undertakings, may deserve
Reward or favour from the commonwealth,   75
Actors may put in for as large a share
As all the sects of the philosophers;
They with cold precepts (perhaps seldom read)
Deliver what an honourable thing
The active virtue is. But does that fire   80
The blood, or swell the veins with emulation
To be both good and great, equal to that
Which is presented on our theatres?
Let a good actor, in a lofty scene,
Show great Alcides honour'd in the sweat   85
Of his twelve labours; or a bold Camillus,
Forbidding Rome to be redeem'd with gold
From the insulting Gauls; or Scipio
After his victories imposing tribute
On conquer'd Carthage: if done to the life,   90
As if they saw their dangers, and their glories,
And did partake with them in their rewards,

79 deliver] expound

336

All that have any spark of Roman in them,
The slothful arts laid by, contend to be
Like those they see presented.

   Rust.   He has put   **95**
The consuls to their whisper.

   Par.   But 'tis urg'd
That we corrupt youth, and traduce superiors.
When do we bring a vice upon the stage,
That does go off unpunish'd? Do we teach,
By the success of wicked undertakings,   **100**
Others to tread in their forbidden steps?
We show no arts of Lydian pandarism,
Corinthian poisons, Persian flatteries,
But mulcted so in the conclusion that
Even those spectators that were so inclin'd   **105**
Go home chang'd men. And, for traducing such
That are above us, publishing to the world
Their secret crimes, we are as innocent
As such as are born dumb. When we present
An heir that does conspire against the life   **110**
Of his dear parent, numb'ring every hour
He lives as tedious to him, if there be
Among the auditors one whose conscience tells him
He is of the same mould,—we cannot help it.
Or, bringing on the stage a loose adult'ress,   **115**
That does maintain the riotous expense
Of him that feeds her greedy lust, yet suffers
The lawful pledges of a former bed
To starve the while for hunger; if a matron,
However great in fortune, birth, or titles,   **120**
Guilty of such a foul unnatural sin,
Cry out, 'Tis writ by me,—we cannot help it.
Or, when a covetous man's express'd, whose wealth
Arithmetic cannot number, and whose lordships

     122 writ by] written about, modelled on

A falcon in one day cannot fly over,   125
Yet he so sordid in his mind, so griping,
As not to afford himself the necessaries
To maintain life; if a patrician,
(Though honour'd with a consulship,) find himself
Touch'd to the quick in this,—we cannot help it.   130
Or, when we show a judge that is corrupt,
And will give up his sentence as he favours
The person, not the cause; saving the guilty,
If of his faction, and as oft condemning
The innocent, out of particular spleen;   135
If any in this reverend assembly,
Nay, e'en yourself, my lord, that are the image
Of absent Cæsar, feel something in your bosom,
That puts you in remembrance of things past,
Or things intended,—'tis not in us to help it.   140
I have said, my lord; and now, as you find cause,
Or censure us, or free us with applause.
    Lat. Well pleaded, on my life! I never saw him
Act an orator's part before.
    Æsop.   We might have given
Ten double fees to Regulus, and yet   145
Our cause delivered worse.   [*A shout within.*
                Enter Parthenius.
    Aret.   What shout is that?
    Parth. Cæsar, our lord, married to conquest, is
Return'd in triumph.
    Ful.   Let's all haste to meet him.
    Aret. Break up the court; we will reserve to him
The censure of this cause.
    All.   Long life to Cæsar!   150
                                        [*Exeunt.*

135 particular] partisan   149 censure] judgement

338 as footer

ACTUS I, SCÆNA 4

Enter Julia, Cænis, Domitilla, *and* Domitia.

Cænis. Stand back—the place is mine.
Jul.   Yours! Am I not
Great Titus' daughter, and Domitian's niece?
Dares any claim precedence?
Cænis.   I was more,—
The mistress of your father, and in his right
Claim duty from you.
Jul.   I confess you were useful   5
To please his appetite—
Dom.   To end the controversy,
For I'll have no contending, I'll be bold
To lead the way myself.
Domitil.   You, minion!
Dom.   Yes;
And all ere long shall kneel to catch my favours.
Jul. Whence springs this flood of greatness?
Dom.   You shall know 10
Too soon, for your vexation, and perhaps
Repent too late, and pine with envy, when
You see whom Cæsar favours.
Jul.   Observe the sequel.

[*Enter Captains with laurels,* Domitian *in his triumphant
   chariot,* Parthenius, Paris, Latinus, *and* Æsopus, *met
   by* Aretinus, Sura, Lamia, Rusticus, Fulcinius;
   prisoners led by him.

Cæs. As we now touch the height of human glory,
Riding in triumph to the Capitol,   15
Let these, whom this victorious arm hath made
The scorn of fortune, and the slaves of Rome,
Taste the extremes of misery. Bear them off

To the common prisons, and there let them prove
How sharp our axes are.   [*Exeunt with prisoners.*
   Rust.   —A bloody entrance!   20
   Cæs. To tell you, you are happy in your prince,
Were to distrust your love, or my desert;
And either were distasteful. Or to boast
How much, not by my deputies, but myself,
I have enlarg'd the empire; or what horrors   25
The soldier in our conduct hath broke through,
Would better suit the mouth of Plautus' braggart,
Than the adored monarch of the world.
   Sura.—This is no boast!
   Cæs.   When I but name the Daci,
And gray-ey'd Germans, whom I have subdu'd,   30
The ghost of Julius will look pale with envy,
And great Vespasian's and Titus' triumph,
(Truth must take place of father and of brother,)
Will be no more rememb'red. I am above
All honours you can give me; and the style   35
Of Lord and God, which thankful subjects give me,
(Not my ambition,) is deserv'd.
   Aret.   At all parts
Celestial sacrifice is fit for Cæsar,
In our acknowledgment.
   Cæs.   Thanks, Aretinus;
Still hold our favour. Now, the god of war,   40
And famine, blood, and death, Bellona's pages,
Banish'd from Rome to Thrace, in our good fortune,
With justice he may taste the fruits of peace
Whose sword hath plough'd the ground, and reap'd
      the harvest
Of your prosperity. Nor can I think   45
That there is one among you so ungrateful,
Or such an enemy to thriving virtue,

19 prove] experience

That can esteem the jewel he holds dearest
Too good for Cæsar's use.

    Sura.   All we possess—
    Lam. Our liberties—
    Ful.   Our children—
    Parth.   Wealth—
    Aret.   And throats, 50
Fall willingly beneath his feet.

    Rust.   —Base flattery!
What Roman can endure this!

    Cæs.   This calls on
My love to all, which spreads itself among you.—
The beauties of the time! Receive the honour

                           [*To the ladies.*
To kiss the hand which, rear'd up thus, holds thunder; 55
To you 'tis an assurance of a calm.
Julia, my niece, and Cænis, the delight
Of old Vespasian; Domitilla, too,
A princess of our blood.

    Rust.   'Tis strange his pride
Affords no greater courtesy to ladies   60
Of such high birth and rank.

    Sura.   Your wife's forgotten.
    Lam. No, she will be rememb'red, fear it not;
She will be grac'd, and greas'd.

    Cæs.   But, when I look on
Divine Domitia, methinks we should meet
(The lesser gods applauding the encounter)   65
As Jupiter, the Giants lying dead
On the Phlegræan plain, embrac'd his Juno.
Lamia, 'tis your honour that she's mine.

    Lam. You are too great to be gainsaid.
    Cæs.   Let all
That fear our frown, or do affect our favour,   70

        70 affect] esteem, value

Without examining the reason why,
Salute her (by this kiss I make it good)
With the title of Augusta.
 Dom.   Still your servant.
 All. Long live Augusta, great Domitian's empress!
 Cæs. Paris, my hand.
 Par.   The góds still honour Cæsar! 75
 Cæs. The wars are ended, and, our arms laid by,
We are for soft delights. Command the poets
To use their choicest and most rare invention
To entertain the time, and be you careful
To give it action: we'll provide the people   80
Pleasures of all kinds.—My Domitia, think not
I flatter, though thus fond.—On to the Capitol;
'Tis death to him that wears a sullen brow.
This 'tis to be a monarch, when alone
He can command all, but is aw'd by none. [*Exeunt.* 85

ACTUS II, SCÆNA I

Enter Philargus, Parthenius.

 Phil. My son to tutor me! Know your obedience,
And question not my will.
 Parth.   Sir, were I one
Whom want compell'd to wish a full possession
Of what is yours; or had I ever numb'red
Your years, or thought you liv'd too long, with reason 5
You then might nourish ill opinions of me:
Or did the suit that I prefer to you
Concern myself, and aim'd not at your good,
You might deny, and I sit down with patience,
And after never press you.

    9 sit down] endure

Phil.   I' the name of Pluto,   10
What wouldst thou have me do?
   Parth.   Right to yourself;
Or suffer me to do it. Can you imagine
This nasty hat, this tatter'd cloak, rent shoe,
This sordid linen, can become the master
Of your fair fortunes? whose superfluous means,   15
(Though I were burthensome,) could clothe you in
The costliest Persian silks, studded with jewels,
The spoils of provinces, and every day
Fresh change of Tyrian purple.
   Phil.   Out upon thee!
My moneys in my coffers melt to hear thee.   20
Purple! hence, prodigal! Shall I make my mercer
Or tailor my heir? or see my jeweller purchase?
No, I hate pride.
   Parth.   Yet decency would do well.
Though for your outside you will not be alter'd,
Let me prevail so far yet, as to win you   25
Not to deny your belly nourishment;
Neither to think you have feasted, when 'tis cramm'd
With mouldy barley-bread, onions and leeks,
And the drink of bondmen, water.
   Phil.   Wouldst thou have me
Be an Apicius or a Lucullus,   30
And riot out my state in curious sauces?
Wise nature with a little is contented;
And, following her, my guide, I cannot err.
   Parth. But you destroy her in your want of care
(I blush to see, and speak it) to maintain her   35
In perfect health and vigour, when you suffer
(Frighted with the charge of physic) rheums, catarrhs,
The scurf, ache in your bones, to grow upon you,
And hasten on your fate with too much sparing;

   22 purchase] *sc. land (evidence of solid wealth)*

When a cheap purge, a vomit, and good diet,   40
May lengthen it. Give me but leave to send
The emperor's doctor to you.
  Phil.   I'll be borne first
Half-rotten to the fire that must consume me!
His pills, his cordials, his electuaries,
His syrups, juleps, bezoar stone, nor his   45
Imagin'd unicorn's horn, comes in my belly;
My mouth shall be a draught first. 'Tis resolv'd.
No; I'll not lessen my dear golden heap,
Which every hour increasing does renew
My youth and vigour; but, if lessen'd, then,   50
Then my poor heart-strings crack. Let me enjoy it,
And brood o'er 't, while I live, it being my life,
My soul, my all. But when I turn to dust,
And part from what is more esteem'd by me
Than all the gods Rome's thousand altars smoke to,   55
Inherit thou my adoration of it,
And, like me, serve my idol.   *[Exit.*
  Parth.   What a strange torture
Is avarice to itself! What man, that looks on
Such a penurious spectacle, but must
Know what the fable meant of Tantalus,   60
Or the ass whose back is crack'd with curious viands,
Yet feeds on thistles? Some course I must take,
To make my father know what cruelty
He uses on himself.
           [Enter Paris.

  Par.   Sir, with your pardon,
I make bold to inquire the emperor's pleasure;   65
For, being by him commanded to attend,
Your favour may instruct us what's his will
Shall be this night presented.

  44 electuaries] syrupy medicines (*Symons*) 45 bezoar stone]
antidote to poison

344

   Parth.   My lov'd Paris,
Without my intercession, you well know,
You may make your own approaches, since his ear   70
To you is ever open.
   Par.   I acknowledge
His clemency to my weakness, and if ever
I do abuse it, lightning strike me dead!
The grace he pleases to confer upon me,
(Without boast I may say so much,) was never   75
Employ'd to wrong the innocent, or to incense
His fury.
   Parth. 'Tis confess'd many men owe you
For provinces they ne'er hop'd for; and their lives,
Forfeited to his anger:—you being absent,
I could say more.
   Par.   You still are my good patron;   80
And, lay it in my fortune to deserve it,
You should perceive the poorest of your clients
To his best abilities thankful.
   Parth.   I believe so.
Met you my father?
   Par.   Yes, sir, with much grief,
To see him as he is. Can nothing work him
To be himself?   85
   Parth.   Oh, Paris, 'tis a weight
Sits heavy here; and could this right hand's loss
Remove it, it should off; but he is deaf
To all persuasion.
   Par.   Sir, with your pardon,
I'll offer my advice: I once observ'd
In a tragedy of ours in which a murder   90
Was acted to the life, a guilty hearer
Forc'd by the terror of a wounded conscience
To make discovery of that which torture

Could not wring from him. Nor can it appear   95
Like an impossibility, but that
Your father, looking on a covetous man
Presented on the stage, as in a mirror,
May see his own deformity, and loathe it.
Now, could you but persuade the emperor   100
To see a comedy we have, that's styl'd
The Cure of Avarice, and to command
Your father to be a spectator of it,
He shall be so anatomiz'd in the scene,
And see himself so personated, the baseness   105
Of a self-torturing miserable wretch
Truly describ'd, that I much hope the object
Will work compunction in him.
     Parth.   There's your fee;
I ne'er bought better counsel. Be you in readiness,
I will effect the rest.
     Par.   Sir, when you please,   110
We'll be prepar'd to enter.—Sir, the emperor.   [*Exit.*

               Enter Cæsar, Aretinus, *Guard*

     Cæs. Repine at us!
     Aret.   'Tis more, or my informers,
That keep strict watch upon him, are deceiv'd
In their intelligence: there is a list
Of malcontents, as Junius Rusticus,   115
Palphurius Sura, and this Ælius Lamia,
That murmur at your triumphs as mere pageants;
And at their midnight meetings tax your justice,
(For so I style what they call tyranny,)
For Pætus Thrasea's death, as if in him   120
Virtue herself were murther'd; nor forget they
Agricola, who, for his service done
In the reducing Britain to obedience,
They dare affirm to be remov'd with poison;

And he compell'd to write you a coheir   125
With his daughter, that his testament might stand,
Which else you had made void. Then your much love
To Julia your niece, censur'd as incest,
And done in scorn of Titus, your dead brother;
But the divorce Lamia was forc'd to sign   130
To her you honour with Augusta's title
Being only nam'd, they do conclude there was
A Lucrece once, a Collatine, and a Brutus;
But nothing Roman left now but in you
The lust of Tarquin.

Cæs.   Yes. His fire, and scorn   135
Of such as think that our unlimited power
Can be confin'd. Dares Lamia pretend
An interest to that which I call mine?
Or but remember she was ever his,
That's now in our possession? Fetch him hither.   140
                        [The Guard go off.
I'll give him cause to wish he rather had
Forgot his own name than e'er mention'd hers.
Shall we be circumscrib'd? Let such as cannot
By force make good their actions, though wicked,
Conceal, excuse, or qualify their crimes!   145
What our desires grant leave and privilege to,
Though contradicting all divine decrees,
Or laws confirm'd by Romulus, and Numa,
Shall be held sacred.

Aret.   You should else take from
The dignity of Cæsar.

Cæs.   Am I master   150
Of two and thirty legions, that awe
All nations of the triumphed world,
Yet tremble at our frown, yield an account

150–4 Am I . . . man?] *Editors should not tidy Domitian's ungrammatical explosion.*

347

Of what's our pleasure to a private man?
Rome perish first, and Atlas' shoulders shrink,   155
Heav'n's fabric fall; the sun, the moon, the stars
Losing their light and comfortable heat;
Ere I confess that any fault of mine
May be disputed!
   Aret.   So you preserve your power,
As you should, equal and omnipotent here   160
With Jupiter's above.

               [Parthenius *kneeling, whispers* Cæsar.

   Cæs.   Thy suit is granted,
Whate'er it be, Parthenius, for thy service
Done to Augusta.——Only so? a trifle:
Command him hither. If the comedy fail
To cure him, I will minister something to him   165
That shall instruct him to forget his gold,
And think upon himself.
   Parth.   May it succeed well,
Since my intents are pious!   [*Exit.*
   Cæs.   We are resolv'd
What course to take, and therefore, Aretinus,
Inquire no farther. Go you to my empress,   170
And say I do entreat (for she rules him
Whom all men else obey) she would vouchsafe
The music of her voice at yonder window,
When I advance my hand, thus. I will blend

               [*Exit* Aretinus.

My cruelty with some scorn, or else 'tis lost;   175
Revenge, when it is unexpected, falling
With greater violence; and hate clothed in smiles,
Strikes, and with horror, dead the wretch that comes
    not
Prepared to meet it.—
               [*Enter* Lamia *with the Guard.*

        Our good Lamia, welcome.
So much we owe you for a benefit,   180
With willingness on your part conferr'd upon us,
That 'tis our study, we that would not live
Engag'd to any for a courtesy,
How to return it.
  Lam.   'Tis beneath your fate
To be oblig'd, that in your own hand grasp 185
The means to be magnificent.
  Cæs.   Well put off;
But yet it must not do: the empire, Lamia,
Divided equally, can hold no weight,
If balanc'd with your gift in fair Domitia—
You, that could part with all delights at once, 190
The magazine of rich pleasures being contain'd
In her perfections, uncompell'd, deliver'd
As a present fit for Cæsar. In your eyes,
With tears of joy, not sorrow, 'tis confirm'd
You glory in your act.
  Lam.   Derided too!   195
Sir, this is more—
  Cæs.   More than I can requite:
It is acknowledg'd, Lamia. There's no drop
Of melting nectar I taste from her lip,
But yields a touch of immortality
To the blest receiver; every grace and feature, 200
Priz'd to the worth, bought at an easy rate,
If purchas'd for a consulship. Her discourse
So ravishing, and her action so attractive,
That I would part with all my other senses,
Provided I might ever see and hear her.   205
The pleasures of her bed I dare not trust
The winds or air with, for that would draw down,
In envy of my happiness, a war

  186 magnificent] greatly munificent

From all the gods, upon me.

    Lam.   Your compassion

To me, in your forbearing to insult   210

On my calamity, which you make your sport,

Would more appease those gods you have provok'd

Than all the blasphemous comparisons

You sing unto her praise.

    Cæs.   I sing her praise!

'Tis far from my ambition to hope it,   215

It being a debt she only can lay down,

And no tongue else discharge.

                            [*Music above and a song.*

                        Hark! I think, prompted

With my consent that you once more should hear her,

She does begin. An universal silence

Dwell on this place! 'Tis death, with ling'ring tor-

    ments,   220

To all that dare disturb her.—

                    [*The song ended,* Cæsar *go on.*

                       Who can hear this,

And falls not down and worships? In my fancy,

Apollo being judge, on Latmos' hill

Fair-hair'd Calliope, on her ivory lute,

(But something short of this,) sung Ceres' praises,   225

And grisly Pluto's rape on Proserpine.

The motion of the spheres are out of time,

Her musical notes but heard. Say, Lamia, say,

Is not her voice angelical?

    Lam.   To your ear:

But I, alas! am silent.

    Cæs.   Be so ever,   230

That without admiration canst hear her!

Malice to my felicity strikes thee dumb,

And, in thy hope, or wish, to repossess

What I love more than empire, I pronounce thee

Guilty of treason.—Off with his head! Do you stare?   235
By her that is my patroness, Minerva,
(Whose statue I adore of all the gods)
If he but live to make reply, thy life
Shall answer it!

        [*The Guard lead off* Lamia, *stopping his mouth.*

            My fears of him are freed now;
And he that liv'd to upbraid me with my wrong,   240
For an offence he never could imagine,
In wantonness remov'd.—Descend, my dearest.
Plurality of husbands shall no more
Breed doubts or jealousies in you. 'Tis dispatch'd,
And with as little trouble here, as if   245
I had kill'd a fly.

   [*Enter* Domitia, *usher'd in by* Aretinus, *her train with*
     all state borne up by Julia, Cænis, *and* Domitilla.

           Now you appear, and in
That glory you deserve! and these, that stoop
To do you service, in the act much honour'd!
Julia, forget that Titus was thy father;
Cænis, and Domitilla, ne'er remember   250
Sabinus, or Vespasian. To be slaves
To her is more true liberty than to live
Parthian or Asian queens. As lesser stars,
That wait on Phœbe in her full of brightness,
Compar'd to her, you are! Thus I seat you   255
By Cæsar's side, commanding these, that once
Were the adored glories of the time,
(To witness to the world they are your vassals)
At your feet to attend you.

   Dom.   'Tis your pleasure,
And not my pride. And yet, when I consider   260
That I am yours, all duties they can pay
I do receive as circumstances due
To her you please to honour.

Enter Parthenius *and* Philargus.

Parth.   Cæsar's will
Commands you hither, nor must you gainsay it.
  Phil. Lose time to see an interlude! must I pay too 265
For my vexation?
  Parth.   Not in the court;
It is the emperor's charge.
  Phil.   I shall endure
My torment then the better.
  Cæs.   Can it be
This sordid thing, Parthenius, is thy father?
No actor can express him. I had held   270
The fiction for impossible in the scene,
Had I not seen the substance.—Sirrah, sit still,
And give attention; if you but nod,
You sleep for ever.—Let them spare the prologue,
And all the ceremonies proper to ourself,   275
And come to the last act—there where the cure
By the doctor is made perfect. The swift minutes
Seem years to me, Domitia, that divorce thee
From my embraces: my desires increasing
As they are satisfied, all pleasures else   280
Are tedious as dull sorrows. Kiss me;—again:
If I now wanted heat of youth, these fires,
In Priam's veins, would thaw his frozen blood,
Enabling him to get a second Hector
For the defence of Troy.
  Dom.   You are wanton, sir!   285
Pray you, forbear. Let me see the play.
  Cæs.   Begin there.

Enter Paris *like a Doctor of Physic,* Æsopus. Latinus
  brought forth asleep in a chair, a key in his mouth.

271 in the scene] on the stage

352

Æsop. O master doctor, he is past recovery;
A lethargy hath seiz'd him; and, however
His sleep resemble death, his watchful care
To guard that treasure he dares make no use of   290
Works strongly in his soul.
    Par.   What 's that he holds
So fast between his teeth?
    Æsop.   The key that opens
His iron chests, cramm'd with accursed gold,
Rusty with long imprisonment. There 's no duty
In me, his son, nor confidence in friends,   295
That can persuade him to deliver up
That to the trust of any.
    Phil.   —He is the wiser!
We were fashion'd in one mould.—
    Æsop.   He eats with it:
And when devotion calls him to the temple
Of Mammon, whom, of all the gods, he kneels to,   300
That held thus still, his orisons are paid;
Nor will he, though the wealth of Rome were pawn'd
For the restoring of it, for one short hour
Be won to part with it.
    Phil.   —Still, still myself!
And if like me he love his gold, no pawn   305
Is good security.—
    Par.   I'll try if I can force it——
It will not be. His avaricious mind,
(Like men in rivers drown'd) makes him gripe fast
To his last gasp, what he in life held dearest;
And, if that it were possible in nature,   310
Would carry it with him to the other world.
    Phil. —As I would do to hell, rather than leave it.—
    Æsop. Is he not dead?
    Par.   Long since to all good actions,
Or to himself or others, for which wise men

Desire to live. You may with safety pinch him,   315
Or under his nails stick needles, yet he stirs not.
Anxious fear to lose what his soul dotes on
Renders his flesh insensible. We must use
Some means to rouse the sleeping faculties
Of his mind, there lies the lethargy. Take a trumpet, 320
And blow it into his ears; 'tis to no purpose;
The roaring noise of thunder cannot wake him:—
And yet despair not, I have one trick left yet.
 Æsop. What is it?
 Par.   I will cause a fearful dream
To steal into his fancy, and disturb it   325
With the horror it brings with it, and so free
His body's organs.
 Dom.   —'Tis a cunning fellow;
If he were indeed a doctor, as the play says,
He should be sworn my servant, govern my slumbers,
And minister to me waking.—   [*A chest brought in.*
 Par.   If this fail,   330
I'll give him o'er. So; with all violence
Rend ope this iron chest. For here his life lies
Bound up in fetters, and in the defence
Of what he values higher, 'twill return,
And fill each vein and artery.—Louder yet!   335
—'Tis open, and already he begins
To stir; mark with what trouble.
        [Latinus *stretches himself.*
 Phil.   —As you are Cæsar,
Defend this honest, thrifty man! they are thieves,
And come to rob him.
 Parth.   Peace! the emperor frowns.—
 Par. So; now pour out the bags upon the table; 340
Remove his jewels, and his bonds.—Again,
Ring a second golden peal. His eyes are open;
He stares as he had seen Medusa's head,

And were turn'd marble.—Once more.

  Lat.   Murther! murther!

They come to murther me. My son in the plot? 345

Thou worse than parricide! if it be death

To strike thy father's body, can all tortures

The Furies in hell practise be sufficient

For thee, that dost assassinate my soul?—

My gold! my bonds! my jewels! dost thou envy 350

My glad possession of them for a day?

Extinguishing the taper of my life

Consum'd unto the snuff?

  Par.   Seem not to mind him.

  Lat. Have I, to leave thee rich, denied myself

The joys of human being; scrap'd and hoarded 355

A mass of treasure, which had Solon seen,

The Lydian Crœsus had appear'd to him

Poor as the beggar Irus? And yet I,

Solicitous to increase it, when my entrails

Were clemm'd with keeping a perpetual fast, 360

Was deaf to their loud windy cries, as fearing,

Should I disburse one penny to their use,

My heir might curse me. And, to save expense

In outward ornaments, I did expose

My naked body to the winter's cold, 365

And summer's scorching heat. Nay, when diseases

Grew thick upon me, and a little cost

Had purchas'd my recovery, I chose rather

To have my ashes clos'd up in my urn,

By hasting on my fate, than to diminish 370

The gold my prodigal son, while I am living,

Carelessly scatters.

  Æsop. Would you would dispatch and die once!

Your ghost should feel in hell, that is my slave

Which was your master.

Phil.   —Out upon thee, varlet!—
Par. And what then follows all your cark and caring, 375
And self-affliction, when your starv'd trunk is
Turn'd to forgotten dust? This hopeful youth
Urines upon your monument, ne'er rememb'ring
How much for him you suffer'd; and then tells
To the companions of his lusts and riots,   380
The hell you did endure on earth, to leave him
Large means to be an epicure, and to feast
His senses all at once, a happiness
You never granted to yourself. Your gold, then,
(Got with vexation, and preserv'd with trouble,)   385
Maintains the public stews, panders, and ruffians,
That quaff damnations to your memory,
For living so long here.
     Lat.   'Twill be so; I see it—
Oh, that I could redeem the time that's past!
I would live and die like myself; and make true use   390
Of what my industry purchas'd.
     Par.   Covetous men,
Having one foot in the grave, lament so ever.
But grant that I by art could yet recover
Your desperate sickness, lengthen out your life
A dozen of years, as I restore your body   395
To perfect health, will you with care endeavour
To rectify your mind?
     Lat.   I should so live then,
As neither my heir should have just cause to think
I liv'd too long, for being close-handed to him,
Or cruel to myself.
     Par.   Have your desires.   400
Phœbus assisting me, I will repair
The ruin'd building of your health; and think not
You have a son that hates you; the truth is,
This means, with his consent, I practis'd on you

356

To this good end: it being a device,   405
In you to show the *Cure of Avarice*.
                    [*Exeunt* Paris, Latinus, Æsopus.
   Phil. An old fool, to be gull'd thus! had he died
As I resolve to do, not to be alter'd,
It had gone off twanging.
   Cæs.   How approve you, sweetest,
Of the matter, and the actors?
   Dom.   For the subject,   410
I like it not; it was filch'd out of Horace.
—Nay, I have read the poets:—but the fellow
That play'd the doctor did it well, by Venus!
He had a tuneable tongue and neat delivery;
And yet, in my opinion, he would perform   415
A lover's part much better. Prithee, Cæsar,
For I grow weary, let us see, to-morrow,
Iphis and Anaxarete.
   Cæs.   Anything
For thy delight, Domitia. To your rest,
Till I come to disquiet you. Wait upon her.   420
There is a business that I must dispatch,
And I will straight be with you,
        [*Exeunt* Aretinus, Domitia, Julia, Cænis, Domitilla.
   Parth.   Now, my dread sir,
Endeavour to prevail.
   Cæs.   One way or other
We'll cure him, never doubt it. Now, Philargus,
Thou wretched thing, hast thou seen thy sordid base-
     ness,   425
And but observ'd what a contemptible creature
A covetous miser is? Dost thou in thyself
Feel true compunction, with a resolution
To be a new man?
   Phil.   This craz'd body's Cæsar's,
But for my mind—

Cæs.   Trifle not with my anger.   430
Canst thou make good use of what was now presented?
And imitate, in thy sudden change of life,
The miserable rich man, that express'd
What thou art to the life?
　　Phil.   Pray you, give me leave
To die as I have liv'd. I must not part with   435
My gold; it is my life: I am past cure.
　　Cæs. No; by Minerva, thou shalt never more
Feel the least touch of avarice. Take him hence,
And hang him instantly. If there be gold in hell,
Enjoy it:—thine here and thy life together   440
Is forfeited.
　　Phil.   Was I sent for to this purpose?
　　Parth. Mercy for all my service, Cæsar, mercy!
　　Cæs. Should Jove plead for him, 'tis resolv'd he dies,
And he that speaks one syllable to dissuade me;
And therefore tempt me not. It is but justice: 445
Since such as wilfully will hourly die,
Must tax themselves, and not my cruelty.   [*Exeunt.*

ACTUS III, SCÆNA 1

Enter Julia, Domitilla, Stephanos.

Jul. No, Domitilla; if you but compare
What I have suffer'd with your injuries,
(Though great ones, I confess,) they will appear
Like molehills to Olympus.
　　Domitil.   You are tender
Of your own wounds, which makes you lose the feeling 5
And sense of mine. The incest he committed
With you, and publicly profess'd, in scorn
Of what the world durst censure, may admit
Some weak defence, as being borne headlong to it,

But in a manly way, to enjoy your beauties.   10
Besides, won by his perjuries that he would
Salute you with the title of Augusta,
Your faint denial showed a full consent,
And grant to his temptations. But poor I,
That would not yield, but was with violence forc'd   15
To serve his lusts, and in a kind Tiberius
At Capreæ never practis'd, have not here
One conscious touch to rise up my accuser,
I in my will being innocent.
   Steph.   Pardon me,
Great princesses, though I presume to tell you,   20
Wasting your time in childish lamentations,
You do degenerate from the blood you spring from:
For there is something more in Rome expected
From Titus' daughter, and his uncle's heir,
Than womanish complaints, after such wrongs   25
Which mercy cannot pardon. But you'll say
Your hands are weak, and should you but attempt
A just revenge on this inhuman monster,
This prodigy of mankind, bloody Domitian,
Hath ready swords at his command, as well   30
As islands to confine you, to remove
His doubts and fears, did he but entertain
The least suspicion you contriv'd or plotted
 Against his person.
   Jul.   'Tis true, Stephanos;
The legions that sack'd Jerusalem   35
Under my father Titus are sworn his,
And I no more rememb'red.
   Domitil.   And to lose
Ourselves by building on impossible hopes,
Were desperate madness.
   Steph.   You conclude too fast.
One single arm, whose master does contemn   40

His own life, holds a full command o'er his,
Spite of his guards. I was your bondman, lady,
And you my gracious patroness; my wealth
And liberty your gift; and, though no soldier,
To whom or custom or example makes   45
Grim death appear less terrible, I dare die
To do you service in a fair revenge;
And it will better suit your births and honours
To fall at once, than to live ever slaves
To his proud empress, that insults upon   50
Your patient sufferings. Say but you, 'Go on!'
And I will reach his heart, or perish in
The noble undertaking.

  Domitil.   Your free offer
Confirms your thankfulness, which I acknowledge
A satisfaction for a greater debt   55
Than what you stand engag'd for; but I must not,
Upon uncertain grounds, hazard so grateful
And good a servant. The immortal Powers
Protect a prince, though sold to impious acts,
And seem to slumber, till his roaring crimes   60
Awake their justice; but then, looking down,
And with impartial eyes, on his contempt
Of all religion and moral goodness,
They, in their secret judgments, do determine
To leave him to his wickedness, which sinks him   65
When he is most secure.

  Jul.   His cruelty
Increasing daily, of necessity
Must render him as odious to his soldiers,
Familiar friends, and freemen, as it hath done
Already to the Senate; then, forsaken   70
Of his supporters, and grown terrible
Ev'n to himself, and her he now so dotes on,

66 secure] confident

360

We may put into act what now with safety
We cannot whisper.

   Steph.   I am still prepar'd
To execute, when you please to command me: 75
Since I am confident he deserves much more
That vindicates his country from a tyranne
Than he that saves a citizen.

                           [*Enter* Cænis.
   Jul.   Oh, here's Cænis.
   Domitil. Whence come you?
   Cænis.   From the empress, who seems mov'd
In that you wait no better. Her pride's grown   80
To such a height that she disdains the service
Of her own women, and esteems herself
Neglected when the princesses of the blood,
On every coarse employment, are not ready
To stoop to her commands.

   Domitil.   Where is her greatness? 85
   Cænis. Where you would little think she could
      descend
To grace the room or persons.

   Jul.   Speak, where is she?
   Cænis. Among the players: where, all state laid by,
She does inquire who plays this part, who that,
And in what habits? blames the tire-women   90
For want of curious dressings;—and, so taken
She is with Paris the tragedian's shape,
That is to act a lover, I thought once
She would have courted him.

   Domitil.   In the mean time
How spends the emperor his hours?

   Cænis.   As ever   95

    74 still] always   77 vindicates] frees   tyranne] tyrant (*Mas-singer's preferred spelling; cf.* v. i. 27, *&c.*)   91 curious]
careful, elaborate

He hath done heretofore, in being cruel
To innocent men, whose virtues he calls crimes.
And, but this morning, if 't be possible,
He hath outgone himself, having condemn'd,
At Aretinus his informer's suit,   100
Palphurius Sura and good Junius Rusticus,
Men of the best repute in Rome for their
Integrity of life; no fault objected,
But that they did lament his cruel sentence
On Pætus Thrasea, the philosopher,   105
Their patron and instructor.
   Steph.   Can Jove see this,
And hold his thunder!
   Domitil.   Nero and Caligula
Commanded only mischiefs; but our Cæsar
Delights to see 'em.
   Jul.   What we cannot help,
We may deplore with silence.
   Cænis.   We are call'd for   110
By our proud mistress.
   Domitil.   We a while must suffer.
   Steph. It is true fortitude to stand firm against
All shocks of fate, when cowards faint and die
In fear to suffer more calamity.   [*Exeunt.*

ACTUS III, SCÆNA 2

Enter Cæsar, Parthenius.

   Cæs. They are then in fetters?
   Parth.   Yes, sir, but—
   Cæs.   But? What?
I'll have thy thoughts. Deliver them.

98 but] only   **103** objected] advanced **or** charged *against them*

Parth.   I shall, sir;
But still submitting to your god-like pleasure,
Which cannot be instructed—
   Cæs.   To the point.
   Parth. Nor let your sacred majesty believe   5
Your vassal, that with dry eyes look'd upon
His father dragg'd to death by your command,
Can pity these, that durst presume to censure
What you decreed.
   Cæs.   Well. Forward.
   Parth.   'Tis my zeal
Still to preserve your clemency admir'd,   10
Temper'd with justice, that emboldens me
To offer my advice. Alas! I know, sir,
These bookmen, Rusticus and Palphurius Sura,
Deserve all tortures; yet, in my opinion,
They being popular senators, and cried up   15
With loud applauses of the multitude,
For foolish honesty, and beggarly virtue,
'Twould relish more of policy, to have them
Made away in private, with what exquisite torments
You please,—it skills not,—than to have them drawn 20
To the Degrees in public; for 'tis doubted
That the sad object may beget compassion
In the giddy rout, and cause some sudden uproar
That may disturb you.
   Cæs.   Hence, pale-spirited coward!
Can we descend so far beneath ourself,   25
As, or to court the people's love, or fear
Their worst of hate? Can they, that are as dust
Before the whirlwind of our will and power,
Add any moment to us? or thou think,

20 skills] matters   21 Degrees] *the* Gemonies *of* 1. i. 95
doubted] suspected, feared   29 moment] importance (*cf.*
'*momentous*')

363

If there are gods above, or goddesses,   30
(But wise Minerva, that's mine own, and sure,)
That they have vacant hours to take into
Their serious protection, or care,
This many-headed monster? Mankind lives
In few, as potent, monarchs, and their peers;   35
And all those glorious constellations
That do adorn the firmament, appointed,
Like grooms, with their bright influence to attend
The actions of kings, and emperors,
They being the greater wheels that move the less.   40
Bring forth those condemn'd wretches; let me see
One man so lost as but to pity 'em,
And though there lay a million of souls
Imprison'd in his flesh my hangmen's hooks
Should rend it off and give 'em liberty.   45
Cæsar hath said it.   [*Exit* Parthenius.

[*Enter* Parthenius, Aretinus, *and the Guard; Hangmen
     dragging in* Junius Rusticus, *and* Palphurius Sura,
     bound back to back.

   Aret.   'Tis great Cæsar's pleasure
That with fix'd eyes you carefully observe
The people's looks. Charge upon any man
That with a sigh or murmur does express
A seeming sorrow for these traitors' deaths.   50
You know his will, perform it.
   Cæs.   A good bloodhound,
And fit for my employments.
   Sura.   Give us leave
To die, fell tyrant.
   Rust.   For, beyond our bodies,
Thou hast no power.

    40 greater wheels ... less] *As in clockworks; cf.* The Duchess
of Malfi, III. ii. 177 *n.*

Cæs.   Yes; I'll afflict your souls,
And force them groaning to the Stygian lake,   55
Prepar'd for such to howl in that blaspheme
The power of princes, that are gods on earth.
Tremble to think how terrible the dream is
After this sleep of death.
   Rust.   To guilty men
It may bring terror, not to us, that know   60
What 'tis to die, well taught by his example
For whom we suffer. In my thought I see
The substance of that pure untainted soul
Of Thrasea, our master, made a star,
That with melodious harmony invites us   65
(Leaving this dunghill Rome, made hell by thee)
To trace his heavenly steps, and fill a sphere
Above yon crystal canopy.
   Cæs.   Do, invoke him
With all the aids his sanctity of life
Have won on the rewarders of his virtue;   70
They shall not save you.—Dogs, do you grin? torment
   'em.   [*The Hangmen torment 'em, they still smiling.*
So, take a leaf of Seneca now, and prove
If it can render you insensible
Of that which but begins here. Now an oil,
Drawn from the Stoics' frozen principles,   75
Predominant over fire, were useful for you.
Again, again. You trifle. Not a groan!—
Is my rage lost? What cursed charms defend 'em!
Search deeper, villains. Who looks pale? or thinks
That I am cruel?
   Aret.   Over-merciful: 80
'Tis all your weakness, sir.
   Parth.   I dare not show
A sign of sorrow; yet my sinews shrink,
The spectacle is so horrid.   [*Aside.*

Cæs.   I was never
O'ercome till now. For my sake roar a little,
And show you are corporeal, and not turn'd   85
Aerial spirits.—Will it not do? By Pallas,
It is unkindly done to mock his fury
Whom the world styles omnipotent! I am tortur'd
In their want of feeling torments. Marius' story,
That does report him to have sat unmov'd,   90
When cunning chirurgeons ripp'd his arteries
And veins, to cure his gout, compar'd to this,
Deserves not to be nam'd. Are they not dead?
If so, we wash an Æthiop.
    Sura.   No, we live.
    Rust. Live to deride thee, our calm patience treading 95
Upon the neck of tyranny. That securely,
(As 'twere a gentle slumber,) we endure
Thy hangmen's studied tortures, is a debt
We owe to grave philosophy, that instructs us
The flesh is but the clothing of the soul,   100
Which growing out of fashion, though it be
Cast off, or rent, or torn, like ours, 'tis then,
Being itself divine, in her best lustre.
But unto such as thou, that have no hopes
Beyond the present, every little scar,   105
The want of rest, excess of heat or cold,
That does inform them only they are mortal,
Pierce through and through them.
    Cæs.   We will hear no more.
    Rust. This only, and I give thee warning of it.
Though it is in thy will to grind this earth   110
As small as atoms, they thrown in the sea too,
They shall seem re-collected to thy sense,
And when the sandy building of thy greatness

86 Pallas] *sc.* Athene, = Minerva   91 chirurgeons] surgeons
(*pronounced as two syllables*)   96 securely] carelessly

366

Shall with its own weight totter, look to see me
As I was yesterday, in my perfect shape;   115
For I'll appear in horror.
   Cæs.   By my shaking
I am the guilty man, and not the judge.
Drag from my sight these cursed ominous wizards,
That, as they are now, like to double-fac'd Janus,
Which way soe'er I look, are Furies to me.   120
Away with 'em! first show them death, then leave
No memory of their ashes. I'll mock fate.
       [*Exeunt Hangmen with* Rusticus *and* Sura.
Shall words fright him, victorious armies circle?
No, no, the fever doth begin to leave me.

      Enter Domitia, Julia, *and* Cænis; Stephanos
             following.

Or, were it deadly, from this living fountain   125
I could renew the vigour of my youth,
And be a second Virbius. O my glory!
My life! command! my all!
   Dom.   As you to me are.
        [*Embracing and kissing mutually.*
I heard you were sad; I have prepar'd you sport
Will banish melancholy. Sirrah, Cæsar,   130
(I hug myself for't), I have been instructing
The players how to act, and to cut off
All tedious impertinency, have contracted
The tragedy into one continued scene.
I have the art of't, and am taken more   135
With my ability that way, than all knowledge
I have, but of thy love.
   Cæs.   Thou art still thyself,
The sweetest, wittiest—

   115 shape] appearance   127 Virbius] *Name given to the*
resurrected Hippolytus.

Dom.   When we are a-bed
I'll thank your good opinion. Thou shalt see
Such an Iphis of thy Paris!—and, to humble   140
The pride of Domitilla, that neglects me
(Howe'er she is your cousin), I have forc'd her
To play the part of Anaxarete.
You are not offended with it?

  Cæs.   Any thing
That does content thee yields delight to me.   145
My faculties and powers are thine.

  Dom.   I thank you.
Prithee let's take out places. Bid 'em enter
Without more circumstance. How do you like

        [*After a short flourish enter* Paris *as* Iphis.

That shape? methinks it is most suitable
To the aspect of a despairing lover.   150
The seeming late-fallen, counterfeited tears
That hang upon his cheeks, was my device.

  Cæs. And all was excellent.

  Dom.   Now hear him speak.

  Par. That she is fair (and that an epithet
Too foul to express her), or descended nobly,   155
Or rich, or fortunate, are certain truths
In which poor Iphis glories. But that these
Perfections, in no other virgin found,
Abus'd, should nourish cruelty and pride
In the divinest Anaxarete,   160
Is, to my love-sick, languishing soul, a riddle—
And with more difficulty to be dissolv'd
Than that the monster Sphinx, from the steep rock,
Offer'd to Œdipus. Imperious Love,
As at thy ever-flaming altars Iphis,   165
Thy never-tired votary, hath presented,
With scalding tears, whole hecatombs of sighs,

        150 aspect] *pronounced* aspéct

Preferring thy power, and thy Paphian mother's,
Before the Thunderer's, Neptune's, or Pluto's
(That, after Saturn, did divide the world,   170
And had the sway of things, yet were compell'd
By thy unevitable shafts to yield,
And fight under thy ensigns), be auspicious
To this last trial of my sacrifice
Of love and service!

    Dom.   —Does he not act it rarely?   175
Observe with what a feeling he delivers
His orisons to Cupid; I am rapt with't.—

    Par. And from thy never-emptied quiver take
A golden arrow, to transfix her heart
And force her love like me, or cure my wound   180
With a leaden one, that may beget in me
Hate and forgetfulness of what's now my idol—
But I call back my prayer; I have blasphem'd
In my rash wish. 'Tis I that am unworthy,
But she all merit, and may in justice challenge,   185
From the assurance of her excellencies,
Not love, but adoration. Yet bear witness
All-knowing Powers, I bring along with me,
As faithful advocates to make intercession,
A loyal heart with pure and holy flames,   190
With the foul fires of lust never polluted.
And, as I touch her threshold, (which with tears,
My limbs benumb'd with cold, I oft have wash'd,)
With my glad lips I kiss this earth, grown proud
With frequent favours from her delicate feet.   195

    Dom. —By Cæsar's life he weeps! and I forbear
Hardly to keep him company.—

    Par. Blest ground, thy pardon,
If I profane it with forbidden steps.
I must presume to knock—and yet attempt it   200

168 Paphian mother] Venus

369

With such a trembling reverence, as if
My hands held up for expiation
To the incensed gods to spare a kingdom.
Within there, ho! something divine come forth
To a distressed mortal.

                        [*Enter* Latinus *as a Porter.*

Lat.   Ha! Who knocks there?   205
Dom. —What a churlish look this knave has!—
Lat.   Is't you, sirrah?
Are you come to pule and whine? Avaunt, and quickly;
Dog-whips shall drive you hence else.
Dom.   —Churlish devil!
But that I should disturb the scene, as I live
I would tear his eyes out.
Cæs.   'Tis in jest, Domitia.   210
Dom. I do not like such jesting; if he were not
A flinty-hearted slave, he could not use
One of his form so harshly. How the toad swells
At the other's sweet humility!
Cæs.   'Tis his part:
Let 'em proceed.
Dom.   A rogue's part, will ne'er leave him.— 215
Par. As you have, gentle sir, the happiness
(When you please) to behold the figure of
The masterpiece of nature, limn'd to the life,
In more than human Anaxarete,
Scorn not your servant, that with suppliant hands   220
Takes hold upon your knees, conjuring you,
As you are a man, and did not suck the milk
Of wolves and tigers, or a mother of
A tougher temper, use some means these eyes,
Before they are wept out, may see your lady.   225
Will you be gracious, sir?
Lat.   Though I lose my place for't,

202 expiation] *Five syllables*, ex-pi-at-i-on

I can hold out no longer.

   Dom.   —Now he melts,
There is some little hope he may die honest.—

   Lat. Madam!   [*Enter* Domitilla *for* Anaxarete.

   Domitil.   Who calls? What object have we here?

   Dom. —Your cousin keeps her proud state still; I
    think   230
I have fitted her for a part.—

   Domitil.   Did I not charge thee
I ne'er might see this thing more?

   Par.   I am indeed
What thing you please; a worm that you may tread on,
Lower I cannot fall to show my duty,
Till your disdain hath digg'd a grave to cover   235
This body with forgotten dust; and, when
I know your sentence (cruellest of women),
I'll by a willing death remove the object
That is an eyesore to you.

   Domitil.   Wretch, thou dar'st not.
That were the last and greatest service to me   240
Thy doting love could boast of. What dull fool
But thou could nourish any flattering hope,
One of my height in youth, in birth and fortune,
Could e'er descend to look upon thy lowness?
Much less consent to make my lord of one   245
I'd not accept, though offer'd for my slave.
My thoughts stoop not so low.

   Dom.   —There's her true nature,
No personated scorn.—

   Domitil.   I wrong my worth,
Or to exchange a syllable or look
With one so far beneath me.

   Par.   Yet take heed,   250
Take heed of pride, and curiously consider

251 curiously] carefully

371

How brittle the foundation is, on which
You labour to advance it. Niobe,
Proud of her numerous issue, durst contemn
Latona's double burthen; but what follow'd?   255
She was left a childless mother, and mourn'd to marble.
The beauty you o'erprize so, time or sickness
Can change to loath'd deformity; your wealth
The prey of thieves; queen Hecuba, Troy fir'd,
Ulysses' bondwoman: but the love I bring you   260
Nor time, nor sickness, violent thieves, nor fate,
Can ravish from you.
    Dom.   —Could the oracle
Give better counsel!—
    Par.   Say will you relent yet?
Revoking your decree that I should die?
Or shall I do what you command? Resolve;   265
I am impatient of delay.
    Domitil.   Dispatch then:
I shall look on your tragedy unmov'd,
Peradventure laugh at it, for it will prove
A comedy to me.
    Dom.   —Oh devil! devil!—
    Par. Then thus I take my last leave. All the curses   270
Of lovers fall upon you; and hereafter
When any man, like me contemn'd, shall study
In the anguish of his soul to give a name
To a scornful, cruel mistress, let him only
Say, 'This most bloody woman is to me   275
As Anaxarete was to wretched Iphis!'——
Now feast your tyrannous mind, and glory in
The ruins you have made: for Hymen's bands,
That should have made us one, this fatal halter
For ever shall divorce us; at your gate,   280
As a trophy of your pride and my affliction,

    265 Resolve] decide

I'll presently hang myself.

Dom.   —Not for the world!
Restrain him, as you love your lives!

Cæs.   Why are you
Transported thus, Domitia? 'tis a play;
Or, grant it serious, it at no part merits   285
This passion in you.

Par.   I ne'er purpos'd, madam,
To do the deed in earnest; though I bow
To your care and tenderness of me.

Dom.   Let me, sir,
Entreat your pardon; what I saw presented,
Carried me beyond myself.

Cæs.   To your place again,   290
And see what follows.

Dom.   No, I am familiar
With the conclusion; besides, upon the sudden
I feel myself much indispos'd.

Cæs.   To bed then;
I'll be thy doctor.

Aret.   There is something more
In this than passion, which I must find out,   295
Or my intelligence freezes.

Dom.   Come to me, Paris,
To-morrow, for your reward.

Steph.   —Patroness, hear me;
Will you not call for your share? Sit down with this,
And, the next action, like a Gaditane strumpet,
I shall look to see you tumble!

Domitil.   —Prithee be patient.   300
I, that have suffer'd greater wrongs, bear this:
And that, till my revenge, my comfort is.   [*Exeunt.*

298 call for your share] resign from the acting profession (*into
which she is being forced*)   Sit down with] endure   299
action] performance (*with an implication of advanced realism*)

ACTUS IV, SCÆNA I

Enter Parthenius, Julia, Domitilla, Cænis.

Parth. Why, 'tis impossible!—Paris?

Jul.   You observ'd not,
(As it appears) the violence of her passion,
When, personating Iphis, he pretended,
(For your contempt, fair Anaxarete,)
To hang himself.

    Parth.   Yes, yes, I noted that;   5
But never could imagine it could work her
To such a strange intemperance of affection
As to dote on him.

    Domitil.   By my hopes, I think
That she respects not, though all here saw and mark'd
    it,
Presuming she can mould the emperor's will   10
Into what form she likes, though we, and all
Th' informers of the world, conspir'd to cross it.

    Cænis. Then with what eagerness, this morning,
    urging
The want of health and rest, she did entreat
Cæsar to leave her!

    Domitil.   Who no sooner absent,   15
But she calls, 'Dwarf!' (so in her scorn she styles me)
'Put on my pantofles; fetch pen and paper,
I am to write':—and with distracted looks,
In her smock, impatient of so short delay
As but to have a mantle thrown upon her,   20
She seal'd I know not what, but 'twas indors'd,
'To my lov'd Paris.'

    Jul.   Add to this, I heard her
Say, when a page receiv'd it, 'Let him wait me,

9 respects] cares   17 pantofles] slippers

374

And carefully, in the walk call'd our Retreat,'
Where Cæsar, in his fear to give offence,   25
Unsent for, never enters.
    Parth.   This being certain,
(For these are more than jealous suppositions,)
Why do not you, that are so near in blood,
Discover it?
    Domitil.   Alas! you know we dare not.
'Twill be received for a malicious practice   30
To free us from that slavery which her pride
Imposes on us. But if you would please
To break the ice, on pain to be sunk ever,
We would aver it.
    Parth.   I would second you,
But that I am commanded with all speed   35
To fetch in Ascletario the Chaldæan;
Who in his absence is condemn'd of treason,
For calculating the nativity
Of Cæsar, with all confidence foretelling,
In every circumstance, when he shall die   40
A violent death. Yet, if you could approve
Of my directions I would have you speak
As much to Aretinus, as you have
To me deliver'd. He in his own nature
Being a spy, on weaker grounds, no doubt,   45
Will undertake it, not for goodness' sake,
(With which he never yet held correspondence,)
But to endear his vigilant observings
Of what concerns the emperor, and a little
To triumph in the ruins of this Paris,   50
That cross'd him in the Senate-house. Here he comes,
                          [*Enter* Aretinus.
His nose held up; he hath something in the wind,
Or I much err, already. My designs

      29 Discover] reveal   30 practice] trick

Command me hence, great ladies; but I leave
My wishes with you.   [*Exit* Parthenius.
   Aret.   Have I caught your Greatness   55
In the trap, my proud Augusta!
   Domitil.   What is't raps him?
   Aret. And my fine Roman Actor! Is't even so?
No coarser dish to take your wanton palate,
Save that which, but the emperor, none durst taste of!
'Tis very well. I needs must glory in   60
This rare discovery, but the rewards
Of my intelligence bid me think, even now,
By an edict from Cæsar, I have power
To tread upon the neck of slavish Rome,
Disposing offices and provinces   65
To my kinsmen, friends, and clients.
   Domitil.   This is more
Than usual with him.
   Jul.   Aretinus!
   Aret.   How!
No more respect and reverence tender'd to me,
But 'Aretinus'! 'Tis confess'd that title,
When you were princesses, and commanded all,   70
Had been a favour; but being as you are
Vassals to a proud woman, the worst bondage,
You stand oblig'd with as much adoration
To entertain him that comes arm'd with strength
To break your fetters, as tann'd galley-slaves   75
Pay such as do redeem them from the oar.
I come not to entrap you; but aloud
Pronounce that you are manumiz'd: and to make
Your liberty sweeter, you shall see her fall,
(This empress, this Domitia, what you will,)   80
That triumph'd in your miseries.
   Domitil.   Were you serious,

56 raps] absorbs (*cf.* rapt)

To prove your accusation I could lend
Some help.
 Cænis. And I.
 Jul.   And I.
 Aret.   No atom to me.
My eyes and ears are everywhere; I know all,
To the line and action in the play that took her; **85**
Her quick dissimulation to excuse
Her being transported, with her morning passion.
I brib'd the boy that did convey the letter,
And, having perus'd it, made it up again:
Your griefs and angers are to me familiar; **90**
That Paris is brought to her, and how far
He shall be tempted.
 Domitil.   This is above wonder.
 Aret. My gold can work much stranger miracles
Than to corrupt poor waiters. Here, join with me—
          [*Offers a paper.*
'Tis a complaint to Cæsar. This is that 95
Shall ruin her and raise you. Have you set your hands
To the accusation?
 Jul.   And will justify
What we have subscrib'd to.
 Cænis.   And with vehemency.
 Domitil. I will deliver it.
 Aret.   Leave the rest to me then.

   Enter Cæsar *with his Guard.*

 Cæs. Let our lieutenants bring us victory, **100**
While we enjoy the fruits of peace at home,
And, being secur'd from our intestine foes
(Far worse than foreign enemies), doubts and fears,
Though all the sky were hung with blazing meteors,
Which fond astrologers give out to be **105**

   105 fond] foolish

      377

Assur'd presages of the change of empires
And deaths of monarchs, we, undaunted yet,
Guarded with our own thunder, bid defiance
To them and fate, we being too strongly arm'd
For them to wound us.

   Aret.   Cæsar!
   Jul.   As thou art   110
More than a man——
   Cænis.   Let not thy passions be
Rebellious to thy reason——

                         The petition deliver'd.

   Domitil.   But receive
This trial of your constancy, as unmov'd
As you go to or from the Capitol,
Thanks given to Jove for triumphs.
   Cæs.   Ha!
   Domitil.   Vouchsafe 115
A while to stay the lightning of your eyes,
Poor mortals dare not look on.
   Aret.   There's no vein
Of yours that rises high with rage, but is
An earthquake to us.
   Domitil.   And, if not kept clos'd
With more than human patience, in a moment   120
Will swallow us to the centre.
   Cænis.   Not that we
Repine to serve her, are we her accusers.
   Jul. But that she's fall'n so low.
   Aret.   Which on sure proofs
We can make good.
   Domitil.   And show she is unworthy
Of the least spark of that diviner fire   125
You have conferr'd upon her.
   Cæs.   I stand doubtful,

And unresolv'd what to determine of you.
In this malicious violence you have offer'd
To the altar of her truth and pureness to me,
You have but fruitlessly labour'd to sully   130
A white robe of perfection, black-mouth'd envy
Could belch no spot on.—But I will put off
The deity you labour to take from me,
And argue out of probabilities with you,
As if I were a man. Can I believe   135
That she, that borrows all her light from me,
And knows to use it, would betray her darkness
To your intelligence; and make that apparent
Which, by her perturbations in a play,
Was yesterday but doubted, and find none   140
But you, that are her slaves, and therefore hate her,
Whose aids she might employ to make way for her?
Or Aretinus, whom long since she knew
To be the cabinet counsellor, nay, the key
Of Cæsar's secrets? Could her beauty raise her   145
To this unequall'd height, to make her fall
The more remarkable? or must my desires
To her, and wrongs to Lamia, be reveng'd
By her, and on herself, that drew on both?
Or she leave our imperial bed, to court   150
A public actor?
    Aret.   Who dares contradict
These more than human reasons, that have power
To clothe base guilt in the most glorious shape
Of innocence?
    Domitil.   Too well she knew the strength
And eloquence of her patron to defend her,   155
And, thereupon presuming, fell securely,
Not fearing an accuser, nor the truth
Produc'd against her, which your love and favour

140 doubted] suspected   156 securely] carelessly

Will ne'er discern from falsehood.

Cæs.   I'll not hear
A syllable more that may invite a change   160
In my opinion of her. You have rais'd
A fiercer war within me by this fable,
(Though with your lives you vow to make it story,)
Than if, and at one instant, all my legions
Revolted from me, and came arm'd against me.   165
Here in this paper are the swords predestin'd
For my destruction; here the fatal stars,
That threaten more than ruin; this the death's head
That does assure me, if she can prove false,
That I am mortal, which a sudden fever   170
Would prompt me to believe, and faintly yield to.
But now in my full confidence what she suffers,
In that, from any witness but myself,
I nourish a suspicion she's untrue,
My toughness returns to me. Lead on, monsters,   175
And, by the forfeit of your lives, confirm
She is all excellence, as you all baseness;
Or let mankind, for her fall, boldly swear
There are no chaste wives now, nor ever were.
                                          [*Exeunt.*

ACTUS IV, SCÆNA 2

Enter Domitia, Paris, *Servants.*

Dom. Say we command, that none presume to dare,
On forfeit of our favour, that is life,
Out of a saucy curiousness, to stand
Within the distance of their eyes or ears,
Till we please to be waited on. And, sirrah,   5
                                  [*Exeunt Servants.*

163 story] history, truth

Howe'er you are excepted, let it not
Beget in you an arrogant opinion
'Tis done to grace you.

    Par.   With my humblest service
I but obey your summons, and should blush else
To be so near you.

    Dom.   'Twould become you rather   10
To fear the greatness of the grace vouchsaf'd you
May overwhelm you, and 'twill do no less,
If, when you are rewarded, in your cups
You boast this privacy.

    Par.   That were, mightiest empress,
To play with lightning.

    Dom.   You conceive it right.   15
The means to kill, or save, is not alone
In Cæsar circumscrib'd, for, if incens'd,
We have our thunder too, that strikes as deadly.

    Par. 'Twould ill become the lowness of my fortune
To question what you can do, but with all   20
Humility to attend what is your will,
And then to serve it.

    Dom.   And would not a secret,
(Suppose we should commit it to your trust,)
Scald you to keep it?

    Par.   Though it rag'd within me
Till I turn'd cinders, it should ne'er have vent.   25
To be an age a-dying, and with torture,
Only to be thought worthy of your counsel,
Or actuate whatever you command me,
A wretched obscure thing, not worth your knowledge,
Were a perpetual happiness.

    Dom.   We could wish   30
That we could credit thee, and cannot find
In reason but that thou, whom oft I have seen

28 actuate] put in action

381

To personate a gentleman, noble, wise,
Faithful, and gamesome and what virtue else
The poet pleases to adorn you with,   35
But that (as vessels still partake the odour
Of the sweet precious liquors they contain'd)
Thou must be really, in some degree,
The thing thou dost present.—Nay, do not tremble;
We seriously believe it, and presume   40
Our Paris is the volume in which all
Those excellent gifts the stage hath seen him grac'd
     with
Are curiously bound up.
     Par.   The argument
Is the same, great Augusta, that I acting
A fool, a coward, a traitor, or cold cynic,   45
Or any other weak and vicious person,
Of force I must be such. O gracious madam,
How glorious soever, or deform'd,
I do appear in the scene, my part being ended,
And all my borrowed ornaments put off,   50
I am no more, nor less, than what I was
Before I enter'd.
     Dom.   Come, you would put on
A wilful ignorance, and not understand
What 'tis we point at. Must we in plain language,
Against the decent modesty of our sex,   55
Say that we love thee, love thee to enjoy thee,
Or that in our desires thou art preferr'd,
And Cæsar but thy second? Thou in justice,
(If from the height of majesty we can
Look down upon thy lowness, and embrace it,)   60
Art bound with fervour to look up to me.

34 gamesome] wanton, spirited (*a favourite adjective with
Massinger; the original reads* gainsome *which makes poor sense*)
47 of force] perforce

Par. O madam! hear me with a patient ear,
And be but pleas'd to understand the reasons
That do deter me from a happiness
Kings would be rivals for. Can I, that owe   65
My life, and all that's mine, to Cæsar's bounties,
Beyond my hopes or merits, show'r'd upon me,
Make payment for them with ingratitude,
Falsehood and treason! Though you have a shape
Might tempt Hippolytus, and larger power   70
To help or hurt than wanton Phædra had,
Let loyalty and duty plead my pardon,
Though I refuse to satisfy—
    Dom.   You are coy,
Expecting I should court you. Let mean ladies
Use prayers and entreaties to their creatures   75
To rise up instruments to serve their pleasures;
But for Augusta so to lose herself,
That holds command o'er Cæsar and the world,
Were poverty of spirit. Thou must—thou shalt!
The violence of my passions knows no mean,   80
And in my punishments and my rewards
I'll use no moderation. Take this only,
As a caution from me: threadbare chastity
Is poor in the advancement of her servants,
But wantonness magnificent; and 'tis frequent   85
To have the salary of vice weigh down
The pay of virtue. So, without more trifling,
Thy sudden answer.
    Par.   In what a strait am I brought in!
Alas! I know that the denial's death;
Nor can my grant, discover'd, threaten more.   90
Yet to die innocent, and have the glory
For all posterity to report that I
Refus'd an empress, to preserve my faith

88 sudden] immediate

383

To my great master, in true judgment must
Show fairer than to buy a guilty life   95
With wealth and honours. 'Tis the base I build on.
I dare not, must not, will not.
   Dom.   How! contemn'd?
—Since hopes, nor fears, in the extremes, prevail not,
I must use a mean.—Think who 'tis sues to thee!
Deny not that yet, which a brother may   100
Grant to a sister: as a testimony
      [*Cæsar, Aretinus, Julia, Domitilla, Cænis, above.*
I am not scorn'd, kiss me. Kiss me again.
Kiss closer. Thou art now my Trojan Paris,
And I thy Helen.
   Par.   Since it is your will.
   Cæs. And I am Menelaus. But I shall be   105
      [*Cæsar descends.*
Something I know not yet.
   Dom.   Why lose we time
And opportunity? These are but salads
To sharpen appetite. Let us to the feast,
      [*Courting* Paris *wantonly.*
Where I shall wish that thou wert Jupiter,
And I Alcmena, and that I had power   110
To lengthen out one short night into three,
And so beget a Hercules.
   Cæs.   While Amphitrio
Stands by, and draws the curtains.
   Par.   Oh!——
      [*Falls on his face.*
   Dom.   Betray'd!
   Cæs. No, taken in a net of Vulcan's filing,
Where, in myself, the theatre of the gods   115
Are sad spectators, not one of them daring
To witness, with a smile, he does desire
To be so sham'd for all the pleasure that

384

You have sold your being for! What shall I name thee?
Ingrateful, treacherous, insatiate, all   120
Invectives which, in bitterness of spirit,
Wrong'd men have breath'd out against wicked
    women,
Cannot express thee! Have I rais'd thee from
Thy low condition to the height of greatness,
Command, and majesty, in one base act   125
To render me, that was, before I hugg'd thee,
An adder, in my bosom, more than man,
A thing beneath a beast! Did I force these
Of mine own blood, as handmaids to kneel to
Thy pomp and pride, having myself no thought   130
But how with benefits to bind thee mine;
And am I thus rewarded! Not a knee?
Nor tear? nor sign of sorrow for thy fault?
Break, stubborn silence: what canst thou allege
To stay my vengeance?
    Dom.   This. Thy lust compell'd me 135
To be a strumpet, and mine hath return'd it
In my intent and will, though not in act,
To cuckold thee.
    Cæs.   O impudence! take her hence,
And let her make her entrance into hell,
By leaving life with all the tortures that   140
Flesh can be sensible of. Yet stay. What power
Her beauty still holds o'er my soul, that wrongs
Of this unpardonable nature cannot teach me
To right myself, and hate her!—Kill her.—Hold!
Oh that my dotage should increase from that   145
Which should breed detestation! By Minerva,
If I look on her longer, I shall melt,
And sue to her, my injuries forgot,
Again to be receiv'd into her favour;
Could honour yield to it! Carry her to her chamber; 150

Be that her prison, till in cooler blood
I shall determine of her.   [*Exit Guard with* Domitia.
   Aret.   Now step I in,
While he's in this calm mood, for my reward.—
Sir, if my service hath deserv'd——
   Cæs.   Yes, yes:
And I'll reward thee. Thou hast robb'd me of   155
All rest and peace, and been the principal means
To make me know that, of which if again
                            [*Enter Guard.*
I could be ignorant of, I would purchase it
With the loss of empire. Strangle him; take these hence
    too,
And lodge them in the dungeon. Could your reason,   160
Dull wretches, flatter you with hope to think
That this discovery, that hath shower'd upon me
Perpetual vexation, should not fall
Heavy on you? Away with 'em!—stop their mouths;
I will hear no reply. O, Paris, Paris,   165
       [*Exit Guard,* Aretinus, Julia, Cænis, Domitilla.
How shall I argue with thee? how begin
To make thee understand, before I kill thee,
With what grief and unwillingness 'tis forc'd from me?
Yet, in respect I have favour'd thee, I will hear
What thou canst speak to qualify or excuse   170
Thy readiness to serve this woman's lust,
And wish thou couldst give me such satisfaction,
As I might bury the remembrance of it.
Look up: we stand attentive.
   Par.   O dread Cæsar!
To hope for life, or plead in the defence   175
Of my ingratitude, were again to wrong you.
I know I have deserv'd death; and my suit is,
That you would hasten it: yet, that your highness,
When I am dead, (as sure I will not live,)

May pardon me, I'll only urge my frailty,   180
Her will, and the temptation of that beauty
Which you could not resist. How could poor I, then,
Fly that which follow'd me, and Cæsar su'd for?
This is all. And now your sentence.
    Cæs.   Which I know not
How to pronounce. Oh that thy fault had been   185
But such as I might pardon! If thou hadst
In wantonness, like Nero, fir'd proud Rome,
Betray'd an army, butcher'd the whole Senate,
Committed sacrilege, or any crime
The justice of our Roman laws calls death,   190
I had prevented any intercession,
And freely sign'd thy pardon.
    Par.   But for this
Alas you cannot, nay, you must not, sir.
Nor let it to posterity be recorded,
That Cæsar, unreveng'd, suffer'd a wrong   195
Which, if a private man should sit down with it,
Cowards would baffle him.
    Cæs.   With such true feeling
Thou arguest against thyself, that it
Works more upon me than if my Minerva,
(The grand protectress of my life and empire,)   200
On forfeit of her favour, cri'd aloud,
'Cæsar, show mercy!' and, I know not how,
I am inclin'd to it. Rise. I'll promise nothing;
Yet clear thy cloudy fears, and cherish hopes.
What we must do, we shall do; we remember   205
A tragedy we oft have seen with pleasure,
Call'd the *False Servant*.
    Par.   Such a one we have, sir.
    Cæs. In which a great lord takes to his protection
A man forlorn, giving him ample power

    191 prevented] forestalled   197 baffle] jeer at

To order and dispose of his estate   210
In his absence, (he pretending then a journey,)
But yet with this restraint, that on no terms
(This lord suspecting his wife's constancy,
She having play'd false to a former husband)
The servant, though solicited, should consent,   215
Though she commanded him, to quench her flames.
  Par. That was, indeed, the argument.
  Cæs.   And what
Didst thou play in it?
  Par.   The false servant, sir.
  Cæs. Thou didst indeed. Do the players wait with-
   out?
  Par. They do, sir, and prepar'd to act the story   220
Your majesty mention'd.
  Cæs.   Call them in. Who presents
The injur'd lord?

  Enter Æsopus, Latinus, *a Boy dress'd for a* Lady.

  Æsop.   'Tis my part, sir.
  Cæs.   Thou didst not
Do it to the life. We can perform it better.
Off with my robe, and wreath: since Nero scorn'd not
The public theatre, we in private may   225
Disport ourselves. This cloak and hat, without
Wearing a beard, or other property,
Will fit the person.
  Æsop.   Only, sir, a foil,
The point and edge rebutted, when you are
To do the murther. If you please to use this,   230
And lay aside your own sword.
  Cæs.   By no means:
In jest or earnest this parts never from me.
We'll have but one short scene—that where the lady

    229 rebutted] blunted

In an imperious way commands the servant
To be unthankful to his patron: when   235
My cue's to enter, prompt me.—Nay, begin,
And do it sprightly: though but a new actor,
When I come to execution, you shall find
No cause to laugh at me.
  Lat.   In the name of wonder,
What's Cæsar's purpose!
  Æsop.   There is no contending.   240
  Cæs. Why, when?—
  Par.   I am arm'd:
And, stood Death now within my view, and his
Unevitable dart aim'd at my breast,
His cold embraces should not bring an ague
To any of my faculties, till his pleasures   245
Were serv'd and satisfied; which done, Nestor's years
To me would be unwelcome.
  Boy.   Must we entreat,
That were born to command? or court a servant,
That owes his food and clothing to our bounty,
For that which thou ambitiously shouldst kneel for? 250
Urge not, in thy excuse, the favours of
Thy absent lord, or that thou stand'st engag'd
For thy life to his charity; nor thy fears
Of what may follow, it being in my power
To mould him any way.
  Par.   As you may me,   255
In what his reputation is not wounded,
Nor I, his creature, in my thankfulness suffer.
I know you're young, and fair; be virtuous too,
And loyal to his bed, that hath advanc'd you
To the height of happiness.
  Boy.   Can my love-sick heart 260
Be cur'd with counsel? or durst reason ever
  241 Why, when?] *Impatient exclamation.*

Offer to put in an exploded plea
In the court of Venus? My desires admit not
The least delay; and therefore instantly
Give me to understand what I shall trust to.   265
For if I am refus'd and not enjoy
Those ravishing pleasures from thee I run mad for,
I'll swear unto my lord at his return
(Making what I deliver good with tears,)
That brutishly thou wouldst have forc'd from me   270
What I make suit for. And then but imagine
What 'tis to die, with these words, 'slave' and 'traitor,'
With burning corrosives writ upon thy forehead,
And live prepared for't.
    Par.   —This he will believe
Upon her information, 'tis apparent;   275
And then I am nothing; and of two extremes,
Wisdom says, choose the less.—Rather than fall
Under your indignation, I will yield.
This kiss, and this, confirms it.
    Æsop.   —Now, sir, now.
    Cæs. I must take them at it?
    Æsop.   Yes, sir; be but perfect. 280
    Cæs. 'O villain! thankless villain!'—I should talk
    now;
But I have forgot my part. But I can do:
Thus, thus, and thus.   [*Kills* Paris.
    Par.   Oh! I am slain in earnest.
    Cæs. 'Tis true; and 'twas my purpose, my good
    Paris.
And yet, before life leave thee, let the honour   285
I have done thee in thy death bring comfort to thee.
If it had been within the power of Cæsar,
(His dignity preserv'd,) he had pardon'd thee,
But cruelty of honour did deny it.
Yet, to confirm I lov'd thee, 'twas my study   290

To make thy end more glorious, to distinguish
My Paris from all others; and in that
Have shown my pity. Nor would I let thee fall
By a centurion's sword, or have thy limbs
Rent piecemeal by the hangman's hook, (however   295
Thy crime deserv'd it); but, as thou didst live
Rome's bravest actor, 'twas my plot that thou
Shouldst die in action, and to crown it die
With an applause enduring to all times,
By our imperial hand.—His soul is freed   300
From the prison of his flesh; let it mount upward!
And for this trunk, when that the funeral pile
Hath made it ashes, we'll see it enclos'd
In a golden urn. Poets adorn his hearse
With their most ravishing sorrows, and the stage   305
For ever mourn him, and all such as were
His glad spectators weep his sudden death,
The cause forgotten in his epitaph.
        [*Exeunt. A sad music, the Players bearing off* Paris' *body,*
                    Cæsar *and the rest following.*

ACTUS V, SCÆNA I

Enter Parthenius, Stephanos, *Guard.*

Parth. Keep a strong guard upon him, and admit not
Access to any, to exchange a word
Or syllable with him, till the emperor pleases
To call him to his presence.—The relation
That you have made me, Stephanos, of these late   5
Strange passions in Cæsar, much amaze me.
The informer Aretinus put to death
For yielding him a true discovery
Of the empress' wantonness; poor Paris kill'd first,

        1 him] *Sc.* Ascletario; *see l.* 106.

And now lamented; and the princesses   10
Confined to several islands; yet Augusta,
(The machine on which all this mischief moved,)
Receiv'd again to grace!

   Steph.   Nay, courted to it:
Such is the impotence of his affection!
Yet, to conceal his weakness, he gives out   15
The people made suit for her, whom they hate more
Than civil war, or famine. But take heed,
My lord, that, nor in your consent nor wishes,
You lent or furtherance or favour to
The plot contriv'd against her; should she prove it,   20
Nay, doubt it only, you are a lost man,
Her power o'er doting Cæsar being now
Greater than ever.

   Parth.   'Tis a truth I shake at;
And, when there's opportunity——

   Steph.   Say but, Do:
I am yours, and sure.

   Parth.   I will stand one trial more,   25
And then you shall hear from me.

   Steph.   Now observe
The fondness of this tyranne, and her pride.

       Enter Cæsar *and* Domitia.

Cæs. Nay, all's forgotten.

   Dom.   It may be, on your part.

   Cæs. Forgiven too, Domitia; 'tis a favour
That you should welcome with more cheerful looks.   30
Can Cæsar pardon what you durst not hope for,
That did the injury, and yet must sue

   11 several] different   14 impotence] uncontrollableness
17–19 take heed . . . You lent] 'Take care you didn't' *is spirited
English for* 'Take care if you did'. *Editors perversely change to* lend,
but the action is past.   21 doubt] suspect   27 Fondness]
foolishness   tyranne] tyrant. *See* III. i. 77 *note*.

To her whose guilt is wash'd off by his mercy
Only to entertain it?

   Dom.   I ask'd none:
And I should be more wretched to receive   35
Remission for what I hold no crime,
But by a bare acknowledgment, than if,
By slighting and contemning it, as now,
I dar'd thy utmost fury. Though thy flatterers
Persuade thee that thy murthers, lusts, and rapes, 40
Are virtues in thee, and what pleases Cæsar
Though never so unjust is right and lawful;
Or work in thee a false belief that thou
Art more than mortal, yet I to thy teeth
(When circl'd with thy guards, thy rods, thy axes, 45
And all the ensigns of thy boasted power,)
Will say, Domitian, nay, add to it Cæsar,
Is a weak, feeble man, a bondman to
His violent passions, and in that my slave,
Nay, more my slave than my affections made me 50
To my lov'd Paris.

   Cæs.   Can I live, and hear this?
Or hear, and not revenge it? Come, you know
The strength that you hold on me; do not use it
With too much cruelty; for, though 'tis granted
That Lydian Omphale had less command   55
O'er Hercules than you usurp o'er me,
Reason may teach me to shake off the yoke
Of my fond dotage.

   Dom.   Never; do not hope it;
It cannot be. Thou being my beauty's captive,
And not to be redeem'd, my empire's larger   60
Than thine, Domitian, which I'll exercise
With rigour on thee, for my Paris' death.
And, when I have forc'd those eyes, now red with fury,
To drop down tears, in vain spent to appease me,

I know thy fervour such to my embraces,   65
(Which shall be, though still kneel'd for, still deni'd thee,)
That thou with languishment shalt wish my actor
Did live again, so thou mightst be his second
To feed upon those delicates, when he's sated.
    Cæs. O my Minerva!
    Dom.   There she is, invoke her: 70
                            [*Image of* Minerva.
She cannot arm thee with ability
To draw thy sword on me, my power being greater;
Or only say to thy centurions,
'Dare none of you do what I shake to think on?
And, in this woman's death, remove the Furies   75
That every hour afflict me?'—Lamia's wrongs,
When thy lust forc'd me from him, are, in me,
At the height reveng'd; nor would I outlive Paris.
But that thy love, increasing with my hate,
May add unto thy torments; so, with all   80
Contempt I can, I leave thee.   [*Exit.*
    Cæs.   I am lost;
Nor am I Cæsar. When I first betray'd
The freedom of my faculties and will
To this imperious siren, I laid down
The empire of the world, and of myself,   85
At her proud feet. Sleep all my ireful powers?
Or is the magic of my dotage such,
That I must still make suit to hear those charms
That do increase my thraldom? Wake, my anger!
For shame, break through this lethargy, and appear   90
With usual terror, and enable me,
(Since I wear not a sword to pierce her heart,
Nor have a tongue to say this, 'Let her die,')
Though 'tis done with a fever-shaken hand,
                      [*Pulls out a table-book.*

94 s.d. table-book] notebook

To sign her death. Assist me, great Minerva,   95
And vindicate thy votary!—So; she's now
Among the list of those I have proscrib'd,
And are, to free me of my doubts and fears,
To die to-morrow.   [*Writes.*
   Steph.   That same fatal book
Was never drawn yet, but some men of rank   100
Were mark'd out for destruction.   [*Exit.*
   Parth.   I begin
To doubt myself.
   Cæs.   Who waits there?
   Parth.   Cæsar.
   Cæs.   So!
These that command arm'd troops, quake at my
    frowns,
And yet a woman slights 'em. Where's the wizard
We charg'd you to fetch in?
   Parth.   Ready to suffer   105
What death you please to appoint him.
   Caes.   Bring him in.

      Enter Ascletario, *Tribunes, Guard.*

We'll question him ourself. Now, you, that hold
Intelligence with the stars, and dare prefix
The day and hour in which we are to part
With life and empire, punctually foretelling   110
The means and manner of our violent end,
As you would purchase credit to your art,
Resolve me, since you are assur'd of us,
What fate attends yourself?
   Ascle.   I have had long since
A certain knowledge, and as sure as thou   115
Shalt die to-morrow, being the fourteenth of
The kalends of October, the hour five,

   108 prefix] ascertain in advance   113 Resolve] inform

Spite of prevention, this carcass shall be
Torn and devour'd by dogs;—and let that stand
For a firm prediction.

  Cæs.   May our body, wretch, 120
Find never nobler sepulchre, if this
Fall ever on thee! Are we the great disposer
Of life and death, yet cannot mock the stars
In such a trifle? Hence with the impostor,
And having cut his throat erect a pile   125
Guarded with soldiers, till his cursed trunk
Be turn'd to ashes: upon forfeit of
Your life, and theirs, perform it.

  Ascle.   'Tis in vain.
When what I have foretold is made apparent,
Tremble to think what follows.

  Cæs.   Drag him hence, 130
      [*The Guard bear off* Ascletario.
And do as I command you. I was never
Fuller of confidence; for having got
The victory of my passions in my freedom
From proud Domitia, (who shall cease to live
Since she disdains to love,) I rest unmov'd, 135
And in defiance of prodigious meteors,
Chaldæans' vain predictions, jealous fears
Of my near friends and freemen, certain hate
Of kindred and alliance, or all terrors
The soldier's doubted faith, or people's rage, 140
Can bring to shake my constancy, I am arm'd.
That scrupulous thing styl'd conscience is sear'd up,
And I insensible of all my actions,
For which, by moral and religious fools,
I stand condemn'd, as they had never been. 145
And, since I have subdu'd triumphant love,
I will not deify pale captive fear,

    118 prevention] precautions

Nor in a thought receive it. For till thou,
Wisest Minerva, that from my first youth
Hast been my sole protectress, dost forsake me,   150
Not Junius Rusticus' threat'ned apparition,
Nor what this soothsayer but ev'n now foretold,
(Being things impossible to human reason)
Shall in a dream disturb me. Bring my couch there;
A sudden but a secure drowsiness   155
Invites me to repose myself. Let music

           [*Enter with couch.*

With some choice ditty second it.

           I' the mean time,
Rest there, dear book, which open'd when I wake

           [*Lays the book under his pillow.*

Shall make some sleep for ever.

           [*The music and a song*. Cæsar *sleeps.*

         Enter Parthenius *and* Domitia.

Dom.   Write my name
In his bloody scroll, Parthenius? the fear's idle;   160
He durst not, could not.
    Parth.   I can assure nothing;
But I observ'd, when you departed from him,
After some little passion, but much fury,
He drew it out; whose death he sign'd, I know not,
But in his looks appear'd a resolution   165
Of what before he stagger'd at. What he hath
Determin'd of is uncertain, but too soon
Will fall on you, or me, or both, or any,
His pleasure known to the tribunes and centurions,
Who never use to inquire his will, but serve it.   170
Now if out of the confidence of your power,
The bloody catalogue being still about him,
As he sleeps you dare peruse it, or remove it,

       155 secure] carefree (*pronounced* sécure)

               397

You may instruct yourself, or what to suffer,
Or how to cross it.
    Dom.   I would not be caught   175
With too much confidence. By your leave, sir. Ha!
No motion!—you lie uneasy, sir,
Let me mend your pillow.
    Parth.   Have you it?
    Dom.   'Tis here.
    Cæs. Oh!
    Parth.   You have wak'd him; softly, gracious
    madam,
While we are unknown, and then consult at leisure.   180
                      [*Exeunt* Parthenius *and* Domitia.

A dreadful music sounding, enter Junius Rusticus *and*
    Palphurius Sura, *with bloody swords; they wave them*
    over his head. Cæsar *in his sleep troubled, seems to pray*
    to the image; they scornfully take it away.

    Cæs. Defend me, goddess, or this horrid dream
Will force me to distraction! whither have
These Furies borne thee? Let me rise and follow.
I am bath'd o'er with the cold sweat of death,
And am depriv'd of organs to pursue   185
These sacrilegious spirits. Am I at once
Robb'd of my hopes and being? No, I live—
                    [*Rises distractedly.*
Yes, live, and have discourse, to know myself
Of gods and men forsaken. What accuser
Within me cries aloud, I have deserv'd it,   190
In being just to neither? Who dares speak this?
Am I not Cæsar?—How! again repeat it?
Presumptuous traitor, thou shalt die!—What traitor?
He that hath been a traitor to himself,
And stands convicted here. Yet who can sit   195
           188 discourse] reason

A competent judge o'er Cæsar? Cæsar. Yes,
Cæsar by Cæsar's sentenc'd, and must suffer.
Minerva cannot save him. Ha! where is she?
Where is my goddess? vanish'd! I am lost then.
No, 'twas no dream, but a most real truth,   200
That Junius Rusticus and Palphurius Sura,
Although their ashes were cast in the sea,
Were by their innocence made up again,
And in corporeal forms but now appear'd,
Waving their bloody swords above my head,   205
As at their deaths they threat'ned. And methought
Minerva, ravish'd hence, whisper'd that she
Was, for my blasphemies, disarm'd by Jove,
And could no more protect me. Yes, 'twas so.
                              [*Thunder and lightning.*
His thunder does confirm it, against which,   210
Howe'er it spare the laurel, this proud wreath
Is no assurance.—Ha! come you resolv'd
                              [*Enter 3 Tribunes.*
To be my executioners?
    1. *Trib.*   Allegiance
And faith forbid that we should lift an arm
Against your sacred head.
    2. *Trib.*   We rather sue   215
For mercy.
    3. *Trib.* And acknowledge that in justice
Our lives are forfeited for not performing
What Cæsar charg'd us.
    1. *Trib.*   Nor did we transgress it
In our want of will, or care; for, being but men,
It could not be in us to make resistance,   220
The gods fighting against us.
    Cæs.   Speak, in what
Did they express their anger? we will hear it,
But dare not say, undaunted.

1. *Trib.*   In brief thus, sir:
The sentence given by your imperial tongue
For the astrologer Ascletario's death   225
With speed was put in execution.
    Cæs.   Well.
    1. *Trib.* For, his throat cut, his legs bound, and his
        arms
Pinion'd behind his back, the breathless trunk
Was with all scorn dragg'd to the Field of Mars,
And there, a pile being rais'd of old dry wood,   230
Smear'd o'er with oil, and brimstone, or what else
Could help to feed, or to increase the fire,
The carcass was thrown on it; but no sooner
The stuff, that was most apt, began to flame,
But suddenly, to the amazement of   235
The fearless soldier, a sudden flash
Of lightning, breaking through the scatter'd clouds,
With such a horrid violence forc'd its passage,
And as disdaining all heat but itself,
In a moment quench'd the artificial fire.   240
And before we could kindle it again
A clap of thunder follow'd, with such noise
As if then Jove, incens'd against mankind,
Had in his secret purposes determin'd
An universal ruin to the world.   245
This horror past, not at Deucalion's flood
Such a stormy shower of rain (and yet that word is
Too narrow to express it) was e'er seen.
Imagine rather, sir, that with less fury
The waves rush down the cataracts of Nile;   250
Or that the sea, spouted into the air
By the angry Orc, endangering tall ships
But sailing near it, so falls down again.
Yet here the wonder ends not, but begins;
For as in vain we labour'd to consume   255

The witch's body, all the dogs of Rome,
Howling and yelling like to famish'd wolves,
Brake in upon us; and though thousands were
Kill'd in th' attempt, some did ascend the pile,
And with their eager fangs seiz'd on the carcass.   260
    Cæs. But have they torn it?
    1. *Trib.*   Torn it, and devour'd it.
    Cæs. I then am a dead man, since all predictions
Assure me I am lost. O my lov'd soldiers,
Your emperor must leave you! yet, however
I cannot grant myself a short reprieve,   265
I freely pardon you. The fatal hour
Steals fast upon me. I must die this morning
By five, my soldiers; that's the latest hour
You e'er must see me living.
    1. *Trib.*   Jove avert it!
In our swords lies your fate, and we will guard it.   270
    Cæs. Oh no, it cannot be; it is decreed
Above, and by no strengths here to be alter'd.
Let proud mortality but look on Cæsar,
Compass'd of late with armies, in his eyes
Carrying both life and death, and in his arms   275
Fadoming the earth; that would be styl'd a god,
And is for that presumption cast beneath
The low condition of a common man,
Sinking with mine own weight.——
    1. *Trib.*   Do not forsake
Yourself, we'll never leave you.
    2. *Trib.*   We'll draw up   280
More cohorts of your guard, if you doubt treason.
    Cæs. They cannot save me. The offended gods,
That now sit judges on me, from their envy
Of my power and greatness here, conspire against me.
    1. *Trib.* Endeavour to appease them.

256 witch] *Used of man or woman.*   281 doubt] suspect

Cæs.   'Twill be fruitless: 285
I am past hope of remission. Yet could I
Decline this dreadful hour of five, these terrors
That drive me to despair would soon fly from me;
And could you but till then assure me——
   1. *Trib.*   Yes, sir;
Or we'll fall with you, and make Rome the urn   290
In which we'll mix our ashes.
   Cæs.   'Tis said nobly:
I am something comforted. Howe'er, to die
Is the full period of calamity.   [*Exeunt.*

ACTUS V, SCÆNA 2

Enter Parthenius, Domitia, Julia, Cænis, Domitilla,
    Stephanos, Sejeius, Entellus.

   Parth. You see we are all condemn'd, there's no
    evasion,
We must do, or suffer.
   Steph.   But it must be sudden;
The least delay is mortal.
   Dom.   Would I were
A man, to give it action!
   Domitil. Could I make my approaches, though my
    stature   5
Does promise little, I have a spirit as daring
As hers that can reach higher.
   Steph.   I will take
That burthen from you, madam. All the art is,
To draw him from the tribunes that attend him;
For, could you bring him but within my sword's reach, 10
The world should owe her freedom from a tyranne
To Stephanos.

   287 Decline] avoid, escape, avert   **1** evasion] escape

Sej.   You shall not share alone
The glory of a deed that will endure
To all posterity.

Ent.   I will put in
For a part, myself.

Parth.   Be resolute, and stand close.   15
I have conceiv'd a way, and with the hazard
Of my life I'll practise it, to fetch him hither.
But then no trifling.

Steph.   We'll dispatch him, fear not:
A dead dog never bites.

Parth.   Thus then at all—
          [Parthenius *goes off; the rest stand aside.*

          Enter Cæsar *and Tribunes.*

Cæs. How slow-pac'd are these minutes! in extremes, 20
How miserable is the least delay!
Could I imp feathers to the wings of time,
Or with as little ease command the sun
To scourge his coursers up heaven's eastern hill,
Making the hour I tremble at, past recalling,   25
As I can move this dial's tongue to six,
My veins and arteries, emptied with fear,
Would fill and swell again. How do I look?
Do you yet see Death about me?

I. Trib.   Think not of him;
There is no danger; all these prodigies   30
That do affright you, rise from natural causes,
And though you do ascribe them to yourself,
Had you ne'er been, had happen'd.

Cæs.   'Tis well said,
Exceeding well, brave soldier. Can it be,
That I, that feel myself in health and strength,   35

15 close] concealed   23 little ease] *The sense demands*
little trouble *or* much ease. *Perhaps read* little care.

403

Should still believe I am so near my end,
And have my guards about me? Perish all
Predictions! I grow constant they are false,
And built upon uncertainties.
    1. *Trib.*   This is right;
Now Cæsar's heard like Cæsar.
    Cæs.   We will to   40
The camp, and having there confirm'd the soldier
With a large donative, and increase of pay,
Some shall——I say no more.
                   Enter Parthenius.
    Parth.   All happiness,
Security, long life, attend upon
The monarch of the world!
    Cæs.   Thy looks are cheerful.   45
    Parth. And my relation full of joy and wonder.
Why is the care of your imperial body,
My lord, neglected, the fear'd hour being past,
In which your life was threat'ned?
    Cæs.   Is't past five?
    Parth. Past six, upon my knowledge; and in justice 50
Your clock-master should die, that hath deferr'd
Your peace so long. There is a post new lighted,
That brings assur'd intelligence that your legions
In Syria have won a glorious day,
And much enlarg'd your empire. I have kept him   55
Conceal'd, that you might first partake the pleasure
In private, and the Senate from yourself
Be taught to understand how much they owe
To you and to your fortune.
    Cæs.   Hence, pale fear, then!
Lead me, Parthenius.
    1. *Trib.*   Shall we wait you?
    Cæs.   No.   60

38 constant] confident

After losses guards are useful. Know your distance.

[Exeunt Cæsar *and* Parthenius.

2. *Trib.* How strangely hopes delude men! as I live,
The hour is not yet come.

1. *Trib.*   Howe'er, we are
To pay our duties, and observe the sequel.

[Exeunt Tribunes.

Dom. I hear him coming. Be constant.

Enter Cæsar *and* Parthenius.

Cæs.   Where, Parthenius, 65
Is this glad messenger?

Steph.   Make the door fast.—Here;
A messenger of horror.

Cæs.   How! betray'd?

Dom. No; taken, tyranne.

Cæs.   My Domitia
In the conspiracy!

Parth.   Behold this book.

Cæs. Nay, then I am lost. Yet, though I am unarm'd, 70
I'll not fall poorly.   *[Overthrows* Stephanos.

Steph.   Help me.

Ent.   Thus, and thus!

Sej. Are you so long a-falling?

Cæs.   'Tis done basely.

[Falls and dies.

Parth. This for my father's death.

Dom.   This for my Paris.

Jul. This for thy incest.

Domitil.   This for thy abuse

[They severally stab him.

Of Domitilla.

Enter Tribunes.

1. *Trib.*   Force the doors! O Mars!   75
What have you done?

61 After . . . useful] *Sc. not after victory.*

Parth.   What Rome shall give us thanks for.
Steph. Dispatch'd a monster.
    1. *Trib.*   Yet he was our prince,
However wicked; and, in you, 'tis murder,
Which whosoe'er succeeds him will revenge;
Nor will we, that serv'd under his command,   80
Consent that such a monster as thyself,
(For in thy wickedness, Augusta's title
Hath quite forsook thee,) thou that wert the ground
Of all these mischiefs, shall go hence unpunish'd.
Lay hands on her and drag her to her sentence.—   85
We will refer the hearing to the Senate,
Who may at their best leisure censure you.
Take up his body. He in death hath paid
For all his cruelties. Here's the difference,
Good kings are mourn'd for after life; but ill,   90
And such as govern'd only by their will,
And not their reason, unlamented fall;
No good man's tear shed at their funeral.
                                        [*Exeunt omnes.*

                Flourish

            FINIS

87 censure] judge.

'Tis Pity She's a Whore

BY

JOHN FORD

JOHN FORD (1586–1639)

'Tis Pity She's a Whore

Acted first between 1626 and 1633; printed in the latter
year.

[*Dramatic Works*, ed. W. Gifford, 2 vols., 1827, revised
A. Dyce, 3 vols., 1869, revised A. H. Bullen, 3 vols.,
1895; *Dramatic Works*, ed. W. Bang and H. De Vocht,
Louvain, 1908, 1927 (reprinted), reproduces the original
editions in facsimile with a critical introduction by S. P.
Sherman (first published 1915). There are recent new
editions of *'Tis Pity She's a Whore*, ed. N. W. Bawcutt,
1964 (Regents Renaissance Drama Series), with a
chronology of Ford and his contemporaries, and ed.
Brian Morris, 1968 (New Mermaid).]

·TIS
Pitty Shee's a Whore

Acted by the *Queenes* Maiesties Seruants, *at The Phænix in Drury-Lane.*

LONDON,
Printed by *Nicholas* Okes for *Richard Collins*, and are to be sold at his shop in *Pauls* Church-yard, at the signe of the three Kings. 1633.

The Scene PARMA

DRAMATIS PERSONÆ

The Actors' Names.

BONAVENTURA,	*A Friar.*
A CARDINAL,	*Nuncio to the Pope.*
SORANZO,	*A Nobleman.*
FLORIO,	*A citizen of Parma.*
DONADO,	*Another citizen.*
GRIMALDI,	*A Roman Gentleman.*
GIOVANNI,	*Son to* FLORIO.
BERGETTO,	*Nephew to* DONADO.
RICHARDETTO,	*A suppos'd Physician.*
VASQUES,	*Servant to* SORANZO.
POGGIO,	*Servant to* BERGETTO.

Banditti, Officers, Attendants, Servants, &c.

Women.

ANNABELLA,	*Daughter to* FLORIO.
HIPPOLITA,	*Wife to* RICHARDETTO.
PHILOTIS,	*His niece.*
PUTANA,	*Tut'ress to* ANNABELLA.

To the Truly Noble

JOHN, EARL OF PETERBOROUGH, LORD MORDAUNT, BARON OF TURVEY

My Lord,

W HERE a truth of merit hath a general warrant, 5
there love is but a debt, acknowledgment a
justice. Greatness cannot often claim virtue by in-
heritance; yet, in this, yours appears most eminent,
for that you are not more rightly heir to your fortunes
than glory shall be to your memory. Sweetness of dis- 10
position ennobles a freedom of birth; in both, your
lawful interest adds honour to your own name, and
mercy to my presumption. Your noble allowance of
these first fruits of my leisure in the action emboldens
my confidence of your as noble construction in this 15
presentment; especially since my service must ever
owe particular duty to your favours by a particular
engagement. The gravity of the subject may easily
excuse the lightness of the title, otherwise I had been
a severe judge against mine own guilt. Princes have 20
vouchsaf'd grace to trifles off'red from a purity of devotion; your lordship may likewise please to admit into
your good opinion, with these weak endeavours, the
constancy of affection from the sincere lover of your
deserts in honour,   25

JOHN FORD.

dedication] John, Lord Mordaunt (*d.* 1642), 1st Earl of
Peterborough.   13 allowance] approval   14 in the
action] when acted   15–6 construction . . . presentment]
interpretation . . . presentation (*sc. in print*)

ACTUS I, SCÆNA I

Enter Friar *and* Giovanni.

Friar. Dispute no more in this, for know, young
    man,
These are no school-points; nice philosophy
May tolerate unlikely arguments,
But Heaven admits no jest; wits that presum'd
On wit too much, by striving how to prove   5
There was no God, with foolish grounds of art,
Discover'd first the nearest way to hell,
And fill'd the word with devilish atheism.
Such questions, youth, are fond; for better 'tis
To bless the sun, than reason why it shines;   10
Yet He thou talk'st of is above the sun.
No more! I may not hear it.
    Gio.   Gentle father,
To you I have unclasp'd my burthened soul,
Empti'd the storehouse of my thoughts and heart,
Made myself poor of secrets; have not left   15
Another word untold, which hath not spoke
All what I ever durst or think or know;
And yet is here the comfort I shall have?
Must I not do what all men else may,—love?
    Friar. Yes, you may love, fair son.
    Gio.   Must I not praise 20
That beauty which, if fram'd anew, the gods
Would make a god of, if they had it there,
And kneel to it, as I do kneel to them?
    Friar. Why, foolish madman!
    Gio.   Shall a peevish sound,
A customary form, from man to man,   25

    I. i] *The acts are marked and numbered in the quarto but the*
scenes are not.   9 fond] foolish

Of brother and of sister, be a bar
'Twixt my perpetual happiness and me?
Say that we had one father, say one womb
(Curse to my joys!) gave both us life and birth;
Are we not therefore each to other bound   30
So much the more by nature? by the links
Of blood, of reason? nay, if you will have't,
Even of religion, to be ever one,
One soul, one flesh, one love, one heart, one all?
   Friar. Have done, unhappy youth! for thou art lost. 35
   Gio. Shall, then, (for that I am her brother born)
My joys be ever banish'd from her bed?
No, father; in your eyes I see the change
Of pity and compassion; from your age,
As from a sacred oracle, distils   40
The life of counsel: tell me, holy man,
What cure shall give me ease in these extremes?
   Friar. Repentance, son, and sorrow for this sin:
For thou hast mov'd a Majesty above
With thy unranged (almost) blasphemy.   45
   Gio. Oh, do not speak of that, dear confessor!
   Friar. Art thou, my son, that miracle of wit
Who once, within these three months, wert esteem'd
A wonder of thine age throughout Bononia?
How did the University applaud   50
Thy government, behaviour, learning, speech,
Sweetness, and all that could make up a man!
I was proud of my tutelage, and chose
Rather to leave my books than part with thee;
I did so:—but the fruits of all my hopes   55
Are lost in thee, as thou art in thyself.
O, Giovanni! hast thou left the schools
Of knowledge to converse with lust and death?

   51 government] way of life   57 Giovanni] *Ford makes*
it four syllables.

For death waits on thy lust. Look through the world,
And thou shalt see a thousand faces shine   60
More glorious than this idol thou ador'st:
Leave her, and take thy choice, 'tis much less sin;
Though in such games as those they lose that win.

  Gio. It were more ease to stop the ocean
From floats and ebbs than to dissuade my vows.   65

  Friar. Then I have done, and in thy wilful flames
Already see thy ruin; Heaven is just.
Yet hear my counsel.

  Gio.   As a voice of life.

  Friar. Hie to thy father's house, there lock thee fast
Alone within thy chamber, then fall down   70
On both thy knees, and grovel on the ground:
Cry to thy heart, wash every word thou utter'st
In tears (and if't be possible) of blood:
Beg Heaven to cleanse the leprosy of lust
That rots thy soul, acknowledge what thou art,   75
A wretch, a worm, a nothing: weep, sigh, pray
Three times a-day, and three times every night:
For seven days' space do this; then if thou find'st
No change in thy desires, return to me:
I'll think on remedy. Pray for thyself   80
At home, whilst I pray for thee here.—Away!
My blessing with thee! we have need to pray.

  Gio. All this I'll do, to free me from the rod
Of vengeance, else I'll swear my fate's my god.

                                       [*Exeunt.*

ACTUS I, SCÆNA 2

Enter Grimaldi *and* Vasques, *ready to fight.*

  Vas. Come sir, stand to your tackling, if you prove
craven, I'll make you run quickly.

65 vows] wishes, prayers (*Latin vota*)   1 tackling] weapons

Grim. Thou art no equal match for me.

Vas. Indeed I never went to the wars to bring home
news, nor cannot play the mountebank for a meal's 5
meat, and swear I got my wounds in the field. See you
these gray hairs? they'll not flinch for a bloody nose.
Wilt thou to this gear?

Grim. Why, slave, think'st thou I'll balance my reputation with a cast-suit? Call thy master; he shall 10
know that I dare—

Vas. Scold like a cot-quean;—that's your profession.
Thou poor shadow of a soldier, I will make thee know
my master keeps servants thy betters in quality and
performance. Com'st thou to fight or prate?   15

Grim. Neither, with thee. I am a Roman and a
gentleman; one that have got mine honour with expense of blood.

Vas. You are a lying coward and a fool. Fight, or
by these hilts, I'll kill thee:—brave my lord!—you'll 20
fight?

Grim. Provoke me not, for if thou dost—

Vas.   Have at you!

[*They fight;* Grimaldi *hath the worst.*

Enter Florio, Donado, Soranzo.

Flo. What mean these sudden broils so near my
          doors?
Have you not other places but my house
To vent the spleen of your disordered bloods?   25
Must I be haunted still with such unrest
As not to eat or sleep in peace at home?
Is this your love, Grimaldi? Fie, 'tis naught.

Don. And, Vasques, I may tell thee 'tis not well

---

8 gear] business (*sc. fighting*)   10 cast-suit] dependent
(*dressed in his master's old clothes*   12 cot-quean] shrew,
hussy (*Sherman*)

To broach these quarrels; you are ever forward   30
In seconding contentions.

Enter above Annabella *and* Putana.

Flo.   What's the ground?
  Sor. That, with your patience signiors, I'll resolve:
This gentleman, whom fame reports a soldier,
(For else I know not,) rivals me in love
To Signior Florio's daughter; to whose ears   35
He still prefers his suit, to my disgrace;
Thinking the way to recommend himself
Is to disparage me in his report:—
But know, Grimaldi, though, may be, thou art
My equal in thy blood, yet this bewrays   40
A lowness in thy mind, which, wert thou noble,
Thou wouldst as much disdain as I do thee
For this unworthiness:—and on this ground
I will'd my servant to correct his tongue,
Holding a man so base, no match for me.   45
  Vas. And had not your sudden coming prevented us,
I had let my gentleman blood under the gills:—I should
have worm'd you, sir, for running mad.
  Grim. I'll be reveng'd, Soranzo.
  Vas. On a dish of warm broth to stay your stomach 50
—do, honest innocence, do! spoon-meat is a whole-
somer diet than a Spanish blade.
  Grim. Remember this!
  Sor.   I fear thee not, Grimaldi.
                    [*Exit* Grimaldi.
  Flo. My Lord Soranzo, this is strange to me,
Why you should storm, having my word engag'd: 55
Owing her heart, what need you doubt her ear?

  31 s.d. *above*] on the upper stage   48 worm'd . . . mad]
Reference to a surgical treatment of dogs to prevent madness.
56 owing] owning

Losers may talk by law of any game.

Vas. Yet the villainy of words, Signior Florio, may
be such as would make any unspleen'd dove choleric.
Blame not my lord in this.   60

Flo. Be you more silent:
I would not for my wealth, my daughter's love
Should cause the spilling of one drop of blood.
Vasques, put up, let's end this fray in wine. [*Exeunt.*

Put. How like you this, child? here's threat'ning,   65
challenging, quarrelling, and fighting on every side;
and all is for your sake: you had need look to yourself,
charge; you'll be stol'n away sleeping else shortly.

Ann. But, tut'ress, such a life gives no content
To me; my thoughts are fix'd on other ends.   70
Would you would leave me!

Put. Leave you! no marvel else; leave me no leaving,
charge; this is love outright. Indeed, I blame you not;
you have choice fit for the best lady in Italy.

Ann. Pray do not talk so much.   75

Put. Take the worst with the best, there's Grimaldi
the soldier, a very well-timb'red fellow. They say he is
a Roman, nephew to the Duke Montferrato; they say
he did good service in the wars against the Milanese;
but, 'faith, charge, I do not like him, an't be for nothing   80
but for being a soldier: not one amongst twenty of
your skirmishing captains but have some privy maim
or other that mars their standing upright. I like him
the worse, he crinkles so much in the hams: though he
might serve if there were no more men, yet he's not   85
the man I would choose.

Ann. Fie, how thou prat'st.

Put. As I am a very woman, I like Signior Soranzo
well; he is wise, and what is more, rich; and what is

59 unspleen'd] without spleen or anger   64 put up]
sheath your sword

more than that, kind; and what is more that all this, 90
a nobleman: such a one, were I the fair Annabella myself, I would wish and pray for. Then he is bountiful;
besides, he is handsome, and, by my troth, I think,
wholesome,—and that's news in a gallant of three-
and-twenty; liberal, that I know; loving, that you 95
know; and a man sure, else he could never ha' purchas'd such a good name with Hippolita, the lusty
widow, in her husband's lifetime: an 'twere but for
that report, sweetheart, would 'a were thine! Commend a man for his qualities, but take a husband as he 100
is a plain, sufficient, naked man: such a one is for your
bed, and such a one is Signior Soranzo, my life for't.

Ann. Sure the woman took her morning's draught
too soon.

Enter Bergetto *and* Poggio.

Put. But look, sweetheart, look what thing comes 105
now! Here's another of your ciphers to fill up the
number: Oh, brave old ape in a silken coat! Observe.

Ber. Didst thou think, Poggio, that I would spoil
my new clothes, and leave my dinner, to fight?

Pog. No, sir, I did not take you for so arrant a baby. 110

Ber. I am wiser than so: for I hope, Poggio, thou
never heardst of an elder brother that was a coxcomb;
didst, Poggio?

Pog. Never indeed sir, as long as they had either
land or money left them to inherit. 115

Ber. Is it possible, Poggio? Oh, monstrous! Why,
I'll undertake with a handful of silver to buy a headful
of wit at any time: but, sirrah, I have another purchase
in hand; I shall have the wench, mine uncle says. I will
but wash my face and shift socks, and then have at her, 120
i'faith!—Mark my pace, Poggio!

[*Exit.*

Pog. Sir!—I have seen an ass and a mule trot the Spanish pavin with a better grace, I know not how often.   [*Exit.*

Ann. This idiot haunts me too.   125

Put. Ay, ay, he needs no description. The rich magnifico that is below with your father, charge, Signior Donado his uncle, for that he means to make this his cousin a golden calf, thinks that you will be a right Israelite, and fall down to him presently: but I hope I   130
have tutor'd you better. They say a fool's bauble is a lady's playfellow; yet you having wealth enough, you need not cast upon the dearth of flesh, at any rate. Hang him, innocent!

Enter Giovanni.

Ann. But see, Putana, see! what blessed shape   135
Of some celestial creature now appears!
What man is he, that with such sad aspect
Walks careless of himself?
    Put.   Where?
    Ann.   Look below.
    Put. Oh, 'tis your brother, sweet.
    Ann.   Ha!
    Put.   'Tis your brother.
    Ann. Sure, 'tis not he; this is some woful thing   140
Wrapp'd up in grief, some shadow of a man.
Alas, he beats his breast and wipes his eyes,
Drown'd all in tears: methinks I hear him sigh.
Let's down, Putana, and partake the cause.
I know my brother, in the love he bears me,   145
Will not deny me partage in his sadness,
My soul is full of heaviness and fear.
                     [*Exeunt* Annabella, Putana.

123 pavin] *A stately dance*   129 cousin] kinsman (*in general; here nephew*)   134 innocent] simpleton   134 s.d. *Enter* Giovanni] *on the main stage*

Gio. Lost! I am lost! my fates have doom'd my
    death:
The more I strive, I love; the more I love,
The less I hope: I see my ruin, certain.   150
What judgment or endeavours could apply
To my incurable and restless wounds,
I throughly have examin'd, but in vain.
Oh that it were not in religion sin
To make our love a god, and worship it!   155
I have even wearied Heaven with prayers, dried up
The spring of my continual tears, even starv'd
My veins with daily fasts: what wit or art
Could counsel, I have practis'd; but alas
I find all these but dreams, and old men's tales,   160
To fright unsteady youth; I'm still the same:
Or I must speak, or burst. 'Tis not, I know,
My lust, but 'tis my fate that leads me on.
Keep fear and low faint-hearted shame with slaves!
I'll tell her that I love her, though my heart   165
Were rated at the price of that attempt.—
Oh me! she comes.

Enter Annabella *and* Putana.

Ann.   Brother!
Gio.   —If such a thing
As courage dwell in men, ye heavenly powers,
Now double all that virtue in my tongue!
Ann. Why, brother, will you not speak to me?   170
Gio. Yes; how d'ye, sister?
Ann. However I am, methinks you are not well.
Put. Bless us, why are you so sad, sir?

147–8] *Gifford marked a new scene here, but the action is con-*
tinuous; Giovanni is already visible on the main stage, and speaks
while the others are coming down from above.   164 Keep]
live

Gio. Let me entreat you, leave us a while, Putana.—
Sister, I would be private with you.   175
  Ann. Withdraw, Putana.
  Put. I will.—If this were any other company for her,
I should think my absence an office of some credit; but
I will leave them together.   [*Exit* Putana.
  Gio. Come, sister, lend your hand: let's walk to-
    gether!   180
I hope you need not blush to walk with me;
Here's none but you and I.
  Ann.   How's this?
  Gio.   Faith,
I mean no harm.
  Ann.   Harm?
  Gio.   No, good faith.
How is't with ye?
  Ann.   —I trust he be not frantic.—
I am very well, brother.   185
  Gio. Trust me, but I am sick; I fear so sick
'Twill cost my life.
  Ann. Mercy forbid it! 'tis not so, I hope.
  Gio. I think you love me, sister.
  Ann.   Yes, you know
I do.
  Gio. I know't, indeed.—Y'are very fair.   190
  Ann. Nay then I see you have a merry sickness.
  Gio. That's as it proves. The poets feign, I read,
That Juno for her forehead did exceed
All other goddesses; but I durst swear
Your forehead exceeds hers, as hers did theirs.   195
  Ann. 'Troth, this is pretty!
  Gio.   Such a pair of stars
As are thine eyes would, like Promethean fire,
If gently glanc'd, give life to senseless stones.

                184 frantic] mad

                        422

Ann. Fie upon ye!

Gio. The lily and the rose, most sweetly strange,   200
Upon your dimpled cheeks do strive for change.
Such lips would tempt a saint; such hands as those
Would make an anchorite lascivious.

Ann. D'ye mock me, or flatter me?

Gio. If you would see a beauty more exact   205
Than art can counterfeit, or nature frame,
Look in your glass, and there behold your own.

Ann. Oh, you are a trim youth!

Gio. Here!   [*Offers his dagger to her.*

Ann.   What to do?

Gio.   And here's my breast; strike home!
Rip up my bosom; there thou shalt behold   210
A heart in which is writ the truth I speak.
Why stand ye?

Ann.   Are you earnest?

Gio.   Yes, most earnest.
You cannot love?

Ann.   Whom?

Gio.   Me. My tortur'd soul
Hath felt affliction in the heat of death.
O Annabella, I am quite undone!   215
The love of thee, my sister, and the view
Of thy immortal beauty have untun'd
All harmony both of my rest and life.
Why d'ye not strike?

Ann.   Forbid it, my just fears!
If this be true, 'twere fitter I were dead.   220

Gio. True, Annabella! 'tis no time to jest.
I have too long suppress'd the hidden flames
That almost have consum'd me; I have spent
Many a silent night in sighs and groans,
Ran over all my thoughts, despis'd my fate,   225
Reason'd against the reasons of my love,

Done all that smooth'd-cheek virtue could advise;
But found all bootless: 'tis my destiny
That you must either love, or I must die.
   Ann. Comes this in sadness from you?
   Gio.   Let some mischief 230
Befall me soon, if I dissemble aught.
   Ann. You are my brother Giovanni.
   Gio.   You
My sister Annabella; I know this,
And could afford you instance why to love
So much the more for this; to which intent   235
Wise nature first in your creation meant
To make you mine; else't had been sin and foul
To share one beauty to a double soul.
Nearness in birth or blood doth but persuade
A nearer nearness in affection.   240
I have ask'd counsel of the holy church,
Who tells me I may love you, and 'tis just
That since I may, I should; and will, yes, will.
Must I now live or die?
   Ann.   Live; thou hast won
The field, and never fought: what thou hast urg'd   245
My captive heart had long ago resolv'd.
I blush to tell thee,—but I'll tell thee now,—
For every sigh that thou hast spent for me
I have sigh'd ten; for every tear shed twenty:
And not so much for that I lov'd, as that   250
I durst not say I lov'd, nor scarcely think it.
   Gio. Let not this music be a dream, ye gods,
For pity's sake, I beg ye!
   Ann.   On my knees, [*She kneels.*
Brother, even by our mother's dust, I charge you,

227 smooth'd-cheek] *Dyce changed to* smooth-cheek'd   230
sadness] seriousness   250 for that] for the reason that,
because

Do not betray me to your mirth or hate: 255
Love me or kill me, brother.
   Gio.   On my knees,   [*He kneels.*
Sister, even by my mother's dust, I charge you,
Do not betray me to your mirth or hate:
Love me or kill me, sister.
   Ann. You mean good sooth, then?
   Gio.   In good troth, I do; 260
And so do you, I hope: say, I'm in earnest.
   Ann. I'll swear 't, I.
   Gio.   And I; and by this kiss,—
                              [*Kisses her.*
Once more, yet once more:—now let's rise by this,
I would not change this minute for Elysium.
What must we now do?
   Ann.   What you will.
   Gio.   Come, then; 265
After so many tears as we have wept,
Let's learn to court in smiles, to kiss, and sleep.
                               [*Exeunt.*

ACTUS I, SCÆNA 3

Enter Florio *and* Donado.

   Flo. Signior Donado, you have said enough,
I understand you, but would have you know
I will not force my daughter 'gainst her will.
You see I have but two, a son and her;
And he is so devoted to his book,   5
As I must tell you true, I doubt his health:
Should he miscarry, all my hopes rely
Upon my girl. As for worldly fortune,
I am, I thank my stars, bless'd with enough.
My care is, how to match her to her liking: 10

I would not have her marry wealth, but love,
And if she like your nephew, let him have her.
Here's all that I can say.

    Don.   Sir, you say well,
Like a true father, and for my part I,
If the young folks can like,—'twixt you and me,—   15
Will promise to assure my nephew presently
Three thousand florins yearly during life,
And after I am dead my whole estate.

    Flo. 'Tis a fair proffer, sir; meantime your nephew
Shall have free passage to commence his suit: 20
If he can thrive, he shall have my consent.
So for this time I'll leave you, signior.   [*Exit.*

    Don.   Well,
Here's hope yet, if my nephew would have wit;
But he is such another dunce, I fear
He'll never win the wench. When I was young,   25
I could have done't, i'faith; and so shall he,
If he will learn of me; and, in good time,
He comes himself.

Enter Bergetto *and* Poggio.

How now, Bergetto, whither away so fast?

    Ber. Oh, uncle, I have heard the strangest news 30
that ever came out of the mint!—Have I not, Poggio?

    Pog. Yes, indeed, sir.

    Don. What news, Bergetto?

    Ber. Why, look ye, uncle! my barber told me just
now that there is a fellow come to town who under- 35
takes to make a mill go without the mortal help of any
water or wind, only with sand-bags: and this fellow
hath a strange horse, a most excellent beast, I'll assure
you uncle, my barber says, whose head, to the wonder
of all Christian people, stands just behind where his 40
tail is.—Is't not true, Poggio?

Pog. So the barber swore, forsooth.

Don. And you are running thither?

Ber. Ay, forsooth, uncle.

Don. Wilt thou be a fool still? Come, sir, you shall 45
not go, you have more mind of a puppet-play than on
the business I told ye. Why, thou great baby, wilt
never have wit? wilt make thyself a May-game to all
the world?

Pog. Answer for yourself, master.   50

Ber. Why, uncle, should I sit at home still, and not
go abroad to see fashions like other gallants?

Don. To see hobby-horses! What wise talk, I pray,
had you with Annabella, when you were at Signior
Florio's house?   55

Ber. Oh, the wench,—Ud's sa'me, uncle, I tickled
her with a rare speech, that I made her almost burst
her belly with laughing.

Don. Nay, I think so; and what speech was't?

Ber. What did I say, Poggio?   60

Pog. Forsooth, my master said, that he loved her
almost as well as he loved Parmasent, and swore—I'll
be sworn for him—that she wanted but such a nose as
his was, to be as pretty a young woman as any was in
Parma.   65

Don. Oh, gross!

Ber. Nay, uncle:—then she ask'd me whether my
father had any more children than myself; and I said
'No; 'twere better he should have had his brains
knock'd out first.'   70

Don. This is intolerable.

Ber. Then said she, 'Will Signior Donado, your
uncle, leave you all his wealth?'

Don. Ha! that was good; did she harp upon that
string?   75

51 still] always   62 Parmasent] Parmesan (*cheese*)

427

Ber. Did she harp upon that string! ay, that she did. I answered, 'Leave me all his wealth! why, woman, he hath no other wit; if he had, he should hear on't to his everlasting glory and confusion: I know,' quoth I, 'I am his white boy, and will not be gull'd:' and with that she fell into a great smile, and went away. Nay, I did fit her.   80

Don. Ah, sirrah, then I see there is no changing of nature. Well, Bergetto, I fear thou wilt be a very ass still.   85

Ber. I should be sorry for that, uncle.

Don. Come, come you home with me: since you are no better a speaker, I'll have you write to her after some courtly manner, and enclose some rich jewel in the letter.   90

Ber. Ay, marry, that will be excellent.

Don. Peace, innocent!
Once in my time I'll set my wits to school:
If all fail, 'tis but the fortune of a fool.

Ber. Poggio, 'twill do, Poggio.   [*Exeunt.* 95

ACTUS II, SCÆNA I

Enter Giovanni *and* Annabella, *as from their Chamber.*

Gio. Come, Annabella,—no more sister now,
But love, a name more gracious,—do not blush,
Beauty's sweet wonder, but be proud to know
That yielding thou hast conquer'd, and inflam'd
A heart whose tribute is thy brother's life.   5

Ann. And mine is his. Oh, how these stol'n contents
Would print a modest crimson on my cheeks,
Had any but my heart's delight prevail'd!

80 white boy] favourite, 'white-haired boy'   92 innocent]
simpleton

428

Gio. I marvel why the chaster of your sex
Should think this pretty toy call'd maidenhead   10
So strange a loss, when, being lost, 'tis nothing,
And you are still the same.
Ann.   'Tis well for you;
Now you can talk.
Gio.   Music as well consists
In th' ear as in the playing.
Ann.   Oh, you're wanton!
Tell on't, you're best, do!
Gio.   Thou wilt chide me, then. 15
Kiss me:—so! Thus hung Jove on Leda's neck,
And suck'd divine ambrosia from her lips.
I envy not the mightiest man alive,
But hold myself in being king of thee,
More great than were I king of all the world.   20
But I shall lose you sweetheart.
Ann.   But you shall not.
Gio. You must be married, mistress.
Ann.   Yes, to whom?
Gio. Some one must have you.
Ann.   You must.
Gio.   Nay, some other.
Ann. Now, prithee do not speak so: without jesting
You'll make me weep in earnest.
Gio.   What, you will not! 25
But tell me, sweet, canst thou be dar'd to swear
That thou wilt live to me, and to no other?
Ann. By both our loves I dare; for didst thou know,
My Giovanni, how all suitors seem
To my eyes hateful, thou wouldst trust me then.   30
Gio. Enough, I take thy word; sweet, we must part:
Remember what thou vow'st; keep well my heart.
Ann. Will you be gone?
Gio.   I must.

Ann.   When to return?

Gio. Soon.

Ann.   Look you do.

Gio.   Farewell.   [*Exit.*

Ann. Go where thou wilt, in mind I’ll keep thee
  here,   35
And where thou art, I know I shall be there.
Guardian!

Enter Putana.

Put. Child, how is’t, child? well, thank Heaven, ha!

Ann. O guardian, what a paradise of joy
Have I pass’d over!   40

Put. Nay, what a paradise of joy have you pass’d
under! Why, now I commend thee, charge. Fear
nothing, sweetheart: what though he be your brother?
your brother’s a man, I hope, and I say still, if a young
wench feel the fit upon her, let her take anybody, 45
father or brother, all is one.

Ann. I would not have it known for all the world.

Put. Nor I, indeed; for the speech of the people; else
’twere nothing.

Flo. [*Within.*] Daughter Annabella!   50

Ann. Oh me, my father!—Here, sir!—Reach my
work.

Flo. [*Within.*] What are you doing?

Ann.   So: let him come now.

Enter Florio, Richardetto *like a Doctor of Physic,*
and Philotis *with a lute in her hand.*

Flo. So hard at work, that’s well! you lose no time.
Look, I have brought you company; here’s one,
A learned doctor lately come from Padua,   55
Much skill’d in physic; and, for that I see
You have of late been sickly, I entreated
This reverend man to visit you some time.

Ann. You're very welcome, sir.

Rich.   I thank you, mistress.
Loud fame in large report hath spoke your praise,   60
As well for virtue as perfection:
For which I have been bold to bring with me
A kinswoman of mine, a maid, for song
And music, one perhaps will give content:
Please you to know her.

Ann.   They are parts I love.   65
And she for them most welcome.

Phi.   Thank you, lady.

Flo. Sir, now you know my house, pray make not
    strange;
And if you find my daughter need your art,
I'll be your pay-master.

Rich.   Sir, what I am
She shall command.

Flo.   You shall bind me to you.— 70
Daughter, I must have conference with you
About some matters that concerns us both.—
Good Master Doctor, please you but walk in,
We'll crave a little of your cousin's cunning:
I think my girl hath not quite forgot   75
To touch an instrument; she could have done't:
We'll hear them both.

Rich.   I'll wait upon you, sir.   [*Exeunt.*

Actus II, Scæna 2

Enter Soranzo *in his study, reading a book.*

Sor. Love's measure is extreme, the comfort pain;
    The life unrest, and the reward disdain.
What's here? look't o'er again.—'Tis so; so writes

74 cunning] skill

This smooth, licentious poet in his rhymes.
But, Sannazar, thou liest; for, had thy bosom   5
Felt such oppression as is laid on mine,
Thou wouldst have kiss'd the rod that made thee
     smart.
To work, then, happy Muse, and contradict
What Sannazar hath in his envy writ.
     Love's measure is the mean, sweet his annoys,   10
     His pleasures life, and his reward all joys.
Had Annabella liv'd when Sannazar
Did, in his brief *Encomium*, celebrate
Venice, that queen of cities, he had left
That verse which gain'd him such a sum of gold,   15
And for one only look from Annabel
Had writ of her, and her diviner cheeks.
Oh, how my thoughts are—
     Vas. [*Within.*] Pray, forbear, in rules of civility, let
me give notice on't: I shall be tax'd of my neglect of 20
duty and service.
     Sor. What rude intrusion interrupts my peace?
Can I be no where private?
     Vas. [*Within.*] Troth, you wrong your modesty.
     Sor. What's the matter, Vasques? who is't?

Enter Hippolita *and* Vasques.

     Hip.   'Tis I;   25
Do you know me now? Look, perjur'd man, on her
Whom thou and thy distracted lust have wrong'd.
Thy sensual rage of blood hath made my youth
A scorn to men and angels; and shall I
Be now a foil to thy unsated change?   30
Thou know'st, false wanton, when my modest fame
Stood free from stain or scandal, all the charms

     5 Sannazar] Jacopo Sannazaro (1450–1530), *a Neapolitan poet
of European fame*   20 tax'd] blamed for

Of hell or sorcery could not prevail
Against the honour of my chaster bosom.
Thine eyes did plead in tears, thy tongue in oaths,   35
Such and so many, that a heart of steel
Would have been wrought to pity, as was mine:
And shall the conquest of my lawful bed,
My husband's death, urg'd on by his disgrace,
My loss of womanhood, be ill-rewarded   40
With hatred and contempt? No; know, Soranzo,
I have a spirit doth as much distaste
The slavery of fearing thee, as thou
Dost loathe the memory of what hath pass'd.
   Sor. Nay, dear Hippolita,—
   Hip.   Call me not dear,   45
Nor think with supple words to smooth the grossness
Of my abuses: 'tis not your new mistress,
Your goodly madam-merchant, shall triumph
On my dejection; tell her thus from me,
My birth was nobler, and by much more free.   50
   Sor. You are too violent.
   Hip.   You are too double
In your dissimulation. Seest thou this,
This habit, these black mourning weeds of care?
'Tis thou art cause of this; and hast divorc'd
My husband from his life, and me from him,   55
And made me widow in my widowhood.
   Sor. Will you yet hear?
   Hip.   More of thy perjuries?
Thy soul is drown'd too deeply in those sins;
Thou need'st not add to th' number.
   Sor.   Then I'll leave you;
You are past all rules of sense.
   Hip.   And thou of grace.   60
   Vas. Fie, mistress, you are not near the limits of

42 distaste] dislike   48 triumph] *pronounced* triúmph

433

reason; if my lord had a resolution as noble as virtue
itself, you take the course to unedge it all.—Sir, I beseech you do not perplex her; griefs, alas, will have a
vent; I dare undertake Madam Hippolita will now 65
freely hear you.

Sor. Talk to a woman frantic!—Are these the fruits
of your love?

Hip. They are the fruits of thy untruth, false man!
Didst thou not swear, whilst yet my husband liv'd,   70
That thou wouldst wish no happiness on earth
More than to call me wife? didst thou not vow,
When he should die, to marry me? for which
The devil in my blood, and thy protests,
Caus'd me to counsel him to undertake   75
A voyage to Leghorn, for that we heard
His brother there was dead, and left a daughter
Young and unfriended, who, with much ado,
I wish'd him to bring hither; he did so,
And went; and, as thou know'st, died on the way.   80
Unhappy man, to buy his death so dear,
With my advice! yet thou, for whom I did it,
Forgett'st thy vows, and leav'st me to my shame.

Sor. Who could help this?

Hip.   Who? perjur'd man, thou couldst,
If thou hadst faith or love.

Sor.   You are deceiv'd;   85
The vows I made, (if you remember well,)
Were wicked and unlawful; 'twere more sin
To keep them than to break them; as for me,
I cannot mask my penitence. Think thou
How much thou hast digress'd from honest shame   90
In bringing of a gentleman to death
Who was thy husband; such a one as he,
So noble in his quality, condition,

67 frantic] mad

Learning, behaviour, entertainment, love,
As Parma could not show a braver man.   95
   Vas. You do not well; this was not your promise.
   Sor. I care not; let her know her monstrous life.
Ere I'll be servile to so black a sin,
I'll be a corse.—Woman, come here no more;
Learn to repent, and die; for, by my honour,   100
I hate thee and thy lust: you have been too foul.
                              [*Exit.*

   Vas. —This part has been scurvily play'd.
   Hip. How foolishly this beast contemns his fate,
And shuns the use of that which I more scorn
Than I once lov'd, his love! But let him go;   105
My vengeance shall give comfort to his woe.
                   [*She offers to go away.*
   Vas. Mistress, mistress, Madam Hippolita! pray, a
word or two.
   Hip. With me, sir?
   Vas. With you, if you please.   110
   Hip. What is't?
   Vas. I know you are infinitely mov'd now, and you
think you have cause; some I confess you have, but
sure not so much as you imagine.
   Hip. Indeed!   115
   Vas. Oh, you were miserably bitter, which you fol-
lowed even to the last syllable; 'faith, you were some-
what too shrewd: by my life, you could not have took
my lord in a worse time since I first knew him; to-
morrow you shall find him a new man.   120
   Hip. Well, I shall wait his leisure.
   Vas. Fie, this is not a hearty patience; it comes
sourly from you; 'troth, let me persuade you for once.

   99 corse] corpse (*The quarto spells* coarse *and modern editors
read* curse *without explaining it.*)   118 shrewd] shrewish,
scolding

Hip. —I have it, and it shall be so; thanks, opportunity!—Persuade me! to what? 125

Vas. Visit him in some milder temper. Oh, if you could but master a little your female spleen, how might you win him!

Hip. He will never love me. Vasques, thou hast been a too trusty servant to such a master, and I believe thy 130 reward in the end will fall out like mine.

Vas. So perhaps too.

Hip. Resolve thyself it will. Had I one so true, so truly honest, so secret to my counsels, as thou hast been to him and his, I should think it a slight acquit- 135 tance, not only to make him master of all I have, but even of myself.

Vas. Oh, you are a noble gentlewoman!

Hip. Wilt thou feed always upon hopes? well, I know thou art wise, and seest the reward of an old servant 140 daily, what it is.

Vas. Beggary and neglect.

Hip. True, but Vasques, wert thou mine, and wouldst be private to me and my designs, I here pro- test, myself and all what I can else call mine should be 145 at thy dispose.

Vas. —Work you that way, old mole? then I have the wind of you.—I were not worthy of it by any desert that could lie within my compass: if I could—

Hip. What then? 150

Vas. I should then hope to live in these my old years with rest and security.

Hip. Give me thy hand! now promise but thy silence,
And help to bring to pass a plot I have,
And here, in sight of heaven, (that being done,) 155
I make thee lord of me and mine estate.

133 Resolve] assure

Vas. Come, you are merry; this is such a happiness
that I can neither think or believe.

Hip. Promise thy secrecy, and 'tis confirm'd.

Vas. Then here I call our good genii for witnesses, 160
whatsoever your designs are, or against whomsoever,
I will not only be a special actor therein, but never disclose it till it be effected.

Hip. I take thy word, and, with that, thee for mine;
Come, then, let's more confer of this anon.—   165
On this delicious bane my thoughts shall banquet:
Revenge shall sweeten what my griefs have tasted.

                                        [*Exeunt.*

ACTUS II, SCÆNA 3

Enter Richardetto *and* Philotis.

Rich. Thou seest, my lovely niece, these strange
    mishaps,
How all my fortunes turn to my disgrace,
Wherein I am but as a looker-on,
Whiles others act my shame, and I am silent.

  Phi. But, uncle, wherein can this borrowed shape   5
Give you content?

  Rich.   I'll tell thee, gentle niece:
Thy wanton aunt in her lascivious riots
Lives now secure, thinks I am surely dead
In my late journey to Leghorn for you,
(As I have caused it to be rumour'd out.)   10
Now would I see with what an impudence
She gives scope to her loose adultery,
And how the common voice allows hereof:
Thus far I have prevail'd.

     5 borrowed shape] disguise

                    437

Phi.   Alas, I fear
You mean some strange revenge.
Rich.   Oh, be not troubled; 15
Your ignorance shall plead for you in all;
But to our business.—What! you learn'd for certain
How Signior Florio means to give his daughter
In marriage to Soranzo?
Phi.   Yes, for certain.
Rich. But how find you young Annabella's love   20
Inclin'd to him?
Phi.   For aught I could perceive,
She neither fancies him or any else.
Rich. There's mystery in that, which time must
    show.
She us'd you kindly?
Phi.   Yes.
Rich.   And crav'd your company?
Phi. Often.
Rich.   'Tis well; it goes as I could wish.   25
I am the doctor now; and as for you,
None knows you: if all fail not, we shall thrive.—
But who comes here?
                    Enter Grimaldi.
                    I know him; 'tis Grimaldi.
A Roman and a soldier, near allied
Unto the Duke of Montferrato, one   30
Attending on the nuncio of the pope
That now resides in Parma; by which means
He hopes to get the love of Annabella.
Grim. Save you, sir.
Rich.   And you, sir.
Grim.   I have heard
Of your approv'd skill, which through the city   35
Is freely talk'd of, and would crave your aid.
Rich. For what, sir?

438

Grim. Marry, sir, for this—
But I would speak in private.

Rich.   Leave us, cousin.   [*Exit* Philotis.

Grim. I love fair Annabella, and would know   40
Whether in art there may not be receipts
To move affection.

Rich.   Sir, perhaps there may;
But these will nothing profit you.

Grim.   Not me?

Rich. Unless I be mistook, you are a man
Greatly in favour with the cardinal.   45

Grim. What of that?

Rich.   In duty to his grace,
I will be bold to tell you, if you seek
To marry Florio's daughter, you must first
Remove a bar 'twixt you and her.

Grim.   Who's that?

Rich. Soranzo is the man that hath her heart;   50
And while he lives, be sure you cannot speed.

Grim. Soranzo! what, mine enemy? is't he?

Rich. Is he your enemy?

Grim.   The man I hate
Worse than confusion; I'll kill him straight.

Rich. Nay, then, take mine advice,   55
Even for his grace's sake the cardinal:
I'll find a time when he and she do meet,
Of which I'll give you notice; and to be sure
He shall not 'scape you, I'll provide a poison
To dip your rapier's point in: if he had   60
As many heads as Hydra had, he dies.

Grim. But shall I trust thee, doctor?

Rich.   As yourself;
Doubt not in aught.—Thus shall the fates decree
By me Soranzo falls, that ruin'd me.   [*Exeunt.*

ACTUS II, SCÆNA 4

Enter Donado, Bergetto, *and* Poggio.

Don. Well, sir, I must be content to be both your secretary and your messenger myself. I cannot tell what this letter may work; but, as sure as I am alive, if thou come once to talk with her, I fear thou wilt mar whatsoever I make. 5

Ber. You make, uncle! why am not I big enough to carry mine own letter I pray?

Don. Ay, ay, carry a fool's head o' thy own! why, thou dunce, wouldst thou write a letter, and carry it thyself? 10

Ber. Yes, that I would, and read it to her with my own mouth; for you must think, if she will not believe me myself when she hears me speak, she will not believe another's handwriting. Oh, you think I am a blockhead, uncle. No, sir, Poggio knows I have indited 15 a letter myself, so I have.

Pog. Yes truly sir, I have it in my pocket.

Don. A sweet one, no doubt; pray let's see't.

Ber. I cannot read my own hand very well, Poggio; read it, Poggio. 20

Don. Begin.

Poggio *reads.*

Pog. Most dainty and honey-sweet mistress, I could call you fair, and lie as fast as any that loves you, but my uncle being the elder man, I leave it to him, as more fit for his age, and the colour of his beard; I am wise enough to tell you I can 25 *bourd where I see occasion, or if you like my uncle's wit better than mine you shall marry me; if you like mine better than*

26 bourd] jest

440

*bis, I will marry you, in spite of your teeth. So, commending
my best parts to you, I rest*

Yours upwards and downwards, or you may choose, 30
                                                    Bergetto.

Ber. Ah, ha! here's stuff, uncle!

Don. Here's stuff indeed to shame us all. Pray,
whose advice did you take in this learned letter?

Pog. None, upon my word, but mine own.   35

Ber. And mine, uncle, believe it, nobody's else;
'twas mine own brain, I thank a good wit for't.

Don. Get you home, sir, and look you keep within
doors till I return.

Ber. How! that were a jest indeed! I scorn it, i'faith. 40

Don. What! you do not?

Ber. Judge me, but I do now.

Pog. Indeed, sir, 'tis very unhealthy.

Don. Well, sir, if I hear any of your apish running to
motions and fopperies, till I come back, you were as 45
good no; look to't.   [*Exit* Donado.

Ber. Poggio, shall's steal to see this horse with the
head in's tail?

Pog. Ay, but you must take heed of whipping.

Ber. Dost take me for a child, Poggio? Come, honest 50
Poggio.   [*Exeunt.*

ACTUS II, SCÆNA 5

Enter Friar *and* Giovanni.

Friar. Peace! thou hast told a tale whose every word
Threatens eternal slaughter to the soul;
I'm sorry I have heard it; would mine ears
Had been one minute deaf, before the hour
That thou cam'st to me! O young man, castaway, 5
By the religious number of mine order,

45 motions] puppet-shows   6 religious number] *Meaning
uncertain*

I day and night have wak'd my aged eyes
Above my strength, to weep on thy behalf;
But Heaven is angry, and be thou resolv'd
Thou art a man remark'd to taste a mischief.   10
Look for't; though it come late, it will come sure,
  Gio. Father, in this you are uncharitable;
What I have done I'll prove both fit and good.
It is a principle (which you have taught,
When I was yet your scholar,) that the frame   15
And composition of the mind doth follow
The frame and composition of the body:
So, where the body's furniture is beauty,
The mind's must needs be virtue; which allowed,
Virtue itself is reason but refin'd,   20
And love the quintessence of that; this proves
My sister's beauty, being rarely fair,
Is rarely virtuous; chiefly in her love,
And chiefly in that love, her love to me.
If hers to me, then so is mine to her;   25
Since in like causes are effects alike.
  Friar. O ignorance in knowledge! Long ago,
How often have I warn'd thee this before!
Indeed, if we were sure there were no Deity,
Nor Heaven nor Hell, then to be led alone   30
By Nature's light (as were philosophers
Of elder times) might instance some defence.
But 'tis not so; then, madman, thou wilt find
That Nature is in Heaven's positions blind.
  Gio. Your age o'errules you; had you youth like
    mine,   35
You'd make her love your heaven, and her divine.
  Friar. Nay, then I see thou'rt too far sold to hell,
It lies not in the compass of my prayers
To call thee back; yet let me counsel thee:

9 resolv'd] assured   34 positions] theorems

Persuade thy sister to some marriage.   40

  Gio. Marriage! why, that's to damn her; that's to prove
Her greedy variety of lust.

  Friar. Oh, fearful! if thou wilt not, give me leave
To shrive her, lest she should die unabsolv'd.

  Gio. At your best leisure, father; then she'll tell you   45
How dearly she doth prize my matchless love;
Then you will know what pity 'twere we two
Should have been sund'red from each other's arms.
View well her face, and in that little round
You may observe a world of variety;   50
For colour, lips; for sweet perfumes, her breath;
For jewels, eyes; for threads of purest gold,
Hair; for delicious choice of flowers, cheeks;
Wonder in every portion of that throne.
Hear her but speak, and you will swear the spheres   55
Make music to the citizens in Heaven.
But, father, what is else for pleasure fram'd
Lest I offend your ears, shall go unnam'd.

  Friar. The more I hear, I pity thee the more,
That one so excellent should give those parts   60
All to a second death. What I can do
Is but to pray; and yet I could advise thee,
Wouldst thou be rul'd.

  Gio.   In what?

  Friar.   Why leave her yet;
The throne of mercy is above your trespass;
Yet time is left you both—

  Gio.   To embrace each other,   65
Else let all time be struck quite out of number;
She is like me, and I like her, resolv'd.

  Friar. No more! I'll visit her.—This grieves me most,
Things being thus, a pair of souls are lost.   [*Exeunt*.

ACTUS II, SCÆNA 6

Enter Florio, Donado, Annabella, Putana.

Flo. Where's Giovanni?

Ann.   Newly walk'd abroad,
And, as I heard him say, gone to the friar,
His reverend tutor.

Flo.   That's a blessed man,
A man made up of holiness; I hope
He'll teach him how to gain another world.   5

Don. Fair gentlewoman, here's a letter sent
To you from my young cousin; I dare swear
He loves you in his soul: would you could hear
Sometimes what I see daily, sighs and tears,
As if his breast were prison to his heart!   10

Flo. Receive it, Annabella.

Ann. Alas, good man!

Don. What's that she said?

Put. An't please you, sir, she said, 'Alas, good man!'
Truly I do commend him to her every night before her   15
first sleep, because I would have her dream of him; and
she hearkens to that most religiously.

Don. Say'st so? God-a'-mercy, Putana! there's something for thee, and prithee do what thou canst on his
behalf; sha' not be lost labour, take my word for't.   20

Put. Thank you most heartily, sir: now I have a
feeling of your mind, let me alone to work.

Ann. Guardian!

Put. Did you call?

Ann. Keep this letter.   25

Don. Signior Florio, in any case bid her read it instantly.

Flo. Keep it for what? pray, read it me here right.

Ann. I shall, sir.   *[She reads.*

Don. How d'ye find her inclin'd, signior?

Flo. Troth, sir, I know not how; not all so well   30
As I could wish.

Ann. Sir, I am bound to rest your cousin's debtor.
The jewel I'll return; for if he love,
I'll count that love a jewel.

Don.   Mark you that?
Nay, keep them both, sweet maid.

Ann.   You must excuse me, 35
Indeed I will not keep it.

Flo.   Where's the ring,
That which your mother, in her will, bequeath'd,
And charg'd you on her blessing not to give 't
To any but your husband? send back that.

Ann. I have it not.

Flo.   Ha! have it not! where is't?   40

Ann. My brother in the morning took it from me,
Said he would wear't to-day.

Flo.   Well, what do you say
To young Bergetto's love? are you content
To match with him? speak.

Don.   There 's the point indeed.

Ann. —What shall I do? I must say something now. 45

Flo. What say? why d'ye not speak?

Ann.   Sir, with your leave—
Please you to give me freedom?

Flo.   Yes, you have.

Ann. Signior Donado, if your nephew mean
To raise his better fortunes in his match,
The hope of me will hinder such a hope;   50
Sir, if you love him, as I know you do,
Find one more worthy of his choice than me:
In short, I'm sure I sha' not be his wife.

Don. Why, here's plain dealing; I commend thee
    for't;

And all the worst I wish thee is, Heaven bless thee!   55
Your father yet and I will still be friends,
Shall we not, Signior Florio?

Flo.   Yes; why not?
Look, here your cousin comes.

Enter Bergetto *and* Poggio.

Don. —Oh, coxcomb, what doth he make here?

Ber. Where's my uncle, sirs?   60

Don. What's the news now?

Ber. Save you, uncle, save you!—You must not
think I come for nothing, masters, and how, and how
is't? what, you have read my letter? ah, there I—tickled
you, i'faith.   65

Pog. —But 'twere better you had tickled her in another place.

Ber. Sirrah sweetheart, I'll tell thee a good jest, and
riddle what 'tis.

Ann. You say you'd tell me.   70

Ber. As I was walking just now in the street, I met
a swaggering fellow would needs take the wall of me,
and because he did thrust me, I very valiantly call'd
him rogue. He hereupon bade me draw; I told him I
had more wit than so; but when he saw that I would   75
not, he did so maul me with the hilts of his rapier, that
my head sung whilst my feet caper'd in the kennel.

Don. —Was ever the like ass seen!

Ann. And what did you all this while?

Ber. Laugh at him for a gull, till I saw the blood run   80
about mine ears, and then I could not choose but find
in my heart to cry; till a fellow with a broad beard—
they say he is a new-come doctor—call'd me into his
house, and gave me a plaster, look you, here 'tis:—and,
sir, there was a young wench wash'd my face and hands   85

72 take the wall of] jostle off the pavement   77 kennel] gutter

446

most excellently, i' faith I shall love her as long as I
live for't.—Did she not, Poggio?

Pog. Yes, and kiss'd him too.

Ber. Why, la, now, you think I tell a lie, uncle, I
warrant.   90

Don. Would he that beat thy blood out of thy head
had beaten some wit into it! for I fear thou never wilt
have any.

Ber. Oh, uncle, but there was a wench would have
done a man's heart good to have look'd on her.—By 95
this light, she had a face methinks worth twenty of
you, Mistress Annabella.

Don. —Was ever such a fool born!

Ann. I am glad she lik'd you sir.

Ber. Are you so? by my troth, I thank you, forsooth. 100

Flo. Sure, 'twas the doctor's niece, that was last day
with us here.

Ber. 'Twas she, 'twas she.

Don. How do you know that, simplicity?

Ber. Why, does not he say so? if I should have said 105
no, I should have given him the lie, uncle, and so have
deserv'd a dry beating again; I'll none of that.

Flo. A very modest well-behav'd young maid as I
have seen.

Don. Is she indeed?   110

Flo. Indeed she is, if I have any judgment.

Don. Well, sir, now you are free: you need not care
for sending letters now; you are dismiss'd, your mistress here will none of you.

Ber. No! why, what care I for that? I can have 115
wenches enough in Parma for half-a-crown a-piece,
cannot I, Poggio?

Pog. I'll warrant you, sir.

Don. Signior Florio,

99 lik'd] pleased

447

I thank you for your free recourse you gave   120
For my admittance: and to you, fair maid,
That jewel I will give you 'gainst your marriage.—
Come, will you go, sir?
   Ber. Ay, marry, will I.—Mistress, farewell, mistress;
I'll come again to-morrow; farewell, mistress.   125
             [*Exeunt* Donado, Bergetto, *and* Poggio.

Enter Giovanni.

   Flo. Son, where have you been? what, alone, alone
     still?
I would not have it so; you must forsake
This over-bookish humour. Well, your sister
Hath shook the fool off.
   Gio.   'Twas no match for her.
   Flo. 'Twas not indeed; I meant it nothing less;   130
Soranzo is the man I only like:—
Look on him, Annabella.—Come, 'tis supper-time,
And it grows late.   [*Exit* Florio.
   Gio. Whose jewel's that?
   Ann. Some sweetheart's.
   Gio.   So I think.
   Ann.   A lusty youth,   135
Signior Donado, gave it me to wear
Against my marriage.
   Gio.   But you shall not wear it:
Send it him back again.
   Ann.   What, you are jealous?
   Gio. That you shall know anon, at better leisure.
Welcome sweet night! the evening crowns the day.   140
                         [*Exeunt.*

ACTUS III, SCÆNA I

Enter Bergetto *and* Poggio.

Ber. Does my uncle think to make me a baby still?
No, Poggio; he shall know I have a sconce now.

Pog. Ay, let him not bob you off like an ape with an
apple.

Ber. 'Sfoot, I will have the wench, if he were ten 5
uncles, in despite of his nose, Poggio.

Pog. Hold him to the grindstone, and give not a jot
of ground: she hath in a manner promised you already.

Ber. True, Poggio, and her uncle the doctor swore
I should marry her.   10

Pog. He swore, I remember.

Ber. And I will have her, that's more: didst see the
codpiece-point she gave me and the box of marmalade?

Pog. Very well; and kiss'd you, that my chops
wat'red at the sight on't. There's no way but to clap 15
up a marriage in hugger-mugger.

Ber. I will do't; for I tell thee, Poggio, I begin to
grow valiant methinks, and my courage begins to rise.

Pog. Should you be afraid of your uncle?

Ber. Hang him, old doting rascal! no, I say I will 20
have her.

Pog. Lose no time, then.

Ber. I will beget a race of wise men and constables,
that shall cart whores at their own charges, and break
the duke's peace ere I have done myself.—Come away. 25

                                                      [Exeunt.

2 sconce] head   3 bob] fob   24 cart whores] *Public
exhibition as punishment.*

ACTUS III, SCÆNA 2

Enter Florio, Giovanni, Soranzo, Annabella,
Putana, *and* Vasques.

Flo. My Lord Soranza, though I must confess
The proffers that are made me have been great
In marriage of my daughter, yet the hope
Of your still rising honours have prevail'd
Above all other jointures; here she is,   5
She knows my mind, speak for yourself to her,—
And hear you daughter, see you use him nobly;
For any private speech I'll give you time.—
Come, son, and you the rest; let them alone;
Agree they as they may.
Sor.   I thank you, sir.   10
Gio. —Sister, be not all woman; think on me.
Sor. Vasques!
Vas.   My lord?
Sor.   Attend me without.
             [*Exeunt all but* Soranzo *and* Annabella.
Ann. Sir, what's your will with me?
Sor.   Do you not know
What I should tell you?
Ann.   Yes, you'll say you love me.
Sor. And I will swear it too; will you believe it?   15
Ann. 'Tis not point of faith.

             Enter Giovanni *above.*

Sor.   Have you not will to love?
Ann. Not you.
Sor.   Whom then?
Ann.   That's as the fates infer.
Gio. —Of those I'm regent now.
Sor.   What mean you, sweet?

Ann. To live and die a maid.

Sor.   Oh, that's unfit.

Gio. —Here's one can say that's but a woman's note. 20

Sor. Did you but see my heart, then would you
   swear—

Ann. That you were dead.

Gio.   —That's true, or somewhat near it.

Sor. See you these true love's tears?

Ann.   No.

Gio.   —Now she winks.

Sor. They plead to you for grace.

Ann.   Yet nothing speak.

Sor. Oh, grant my suit!

Ann.   What is 't?

Sor.   To let me live— 25

Ann. Take it.

Sor.   —Still yours.

Ann.   That is not mine to give.

Gio. —One such another word would kill his hopes.

Sor. Mistress, to leave those fruitless strifes of wit,
Know I have lov'd you long and lov'd you truly:
Not hope of what you have, but what you are,   30
Have drawn me on; then let me not in vain
Still feel the rigour of your chaste disdain:
I'm sick, and sick to th' heart.

Ann.   Help, aqua-vitæ!

Sor. What mean you?

Ann.   Why, I thought you had been sick.

Sor. Do you mock my love?

Gio.   —There, sir, she was too nimble. 35

Sor. —'Tis plain, she laughs at me!—These scornful
   taunts
Neither become your modesty, or years.

Ann. You are no looking-glass: or if you were,
I'd dress my language by you.

Gio.   —I'm confirm'd.

Ann. To put you out of doubt, my lord, methinks 40
Your common sense should make you understand
That if I lov'd you, or desir'd your love,
Some way I should have given you better taste:
But since you are a nobleman, and one
I would not wish should spend his youth in hopes, 45
Let me advise you here to forbear your suit,
And think I wish you well, I tell you this.

Sor. Is't you speak this?

Ann.   Yes, I myself; yet know,—
Thus far I give you comfort,—if mine eyes
Could have pick'd out a man (amongst all those 50
That sued to me) to make a husband of,
You should have been that man; let this suffice;
Be noble in your secrecy and wise.

Gio. —Why, now I see she loves me.

Ann.   One word more.
As ever virtue liv'd within your mind, 55
As ever noble courses were your guide,
As ever you would have me know you lov'd me,
Let not my father know hereof by you:
If I hereafter find that I must marry,
It shall be you or none.

Sor.   I take that promise. 60

Ann. Oh, oh, my head!

Sor. What's the matter? not well?

Ann. Oh, I begin to sicken!

Gio.   —Heaven forbid!
                              [*Exit from above.*

Sor. Help, help, within there, ho!

Enter Florio, Giovanni, Putana.

Look to your daughter, Signior Florio. 65
Flo. Hold her up, she swoons.

Gio. Sister, how d'ye?

Ann.   Sick,—brother, are you there?

Flo. Convey her to her bed instantly, whilst I send
for a physician; quickly, I say.

Put. Alas, poor child!   [*Exeunt, manet* Soranzo. 70

Enter Vasques.

Vas. My lord,—

Sor. Oh, Vasques, now I doubly am undone
Both in my present and my future hopes!
She plainly told me that she could not love,
And thereupon soon sick'ned; and I fear   75
Her life's in danger.

Vas. —By'r lady, sir, and so is yours, if you knew all.—
'Las, sir, I am sorry for that; may be 'tis but the maid's-
sickness, an over-flux of youth—and then sir, there is
no such present remedy as present marriage. But hath 80
she given you an absolute denial?

Sor. She hath, and she hath not; I'm full of grief:
But what she said I'll tell thee as we go.   [*Exeunt.*

ACTUS III, SCÆNA 3

Enter Giovanni *and* Putana.

Put. Oh, sir, we are all undone, quite undone,
utterly undone, and sham'd for ever! your sister, oh,
your sister!

Gio. What of her? for Heaven's sake, speak; how
does she?   5

Put. Oh, that ever I was born to see this day!

Gio. She is not dead, ha? is she?

Put. Dead! no, she is quick; 'tis worse, she is with
child. You know what you have done; Heaven forgive
ye! 'tis too late to repent now, Heaven help us!   10

453

Gio. With child? how dost thou know't?

Put. How do I know't! am I at these years ignorant
what the meanings of qualms and water-pangs be? of
changing of colours, queasiness of stomachs, pukings,
and another thing that I could name? Do not, for her 15
and your credit's sake, spend the time in asking how,
and which way, 'tis so: she is quick, upon my word;
if you let a physician see her water, y'are undone.

Gio. But in what case is she?

Put. Prettily amended; 'twas but a fit, which I soon 20
espi'd, and she must look for often henceforward.

Gio. Commend me to her, bid her take no care;
Let not the doctor visit her, I charge you;
Make some excuse, till I return.—Oh me!
I have a world of business in my head.—   25
Do not discomfort her.—
How do this news perplex me!—If my father
Come to her, tell him she's recover'd well;
Say 'twas but some ill diet—d'ye hear, woman?
Look you to't.   30

Put. I will, sir.   [*Exeunt.*

ACTUS III, SCÆNA 4

Enter Florio *and* Richardetto.

Flo. And how d'ye find her, sir?

Rich.   Indifferent well;
I see no danger, scarce perceive she's sick,
But that she told me she had lately eaten
Melons, and, as she thought, those disagreed
With her young stomach.

Flo.   Did you give her aught? 5

22 take no care] not worry   1 indifferent] fairly

454

Rich. An easy surfeit-water, nothing else.
You need not doubt her health; I rather think
Her sickness is a fulness of the blood,—
You understand me?
Flo.   I do, you counsel well;
And once, within these few days, will so order 't   10
She shall be married ere she know the time.
Rich. Yet let not haste, sir, make unworthy choice;
That were dishonour.
Flo.   Master Doctor, no;
I will not do so neither; in plain words,
My Lord Soranzo is the man I mean.   15
Rich. A noble and a virtuous gentleman.
Flo. As any is in Parma. Not far hence
Dwells Father Bonaventure, a grave friar,
Once tutor to my son; now at his cell
I'll have 'em married.
Rich.   You have plotted wisely.   20
Flo. I'll send one straight to speak with him to-night.
Rich. Soranzo's wise; he will delay no time.
Flo. It shall be so.

Enter Friar *and* Giovanni.

Friar.   Good peace be here and love!
Flo. Welcome, religious friar; you are one
That still bring blessing to the place you come to.   25
Gio. Sir, with what speed I could, I did my best
To draw this holy man from forth his cell
To visit my sick sister, that with words
Of ghostly comfort, in this time of need,
He might absolve her, whether she live or die.   30
Flo. 'Twas well done, Giovanni; thou herein
Hast showed a Christian's care, a brother's love.
Come, father, I'll conduct you to her chamber,

29 ghostly] spiritual

455

And one thing would entreat you.
   Friar.   Say on, sir.
   Flo. I have a father's dear impression   35
And wish, before I fall into my grave,
That I might see her married, as 'tis fit;
A word from you, grave man, will win her more
Than all our best persuasions.
   Friar.   Gentle sir,
All this I'll say, that Heaven may prosper her.   40
                                 [*Exeunt.*

ACTUS III, SCÆNA 5

Enter Grimaldi.

   Grim. Now if the doctor keep his word, Soranzo,
Twenty to one you miss your bride. I know
'Tis an unnoble act, and not becomes
A soldier's valour; but in terms of love,
Where merit cannot sway, policy must.   5
I am resolv'd, if this physician
Play not on both hands, then Soranzo falls.

Enter Richardetto.

   Rich. You're come as I could wish; this very night
Soranzo, 'tis ordain'd, must be affied
To Annabella, and, for aught I know,   10
Married.
   Grim.   How!
   Rich.   Yet your patience:—
The place, 'tis Friar Bonaventure's cell.
Now I would wish you to bestow this night
In watching thereabouts; 'tis but a night:
If you miss now, to-morrow I'll know all.   15

9 affied] affianced

456

Grim. Have you the poison?

Rich.   Here 'tis in this box:
Doubt nothing, this will do't; in any case,
As you respect your life, be quick and sure.

Grim. I'll speed him.

Rich.   Do; away! for 'tis not safe
You should be seen much here—Ever my love!   20

Grim. And mine to you.   [*Exit* Grimaldi.

Rich. So! if this hit, I'll laugh and hug revenge;
And they that now dream of a wedding-feast
May chance to mourn the lusty bridegroom's ruin.
But to my other business.—Niece Philotis!   25

Enter Philotis.

Phi. Uncle?

Rich. My lovely niece!
You have bethought ye?

Phi.   Yes,—and, as you counsell'd,
Fashion'd my heart to love him, but he swears
He will to-night be married; for he fears   30
His uncle else, if he should know the drift,
Will hinder all, and call his coz to shrift.

Rich. To-night! why, best of all; but, let me see—
Ay—ha—yes—so it shall be; in disguise
We'll early to the friar's; I have thought on't.   35

Enter Bergetto *and* Poggio.

Phi. Uncle, he comes.

Rich.   Welcome, my worthy coz.

Ber. Lass, pretty lass, come buss, lass!—A-ha,
Poggio!   [*Kisses her.*

Rich. —There's hope of this yet.—
You shall have time enough; withdraw a little;   40
We must confer at large.

Ber. Have you not sweetmeats or dainty devices for
me?

Phi. You shall have enough, sweetheart.

Ber. Sweetheart! mark that, Poggio!—By my troth, 45
I cannot choose but kiss thee once more for that word,
'sweetheart.'—Poggio, I have a monstrous swelling
about my stomach, whatsoever the matter be.

Pog. You shall have physic for't, sir.

Rich. Time runs apace. 50

Ber. Time's a blockhead.

Rich. Be rul'd: when we have done what's fit to do,
Then you may kiss your fill, and bed her too. [*Exeunt.*

ACTUS III, SCÆNA 6

Enter the Friar *in his study, sitting in a chair,* Annabella
*kneeling and whispering to him; a table before them, and
wax-lights; she weeps, and wrings her hands.*

Friar. I'm glad to see this penance; for, believe me,
You have unripp'd a soul so foul and guilty,
As, I must tell you true, I marvel how
The earth hath borne you up; but weep, weep on,
These tears may do you good; weep faster yet, 5
Whiles I do read a lecture.

Ann.   Wretched creature!

Friar. Ay, you are wretched, miserably wretched,
Almost condemn'd alive. There is a place,—
List, daughter!—in a black and hollow vault,
Where day is never seen; there shines no sun, 10
But flaming horror of consuming fires;
A lightless sulphur, chok'd with smoky fogs
Of an infected darkness; in this place
Dwell many thousand thousand sundry sorts
Of never-dying deaths; there damned souls 15

2 unripp'd] exposed, laid bare

458

Roar without pity; there are gluttons fed
With toads and adders; there is burning oil
Pour'd down the drunkard's throat; the usurer
Is forc'd to sup whole draughts of molten gold;
There is the murtherer forever stabb'd,   20
Yet can he never die; there lies the wanton
On racks of burning steel, whiles in his soul
He feels the torment of his raging lust.
    Ann. Mercy, oh mercy!
    Friar.   There stand these wretched things
Who have dream'd out whole years in lawless sheets   25
And secret incests, cursing one another.
Then you will wish each kiss your brother gave
Had been a dagger's point; then you shall hear
How he will cry, 'oh would my wicked sister
Had first been damn'd, when she did yield to lust!'— 30
But soft, methinks I see repentance work
New motions in your heart; say, how is't with you?
    Ann. Is there no way left to redeem my miseries?
    Friar. There is, despair not; Heaven is merciful,
And offers grace even now. 'Tis thus agreed: 35
First, for your honour's safety, that you marry
My Lord Soranzo; next, to save your soul,
Leave off this life, and henceforth live to him.
    Ann. Ay me!
    Friar.   Sigh not; I know the baits of sin
Are hard to leave; oh, 'tis a death to do't.   40
Remember what must come. Are you content?
    Ann. I am.
    Friar.   I like it well; we'll take the time.—
Who's near us there?

Enter Florio, Giovanni.

Flo.   Did you call, father?
Friar. Is Lord Soranzo come?

Flo.   He stays below

Friar. Have you acquainted him at full?

Flo.   I have,   45
And he is overjoy'd.

Friar.   And so are we.
Bid him come near.

Gio.   —My sister weeping! Ha!
I fear this friar's falsehood.—I will call him.   [*Exit.*

Flo. Daughter, are you resolv'd?

Ann.   Father, I am.

        Enter Giovanni, Soranzo, *and* Vasques.

Flo. My Lord Soranzo, here   50
Give me your hand; for that I give you this.
                   [*Joins their hands.*

Sor. Lady, say you so too?

Ann.   I do, and vow
To live with you and yours.

Friar.   Timely resolv'd:
My blessing rest on both! More to be done,
You may perform it on the morning sun.   [*Exeunt.* 55

ACTUS III, SCÆNA 7

Enter Grimaldi *with his rapier drawn and a dark-lantern.*

Grim. 'Tis early night as yet, and yet too soon
To finish such a work; here I will lie
To listen who comes next.   [*He lies down.*

      Enter Bergetto *and* Philotis *disguis'd, and after*
              Richardetto *and* Poggio.

Ber. We are almost at the place, I hope, sweetheart.

Grim. —I hear them near, and heard one say 'sweet-
    heart.'
                                   5
'Tis he; now guide my hand, some angry justice,

Home to his bosom!—Now have at you, sir!
                    [*Strikes* Bergetto *and exit.*
  Ber. Oh, help! help! here's a stitch fallen in my
guts: Oh for a flesh-tailor quickly!—Poggio!
  Phi. What ails my love?   10
  Ber. I am sure I cannot piss forward and backward,
and yet I am wet before and behind.—Lights! lights!
ho, lights!
  Phi. Alas, some villain here has slain my love!
  Rich. Oh, Heaven forbid it!—Raise up the next
    neighbours   15
Instantly, Poggio, and bring lights.   [*Exit* Poggio.
How is't, Bergetto? slain! It cannot be;
Are you sure y'are hurt?
  Ber. Oh, my belly seethes like a porridge-pot! Some
cold water, I shall boil over else; my whole body is in 20
a sweat, that you may wring my short; feel here—
Why, Poggio!

  Enter Poggio *with Officers and lights and halberts.*

  Pog. Here! Alas, how do you?
  Rich. Give me a light.—What's here? all blood!—
    Oh, sirs,
Signior Donado's nephew now is slain.   25
Follow the murtherer with all the haste
Up to the city, he cannot be far hence;
Follow, I beseech you.
  Off.   Follow, follow, follow! [*Exeunt Officers.*
  Rich. Tear off thy linen, coz, to stop his wounds.—
Be of good comfort, man.   30
  Ber. Is all this mine own blood? nay, then, good
night with me.—Poggio, commend me to my uncle,
dost hear? bid him, for my sake, make much of this
wench.—Oh, I am going the wrong way sure, my belly
aches so.—Oh, farewell, Poggio!—Oh, oh—oh! [*Dies.* 35

Phi. Oh, he is dead!

Pog.   How! dead!

Rich.   He's dead indeed;
'Tis now too late to weep; let's have him home,
And with what speed we may find out the murtherer.

Pog. Oh, my master! my master! my master!

                                                        [*Exeunt.*

ACTUS III, SCÆNA 8

Enter Vasques *and* Hippolita.

Hip. Betroth'd?

Vas. I saw it.

Hip. And when's the marriage-day?

Vas.   Some two days hence.

Hip. Two days! why, man, I would but wish two
    hours
To send him to his last and lasting sleep.
And, Vasques, thou shalt see I'll do it bravely.

Vas. I do not doubt your wisdom, nor, I trust, you
my secrecy; I am infinitely yours.

Hip. I will be thine in spite of my disgrace.—
So soon? Oh, wicked man, I durst be sworn   10
He'd laugh to see me weep.

Vas. And that's a villainous fault in him.

Hip. No, let him laugh; I'm arm'd in my resolves:
Be thou still true.

Vas. I should get little by treachery against so hope- 15
ful a preferment as I am like to climb to.

Hip. Even to my bosom, Vasques. Let my youth
Revel in these new pleasures: if we thrive,
He now hath but a pair of days to live.   [*Exeunt.*

ACTUS III, SCÆNA 9

Enter Florio, Donado, Richardetto, Poggio, *and*
Officers.

Flo. 'Tis bootless now to show yourself a child,
Signior Donado; what is done, is done;
Spend not the time in tears, but seek for justice.

   Rich. I must confess somewhat I was in fault
That had not first acquainted you what love   5
Passed 'twixt him and my niece; but, as I live,
His fortune grieves me as it were mine own.

   Don. Alas, poor creature! he meant no man harm,
That I am sure of.

   Flo.   I believe that too.
But stay, my masters: are you sure you saw   10
The murtherer pass here?

   Off. An it please you, sir, we are sure we saw a
ruffian, with a naked weapon in his hand all bloody, get
into my lord cardinal's grace's gate; that we are sure
of; but for fear of his grace—bless us!—we durst go 15
no further.

   Don. Know you what manner of man he was?

   Off. Yes, sure, I know the man; they say 'a is a
soldier; he that lov'd your daughter, sir, an't please ye;
'twas he for certain.   20

   Flo. Grimaldi, on my life!

   Off.   Ay, ay, the same.

   Rich. The cardinal is noble; he no doubt
Will give true justice.

   Don.   Knock some one at the gate.

   Pog. I'll knock, sir.   [Poggio *knocks.*

   Serv. [*Within.*] What would ye?   25

   Flo. We require speech with the lord cardinal

18 'a] he

463

About some present business; pray inform
His grace that we are here.

Enter Cardinal *and* Grimaldi.

  Car. Why, how now, friends! what saucy mates are
    you
That know nor duty nor civility?   30
Are we a person fit to be your host;
Or is our house become your common inn,
To beat our doors at pleasure? What such haste
Is yours, as that it cannot wait fit times?
Are you the masters of this commonwealth,   35
And know no more discretion? Oh, your news
Is here before you; you have lost a nephew,
Donado, last night by Grimaldi slain:
Is that your business? well, sir, we have knowledge
    on't;
Let that suffice.
  Grim.   In presence of your grace,   40
In thought I never meant Bergetto harm:
But Florio, you can tell, with how much scorn
Soranzo, back'd with his confederates,
Hath often wrong'd me; I, to be reveng'd,
(For that I could not win him else to fight,)   45
Had thought by way of ambush to have kill'd him,
But was unluckily therein mistook;
Else he had felt what late Bergetto did:
And though my fault to him were merely chance,
Yet humbly I submit me to your grace,   50
To do with me as you please.
  Car.   Rise up, Grimaldi.—
You citizens of Parma, if you seek
For justice, know, as nuncio from the pope,
For this offence I here receive Grimaldi

27 present] urgent

464

Into his holiness' protection.   55
He is no common man, but nobly born,
Of princes' blood, though you, Sir Florio,
Thought him too mean a husband for your daughter.
If more you seek for, you must go to Rome,
For he shall thither; learn more wit, for shame.—   60
Bury your dead.—Away, Grimaldi; leave 'em!
                         [*Exeunt* Cardinal *and* Grimaldi.
    Don. Is this a churchman's voice? dwells justice
        here?
    Flo. Justice is fled to Heaven, and comes no nearer.
Soranzo!—was't for him? Oh, impudence!
Had he the face to speak it, and not blush?   65
Come, come, Donado, there's no help in this,
When cardinals think murder's not amiss.
Great men may do their wills, we must obey;
But Heaven will judge them for't another day.
                                         [*Exeunt.*

ACTUS IV, SCÆNA I

A Banquet. Hautboys.

Enter the Friar, Giovanni, Annabella, Philotis, Soranzo,
    Donado, Florio, Richardetto, Putana, *and* Vasques.

    Friar. These holy rites perform'd, now take your
        times
To spend the remnant of the day in feast;
Such fit repasts are pleasing to the saints,
Who are your guests, though not with mortal eyes
To be beheld.—Long prosper in this day,   5
You happy couple, to each other's joy!
    Sor. Father, your prayer is heard; the hand of good-
        ness
Hath been a shield for me against my death:

And, more to bless me, hath enrich'd my life
With this most precious jewel; such a prize   10
As earth hath not another like to this.—
Cheer up, my love, and, gentlemen, my friends,
Rejoice with me in mirth: this day we'll crown
With lusty cups to Annabella's health.

Gio. —Oh torture! were the marriage yet undone,   15
                                                      [*Aside.*

Ere I'd endure this sight, to see my love
Clipp'd by another, I would dare confusion,
And stand the horror of ten thousand deaths.

Vas. Are you not well, sir?

Gio.   Prithee, fellow, wait;
I need not thy officious diligence.   20

Flo. Signior Donado, come, you must forget
Your late mishaps, and drown your cares in wine.

Sor. Vasques!

Vas.   My lord?

Sor.   Reach me that weighty bowl.
Here, brother Giovanni, here's to you;
Your turn come next, though now a bachelor;   25
Here's to your sister's happiness and mine!

Gio. I cannot drink.

Sor.   What!

Gio.   'Twill indeed offend me.

Ann. Pray, do not urge him, if he be not willing.
                                                      [*Hautboys.*

Flo. How now! what noise is this?

Vas. Oh, sir, I had forgot to tell you; certain young   30
maidens of Parma, in honour to Madam Annabella's
marriage, have sent their loves to her in a Masque, for
which they humbly crave your patience and silence.

Sor. We are much bound to them, so much the more
As it comes unexpected; guide them in.   35

17 Clipp'd] embraced

466

Enter Hippolita *and Ladies in white robes with garlands of*
willows, all masked.
Music and a dance.

Thanks, lovely virgins! now might we but know
To whom we have been beholding for this love,
We shall acknowledge it.

   Hip.   Yes, you shall know.   [*Unmasks.*
What think you now?

   All.   Hippolita!

   Hip.   'Tis she;
Be not amaz'd; nor blush, young lovely bride;   40
I come not to defraud you of your man!
'Tis now no time to reckon-up the talk
What Parma long hath rumour'd of us both:
Let rash report run on; the breath that vents it
Will, like a bubble, break itself at last.   45
But now to you, sweet creature; lend's your hand;—
Perhaps it hath been said that I would claim
Some interest in Soranzo, now your lord;
What I have right to do, his soul knows best:
But in my duty to your noble worth,   50
Sweet Annabella, and my care of you,—
Here, take, Soranzo, take this hand from me;
I'll once more join what by the holy church
Is finish'd and allow'd.—Have I done well?

   Sor. You have too much engag'd us.

   Hip.   One thing more. 55
That you may know my single charity,
Freely I here remit all interest
I e'er could claim, and give you back your vows;
And to confirm't,—reach me a cup of wine,—
My Lord Soranzo, in this draught I drink   60
Long rest t'ye!—Look to it, Vasques.

56 single] signal, outstanding

Vas. —Fear nothing.

[*He gives her a poison'd cup.*
[*She drinks.*

Sor. Hippolita, I thank you, and will pledge
This happy union as another life.—
Wine, there!   65

Vas. You shall have none, neither shall you pledge
her.

Hip. How!

Vas. Know now, Mistress She-devil, your own mis-
chievous treachery hath kill'd you; I must not marry 70
you.

Hip. Villain!

All. What's the matter?

Vas. Foolish woman, thou **art** now like a firebrand
that hath kindled others and burnt thyself:—*troppo* 75
sperar, *inganna*,—thy vain hope hath deceiv'd thee;
thou art but dead; if thou hast any grace, pray.

Hip. Monster!

Vas. Die in charity, for shame.—This thing of
malice, this woman, had privately corrupted me with 80
promise of marriage, under this politic reconciliation,
to poison my lord, whiles she might laugh at his confusion on his marriage-day. I promis'd her fair; but I
knew what my reward should have been, and would
willingly have spar'd her life, but that I was acquainted 85
with the danger of her disposition; and now have fitted
her a just payment in her own coin: there she is, she
hath yet——and end thy days in peace, vild woman; as
for life, there's no hope; think not on't.

All. Wonderful justice!   90

Rich. Heaven, thou art righteous.

Hip.   Oh, 'tis true;

75–6 *troppo &c.*] too much hope deceives   88 yet——] *So
printed in the original*   vild] vile

468

I feel my minute coming. Had that slave
Kept promise,—oh, my torment!—thou this hour
Hadst died, Soranzo;—heat above hell-fire!—
Yet, ere I pass away,—cruel, cruel flames!—   95
Take here my curse amongst you; may thy bed
Of marriage be a rack unto thy heart,
Burn blood, and boil in vengeance;—oh my heart,
My flame's intolerable!—mayst thou live
To father bastards; may her womb bring forth   100
Monsters,—and die together in your sins,
Hated, scorn'd, and unpitied!—oh—oh—   [*Dies.*

   Flo. Was e'er so vild a creature!
   Rich.   Here's the end
Of lust and pride.
   Ann.   It is a fearful sight.
   Sor. Vasques, I know thee now a trusty servant,   105
And never will forget thee.—Come, my love,
We'll home, and thank the heavens for this escape.—
Father and friends, we must break up this mirth;
It is too sad a feast.
   Don.   Bear hence the body.
   Friar. —Here's an ominous change!   110
Mark this, my Giovanni, and take heed!—
I fear the event: that marriage seldom's good
Where the bride-banquet so begins in blood. [*Exeunt.*

ACTUS IV, SCÆNA 2

Enter Richardetto *and* Philotis.

   Rich. My wretched wife, more wretched in her
     shame
Than in her wrongs to me, hath paid too soon
The forfeit of her modesty and life.
And I am sure, my niece, though vengeance hover,

Keeping aloof yet from Soranzo's fall,   5
Yet he will fall, and sink with his own weight.
I need not now—my heart persuades me so—
To further his confusion; there is One
Above begins to work, for as I hear
Debates already 'twixt his wife and him   10
Thicken and run to head; she, as 'tis said,
Slightens his love, and he abandons hers;
Much talk I hear. Since things go thus, my niece,
In tender love and pity of your youth,
My counsel is, that you should free your years   15
From hazard of these woes by flying hence
To fair Cremona, there to vow your soul
In holiness, a holy votaress:
Leave me to see the end of these extremes.
All human worldly courses are uneven;   20
No life is blessed but the way to Heaven.
　　Phi. Uncle, shall I resolve to be a nun?
　　Rich. Ay, gentle niece, and in your hourly prayers
Remember me, your poor unhappy uncle.
Hie to Cremona now, as fortune leads,   25
Your home your cloister, your best friends your beads;
Your chaste and single life shall crown your birth:
Who dies a virgin lives a saint on earth.
　　Phi. Then farewell, world, and worldly thoughts,
　　　adieu!
Welcome, chaste vows; myself I yield to you. [*Exeunt.* 30

ACTUS IV, SCÆNA 3

Enter Soranzo *unbrac'd, and* Annabella *dragg'd in.*

　　Sor. Come, strumpet, famous whore! were every drop
Of blood that runs in thy adulterous veins
A life, this sword—dost see't?—should in one blow

ⅳ. iii heading *unbrac'd*] with clothes untied

470

Confound them all. Harlot, rare, notable harlot,
That with thy brazen face maintain'st thy sin,   5
Was there no man in Parma to be bawd
To your loose cunning whoredom else but I?
Must your hot itch and plurisy of lust,
The heyday of your luxury, be fed
Up to a surfeit, and could none but I   10
Be pick'd out to be cloak to your close tricks,
Your belly-sports? Now I must be the dad
To all that gallimaufry that is stuff'd
In thy corrupted bastard-bearing womb!
Say, must I?
 Ann.   Beastly man! why, 'tis thy fate.   15
I sued not to thee; for, but that I thought
Your over-loving lordship would have run
Mad on denial, had ye lent me time,
I would have told ye in what case I was:
But you would needs be doing.
 Sor.   Whore of whores! 20
Dar'st thou tell me this?
 Ann.   Oh yes, why not?
You were deceiv'd in me; 'twas not for love
I chose you, but for honour; yet know this,
Would you be patient yet, and hide your shame,
I'd see whether I could love you.
 Sor.   Excellent quean!   25
Why, art thou not with child?
 Ann.   What needs all this,
When 'tis superfluous? I confess I am.
 Sor. Tell me by whom.
 Ann.   Soft, sir! 'twas not in my bargain.
Yet somewhat, sir, to stay your longing stomach,
I am content t' acquaint you with; the man,   30
The more than man, that got this sprightly boy,—

8 plurisy] excess 9 luxury] lust 11 close] secret

471

For 'tis a boy, that for your glory, sir!
Your heir shall be a son—
  Sor.   Damnable monster!
  Ann. Nay, an you will not hear, I'll speak no more.
  Sor. Yes, speak, and speak thy last.
  Ann.   A match! a match! 35
This noble creature was in every part
So angel-like, so glorious, that a woman
Who had not been but human, as was I,
Would have kneel'd to him, and have begg'd for love.—
You! why, you are not worthy once to name   40
His name without true worship, or, indeed,
Unless you kneel'd, to hear another name him.
  Sor. What was he call'd?
  Ann.   We are not come to that;
Let it suffice that you shall have the glory
To father what so brave a father got.   45
In brief, had not this chance fall'n out as't doth,
I never had been troubled with a thought
That you had been a creature; but for marriage,
I scarce dream yet of that.
  Sor.   Tell me his name.
  Ann. Alas, alas, there's all! will you believe?   50
  Sor. What?
  Ann.   You shall never know.
  Sor.   How!
  Ann.   Never:
If you do, let me be curs'd!
  Sor. Not know it, strumpet! I'll rip up thy heart,
And find it there.
  Ann.   Do, do!
  Sor.   And with my teeth
Tear the prodigious lecher joint by joint.   55
  Ann. Ha, ha, ha! the man's merry.

32 for your glory] *The original reads* for glory

Sor.   Dost thou laugh?
Come, whore, tell me your lover, or, by truth,
I'll hew thy flesh to shreds; who is't?

Ann. [*Sings*] *Che morte più dolce che morire per amore?*

Sor. Thus will I pull thy hair, and thus I'll drag   60
Thy lust-be-lep'red body through the dust.
                                    [*Hales her up and down.*
Yet tell his name.

Ann. [*Sings*] *Morendo in grazia dee morire senza dolore.*

Sor. Dost thou triumph? The treasure of the earth
Shall not redeem thee; were there kneeling kings   65
Did beg thy life, or angels did come down
To plead in tears, yet should not all prevail
Against my rage; dost thou not tremble yet?

Ann. At what? to die! no, be a gallant hangman;
I dare thee to the worst: strike, and strike home;   70
I leave revenge behind, and thou shalt feel't.

Sor. Yet tell me ere thou diest, and tell me truly,
Knows thy old father this?

Ann.   No, by my life.

Sor. Wilt thou confess, and I will spare thy life?

Ann. My life! I will not buy my life so dear.   75

Sor. I will not slack my vengeance.   [*Draws.*

                    Enter Vasques.

Vas.   What d'ye mean, sir?

Sor. Forbear, Vasques; such a damned whore
Deserves no pity.

Vas.   Now the gods forfend!
And would you be her executioner, and kill her in your
rage too? Oh, 'twere most unmanlike. She is your wife: 80
what faults have been done by her before she married
you were not against you; alas, poor lady, what hath

---

59 *Che morte &c.*) what death is sweeter than to die for love
63 *Morendo &c.*] dying in God's grace is to die without pain

she committed, which any lady in Italy, in the like case,
would not? Sir, you must be ruled by your reason, and
not by your fury; that were unhuman and beastly.   85

Sor. She shall not live.

Vas. Come, she must. You would have her confess the
author of her present misfortunes, I warrant ye; 'tis an
unconscionable demand, and she should lose the estima-
tion that I, for my part, hold of her worth, if she had done 90
it; why, sir, you ought not, of all men living, to know
it. Good sir, be reconciled: alas, good gentlewoman!

Ann. Pish, do not beg for me; I prize my life
As nothing; if the man will needs be mad,
Why, let him take it.

Sor.   Vasques, hear'st thou this?   95

Vas. Yes, and commend her for it; in this she shows
the nobleness of a gallant spirit, and beshrew my heart,
but it becomes her rarely.—Sir, in any case, smother
your revenge; leave the scenting-out your wrongs to
me; be rul'd, as you respect your honour, or you mar 100
all.—Sir, if ever my service were of any credit with
you, be not so violent in your distractions: you are
married now; what a triumph might the report of this
give to other neglected suitors! 'Tis as manlike to bear
extremities as godlike to forgive.   105

Sor. Oh, Vasques, Vasques, in this piece of flesh,
This faithless face of hers, had I laid up
The treasure of my heart!—Hadst thou been virtuous,
Fair, wicked woman, not the matchless joys
Of life itself had made me wish to live   110
With any saint but thee; deceitful creature,
How hast thou mock'd my hopes, and in the shame
Of thy lewd womb even buried me alive!
I did too dearly love thee.

Vas.   This is well;   [*Aside.*
Follow this temper with some passion: 115

Be brief and moving; 'tis for the purpose.

Sor. Be witness to my words thy soul and thoughts;
And tell me, didst not think that in my heart
I did too superstitiously adore thee?

Ann. I must confess I know you lov'd me well.   120

Sor. And wouldst thou use me thus! Oh, Annabella,
Be thus assur'd, whatsoe'er the villain was
That thus hath tempted thee to this disgrace,
Well he might lust, but never lov'd like me:
He doted on the picture that hung out   125
Upon thy cheeks to please his humorous eye;
Not on the part I lov'd, which was thy heart,
And, as I thought, thy virtues.

Ann.   Oh, my lord!
These words wound deeper than your sword could do.

Vas. Let me not ever take comfort, but I begin to 130
weep myself, so much I pity him; why, madam, I knew,
when his rage was over-past, what it would come to.

Sor. Forgive me, Annabella. Though thy youth
Hath tempted thee above thy strength to folly,
Yet will not I forget what I should be,   135
And what I am—a husband; in that name
Is hid divinity; if I do find
That thou wilt yet be true, here I remit
All former faults, and take thee to my bosom.

Vas. By my troth, and that's a point of noble charity. 140

Ann. Sir, on my knees—

Sor.   Rise up, you shall not kneel.
Get you to your chamber; see you make no show
Of alteration; I'll be with you straight;
My reason tells me now that "'tis as common
To err in frailty as to be a woman.'   145
Go to your chamber.   [*Exit* Annabella.

Vas. So! this was somewhat to the matter; what do
you think of your heaven of happiness now, sir?

475

Sor. I carry hell about me; all my blood
Is fir'd in swift revenge.   150
   Vas. That may be, but know you how, or on whom?
Alas, to marry a great woman, being made great in the
stock to your hand, is a usual sport in these days; but
to know what ferret it was that haunted your cony-
berry,—there's the cunning.   155
   Sor. I'll make her tell herself, or—
   Vas. Or what? you must not do so; let me yet persuade your sufferance a little while; go to her, use her
mildly; win her, if it be possible, to a voluntary, to a
weeping tune; for the rest, if all hit, I will not miss my 160
mark. Pray, sir, go in: the next news I tell you shall be
wonders.
   Sor. Delay in vengeance gives a heavier blow. [*Exit.*
   Vas. Ah, sirrah, here's work for the nonce! I had a
suspicion of a bad matter in my head a pretty whiles   165
ago; but after my madam's scurvy looks here at home,
her waspish perverseness, and loud fault-finding, then
I rememb'red the proverb, that *Where hens crow, and
cocks hold their peace, there are sorry houses.* 'Sfoot, if the
lower parts of a she-tailor's cunning can cover such a 170
swelling in the stomach, I'll never blame a false stitch
in a shoe whiles I live again. Up, and up so quick? and
so quickly too? 'twere a fine policy to learn by whom:
this must be known; and I have thought on't—Here's
the way, or none.—What, crying, old mistress! alas,   175
alas, I cannot blame ye; we have a lord, Heaven help
us, is so mad as the devil himself, the more shame for
him.

Enter Putana.

   Put. Oh, Vasques, that ever I was born to see this
day! Doth he use thee so too sometimes, Vasques?   180

155 154–5 cony-berry] rabbit warren

Vas. Me? why he makes a dog of me; but if some
were of my mind, I know what we would do. As sure
as I am an honest man, he will go near to kill my lady
with unkindness; say she be with child, is that such a
matter for a young woman of her years to be blam'd for? 185

Put. Alas, good heart, it is against her will full sore.

Vas. I durst be sworn all his madness is for that she
will not confess whose 'tis, which he will know; and
when he doth know it, I am so well acquainted with his
humour, that he will forget all straight. Well, I could 190
wish she would in plain terms tell all, for that's the
way indeed.

Put. Do you think so?

Vas. Foh, I know't; provided that he did not win
her to 't by force. He was once in a mind that you 195
could tell, and meant to have wrung it out of you, but
I somewhat pacified him for that; yet sure you know a
great deal.

Put. Heaven forgive us all, I know a little, Vasques.

Vas. Why should you not? who else should? Upon 200
my conscience, she loves you dearly; and you would
not betray her to any affliction for the world.

Put. Not for all the world, by my faith and troth,
Vasques.

Vas. 'Twere pity of your life if you should; but in 205
this you should both relieve her present discomforts,
pacify my lord, and gain yourself everlasting love and
preferment.

Put. Dost think so, Vasques?

Vas. Nay, I know't; sure 'twas some near and entire 210
friend.

Put. 'Twas a dear friend indeed; but—

Vas. But what? fear not to name him; my life between you and danger; 'faith, I think 'twas no base
fellow.   215

Put. Thou wilt stand between me and harm?

Vas. 'Ud's pity, what else? you shall be rewarded too, trust me.

Put. 'Twas even no worse than her own brother.

Vas. Her brother Giovanni, I warrant ye!   220

Put. Even he, Vasques; as brave a gentleman as ever kiss'd fair lady. Oh, they love most perpetually.

Vas. A brave gentleman indeed! why, therein I commend her choice.—Better and better.—You are sure 'twas he?   225

Put. Sure; and you shall see he will not be long from her too.

Vas. He were to blame if he would: but may I believe thee?

Put. Believe me! why, dost think I am a Turk or a 230 Jew? No, Vasques, I have known their dealings too long to belie them now.

Vas. Where are you there? within, sirs!

Enter Banditti.

Put. How now! what are these?

Vas. You shall know presently.—Come, sirs, take 235 me this old damnable hag, gag her instantly, and put out her eyes, quickly, quickly!

Put. Vasques! Vasques!—

Vas. Gag her, I say; 'sfoot, d'ye suffer her to prate? what d'ye fumble about? let me come to her, I'll help 240 your old gums, you toad-bellied bitch! Sirs, carry her closely into the coal-house, and put out her eyes instantly; if she roars, slit her nose: d'ye hear, be speedy and sure. Why, this is excellent and above expectation—   [*Exeunt with* Putana. 245 Her own brother! Oh, horrible! to what a height of liberty in damnation hath the devil train'd our age!

242 closely] secretly   247 train'd] drawn, enticed

her brother, well! there's yet but a beginning; I must
to my lord, and tutor him better in his points of
vengeance; now I see how a smooth tale goes beyond a 250
smooth tail. But soft!——What thing comes next?

Enter Giovanni.

Giovanni! as I would wish; my belief is strengthened,
'tis as firm as winter and summer.

Gio. Where's my sister?

Vas. Troubled with a new sickness, my lord; she's 255
somewhat ill.

Gio. Took too much of the flesh, I believe.

Vas. Troth, sir, and you, I think, have e'en hit it:
but my virtuous lady—

Gio. Where's she?   260

Vas. In her chamber; please you visit her; she is
alone. [Giovanni *gives him money*.] Your liberality hath
doubly made me your servant, and ever shall, ever—

[*Exit* Giovanni.

Enter Soranzo.

Sir, I am made a man; I have plied my cue with cunning and success; I beseech you let's be private.   265

Sor. My lady's brother's come; now he'll know all.

Vas. Let him know't; I have made some of them fast
enough. How have you dealt with my lady?

Sor. Gently, as thou hast counsell'd; Oh, my soul
Runs circular in sorrow for revenge: 270
But, Vasques, thou shalt know—

Vas. Nay, I will know no more; for now comes your
turn to know; I would not talk so openly with you.—
Let my young master take time enough, and go at
pleasure; he is sold to death, and the devil shall not 275
ransom him.—Sir, I beseech you, your privacy.

Sor. No conquest can gain glory of my fear. [*Exeunt.*

ACTUS V, SCÆNA I

Enter Annabella *above.*

Ann. Pleasures, farewell, and all ye thriftless minutes
Wherein false joys have spun a weary life!
To these my fortunes now I take my leave.
Thou, precious Time, that swiftly rid'st in post
Over the world, to finish up the race   5
Of my last fate, here stay thy restless course,
And bear to ages that are yet unborn
A wretched, woeful woman's tragedy!
My conscience now stands up against my lust
With depositions charact'red in guilt,   [*Enter* Friar. 10
And tells me I am lost: now I confess
Beauty that clothes the outside of the face
Is cursed if it be not cloth'd with grace.
Here like a turtle (mew'd up in a cage,)
Unmated, I converse with air and walls,   15
And descant on my vild unhappiness.
O Giovanni, thou hast had the spoil
Of thine own virtues and my modest fame,
Would thou hadst been less subject to those stars
That luckless reign'd at my nativity!   20
Oh, would the scourge due to my black offence
Might pass from thee, that I alone might feel
The torment of an uncontrolled flame!
Friar. —What's this I hear?
Ann.   That man, that blessed friar,
Who join'd in ceremonial knot my hand   25
To him whose wife I now am, told me oft
I trod the path to death, and showed me how.
But they who sleep in lethargies of lust
Hug their confusion, making Heaven unjust;

14 turtle] *sc.* turtle-dove   16 vild] vile

And so did I.

Friar.   —Here's music to the soul!   30

Ann. Forgive me, my good genius, and this once
Be helpful to my ends; let some good man
Pass this way, to whose trust I may commit
This paper, double-lin'd with tears and blood;
Which being granted, here I sadly vow   35
Repentance, and a leaving of that life
I long have died in.

Friar.   Lady, Heaven hath heard you,
And hath by providence ordain'd that I
Should be his minister for your behoof.

Ann. Ha, what are you?

Friar.   Your brother's friend, the friar; 40
Glad in my soul that I have liv'd to hear
This free confession 'twixt your peace and you.
What would you, or to whom? fear not to speak.

Ann. Is Heaven so bountiful? then I have found
More favour than I hop'd. Here, holy man—   45
                              [*Throws a letter.*
Commend me to my brother; give him that,
That letter; bid him read it, and repent.
Tell him that I (imprison'd in my chamber,
Barr'd of all company, even of my guardian,
Who gives me cause of much suspect,) have time   50
To blush at what hath pass'd; bid him be wise,
And not believe the friendship of my lord:
I fear much more than I can speak: good father,
The place is dangerous, and spies are busy.
I must break off—You'll do't?

Friar.   Be sure I will;   55
And fly with speed—my blessing ever rest
With thee, my daughter; live, to die more blessed!
                              [*Exit* Friar.

35 sadly] seriously

Ann. Thanks to the heavens, who have prolong'd
my breath
To this good use! now I can welcome death.   [*Exit.*

ACTUS V, SCÆNA 2

Enter Soranzo *and* Vasques.

Vas.   Am I to be believ'd now?
First marry a strumpet that cast herself away upon you
but to laugh at your horns, to feast on your disgrace,
riot in your vexations, cuckold you in your bride-bed,
waste your estate upon panders and bawds!   5
Sor. No more, I say, no more!
Vas. A cuckold is a goodly tame beast, my lord.
Sor. I am resolv'd; urge not another word;
My thoughts are great, and all as resolute
As thunder; in mean time I'll cause our lady   10
To deck herself in all her bridal robes,
Kiss her, and fold her gently in my arms.
Begone,—yet hear you, are the banditti ready
To wait in ambush?
Vas. Good sir, trouble not yourself about other 15
business than your own resolution; remember that
time lost cannot be recall'd.
Sor. With all the cunning words thou canst, invite
The states of Parma to my birthday's feast;
Haste to my brother-rival and his father,   20
Entreat them gently, bid them not to fail.
Be speedy, and return.
Vas. Let not your pity betray you till my coming
back; think upon incest and cuckoldry.
Sor. Revenge is all the ambition I aspire;   25
To that I'll climb or fall; my blood's on fire.   [*Exeunt.*

19 states] noblemen

ACTUS V, SCÆNA 3

Enter Giovanni.

Gio. Busy opinion is an idle fool,
That, as a school-rod keeps a child in awe,
Frights the unexperienc'd temper of the mind:
So did it me, who, ere my precious sister
Was married, thought all taste of love would die   5
In such a contract; but I find no change
Of pleasure in this formal law of sports.
She is still one to me, and every kiss
As sweet and as delicious as the first
I reap'd, when yet the privilege of youth   10
Entitled her a virgin. Oh, the glory
Of two united hearts like her and mine!
Let poring book-men dream of other worlds;
My world and all of happiness is here,
And I'd not change it for the best to come: 15
A life of pleasure is elysium.
                    Enter Friar.
Father, you enter on the jubilee
Of my retir'd delights: now I can tell you,
The hell you oft have prompted is nought else
But slavish and fond superstitious fear;   20
And I could prove it too—
    Friar.   Thy blindness slays thee:
Look there, 'tis writ to thee.   [*Gives the letter.*
    Gio. From whom?
    Friar. Unrip the seals and see;
The blood's yet seething hot, that will anon   25
Be frozen harder than congeal'd coral.
Why d'ye change colour, son?
    Gio.   'Fore Heaven, you make
Some petty devil factor 'twixt my love

And your religion-masked sorceries.
Where had you this?
   Friar.   Thy conscience, youth, is sear'd, 30
Else thou wouldst stoop to warning.
   Gio.   'Tis her hand,
I know't; and 'tis all written in her blood.
She writes I know not what. Death! I'll not fear
An armed thunderbolt aim'd at my heart.
She writes, we are discovered:—Pox on dreams 35
Of low faint-hearted cowardice!—discovered?
The devil we are! which way is't possible?
Are we grown traitors to our own delights?
Confusion take such dotage! 'tis but forg'd;
This is your peevish chattering, weak old man! 40
Now, sir, what brings you?

               Enter Vasques.

   Vas. My lord, according to his yearly custom keeping this day a feast in honour of his birthday, by me invites you thither. Your worthy father, with the pope's reverend nuncio, and other magnificoes of 45
Parma, have promis'd their presence: will't please you to be of the number?
   Gio. Yes, tell him I dare come.
   Vas. 'Dare come!'
   Gio. So I said; and tell him more, I will come. 50
   Vas. These words are strange to me.
   Gio. Say I will come.
   Vas. You will not miss?
   Gio. Yet more! I'll come, sir. Are you answer'd?
   Vas. So I'll say.—My service to you. 55
                   [*Exit* Vasques.
   Friar. You will not go, I trust.
   Gio.   Not go! for what?
   Friar. Oh, do not go! this feast, I'll gage my life,

Is but a plot to train you to your ruin.
Be rul'd, you sha' not go.
 Gio.   Not go! stood Death
Threat'ning his armies of confounding plagues,   **60**
With hosts of dangers hot as blazing stars,
I would be there: not go! yes, and resolve
To strike as deep in slaughter as they all;
For I will go.
 Friar. Go where thou wilt: I see
The wildness of thy fate draws to an end,   **65**
To a bad fearful end. I must not stay
To know thy fall; back to Bononia I
With speed will haste, and shun this coming blow.—
Parma, farewell; would I had never known thee,
Or aught of thine!—Well, young man, since no prayer **70**
Can make thee safe, I leave thee to despair.
            [*Exit* Friar.
 Gio. Despair, or tortures of a thousand hells;
All's one to me; I have set up my rest.
Now, now, work serious thoughts on baneful plots!
Be all a man, my soul; let not the curse   **75**
Of old prescription rend from me the gall
Of courage, which enrols a glorious death.
If I must totter like a well-grown oak,
Some under-shrubs shall in my weighty fall
Be crush'd to splits; with me they all shall perish! **8c**
              [*Exit.*

ACTUS V, SCÆNA 4

Enter Soranzo, Vasques *with masks, and* Banditti.

Sor. You will not fail, or shrink in the attempt?
Vas. I will undertake for their parts.—Be sure, my

73 set up my rest] decided my stake (*as in 'standing' in a card-game*)

masters, to be bloody enough, and as unmerciful as
if you were preying upon a rich booty on the very
mountains of Liguria; for your pardons, trust to my 5
lord; but for reward you shall trust none but your own
pockets.

Band. omnes. We'll make a murther.

Sor. Here's gold, here's more; want nothing; what
    you do
Is noble, and an act of brave revenge.   10
I'll make ye rich, banditti, and all free.

Omnes. Liberty! liberty!

Vas. Hold, take every man a vizard; when ye are
withdrawn, keep as much silence as you can possibly.
You know the watchword; till which be spoken, move 15
not; but when you hear that, rush in like a stormy
flood; I need not instruct ye in your own profession.

Omnes. No, no, no.

Vas. In, then; your ends are profit and preferment—
away!   [*Exeunt* Banditti. 20

Sor. The guests will all come, Vasques?

Vas. Yes, sir. And now let me a little edge your
resolution; you see nothing is unready to this great
work, but a great mind in you; call to your remembrance your disgraces, your loss of honour, Hippolita's 25
blood, and arm your courage in your own wrongs; so
shall you best right those wrongs in vengeance, which
you may truly call your own.

Sor. 'Tis well; the less I speak, the more I burn,
And blood shall quench that flame.   30

Vas. Now you begin to turn Italian. This beside:—
when my young incest-monger comes, he will be sharp
set on his old bit: give him time enough, let him have
your chamber and bed at liberty; let my hot hare have
law ere he be hunted to his death, that, if it be possible, 35
he post to hell in the very act of his damnation.

Enter Giovanni.

Sor. It shall be so; and see, as we would wish,
He comes himself first. Welcome, my much-lov'd
    brother,
Now I perceive you honour me; y'are welcome.
But where's my father?

Gio.   With the other states,   40
Attending on the nuncio of the pope,
To wait upon him hither. How's my sister?

Sor. Like a good housewife, scarcely ready yet;
Y'are best walk to her chamber.

Gio.   If you will.

Sor. I must expect my honourable friends;   45
Good brother, get her forth.

Gio.   You are busy, sir.

                          [*Exit* Giovanni.

Vas. Even as the great devil himself would have it!
let him go and glut himself in his own destruction.

                          [*Flourish.*

Hark, the nuncio is at hand; good sir, be ready to
receive him.   50

Enter Cardinal, Florio, Donado, Richardetto, *and*
                    Attendants.

Sor. Most reverend lord, this grace hath made me
    proud,
That you vouchsafe my house; I ever rest
Your humble servant for this noble favour.

Car. You are our friend, my lord; his Holiness
Shall understand how zealously you honour   55
Saint Peter's vicar in his substitute:
Our special love to you.

Sor.   Signiors, to you
My welcome, and my ever best of thanks

45 expect] await

487

For this so memorable courtesy.—
Pleaseth your grace to walk near?
 Car.   My lord, we come 60
To celebrate your feast with civil mirth,
As ancient custom teacheth: we will go.
 Sor. Attend his grace there!—Signiors, keep your
 way.   [*Exeunt.*

ACTUS V, SCÆNA 5

Enter Giovanni *and* Annabella *lying on a bed.*

 Gio. What, chang'd so soon! hath your new sprightly
  lord
Found out a trick in night-games more than we
Could know in our simplicity? Ha! is't so?
Or does the fit come on you, to prove treacherous
To your past vows and oaths?
 Ann.   Why should you jest 5
At my calamity, without all sense
Of the approaching dangers you are in?
 Gio. What danger's half so great as thy revolt?
Thou art a faithless sister, else thou know'st,
Malice, or any treachery beside,   10
Would stoop to my bent brows; why, ⸸ hold fate
Clasp'd in my fist, and could command the course
Of time's eternal motion, hadst thou been
One thought more steady than an ebbing sea.
And what? you'll now be honest, that's resolv'd?   15
 Ann. Brother, dear brother, know what I have been,
And know that now there's but a dying time
'Twixt us and our confusion: let's not waste
These precious hours in vain and useless speech.

 v. v heading *Enter . . . bed*] *The curtain is drawn to reveal them*
in the 'study' or inner stage.

488

Alas, these gay attires were not put on   20
But to some end; this sudden solemn feast
Was not ordain'd to riot in expense;
I, that have now been chamb'red here alone,
Barr'd of my guardian or of any else,
Am not for nothing at an instant freed   25
To fresh access. Be not deceiv'd, my brother;
This banquet is an harbinger of death
To you and me, resolve yourself it is,
And be prepar'd to welcome it.
   Gio.   Well, then;
The schoolmen teach that all this globe of earth   30
Shall be consum'd to ashes in a minute.
   Ann. So I have read too.
   Gio.   But 'twere somewhat strange
To see the waters burn; could I believe
This might be true, I could believe as well
There might be hell or Heaven.
   Ann.   That's most certain. 35
   Gio. A dream, a dream! else in this other world
We should know one another.
   Ann.   So we shall.
   Gio. Have you heard so?
   Ann.   For certain.
   Gio.   But d'ye think
That I shall see you there?—You look on me?—
May we kiss one another, prate or laugh,   40
Or do as we do here?
   Ann.   I know not that.
But good, for the present, what d'ye mean
To free yourself from danger? some way, think
How to escape; I'm sure the guests are come.
   Gio. Look up, look here; what see you in my face? 45
   Ann. Distraction and a troubled countenance.
   Gio. Death, and a swift repining wrath—yet look;

What see you in mine eyes?
Ann.   Methinks you weep.
  Gio. I do indeed; these are the funeral tears
Shed on your grave; these furrow'd up my cheeks   50
When first I lov'd and knew not how to woo.
Fair Annabella, should I here repeat
The story of my life, we might lose time.
Be record all the spirits of the air,
And all things else that are, that day and night,   55
Early and late, the tribute which my heart
Hath paid to Annabella's sacred love
Hath been these tears, which are her mourners now!
Never till now did Nature do her best
To show a matchless beauty to the world,   60
Which in an instant, ere it scarce was seen,
The jealous Destinies requir'd again.
Pray, Annabella, pray! Since we must part,
Go thou, white in thy soul, to fill a throne
Of innocence and sanctity in Heaven.   65
Pray, pray, my sister!
  Ann.   Then I see your drift.—
Ye blessed angels, guard me!
  Gio.   So say I.
Kiss me. If ever after-times should hear
Of our fast-knit affections, though perhaps
The laws of conscience and of civil use   70
May justly blame us, yet when they but know
Our loves, that love will wipe away that rigour
Which would in other incests be abhorr'd.
Give me your hand; how sweetly life doth run
In these well-coloured veins! how constantly   75
These palms do promise health! but I could chide
With Nature for this cunning flattery.
Kiss me again—forgive me.
  Ann.   With my heart.

Gio. Farewell!

Ann.   Will you be gone?

Gio.   Be dark, bright sun,
And make this mid-day night, that thy gilt rays   80
May not behold a deed will turn their splendour
More sooty than the poets feign their Styx!
One other kiss, my sister.

Ann.   What means this?

Gio. To save thy fame, and kill thee in a kiss.

                              [*Stabs her.*

Thus die, and die by me, and by my hand!   85
Revenge is mine; honour doth love command.

Ann. Oh, brother, by your hand!

Gio.   When thou art dead
I'll give my reasons for't; for to dispute
With thy—even in thy death—most lovely beauty,
Would make me stagger to perform this act,   90
Which I most glory in.

Ann. Forgive him, Heaven—and me my sins! Farewell,
Brother unkind, unkind—Mercy, great Heaven!—oh
    —oh!   [*Dies.*

Gio. She's dead, alas, good soul! The hapless fruit
That in her womb receiv'd its life from me   95
Hath had from me a cradle and a grave.
I must not dally. This sad marriage-bed,
In all her best, bore her alive and dead.
Soranzo, thou hast miss'd thy aim in this;
I have prevented now thy reaching plots,   100
And kill'd a love, for whose each drop of blood
I would have pawn'd my heart.—Fair Annabella,
How over-glorious art thou in thy wounds,
Triumphing over infamy and hate!

100 prevented] forestalled

Shrink not, courageous hand, stand up, my heart,   105
And boldly act my last and greater part!

> [*Exit with the body.*

ACTUS V, SCÆNA 6

A Banquet.

Enter Cardinal, Florio, Donado, Soranzo, Richardetto,
Vasques, *and Attendants; they take their places.*

Vas. Remember, sir, what you have to do; be wise
and resolute.

Sor. Enough—my heart is fix'd.—Pleaseth your
  grace
To taste these coarse confections; though the use
Of such set entertainments more consists   5
In custom than in cause; yet, reverend sir,
I am still made your servant by your presence.

Car. And we your friend.

Sor. But where's my brother Giovanni?

> *Enter* Giovanni *with a heart upon his dagger.*

Gio. Here, here, Soranzo! trimm'd in reeking blood, 10
That triumphs over death; proud in the spoil
Of love and vengeance! Fate, or all the powers
That guide the motions of immortal souls,
Could not prevent me.

Car. What means this?   15

Flo. Son Giovanni!

Sor. —Shall I be forestall'd?

Gio. Be not amaz'd: if your misgiving hearts
Shrink at an idle sight, what bloodless fear
Of coward passion would have seiz'd your senses,   20
Had you beheld the rape of life and beauty
Which I have acted!—My sister, oh my sister!

v. vi heading *Banquet*] dessert (*usually in another room*)

492

Flo. Ha! what of her?

Gio.   The glory of my deed
Dark'ned the mid-day sun, made noon as night.
You came to feast, my lords, with dainty fare: 25
I came to feast too; but I digg'd for food
In a much richer mine than gold or stone
Of any value balanc'd; 'tis a heart,
A heart, my lords, in which is mine entomb'd:
Look well upon't; d'ye know't?   30

Vas. —What strange riddle's this?

Gio. 'Tis Annabella's heart, 'tis:—why d'ye startle?—
I vow 'tis hers: this dagger's point plough'd up
Her fruitful womb, and left to me the fame
Of a most glorious executioner.   35

Flo. Why, madman, art thyself?

Gio. Yes, father; and, that times to come may know
How, as my fate, I honoured my revenge,
List, father; to your ears I will yield up
How much I have deserv'd to be your son.   40

Flo. What is't thou say'st?

Gio.   Nine moons have had their changes
Since I first throughly view'd and truly lov'd
Your daughter and my sister,

Flo.   How!—Alas,
My lords, he's a frantic madman!

Gio.   Father, no.
For nine months' space in secret I enjoy'd   45
Sweet Annabella's sheets; nine months I liv'd
A happy monarch of her heart and her.
Soranzo, thou know'st this; thy paler cheek
Bears the confounding print of thy disgrace;
For her too-fruitful womb too soon bewray'd   50
The happy passage of our stol'n delights,
And made her mother to a child unborn.

Car. Incestuous villain!

Flo.   Oh, his rage belies him.

Gio. It does not, 'tis the oracle of truth;
I vow it is so.

Sor.   I shall burst with fury,—   55
Bring the strumpet forth!

Vas. I shall, sir.   [*Exit* Vasques.

Gio.   Do, sir.—Have you all no faith
To credit yet my triumphs? Here I swear
By all that you call sacred, by the love
I bore my Annabella whilst she liv'd,   60
These hands have from her bosom ripp'd this heart.

Enter Vasques.

Is't true or no, sir?

Vas.   'Tis most strangely true.

Flo. Cursed man!—Have I liv'd to—   [*Dies.*

Car.   Hold up, Florio.—
Monster of children! see what thou hast done,
Broke thy old father's heart.—Is none of you   65
Dares venture on him?

Gio.   Let 'em!—oh, my father,
How well his death becomes him in his griefs!
Why, this was done with courage; now survives
None of our house but I, gilt in the blood
Of a fair sister and a hapless father.   70

Sor. Inhuman scorn of men, hast thou a thought
T' outlive thy murthers?

Gio.   Yes, I tell thee, yes;
For in my fists I bear the twists of life.
Soranzo, see this heart, which was thy wife's;
Thus I exchange it royally for thine.   [*They fight.* 75
And thus, and thus!   [Soranzo *falls.*
              Now brave revenge is mine.

Vas. I cannot hold any longer.—You, sir, are you
grown insolent in your butcheries? have at you! [*Fight.*

Gio. Come, I am arm'd to meet thee.

Vas. No! will it not be yet? if this will not, another   80
shall. Not yet? I shall fit you anon.—Vengeance!

Enter Banditti.

Gio. Welcome! come more of you; whate'er you be,
I dare your worst—
Oh, I can stand no longer! feeble arms,
Have you so soon lost strength?   85

Vas. Now you are welcome, sir!—
Away, my masters, all is done; shift for yourselves,
your reward is your own; shift for yourselves.

Band. Away, away!   [*Exeunt* Banditti.

Vas. How d'ye, my lord?—See you this? [*Pointing to* 90
Giovanni.] How is't?

Sor. Dead; but in death well pleased that I have liv'd
To see my wrongs reveng'd on that black devil.
Oh, Vasques, to thy bosom let me give
My last of breath; let not that lecher live—oh! [*Dies.* 95

Vas. The reward of peace and rest be with him, my
ever dearest lord and master!

Gio. Whose hand gave me this wound?

Vas. Mine, sir; I was your first man; have you
    enough?

Gio. I thank thee; thou hast done for me   100
But what I would have else done on myself.
Art sure thy lord is dead?

Vas.   Oh, impudent slave!
As sure as I am sure to see thee die.

Car. Think on thy life and end, and call for mercy.

Gio. Mercy! why, I have found it in this justice.   105

Car. Strive yet to cry to Heaven.

Gio.   Oh, I bleed fast!
Death, thou art a guest long look'd-for; I embrace
Thee and thy wounds: oh, my last minute comes!

Where'er I go, let me enjoy this grace,
Freely to view my Annabella's face.   [*Dies.* 110
   Don. Strange miracle of justice!
   Car. Raise up the city; we shall be murdered all!
   Vas. You need not fear, you shall not; this strange
task being ended, I have paid the duty to the son which
I have vowed to the father.   115
   Car. Speak, wretched villain, what incarnate fiend
Hath led thee on to this?
   Vas. Honesty, and pity of my master's wrongs; for
know, my lord, I am by birth a Spaniard, brought forth
from my country in my youth by Lord Soranzo's father, 120
whom whilst he lived I serv'd faithfully; since whose
death I have been to this man as I was to him. What
I have done was duty, and I repent nothing, but that
the loss of my life had not ransom'd his.
   Car. Say, fellow, know'st thou any yet unnam'd   125
Of counsel in this incest?
   Vas. Yes, an old woman, sometimes guardian to this
murthered lady.
   Car. And what's become of her?
   Vas. Within this room she is! whose eyes, after her 130
confession, I caus'd to be put out, but kept alive, to
confirm what from Giovanni's own mouth you have
heard. Now, my lord, what I have done you may judge
of; and let your own wisdom be a judge in your own
reason.   135
   Car. Peace!—First this woman, chief in these effects,
My sentence is, that forthwith she be ta'en
Out of the city, for example's sake,
There to be burnt to ashes.
   Don.   'Tis most just.
   Car. Be it your charge, Donado, see it done.   140
   Don. I shall.

     127 sometimes] sometime, once

Vas. What for me? if death, 'tis welcome: I have
been honest to the son, as I was to the father.

Car. Fellow, for thee, since what thou didst was
done

Not for thyself, being no Italian,   145
We banish thee for ever; to depart
Within three days: in this we do dispense
With grounds of reason, not of thine offence.

Vas. 'Tis well: this conquest is mine, and I rejoice
that a Spaniard outwent an Italian in revenge. [*Exit.* 150

Car. Take up these slaughtered bodies, see them
buried;

And all the gold and jewels, or whatsoever,
Confiscate by the canons of the church,
We seize upon to the Pope's proper use.

Rich. [*Discovers himself.*] Your grace's pardon: thus
long I liv'd disguis'd,   155
To see the effect of pride and lust at once
Brought both to shameful ends.

Car. What! Richardetto, whom we thought for
dead?

Don. Sir, was it you—

Rich.   Your friend.

Car.   We shall have time
To talk at large of all; but never yet   160
Incest and murther have so strangely met.
Of one so young, so rich in nature's store,
Who could not say, 'TIS PITY SHE'S A WHORE?
[*Exeunt.*

FINIS

The general commendation deserved by the actors in their
presentment of this tragedy may easily excuse such few faults as
are escaped in the printing. A common charity may allow him the
ability of spelling whom a secure confidence assures that he cannot
ignorantly err in the application of sense.